Occupation

The Ordeal of France
1940–1944

The Crime and Mystery Book: A Reader's Companion to the Detective Novel
The Blue Guide to England
The Cambridge Guide to Literature in English
The Blue Guide to Burgundy
James Plumptre's Britain: The Journals of a Tourist in the 1790s
The Englishman's England: Taste, Travel and the Rise of Tourism
The Correspondence of John Ruskin and Charles Eliot Norton
The Blue Guide to Literary Britain and Ireland
Bloodhounds of Heaven: The Detective in English Fiction from Godwin to Doyle

Occupation

The Ordeal of France
1940–1944

IAN OUSBY

JOHN MURRAY
Albemarle Street, London

The maps on pp. xv–xviii were drawn by John Flower

First published in 1997
by John Murray (Publishers) Ltd,
50 Albemarle Street, London W1X 4BD
Reprinted 1998

A catalogue record for this book is available from the British Library

ISBN 0-7195-5670 8

Typeset in 12.25/13.5 Monotype Garamond by Servis Filmsetting Ltd, Manchester

Printed and bound in Great Britain by
The University Press, Cambridge

I will never believe that people are made for war. But I also know that they are not made for servitude either.

Jean Guéhenno, 17 June 1940

Contents

Illustrations

The author and publisher would like to thank the following for permission to reproduce illustrations: Plate 1, Roger Schall; 2, Sygma, London; 3, 11 and 15, Getty Images; 4, © Lapi-Viollet; 5, 6, 7 and 9, © Zucca/Bibliothèque Historique de la Ville de Paris; 12, 13 and 14, Imperial War Museum, London; 16, Photo Doisneau-Rapho.

Preface

I AM ENGLISH. I was born in 1947. I have no formal training as a historian. In other words, I lack all the obvious qualifications for writing about the German occupation of France during the Second World War – a subject jealously guarded first by a generation of writers (usually French) who had lived through the experience and then by a generation of academic historians (not always French) who have built up a complex body of scholarship, still enlarging by the minute. So, to start with, I owe the reader at least a word of explanation about how I came to write this book and what function I intend it to serve.

The second, and more important, matter is simple to explain. My aim has been to write a short history of the Occupation in its various aspects – social and cultural, as well as political and military – for the general reader rather than the specialist. The fact that such a book does not already exist (at least not in English) is no rebuke to the academics who have in recent years done so much to shed new light on the period. Indeed, it is precisely in such times of re-evaluation, when established views are challenged and new ones breed controversy, that general readers tend to get neglected.

I myself certainly began by feeling the consequences of this neglect during my time in France over the last decade. Like so many visitors, I was struck by the imprint that the Occupation, though it is now a good fifty years in the past, has left on contemporary France. It is there most obviously in a habit of official commemoration. Towns name their central squares after the exact day when they were liberated in 1944, or after the day shortly beforehand when local people were massacred. The generals commanding the French divisions in the Allied armies give their names to main streets: the Rue Général Leclerc in the north, the Avenue de Lattre de Tassigny in the south. *Résistants* are remembered everywhere, though on plaques and monuments put up by their surviving comrades rather than on the civic war memorials listing those who died in 1914–18 or during the fall of France in 1940. On the wall of a house in a back street, or beside a busy road, or in the overgrown depths of a wood, one comes across the reminder that this particular *résistant* or this particular group of *résistants* died on this particular spot. The inscriptions often speak in uncompromising terms of cowardly betrayals and barbarous atrocities, and the monuments themselves are always immaculately tended.

To the visitor from England such reminders – local, fragmentary, only partly understood though they may be – bring home the force of the question Jean-Paul Sartre first asked when the events themselves were barely over: 'How can the people of the free countries be made to realize what life was like under the Occupation?' His implied answer, obviously, was that they could not: that *we* could not. And he was undoubtedly right. Even with the greatest imagination, the most careful reconstruction, the most detailed scholarship, the gap between the French experience and the British experience in the Second World War remains unbridgeable. Yet, of course, this is not to say that the effort is worthless. It is perhaps now more tantalizing than ever to make it, and more instructive too.

For the British, consideration of what it meant for France to be occupied has always involved covert self-questioning. If we had been occupied too, what would have happened to us? How would we have behaved? Always uneasy, these questions are now tinged with a sort of speculative guilt prompted by the stock which the French themselves have been taking of their own record. Sartre characterized the different memories separating Britain and France by saying that 'a past which fills London with pride was, for Paris, marked with shame and despair'. This put the matter with a bluntness that was unwelcome so soon after the events. In general the French, understandably, reacted to their ordeal by retreating into a myth (my epilogue shows how it can fairly be called the Gaullist myth) of a people united in hostility to the Nazi occupiers, of a nation of *résistants*. For our part, we in Britain were content to accept the myth – though of course we insisted, in the films and popular literature which flourished in my childhood, on giving British agents a flatteringly prominent role, usually the leading role, in resistance.

Even from the start, however, the myth could not completely stifle the sense of shame and despair to which Sartre testified. Alongside the official commemorations, an act of collective forgetting was also required. It was written quite literally into the title of André Mornet's book published in 1949, *Quatre années à rayer de notre histoire (Four Years to Strike from Our History)*. What had to be forgotten was not France's defeat in 1940 or the brutality of her occupiers, of course. What had to be forgotten was what the French had done to the French. So when, in July 1946, an official monument was unveiled on the spot where the politician Georges Mandel had been killed in the forest of Fontainebleau two years before, its inscription spoke of him as having been 'murdered by the enemies of France' – the bland phrase deliberately failing to specify that his murderers were Frenchmen. And when, a decade later, Alain Resnais made his documentary film about Auschwitz, *Nuit et brouillard (Night and Fog)*, the censors objected to footage which showed that the Jews deported from the camp at Pithiviers were herded into the trains not by German soldiers but by French gendarmes.

The paradoxes inherent even in the attempt to forget were already apparent in Mornet's book: a history of something that should be forgotten which in fact concluded that it could not be forgotten. The attempt to remember and to confront the past began in the 1970s with (to cite two very different but equally influential works) Marcel Ophuls' film *Le Chagrin et la pitié (The Sorrow and the Pity)*, released in 1971, and Robert O. Paxton's scholarly study *Vichy France: Old Guard and New Order, 1940–44*, published in 1972. Most of what has been said and written about the Occupation since then has explored the questions such works opened up. Purely academic inquiry has moved in step with events in French public life which have made headlines outside France: the arrest and trial of French wartime officials for their misdeeds, for example, and the revelations which President Mitterrand chose to make just before his death about the ambiguities of his own past.

A myth of national heroism succeeded by a determination to investigate national shame: even so crude a description of how the French have lived with their past suggests the discomforts that history can hold fifty years afterwards. Yet, in its very crudity, the description hardly begins to answer the important questions about what really happened during the Occupation: what was heroic, what was shameful, in what proportions they flourished in the same soil, and why. These, of course, were precisely the questions which prompted me to embark on this work.

The need to address them in a book designed for an English audience was confirmed by the reactions of various friends. Some, knowing I was writing a history of the Occupation, would still insist on referring to it as a history of the Resistance. Rather more asked me, with some embarrassment, if my research had 'lowered my opinion of the French'. I reminded the former that, sadly, a history of the Occupation is not the same thing as a history of the Resistance. I told the latter that it had not altered my respect for the French, though it had sometimes lowered my opinion of human nature, just as it had sometimes raised it. Those who look at how people in another time and another country behaved in an hour of darkness find no easy clue as to how they themselves might behave should they suffer a similar ordeal. Instead they find what Václav Havel, with his eye on different events altogether, had occasion to remind us in 1990: 'It is extremely shortsighted to believe that the face society happens to be presenting to you at a given moment is its only true face. None of us knows all the potentialities that slumber in the spirit of the population.'

Ian Ousby
Cambridge
February 1997

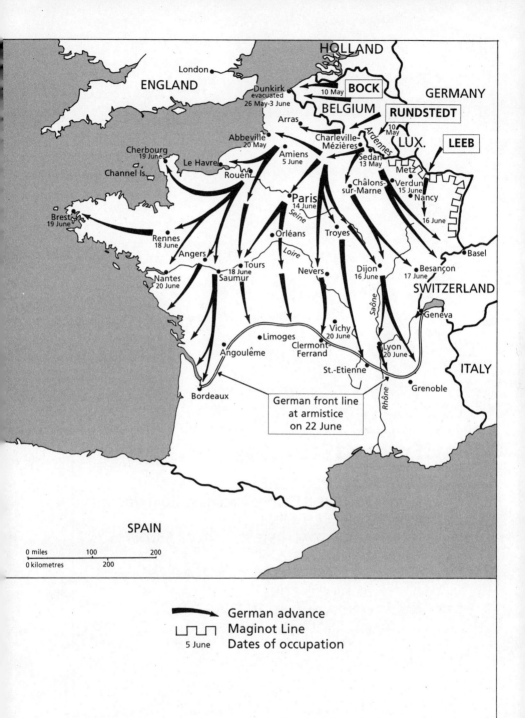

The Invasion of France, 1940

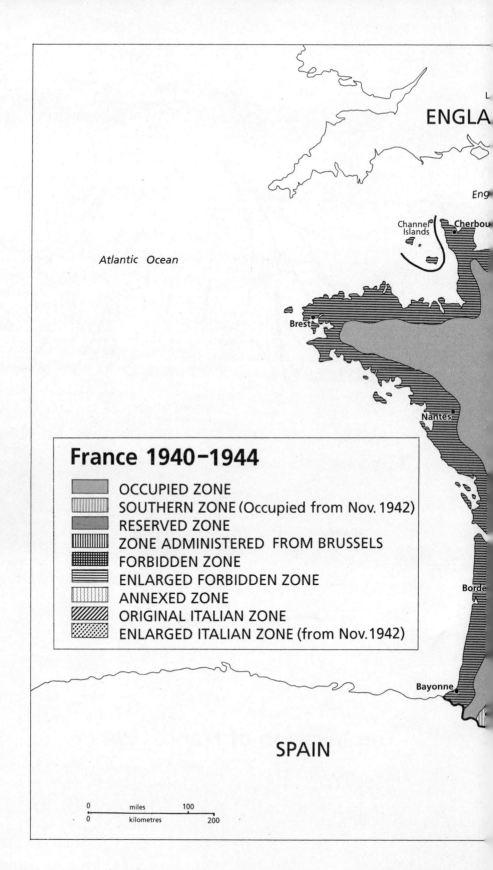

ENGLA

Eng

Channel
Islands   Cherbou

Atlantic Ocean

Brest

Nantes

France 1940–1944

OCCUPIED ZONE
SOUTHERN ZONE (Occupied from Nov. 1942)
RESERVED ZONE
ZONE ADMINISTERED FROM BRUSSELS
FORBIDDEN ZONE
ENLARGED FORBIDDEN ZONE
ANNEXED ZONE
ORIGINAL ITALIAN ZONE
ENLARGED ITALIAN ZONE (from Nov. 1942)

Borde

Bayonne

SPAIN

0   miles   100
0   kilometres   200

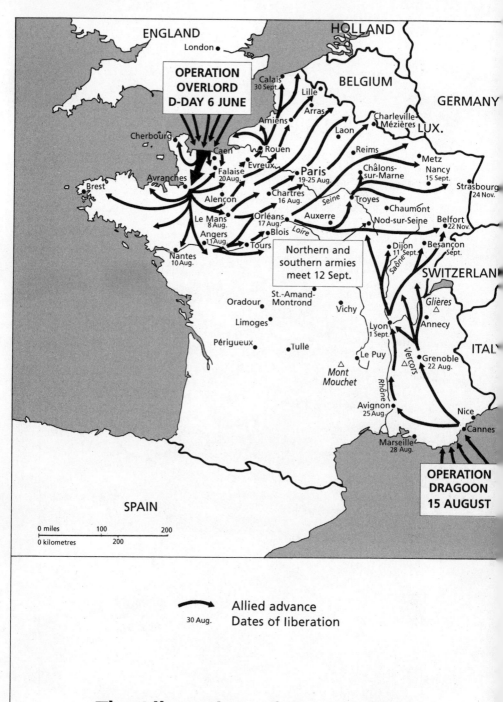

The Liberation of France, 1944

PROLOGUE

Verdun and Its Legacy

This war has marked us for generations. It has left its
imprint upon our souls. All those inflamed nights of
Verdun we shall rediscover one day in the eyes of our
children.

Pierre de Mazenod

IN BRITAIN WE identify the First World War and its legacy above all
with the battle of the Somme. The name engraved on the French
memory is Verdun. Indeed, Verdun might stand as the name for all
the battles and all the wars France has fought over her unstable
eastern border, in the disputed lands between the Meuse and the
Rhine. At the Porte Saint-Paul, the smallest of the town's medieval
gates, a tablet records that Verdun was besieged, damaged or
destroyed in 450, 485, 984, 1047, 1246, 1338, 1552 and 1792, as well as
in 1916. And, of course, the list fails to take account of the Second
World War, unimagined and unimaginable when the tablet was put
up in the 1920s. The most piquant reminder of what happened then
is a plaque beneath the walls of Vauban's fortress, telling visitors that
what is now a car park was, from 1940 until 1944, the site of the
Gestapo headquarters.

The town has its stone and bronze memorials to the battle of
1916, but the scars themselves still show on the ring of hills straddling the Meuse to the north and east. With the river, the hills give
Verdun its strategic importance. At first glance they make a pleasant
change in an otherwise dull stretch of countryside. The forests have
been replanted and, after an absence of fifty years or more, the birds
have returned. Yet, despite being grassed over again, the ground is
still pockmarked with saucer-shaped dips which were shell craters

and criss-crossed with ditches which were trenches. Remnants of artillery positions stand in the midst of the woods; scattered monuments mark where soldiers died or villages stood. On the ridge at Douaumont the skyline is dominated by the ghastliest monument of all, the Ossuaire (or charnel house) built in the shape of a huge artillery shell pointed at the heavens, holding the bones of perhaps 150,000 unidentified soldiers. It faces the military cemetery where a further 15,000 men lie beneath rows of white crosses.

The starkest relic is nearby Fort Douaumont, a sunken fortress showing hardly more than its concrete roof and its gun turrets above ground. Below lies a labyrinth of corridors, barrack rooms, munitions stores and latrines: a dripping, echoing tomb, still a place of nightmare and claustrophobia even though it is now lit by electricity rather than candles and kerosene lamps. It was built in response to the Franco-Prussian War of 1870, when the fall of Verdun had set the seal on France's humiliation after her defeat by Count von Moltke's armies at Sedan, Metz and Strasbourg. The best-designed and best-equipped fortress of its day, it dominated the other forts which formed a three-ringed defence of the hills. These, in turn, were the key to a chain of fortifications which ran from Verdun along the eastern bank of the Meuse down to Toul and then, after a deliberate gap or *trouée de charmes* into which it was hoped the enemy might be enticed, along the Moselle from Epinal to Belfort. The whole system anticipated the Maginot Line of the interwar years in its spirit if not in its details and technology. France reacted to defeat in 1870 as she would to victory in 1918, protecting herself from the possibility of invasion from the east by digging herself sullenly into the soil. 'Rather be buried under the ruins of the fort than surrender' ordered the signs in the underground corridors of Fort Douaumont.

At the beginning of 1916 the military maps showed Verdun, Fort Douaumont and the other forts guarding the surrounding hills as what tacticians call a salient: a little bump sticking out from the Allied front lines which stretched down from the Belgian coast to the Swiss border. Germany's thrust in September 1914 had brought its advance cavalry within 20 kilometres of Paris and the sound of its artillery within hearing of Parisians. Then it had failed: rallying from his original miscalculations and capitalizing on German mistakes, Marshal Joffre had achieved the 'Miracle of the Marne'. The Germans had been pushed back to positions which robbed them of any chance of the quick victory they had sought. As the next four years would show, these positions also deprived the Allies of the same chance. It was, above all, to be a war of stagnation.

For the most part the contours of the battle line were dictated not by natural features but by accidents of the fighting. It was, says Alistair Horne, simply a 'line of exhaustion'. But the salient at Verdun owed more to the defence its hills provided than to the way the French had kept up the elaborate fortifications they had added. The forts were stripped of all but their fixed artillery and Douaumont itself, built for 500 men, had in fact less than sixty to defend it. French public opinion and politicians might have put their faith in defensive walls dug deep into the soil, but French military commanders clung stubbornly to their belief in *attaque à l'outrance*, the romantic bravado of the all-out charge. The discrepancy in military thinking would run through the history of the whole war, and beyond.

So in 1916 Verdun presented, not a soft target (there were no soft targets in the First World War), but an obvious one for any German offensive. The plan put forward by General von Falkenhayn and approved by Kaiser Wilhelm II called for the only major German attack between their unsuccessful thrust in 1914 and General Ludendorff's gamble in March 1918. The guns opened up at dawn on 21 February, announcing the start of a battle fought on the tactical principles which dominated the war. First the artillery laid a heavy barrage to knock out or soften up enemy positions and demoralize survivors. Then the infantry advanced to secure a foothold. Defenders in trenches, machine-gun posts and bunkers on both fronts were all too familiar with the unnerving rhythm: heavy explosions and deafening noise followed by an ominous quiet signalling that the hand-to-hand fighting was about to start.

The bombardment at Verdun was massive. The German artillery had 850 guns (as against the French 250), already supplied with two and a half million shells for the first six days of fighting. They included the Big Berthas, or Gamma Guns, firing shells almost as tall as a man and weighing over a ton. From the air the German lines looked like a single sheet of flame, and the noise could be heard more than 150 kilometres away. Trees were scythed down like so many matchsticks. Whole woods were uprooted and then blown into the air again by the next round of firing. The landscape was on its way to becoming the unearthly wasteland familiar today only through sepia or black-and-white photographs: distant prisms which cannot fully evoke the cloying mud and discoloured pools of water, the reek of smoke, decaying flesh and shit, the ever-present rats and lice that made up the experience of battle.

On the French side, trenches were levelled, artillery positions mangled beyond recognition and machine-gun posts blown out of existence. The survivors were sometimes stunned or driven mad. Some did what soldiers often do after hours of tension: they fell asleep. During the late afternoon the German infantry began its advance in small patrols and raiding parties rather than in massed ranks. Some had flame-throwers fed from petrol canisters on their backs, a new weapon which could scorch men to death and even set fire to the timbers shoring up trenches. If the flame-thrower took an unlucky hit, its carrier turned into a human torch or sprayed his comrades with burning petrol. Darkness ended the hand-to-hand fighting on the first day but renewed the bombardment. Ten months of battle had begun.

At first, the tide seemed to be running wholly in the Germans' favour. On 25 February Fort Douaumont, still intact beneath the bombardment, fell with ludicrous ease: a mere handful of attackers took it without having to fire a shot. The French paid dearly for having neglected its defence. The loss had a devastating effect on the morale of troops in the field, of local civilians (who fled the already depleted town of Verdun virtually *en masse*) and, despite the best efforts of the wartime censors, on the nation as a whole. As for the effect on the course of the battle, one French divisional commander estimated that the loss of Douaumont would cost 100,000 lives.

Yet the German attack was getting bogged down – literally so in some places, for their heavy bombardment ploughed up the ground so effectively that it was often difficult or impossible to move the artillery forward to new positions. Though only about a quarter the size of Fort Douaumont, Fort Vaux proved a much tougher nut to crack; it fell in June after a seven-day siege. Elsewhere the battle had settled into minor fluctuations, local versions of the meaningless ebb and flow between fronts which typified the pattern of the First World War. On the west bank of the Meuse, assault and counter-assault surged over Côte 304 and the hill sinisterly named Le Mort Homme. On the east bank, the village of Vaux is said to have changed hands thirteen times in March. The Ouvrage de Thiaumont, a small fort near the site of the present Ossuaire, changed hands sixteen times during the summer. After the Germans failed to take the fort at Souville, on the middle of the three rings of forts, the Kaiser seized the opportunity to sack Falkenhayn as Chief of the General Staff. His successor, Field Marshal von Hindenburg, ordered a virtual stop to the whole attack. The French recaptured Fort Douaumont in October and Fort Vaux in November. By mid-December they had pushed their front line a few kilometres east beyond Douaumont.

What had the 300 days of fighting cost? The statistics quoted for the battle of Verdun are no more precise or reliable than those for many of the events this book will describe. Yet most modern authorities would agree that the casualties on both sides reached a total of about 700,000, and that the French suffered more heavily than the Germans. Perhaps 162,000 French soldiers and 143,000 German soldiers were dead or missing in action. Taking into account the numbers engaged and the relatively small compass of the battlefield itself, the slaughter was on a scale for which the recorded history of western Europe can offer no parallel. And what purpose had it served? In fact, the Germans did not want Verdun and the French did not need Verdun. If the Germans had taken it, the way to Paris would still not have been open: the war would have continued its already established pattern of trench fighting on a static front. As for the French, they could have yielded Verdun without disadvantage. Indeed, withdrawal from the salient would have shortened their front line and husbanded resources.

The real reasons for the battle lay elsewhere. The German codename for their attack was *Gericht*, which can mean a law court or tribunal but (as Alistair Horne points out) in this context means a place of execution. Falkenhayn's plan had been not so much to take Verdun as to draw the French into a defence which would bleed their army to death. And the French had been obliged to make the defence by a military code of honour which viewed any withdrawal as cowardice, any loss of ground as humiliation. It was a soldier's duty to hold his position, at whatever cost, and if the enemy did push him back it was his duty to try and recapture his position, at whatever cost. 'Do not surrender, do not yield an inch, let yourself be killed where you stand,' General Nivelle was still telling his troops in the summer of 1916.

Such absurdities of doctrine applied with particular force when the ground in question was Verdun, endowed with special meaning since its loss in 1870 had heralded the collapse of France herself. The effect on French morale of losing Verdun by withdrawal or defeat, it was argued, would have been disastrous, perhaps even fatal. In other words, France elected to fight for a symbol. Just as the Germans could for the time being overlook their losses and claim success in bleeding the French army to death, so the French could overlook their losses and claim success in preserving their symbol. France had lived up to the boast Nivelle had made in the order of the day urging his men to repel the attack on Fort Souville: '*Ils ne passeront pas!*' – 'They shall not get through.'

THE FRENCH DID not forget this rallying cry, but above all they remembered Verdun as the epitome of their experience in the war. France had suffered proportionately greater losses than Britain, Germany or the United States; indeed, her losses had been greater than those of any other country except Serbia. Metropolitan France alone – that is to say, just her mainland and not her colonial territories – lost about a million and a half men, more than a tenth of her active male population and roughly one-third of her male population between the ages of 18 and 27. Statistics can be inexpressive, and the twentieth century has taught us that the larger the figures cited the less expressive they become. A contemporary put the death toll more vividly: if the dead rose up and marched by a given point at an ordinary pace, the column would take eleven days and eleven nights to pass.

When France came to select a *soldat inconnu* to be buried beneath the Arc de Triomphe in memory of all these men, it was inevitable that the choice should have been made from the field of Verdun, so appallingly rich in unidentified remains. Yet France did not need to seek only among the dead for reminders. There were the survivors, and something called the Noria guaranteed that there were survivors in virtually every town and village. In both French and English, a noria is an endless chain of buckets on a wheel or loop, used for raising water. In French military jargon it was also the name for the system, introduced at Verdun, of relieving men serving at the front as quickly as possible. The Noria was a sensible precaution in a battle whose pressures could cause psychological breakdown and raise the spectre of mutiny. The result of its use was that seven out of every ten French soldiers who fought in the First World War served at Verdun. So the battle was not just engraved in general terms on the national memory. It was part of the direct experience of innumerable people, including many who went on to enter public life – from Captain Charles de Gaulle, at first reported killed near Douaumont but in fact only wounded and captured, to Sergeant André Maginot.*

Maginot was wounded in the legs and afterwards walked only with the aid of a stick. He became a spokesman for disabled veterans before, as Minister of War, enthusiastically pushing ahead the building of the defensive line which handed his name down to history. The First World War had been a war of heavy shells exploding in mid-air, of grenades splintering into shrapnel, of gas seeping into the chest. As well as its dead, it had left its wounded, its maimed and its disfigured. About four million men, more than half those who had survived the fighting, had suffered some sort of wound, and of them more than a million counted as *grands mutilés* (severely disabled), *mutilés* (disabled), *aveugles de guerre* (those blinded in the war) or *ailes brisées* (literally 'broken wings', or disabled airmen). Shrapnel often caused facial injuries, so there was a sadly distinctive category of *gueules cassées* (literally 'broken faces'). They were not hidden away or looked on with revulsion. Clemenceau insisted that a *gueule cassée* attend the signing of the Treaty of Versailles which formally ended the war. *Grands mutilés* led the great Victory Parade in Paris in July 1919, when the French proudly removed the chains they had installed to prevent the Prussians marching beneath the Arc de Triomphe in 1870. In what Ted Morgan has called a 'cult of the fallen and the maimed' they were venerated as emblems of both the renewed pride and the bitter sacrifice that the war had brought.

So Verdun gave the imagery of French public life its *soldat inconnu*, its *mutilés* and its *gueules cassées*. In Philippe Pétain, appointed to command the battle in February 1916, it also gave France a new hero: a leader to trust, admire, eventually love. That in itself is surprising: the First World War was notorious for breaking the reputations of military commanders from all nations. But Pétain survived his elevation. Wearing his sky-blue uniform and riding a white horse, he was the people's hero at the Victory Parade. To the cheering crowds he stood for everything France had suffered, everything

---

* Apart from these men (and of course Pétain himself) other French veterans of Verdun whom later chapters will mention included the future President Albert Lebrun, the future Admiral Darlan and the future General de Lattre de Tassigny. German veterans included Heinz Guderian, the future General Keitel, the future Field Marshal Paulus and the future General Karl Heinrich von Stülpnagel.

France had achieved. And his reputation endured. While other military men foolishly dabbled in right-wing conspiracies or rushed incautiously into print with memoirs praising themselves and denigrating their colleagues, Pétain remained aloof, immaculate. So, when 1940 brought defeat and the ordeal of occupation, he seemed the natural choice, the only choice, of leader. No other man embodied more completely the legacy of Verdun, transmitted with fatal results to the next generation.

Pétain's rise was surprising in another respect as well. At first inspection he looked merely a nonentity who had greatness thrust upon him. His origins were undistinguished and until the First World War his career was unremarkable. A farmer's son from a shabby village on the edge of the Béthune coalfields in the Pas-de-Calais, he had worked his way up to the military academy at Saint-Cyr, entering as 403rd in a class of 412 and graduating as 229th. Thereafter his fortunes languished in much the way that might have been expected of an officer without private means or family connections. He had been born in 1856 and so when war came in 1914 he was 58, close to retirement but still only a colonel. Behind him lay the reputation among junior officers of a martinet, a peripatetic bachelor existence in one garrison town after another, and a long record of sexual conquests made easy by his curling chestnut hair and china-blue eyes. Ahead, if the war had not come, lay half-pay and the small house he had bought in Saint-Omer. Instead, the rapid turnover of military commanders meant that he was promoted to the rank of general. Eighteen months later the same process put him in command of the defence of Verdun, opening the way to sudden fame and, by the end of the war, the rank of marshal, the highest a French soldier could achieve.

This, at least, is how his career would later be sketched by detractors. They usually took special pleasure in pointing to his lowly position among the cadets at Saint-Cyr. Yet the portrait is too crude. Pétain was far more than a plodding career officer, animated only when he was writing a love letter on coloured notepaper to one of his mistresses. He was known, for example, for his habit of directing sarcastic witticisms at senior officers and politicians: that, surely, is the mark of an intelligent but frustrated man rather than a dull one. Indeed, Pétain had every reason to feel frustrated until February 1916. He held clear and strong views, unfashionable but still refreshing enough to make the young de Gaulle eager to serve under him.

In an era when military thinking was still dominated by belief in *attaque à l'outrance*, Pétain was an advocate of defensive strategy. And in an era when defence was considered largely a matter of standing your ground even if you were cut to pieces, Pétain was an advocate of cautious and well-husbanded defence. Heresy of heresies, he even believed that ground should sometimes be yielded to the enemy. His favourite maxim was that 'firepower kills', and it was on the concentration and deployment of firepower that he placed most emphasis, whether it came from the infantryman's rifle, the machine gun or the heavy guns of the artillery. In effect, he believed in fighting war by attrition, but not the sort of attrition that used men as cannon fodder. 'One does not fight with men against *matériel*,' he liked to say.

Pétain's appointment to command the defence of Verdun seems simply to have been a matter of luck: he and his Second Army happened to be in reserve when the Germans launched their attack. But contemporaries soon came to feel, and historians have largely endorsed their verdict, that he was the ideal choice. From his point of view he had been given a heaven-sent opportunity to put into practice the neglected, if not despised, theories he had advanced during the long years of his obscurity. His brief was marred only by the determination of his superiors that the east bank of the Meuse must be held, however badly depleted and undermanned its defences had become. Left to himself Pétain might well have judged it an occasion for strategic withdrawal.

Characteristically, he set to work improving Verdun's almost strangled lines of communication and supply. Soldiers replaced the narrow-gauge railway with a broad-gauge line. The way from Bar-le-Duc – soon to become famous as the *Voie Sacrée* – was widened, consolidated and assigned permanent crews of road-menders and mechanics. In the field Pétain established a clearly marked 'line of resistance', as well as a secret 'line of panic' closer to Verdun. At every point he sought to plug loopholes in the defence and equip it to capitalize on the attackers' mistakes. '*Courage, on les aura!*' ('Take heart, we'll get them!'), he urged his troops. The words have a fine rhetorical ring to them, partly because of their deliberate echo of Joan of Arc.* Yet they are essentially the words of a commander encouraging his men to settle down to a waiting game.

---

* '*Nos ennemis, fussent-ils pendus aux nuages, nous les aurons! Et nous les bouterons hors de France*' ('Our enemies, even if they hang from the clouds, we shall get them! And we'll drive them out of France').

By the standards of the time Pétain's style of leadership was as unusual as his tactical approach. First World War generals like Joffre slept long hours, leaving aides reluctant to disturb their slumbers with even the most urgent communiqué. Pétain went to bed late and rose early. First World War generals preferred to conduct their battles from as far behind the front line as possible. Pétain made his headquarters at Souilly, only 17 kilometres from Verdun, where he lived at the *mairie* in spartan conditions – a first display of the peasant simplicity he would cultivate later in his career. Though shy of photographers and predictably short with visiting politicians, he took every opportunity to inspect the scene of battle himself: consoling the wounded, pinning medals on heroes, checking the rations were up to standard.

Like his introduction of the Noria, such behaviour showed a grasp of the psychology as well as the mechanics of warfare. The *poilus*, or ordinary soldiers, appreciated Pétain's preference for tactics which avoided the waste of life common elsewhere on the Western Front. They also cherished him as a general with the common touch, a concern for the welfare of his men. He consolidated this reputation when he was called in to quell the mutinies provoked by the disastrous Chemin des Dames offensive in 1917. They are still among the murkier episodes of the war, and dark rumours circulated about the summary justice meted out to some mutineers. But the public record, in which the average Frenchman trusted, told a different story. Pétain approved only a minimum of death sentences. He relied on personal visits of inspection as he had at Verdun, seeing that the living conditions of the troops were improved. Above all, he reassured them that there would be no more rash offensives. His work won him the nickname of *le médecin de l'Armée*, the doctor of the army, which afterwards gave him more pride than that of *le vainqueur de Verdun*, the victor of Verdun.

Yet by 1917 it was becoming clear that, whatever the average *poilu* might think of Pétain, his colleagues and superiors had their doubts. Having been raised from obscurity to fame late in life, he was to be denied supreme recognition. As early as April 1916 Joffre, who resented the demands Pétain's tactics at Verdun put on the rest of the army, made him Commander of the Army Group Centre and gave charge of the Second Army to Nivelle. Pétain, in other words, was kicked upstairs and day-to-day command in the field went to a soldier whose approach promised, falsely, a quicker and easier end.

When Joffre himself fell from grace in December it was Nivelle, not Pétain, who succeeded him. Pétain got the job after Nivelle disgraced himself with the Chemin des Dames offensive, but that was specifically because his touch was needed in handling the mutinies. At the start of the final Allied offensive in the summer of 1918 Foch was appointed over his head as Supreme Commander of all the Allied armies in France. So though Pétain might have been the popular hero of the 1919 Victory Parade it was Foch who enjoyed the place of honour behind the *grands mutilés* at the head of the column.

Pétain was slighted in this fashion because, in Joffre's words, he was '*trop negatif, trop timide*'. Perhaps Joffre and others like him can be dismissed as spokesmen for the older school of military thinking which the war discredited and Pétain himself rejected. Field Marshal Earl Haig's doubts are harder to dismiss since he originally judged Pétain 'business-like, knowledgeable, and brief of speech', the last being a quality he prized greatly but encountered too rarely in Frenchmen. Yet even he reported that, during Ludendorff's spring offensive in 1918, Pétain looked as if he 'was in a funk and had lost his nerve'. The criticism, by one commander of another, albeit a francophobic British commander of a French commander, cannot be lightly set aside.

A safe pair of hands, a master of defence, but a poor leader in an emergency and no sort of leader when attack was the order of the day? Perhaps that is all Pétain had really been from the start. But there is reason to agree with Alistair Horne when he finds in Pétain's mood during the First World War a descent from caution to pessimism and finally to defeatism. Verdun had that effect on people and Verdun was, after all, the first major battle Pétain had ever witnessed, much less commanded. It did not just kill or maim. It did something else, observers noted. It infected men with what Louis Madelin called a *crise de tristesse sombre*, an attack of black sorrow. The British called it 'shellshock' and today we call it 'post-traumatic stress disorder', but *crise de tristesse sombre* is more eloquent than either term. Soldiers deserted without warning, or abandoned positions they were supposed to hold. Some collapsed into a lethargy so deep they lost the will to defend themselves. When they returned from their tour of duty at the front, 'their expressions, indescribably, seemed frozen by a vision of terror; their gait and their postures betrayed a total dejection; they sagged beneath the weight of horrifying memories'.

Pétain himself wrote these words, and the fact that he so vividly noted the air of something broken in his troops suggests that he too, however subtly, may have been touched by it. Verdun did not break him. Indeed, in terms of his public career Verdun made him: later chapters of this book will need to examine the dangerous effect on his ego of such unexpected adulation, coming as it did late in life after years of frustrated obscurity. But Verdun and the rest of the war also diminished, even crushed, something inside a soldier already inclined to caution and sensitive to the suffering of those he commanded. So the trim figure in the sky-blue uniform on the white horse passing beneath the Arc de Triomphe at the Victory Parade embodied not just victory, the glory of France vindicated through sacrifice. It embodied, at whatever private level, a sense of defeat and that, too, was an element in his rapport with the cheering crowds. The sense of defeat ran like a hidden undercurrent through the mood of France in the interwar years. In 1940 it came to the surface again, and Pétain was once more in rapport with the cheering crowds.

N O NATION CAN build its public ceremonies on such a mood, or even acknowledge its existence on these occasions. No politician can appeal to the electorate in its name, or even frame policies to take it openly into account. Officially, the mood was one of pride tempered by sacrifice. Indeed in many respects it was one of pride embittered by sacrifice. *Revanchisme* became the order of the day: revenge not just for the sufferings of 1914–18 but for the humiliation of the 'three absurd weeks' in 1870 as well. The *wagon-lit* at Rethondes in the Forest of Compiègne, where the Germans surrendered to Marshal Foch in November 1918, was moved from its siding and housed in a museum a few yards away. The spot where it had originally stood was marked by a granite slab whose inscription spoke unforgivingly of 'the criminal pride of the German Empire . . . vanquished by the free peoples which it tried to enslave'. At France's insistence the Treaty of Versailles, which dictated the terms of the peace, was negotiated and signed in Louis XIV's great Galerie des Glaces where, after the Franco-Prussian War, the Prussian King had declared himself Kaiser Wilhelm I in 1871.

These symbolic gestures were matched by the actual terms of the treaty, which began by reaffirming Germany's guilt in starting the war. She was to pay reparations (though in the event she ended up paying only about one-eighth of the amount demanded). She was to be stripped of her colonial possessions, which became mandated territories administered, for the most part, by Britain and France under the authority of the League of Nations. She was to be deprived of an ally to the east by the division of the Habsburg Empire into nation states such as Poland and Czechoslovakia. At home, her army was to be reduced to a militia of just 100,000 men, lacking a general staff to command it and conscripts to supply it; heavy artillery, tanks, armoured cars, poison gas, aircraft and zeppelins were banned.

'*Vous n'aurez pas l'Alsace et la Lorraine*': military bands had played the tune enthusiastically throughout the war. Germany was stripped of the disputed provinces she had acquired in 1870, as well as being forced to allow France a fifteen-year foothold in the Saar basin and to submit to the creation of a permanently demilitarized zone stretching 50 kilometres east of the Rhine. Even these terms did not fully satisfy France – or many in Britain, for that matter – but the United States would go no further, to the disgust of men like Marshal Foch. With a twisted sort of prescience he prophesied that, by its failure to treat Germany with proper severity, the Treaty of Versailles would not guarantee lasting peace: it would merely bring about a twenty-year armistice.

How then could France secure her fragile eastern border? 'What haunts us most is the safety of our own hexagonal territory,' de Gaulle wrote in the 1930s. The popular answer (though not de Gaulle's) lay in Pétain's views and the costly lesson taught by the neglect of the Verdun forts in 1916. The Maginot Line – it could as easily and more justly have been called the Pétain Line – was started in 1930 and more or less finished by 1935, the expiry date for the French occupation of the Rhineland stipulated by the Treaty of Versailles. It ran north from the Swiss border near Basel to Longwy, near the junction of France's border with Luxembourg and Belgium. Two stretches judged particularly vulnerable, the area round Metz and Nancy and that looking north over the plains of lower Alsace, were fortified with extra care.

The largest of the forts strung along the course of the Line held a garrison of 1,200 troops in buildings divided in two so that each could fire on the other should it fall into enemy hands. One visitor to the Mont des Welsches outside Metz found 'a great mound of insulating wooded earth whose bald head was studded with bombproof turtle-neck gun-turrets' – in other words, a sight strongly reminiscent of Douaumont and the other Verdun forts. In an age already half in love with Wellsian visions of the shape of things to come, most visitors concentrated their admiration on the futuristic arrangements which reached six or seven storeys below ground. They duly marvelled at the air-conditioned galleries with railway tracks, partitioned at intervals by fireproof sliding doors and guarded by machine-gun posts; the floors with traps that could drop intruders into 18-metre pits; the cinemas and the shower rooms; the handsomely equipped hospitals and the supply rooms crammed with food. If this display of high technology threatened to make people forget the descent of the Maginot forts from Verdun and the experience of 1916, they had only to read the motto emblazoned on them: *Ils ne passeront pas.*

Time treats few things more cruelly than the futuristic fantasies of past generations, particularly when they are actually realized in concrete and steel. Hindsight makes it abundantly clear that the Maginot Line was a foolish misdirection of energy when it was conceived, a dangerous distraction of time and money when it was built, and a pitiful irrelevance when the German invasion did come in 1940. Most glaringly, it concentrated on the Rhineland and left France's 400-kilometre border with Belgium unfortified. In justification the French could point to the fact that Belgium was an ally when the Line was started: one does not put up fortified walls between oneself and the neighbour one has sworn to protect. But Leopold III made the harebrained decision to join Holland and Luxembourg as a neutral country in 1936, and France still did nothing substantial to extend the Maginot Line toward the Channel coast. Conscious of how vastly the original work had overrun its budget, the government just added a few light fortifications between Montmédy, near Sedan, and Dunkirk as a token gesture.

By then France not only had to face the problem of Belgian neutrality: she also had to confront the ominous signs of Hitler's rearmament of Germany, his creation of the Luftwaffe, his bold remilitarization of the Rhineland and his construction of Germany's own Siegfried Line in answer to the Maginot Line. It was not enough to point to the supposed impenetrability of the Ardennes forests or to talk vaguely of French readiness to counter-attack in the flat countryside further north, though Pétain himself duly trotted out both these feeble reassurances. 'This sector is not dangerous,' he insisted in 1934, when he was Minister of War, and his opinion did not alter.

That might sound as if the Maginot Line was begun in complacency and encouraged more complacency. But in fact fear and distrust played a larger part in its history. Fear of Germany, France's old enemy, was obvious and fundamental: however misconceived, the Line was meant as a national bulwark to prevent the *boches* storming across the Rhine and snatching back Alsace and Lorraine, or laying waste the field of Verdun, or bringing their guns within hearing of Paris. Distrust of Britain, France's ally in 1914–18 and the interwar years, is less obvious but was no less important in shaping the Line, as well as the events of 1940 and beyond.

Such distrust had a long history. As the two dominant nation states of western Europe and also its two most ambitious empire-builders, Britain and France were used to treating each other as rivals or enemies rather than as allies. In 1914 a friend of Proust heard a Breton peasant lament that France had picked the wrong people to fight against: 'If it were the English, we would have more heart for it.' If anything, the First World War sharpened rather than dulled this mutual suspicion. Verdun was just one of several occasions which strained the uneasy Franco-British alliance: the British resented the way French concentration on Verdun pulled French troops away from the Somme, and the French resented the way British delays in launching the Somme offensive helped keep German pressure on Verdun. By the end of the war many French felt confirmed in their suspicion that the British furthered their own interests by fighting wars on French rather than British soil and at the expense of more French than British lives.

Fear of Germany and distrust of Britain both helped to determine the popular mood in France during the interwar years. By themselves they might have encouraged a more sensible approach to defence than the Maginot Line. Yet they were overshadowed by a third factor, less tangible but sufficient to blunt the edge of practicality. This was the belief that another war was, quite simply, unthinkable. In Britain it crystallized in the habit of referring to the First World War as 'the war to end all wars'. The French spoke of *la der des ders*, the last of the last. The belief that another war was unthinkable began with the *crise de tristesse sombre* which the troops and perhaps Pétain himself took away with them from Verdun in one form or another. They could not go through that again. It grew into the hope that, with Verdun engraved on its memory, the next generation would know better. Europe must surely have learned its lesson.

Such a reaction shaped the public mood deeply enough to generate disparate and sometimes contradictory results at the level of day-to-day politics. It helped to build a useless line of forts, and it stirred pan-European visions which briefly anticipated the hopes embodied in the creation of the Common Market after the Second World War. It bred the world-weary pacifism voiced in a whole generation of literature about the First World War, and it attracted naïvely well-intentioned recruits to the Franco-German friendly societies which offered useful opportunities to the Nazi propaganda machine. What all these activities had in common was their underlying lack of realism, their belief that, if war was unthinkable, then somehow it was not going to happen. The common result was a lack of preparedness reaching beyond the actions of soldiers and politicians into the national psyche itself. In 1940 France was profoundly ill-prepared not just for the German attack but also for the consequences of her defeat.

PERHAPS THE MOST expressive monument to the mood of France between the wars was not the railway carriage at Rethondes and the nearby inscription denouncing Germany's criminal pride, or the forts of the Maginot Line and their boast that the Germans would not get through. It was, after all, the field of Verdun itself. Energy was spent on making the ravaged landscape into a memorial to victory, certainly, but also into a textbook where Europe might read the lesson that Verdun could not and would not be repeated. Regiments put up memorials to their dead, often speaking of future peace as well as past glory. Identifiable corpses were given decent burial in military cemeteries. Quakers gathered the unidentifiable bones so that they could be heaped in the Ossuaire on the ridge at Douaumont; Pétain laid the foundation stone in 1920 and the building was finally consecrated in 1932.

Only one memorial was lacking. Pétain refused to allow a statue of himself to be put up. Instead, he made known his wish to be buried alongside the men who had served under him, and an appropriate space for his grave was left at the centre of the front row in the cemetery facing the Ossuaire. It seemed a characteristically modest gesture by a man who wanted to be remembered not just as *le vainqueur de Verdun*, the leader who had defended France's honour, but also as *le médecin de l'Armée*, the leader who had taken France's suffering to heart. But the plot was destined to remain vacant. By the time Pétain did eventually die he had been transformed from the embodiment of national pride in the First World War into the embodiment of national disgrace in the Second.

PART I

The Fall of France
and the Path of Collaboration

You take Hitler for another Wilhelm I, the old gentleman who seized Alsace-Lorraine from us, and that was all there was to it. But Hitler is Genghis Khan.

> Paul Reynaud to his cabinet, 12 June 1940

Collaboration means: give me your wristwatch and I will tell you the time.

> Street saying noted by Jean Galtier-Boissière,
> *Mon Journal pendant l'Occupation*, 30 December 1940

I

Invasion and Exodus

We are always the invaded, we are always the ones who
suffer, we are always the ones to be sacrificed.

André Maginot

The peace that is on its way is not the fruit of a decision
reached by man. It spreads apace like a grey leprosy.

Antoine de Saint-Exupéry, *Pilote de guerre* (1942)

IN 1916 THE Germans attacked Verdun for ten months without
taking it; about 162,000 of their troops were killed or reported
missing in action. In 1940 the Germans took Verdun in little more
than a day; they lost fewer than 200 men.* Probably no other detail
so graphically conveys the contrast between France's experience in
the First and Second World Wars or so clearly evokes the sudden and
profound shock that defeat in 1940 inflicted on her.

Like other western democracies, France had continued to hope
against hope that, because another war was unthinkable, it would
also prove impossible. In 1938, when the Third Reich fomented
trouble in the German-speaking Sudetenland of Czechoslovakia, the
French Prime Minister, Edouard Daladier, joined Neville
Chamberlain in fudging the agreement at Munich which their
respective countries greeted with a mixture of shame and relief, cynicism and indifference. In France a contemporary noted: 'There was
a feeling later that if "they" had wriggled out of going to war once,

---

* Among the French wounded and captured was a 24-year-old infantry sergeant, François
Mitterrand. As President, he joined Chancellor Kohl of West Germany (as it then was) in a
ceremony of reconciliation at the battlefield in 1986.

then "they" were quite capable of doing so again – "they" being, as always with the French, the government.' This uneasy yet passive mood had not essentially changed by September 1939 when the Reich invaded Poland, and France was dragged on Britain's coat-tails into declaring war. *'Mourir pour Dantzig?'* ('Why die for Danzig?'):* the rhetorical question Marcel Déat had asked the previous May still summed up the prevailing attitude.

War might have come, but it was still a mere *drôle de guerre*. (The British, belatedly but fractionally more militant, called it 'the funny war' or 'the phoney war'. The Germans called it *Sitzkrieg*, the sitting war, as opposed to *Blitzkrieg*, the lightning war.) France did little or nothing to open a front against Germany which might have relieved the onslaught on Poland. The so-called Saar offensive in September was just a token manoeuvre; British proposals for bombing raids against Germany were vetoed on the grounds that they might provoke retaliation against Paris.

Inevitably France took refuge behind her national bulwark, the Maginot Line, though even here reservists only trickled in to reinforce its garrisons and settled down in a relaxed, if not openly bored, fashion to play football or grow roses. Jean-Paul Sartre's duties consisted largely of sending up balloons and watching them through binoculars:

> This is called 'making a meteorological observation'. Afterwards I phone the battery artillery officers and tell them the wind direction; what they do with this information is their affair. The young ones make some use of the intelligence reports; the old school just shove them straight in the waste-paper basket.

He himself was persuaded that 'there will be no fighting, that it will be a modern war, without massacres as modern painting is without subject, music without melody, physics without matter'. Others talked of having won *la Marne blanche*, a platonic or bloodless battle of the Marne. At best, they hoped for a quick diplomatic settlement. At worst, they foresaw a mild escalation of the sitting war: a drawn-out campaign, like the First World War but this time fought from hygienic bunkers rather than muddy trenches, ending in stalemate on the battlefield and negotiation at the conference table.

---

* Now Gdansk.

Old, vague and timid tactics found their natural leadership in old, vague and timid commanders. General Maurice Gamelin, Chief of the General Staff of National Defence since 1935 and Supreme Commander of French land forces since the outbreak of war, was made to seem older than his 68 years by his reserved and somnolent manner. 'Gagamelin', his subordinate officers called him. He had reacted to Hitler's risky move in remilitarizing the Rhineland in 1936 by overestimating German strength and claiming that a general mobilization would have been needed to oppose it. In effect, he had hummed and hawed and recommended that nothing could be done. In September 1939, torn between his public undertaking to help Poland and his private determination not to risk another Verdun, he enigmatically instructed his commander on the Saar that the tactics to be adopted did not exclude action.

Gamelin responded in much the same fashion when the Reich turned its attention to its western borders in May 1940. His grasp of strategy remained vague, his orders ambiguous and his reports to the cabinet bewildering. 'When Gamelin speaks, it's like running sand through one's fingers,' complained Daladier, himself hardly the most incisive of men. Only Gamelin's air of despondency was eloquent. Gone were the days when the defenders of Verdun could muster rousing or consolatory slogans in time of national emergency. Gone, even, were the days of 1870 when General Ducrot could at least face the prospect of defeat at Sedan with blunt clarity: '*Nous sommes dans un pot de chambre et nous y serons emmerdés!*' ('We're in a chamber pot and we're going to get covered in shit!').

Gamelin owed what prestige he had to his career in the First World War, particularly to his work on Joffre's operations staff during the Miracle of the Marne. In 1940 the instinct of politicians and public alike was to rely on yesterday's men, not even heroes from the previous war but just men associated with heroes from the previous war. When France's military reverses grew into a full-scale *débâcle* during May, it was clear that Gamelin would have to go. But Paul Reynaud, who had succeeded Daladier as Prime Minister shortly before the invasion, delved further into the past. He replaced Gamelin with the 78-year-old General Maxime Weygand, commending him largely on the grounds that he had been Foch's right-hand man, literally by Foch's side at the Victory Parade of 1919. A Catholic right-winger with little enthusiasm for the war, Weygand brought neither a change in tactics nor a change in spirit. His first declaration on taking over was to tell Reynaud that, far from being able to promise victory, he could not offer even the hope of victory.

THE REICH, in contrast, was ready for *Blitzkrieg* rather than *Sitzkrieg*. It had new men, new weaponry and new tactics – a new battle plan with the means and the will to carry it out. Ernst Udet, Ernst Heinkel and Willy Messerschmitt, Gerd von Rundstedt and Heinz Guderian: even the mere roster of its technicians and soldiers is a tribute both to Hitler's shrewdness in surrounding himself with first-rate advisers and to the professionalism of his armed forces. Together, they had seized on the opportunities provided by tanks and planes to transform the art of warfare as it had been practised in 1914–18.

Like all the other major offensives by both sides on the Western Front in the First World War, the German attack on Verdun in 1916 had begun with a bombardment from fixed artillery positions followed by an infantry advance. Tanks, thinly spread out on a long line, had lumbered along in support of the foot soldiers. 'Tanks assist the advance of the infantry, by breaking static obstacles and active resistance put up by the enemy,' Pétain said in 1921, not just summarizing the experience of the past but also laying down military doctrine for the future as well. Even in 1939 he was still insisting that tanks did not change the basic principles of warfare. The country's safety was best guaranteed by a continuous front buttressed with fortification: the Maginot Line. Weygand, shortly before he was recalled to take over the helm from Gamelin, added his reassuring voice: 'There's nothing more to do, everything's in place.'

So France had joined Britain in dismissing the theories of General Fuller and Basil Liddell Hart. De Gaulle, to be sure, had strained his relationship with Pétain, originally his hero and patron, by echoing them in his book *Vers l'armée de métier* (*Towards a Professional Army*, published in 1934).* It envisaged 'an army of manoeuvre and attack, mechanized, armoured, composed of picked men' and looked forward to the day when 'the professional army will move entirely on caterpillar wheels'. His voice was not unique in France any more than it was original – he found useful allies in, for example, the

---

* Belatedly translated into English as *The Army of the Future* (1940).

journalist André Pironneau and the future Prime Minister Paul Reynaud – but it was certainly unpopular. Publishing the book merely spoiled de Gaulle's prospects of rising from the lowly rank of major; he was not promoted colonel until 1937. Like Britain, France went on to misinterpret the example of the civil war in Spain, where General Bergonzoli got the chance to put new tank strategy into action. Because it was only short-lived, the French took the Italian success in penetrating enemy lines as proof that tanks were no good at leading an assault.

The Germans took it as proof that Italians were no good at leading an assault. Hitler continued to encourage Guderian, a veteran of Verdun and future tank commander in the invasion of France, who had studied the writings of Liddell Hart to advantage. Guderian believed in massing tanks, rather than dispersing them, and in using them to make fast, sudden breakthroughs at weak points in the enemy lines. '*Klotzen, nicht kleckern,*' he liked to say: 'Make waves, not ripples.' The Panzer divisions he pioneered were organized around this slogan. Tanks would dictate the attack, and the infantry, carried in armoured vehicles, would support them. The army would advance not at a walking or running pace but at the speed of machines capable of 30 or 40 kilometres an hour.

What role would heavy artillery play in such tactics? The First World War had shown the disadvantages as well as the advantages of the opening bombardment from fixed positions: it might have wrought destruction and panic on a massive scale but it also gave warning of the intention to attack and, besides, it could plough up the terrain which advancing troops needed to cross. Both drawbacks could be fatal to Panzer divisions whose best chance of success lay in surprise and speed. Mobile anti-tank guns supporting the tanks would help, thought Guderian, since he always regarded the tank as the most dangerous enemy of the tank. So would striking at dawn. Yet his Panzers would still be at risk unless a radically new form of artillery was forthcoming.

It was supplied by Ernst Udet in 1935 with the invention of the plane that became known to the Luftwaffe as the Junkers 87 Sturzkampfflugzeug and to the world as the Stuka. During the First World War, in which Udet had served as a pilot, the potential of the plane had been as little developed as that of the tank. Aircraft had been used on the Western Front for support bombing and observation – in spying out, for instance, the German blunders that made the Miracle of the Marne possible – but for little else. Chivalrous clashes between enemy fighters had encouraged the orthodox view that planes were suited more to sport than warfare. Now Udet's Stuka, a single-engined dive-bomber, made artillery airborne. Though vulnerable to anti-aircraft guns and other fighters (as its heavy rate of losses would soon testify) it was tactically superior to the ponderous guns which had lurched through the mud, or sunk into it, on the Western Front. With a top speed of 320 (later 400) kilometres an hour and a range of 160 kilometres, it was highly mobile. It could swoop steeply on its target and deliver its 500-kg load of bombs much more accurately than conventional higher-level bombers like the Heinkel 111 and the Junkers 88. The screech of its siren as it went into its dive added a final demoralizing flourish.

The French had nothing to rival the Stuka or to deal with the threat it posed. Though 1940 would make them joke grimly that they had more airforce generals than planes, their fleet did not compare too unfavourably with the Luftwaffe in terms of strict numbers. But French workshops produced planes more slowly than did German ones and, by failing to pay attention to the Stuka in the same way that the army failed to pay attention to the Panzer, the airforce ordered the wrong planes. As a result, in 1940 it had only fifty planes capable of ground-level attack, hastily brought into service at the last moment. Its best fighter, the Morane 406, lacked firepower and speed, being slower than its German equivalent, the Messerschmitt 109, and barely fast enough to take on the German aircraft it was supposed to deal with. In short, the airforce lacked a coherent strategy or the means to implement it just as badly as the army did, if not more so. The army might have suffered a humiliating defeat in 1940, but the airforce – held in reserve for a long campaign that never developed – hardly got off the runway. Half the planes it lost were destroyed on the ground.

The advantages brought by the combination of the Panzer and the Stuka are obvious to military historians and strategists who enjoy the benefit of hindsight. They were not obvious at the time, and blindness to them was by no means limited to France. In Britain, Winston Churchill could still thank God for the French army, an attitude which looked back to Napoleon's *Grande Armée* rather than forward to the forces commanded by Gamelin and Weygand in 1940. Even Liddell Hart, while conceding that Germany's margin of superiority in numbers put it in a promising position to attack France, could still doubt that it would stand any real chance of success. And such doubts did not go without echo in the German military élite, which, for all its pride in its recent achievements, remained uneasily aware that rearmament under the Reich had a makeshift aspect. It knew, for example, that the remilitarization of the Rhineland had been a risk whose success said more about French passivity than about real German military strength. As for Hitler himself, he was prone to fits of nervousness, yet he was also willing to take risks and particularly willing to take risks which depended on the psychological weaknesses of his enemies.

This readiness to gamble made him urge his commanders to produce a new battle plan for the invasion of France. Thinking on this score had for many years been dominated by the Schlieffen Plan, named after Count von Schlieffen, Chief of the General Staff at the turn of the century. The Rhineland was to be left deliberately weak in order to tempt the French into massing their forces to counter-attack there. The real thrust of the German attack would come further north, from what had always been the weakest point on France's borders: the low-lying countryside of Hainault and Flanders. Here rivers like the Meuse, the Sambre, the Schelde (or Escaut), the Scarpe and the Leie (or Lys) offered convenient routes for an invader, all the more so since they gave access to the Seine, the Marne, the Aisne and the Oise, whose confluence is Paris. Yet in Schlieffen's plan the German army would not head directly for the capital. Instead it would ford the Somme near Amiens and then swing west and south in a wide arc to cross the Seine below Rouen. Paris would be encircled from the west, leaving the German army poised to force the French army back towards the Swiss border.

The plan depended on catching the French on the hop and keeping them guessing. Its potential weakness lay in exposing the right flank of the German army as it turned west and south, as Schlieffen himself was well aware: 'Let the last man brush the Channel with his sleeve,' he urged and, in his dying words, 'Keep the right wing strong.' Its strength lay in creating what Liddell Hart aptly described as a revolving door: the harder the French pushed in the Rhineland, the more they left the way open for the German army wheeling round in the north to catch them from behind. On paper the plan was a classic example of military strategy. Yet it was destined to remain on paper, thanks to the timidity of Schlieffen's successor, the younger Moltke,* and General von Kluck in 1914. Moltke weakened the right flank by failing to attack through Holland as well as Belgium and Luxembourg, and Kluck made things worse by swinging south when he was still short of Paris, exposing his flank to the army guarding the capital. So Joffre had the chance to recover in time to bring about the Miracle of the Marne.

The Reich was not about to make Kluck's mistake again in 1940: that had cost Germany four years of slaughter along a static front and then the humiliation at Versailles in 1919. Nor was it going simply to resurrect the Schlieffen Plan in its original purity. Its armies would come from the north and east, across Holland and Belgium, but the vital attack would drive through the supposedly impenetrable forests of the Ardennes. Rather than advancing directly on Paris or swinging round to the west of the capital, it would head north for the Channel coast near the mouth of the Somme. A 'Panzer corridor', curving across the map of north-eastern France, would chop the defending forces in two. Trapped between the army advancing from the Low Countries and the right flank of the Panzer corridor, the troops in the corner would be pushed into the sea. After consolidating itself against counter-attack, the broad left flank of the Panzer corridor could move on Paris and then mop up the rest of France. Though distantly inspired by the Schlieffen Plan, the strategy of 1940 was bold enough in its innovation to deserve its own name. With a typically melodramatic flourish, the Reich called it *Sichelschnitt*, the cut of the sickle.

SICHELSCHNITT WAS LAUNCHED at dawn on 10 May. In the south General von Leeb's army faced the Maginot Line, encouraging the French to look for attack from that quarter; in fact, it was the weakest of the three German armies deployed and the least active in the coming battle. In the north Field Marshal von Bock's army moved into Belgium and Holland across the Maas (the Flemish name for the Meuse), subjecting them to a combined onslaught of tanks, infantry and bombers, as well as airborne landings which seized bridgeheads. An Allied plan for defending a front running north from Sedan along the Meuse and the Dyle and up to Breda,

---

* Not to be confused with his uncle Count von Moltke, the nineteenth-century commander.

near the Maas estuary, quickly crumbled, but not before it had served its chief purpose in German eyes. It had made the Allies concentrate their strength too far north, as if the Germans were about to follow the Schlieffen Plan, and leave the stretch between Sedan and Namur facing the Ardennes forests defended only by weaker units.

So the attention of Allied leaders, their propaganda machinery and their press had switched from the illusory calm of the Maginot Line to the dramatic events in the north while the Reich made the breakthrough crucial to the success of *Sichelschnitt*. Positioned between Leeb and Bock's forces, Field Marshal von Rundstedt's army came round the top of the Maginot Line at Longwy to strike through the Ardennes. Guderian accompanied the First Division of his Panzer Corps across the Luxembourg border above Vianden and Rommel's Seventh Division entered Belgium to head toward Dinant on the Meuse. On 13 May Rommel crossed the river at Houx, between Namur and Dinant, and Guderian crossed it further south at Sedan, a name already fraught with memories of France's humiliation in 1870. The impenetrable Ardennes had been penetrated.

By 18 May the Panzer divisions of Rundstedt's army had regrouped round Saint-Quentin and, rather than heading west in the direction of Paris, were starting to swing north towards the Channel. They reached the coast at Noyelles, near Abbeville, on 20 May and broadened the corridor they had blazed by taking Boulogne and Calais two days later. Allied plans to nip the advance in a pincer movement – the French attacking from the south and the British Expeditionary Force from the north – began with Major-General Martel's spirited Frankforce operation at Arras on 21 May but soon petered out in confusion and rising ill-will between the French and the British.

At this critical point in the German manoeuvre, Hitler began to vacillate, as he was prone to do when the first stage of a great gamble had worked but the second still lay ahead. He worried about delays in bringing up his infantry to reinforce the southern flank of the Panzer corridor along the Aisne. On 24 May, as the British forces began to fall back on Dunkirk, he ordered a halt to the Panzers' advance. Historians have argued that the decision might actually have originated with Rundstedt rather than Hitler, but this matters less than the obvious point: the German attack had not just succeeded so far but had succeeded with an ease and speed which unnerved Hitler and his high command as much as it did the French and the British.

The resulting three-day lull, followed by a spirited rearguard action from the French round Lille, made it possible for the British to consolidate a bridgehead at Dunkirk and organize an evacuation from the beaches. By the time the last men left, on 3 June, 227,000 British troops – virtually the entire British Expeditionary Force – and 110,000 French troops had been rescued.

Even with this unexpected relief for the British, by the early days of June the ultimate success of *Sichelschnitt* was assured and with its success the fate of France was sealed. Belgium and Holland had already fallen: the Dutch army had surrendered on 14 May and the Belgian army on 28 May. The British had been pushed back across the Channel in disarray, leaving most of their *matériel* and some of their pride behind them. All that remained was for the armies of the Reich to mop up as much of the rest of France as they chose. Their front reached Amiens and the Somme by 5 June. The last battle Weygand had promised behind the Somme and the Aisne proved a mere gesture to satisfy honour, not a serious attempt to prevent defeat, and the front overran Rouen a few days later. An attack in the forests of the Argonne west of Verdun made it more than 300 kilometres long, stretching across the width of France.

The government fled Paris on 10 June, beginning a journey which would take it first to Tours and the châteaux of the Loire valley, then to Bordeaux, and finally via Clermont-Ferrand to Vichy. Weygand declared the capital 'open' on 12 June and contact was made the next day between General Dentz, the French military governor, and his German counterpart, General von Studnitz. The Germans' first demand was that the regimental flags captured from them in the First World War be returned; Dentz had no idea where they were. Studnitz's Eighty-Seventh Infantry Division entered Paris on 14 June without meeting any opposition. 'The terrible thing has come about,' wrote Roger Langeron, *préfet* of police, in his diary:

> An immense, an interminable column of motorized troops has begun to cross Paris. They are coming from Saint-Denis and from the northern suburbs and in the direction of Montrouge. First motorcyclists with side-cars, in their leather overcoats. Then the weight of the armour, of tanks. The streets are virtually empty, and the majority of houses are shuttered.

The swastika replaced the *tricolore* on the Hôtel de Ville by midday. France, André Maurois said, had become a body without a head.

In the shadow of such losses, Italy's declaration of war against

France and Britain on 10 June seemed of minor importance. It brought virtually no military result – the Italian army scarcely dented France's south-eastern border – but simply announced Mussolini's determination to share in the pickings from a German victory. And in the week following the fall of Paris the armies of the Reich went on to consolidate their victory: they reached the tips of the Breton peninsula at Cherbourg in the north and Brest in the west, seized the Atlantic coastline down as far as Bordeaux, crossed the Loire, encircled the troops who had been ordered to abandon the forts on the Maginot Line in the east, and spread beyond Besançon and Lyon to the Swiss border.

Such a recital of dates and place names does no more than hint at the chaos which actually overtook the French army on the ground. In some places the French mistook German soldiers for British simply because they could not believe the enemy had advanced so far into their territory so quickly. In others, French soldiers fell back only to discover that the positions they were retreating to had already been taken. Elsewhere, they just stood by, idle and bewildered spectators rather than participants in the fighting. They surrendered in numbers so great that the Germans worried their progress would be held up: some were just told to throw away their weapons and make themselves scarce. Some did not wait to be told, but discarded their identifying uniforms as well as their weapons. Officers who tried to resist the rout rather than joining it were often unsuccessful and sometimes at risk. On 20 June troops near the Maginot Line killed an officer, Colonel Charly, who ordered them to fight their way out of their encircled position in the village of Tantimont. It is said that a tank officer who wanted to defend Vierzon, on the Cher near Bourges, was lynched by the inhabitants; veterans of the First World War prevented an officer from blowing up a bridge to delay the German advance in the Indre.

France had entered the war with little enough enthusiasm. Under the German onslaught she now became a country of civilians who no longer wanted to be part of any war and of *fuyards*, soldiers not in retreat but in open flight, soldiers who no longer wanted to be soldiers at any price. Not all the army succumbed to panic, of course. There were, for example, the troops (largely north African) who fought stubbornly under General Molinié at Lille until 1 June, buying precious time for the British Expeditionary Force to evacuate Dunkirk. Weygand's last battle may hardly have deserved the name, but it did encourage pockets of resistance which could give trouble to the Germans, including Rommel and his Panzers. Particularly effective were the so-called *hérissons,* or hedgehogs: small groups of soldiers dug in and ordered to stay in position even when the enemy had surrounded or outflanked them.

The French could grasp a few other fragments of consolation from the general collapse. In May 1940 de Gaulle was 49 and still a colonel. Initially he refused a minor post in Reynaud's cabinet and chose to serve on the battlefield. Put in command of the Fourth Armoured Division, based round Laon, he found ample confirmation that the fighting was going as badly as he had feared but also the opportunity to put into practice the tactics he had been advocating since before the war. Mustering his ill-equipped tanks, he set out on 17 May for the road junction at Montcornet, north-east of Laon and a critical point on the flank of the Panzer corridor heading towards the Channel. To start with, his battalions caught by surprise an enemy which no longer expected to see French tanks advancing rather than retreating. They even managed to take some prisoners. But, lacking infantry support, anti-aircraft guns or protection from the air, and suffering heavy attack from Stukas, de Gaulle soon had to order his men to withdraw: they were, he said, 'lost children'.

This unsurprising failure did not deter him from two other assaults on the Panzer corridor. On 19 May he struck out for Crécy-sur-Serre, north of Laon, before finding it prudent to heed his field commander's orders and fall back south of the Aisne. From 27 to 30 May he attacked the German bridgehead round Abbeville, this time managing not just to take prisoners but actually to gain ground: 'an atmosphere of victory hovered over the battlefield. Everyone held his head high. The wounded were smiling. The guns fired gaily. Before us, in a pitched battle, the Germans had retired.' From the enemy point of view the engagement was a mere pinprick which caused nothing like the anxiety Martel's Frankforce attack at Arras did, but de Gaulle had at least contributed raw material to the legends that would soon surround his early career. 'In the course of the battle of France,' he would ask rhetorically in his *Mémoires de guerre,* 'what other ground had been won or would be won, except this strip 14 kilometres deep?'

The behaviour of the Cavalry School at Saumur – founded in the eighteenth century and one of the most prestigious military academies in the country – contributed to a different legend. Bock's

Panzers arrived at the Loire crossing on 18 June. The 2,500 or so cadets from the school opted to hold a front of 26 kilometres covering the bridges, despite all the disadvantages which made resistance hopeless: they were not fully trained, they were armed only with training weapons and they were vastly outnumbered. Their defence managed to halt the German advance for two days, though at a cost of many casualties and considerable damage to the town. At least in one local instance, the reputation for bravery and professionalism of an army which proudly traced its descent from Napoleon's *grognards* and the defenders of Verdun had been vindicated.

Yet it was far too late for such futile heroism, if there ever had been a proper time for it. On the day the cadets began their resistance, the politicians were already suing for an armistice. On 22 June, two days after the Germans crossed the Saumur bridges, the armistice was formally agreed. Since the launch of its western offensive against Luxembourg, Belgium and Holland on 10 May, Germany had lost about 27,000 men, with another 18,000 missing and 111,000 wounded – that is to say, roughly a third of its losses at Verdun in 1916. The total numbers of dead and wounded suffered by the British were 68,000, by the Belgians about 23,000 and by the Dutch about 10,000. As for France, nearly two million of her soldiers, or about 5 per cent of her population, had been taken prisoner. About one and a half million of them would be transported to Germany, making their fate one of the running sores of the Occupation. In all, about 90,000 of her troops had been killed and another 200,000 wounded – figures that come disturbingly close to French losses at Verdun in 1916. But the battle of Verdun had dragged on for ten months: the German offensive of 1940 had lasted just six weeks.

POLITICAL SURRENDER DOES not necessarily follow military defeat, even defeat on the scale France had suffered. Soldiers in neighbouring Holland and Belgium were told to stop shooting and lay down their arms, but their governments did not enter into negotiations with the Reich. Queen Wilhelmina of the Netherlands and her government went into exile. So, snubbing King Leopold, did the Belgian government; so too did the Grand Duchess and the government of Luxembourg. In France, however, the chaos that overtook her armed forces quickly bred a clamour from public, soldiers and politicians alike for negotiation. The announcement that talks with the enemy had begun surprised nobody and the news that an armistice had been agreed came as a relief to most people. Indeed, they greeted it not as a temporary truce but as the prelude to a lasting peace. France was out of the war.

In other words, the public mood which had made France unprepared to resist the savage onslaught on the battlefield had also left her unprepared to resist it in the council chamber. Few governments could have been less equipped to deal with the crisis than those which presided over the last, sorry days of the Third Republic. Their ineffectiveness was aptly embodied in President Albert Lebrun. Constitutionally, he was little more than a figurehead. Personally, he was amiable but alarmingly mild: he cried, Pierre Laval said maliciously, whenever a cloud covered the sun. Edouard Daladier, Prime Minister at the time of the Munich agreement and the outbreak of war, was scarcely better. He led France through the *drôle de guerre* in an appropriately inert fashion, unable to rise or get his colleagues to rise above personal and party rivalries. As a result, he made himself doubly vulnerable: to the charge that he was not prosecuting the war vigorously enough and to the charge that he was bothering to prosecute it at all.

Yet the man who replaced Daladier on 22 March 1940 was of a different mettle. On the face of it, Paul Reynaud was an ideal choice as leader of a country which would shortly need to fight battles vigorously and confront defeat resolutely. Temperamentally he was fiery and quick-witted; his detractors might call him a *Napoléon de poche* but in such desperate times even a pocket Napoleon was valuable. Before 1939 he had allied himself with the military attitudes personified by de Gaulle, who would soon join his cabinet, and with the hostility to Hitler personified by Churchill, who would soon succeed Chamberlain in Britain. 'The stake in this total war is total,' he told the deputies who ratified his appointment: 'To conquer is to save everything. To succumb is to lose everything.' He pledged that his government would strive 'to arouse, reassemble and direct all the energies of France to fight and to conquer'. His bitter failure mirrored the fall of France.

The insuperable problem Reynaud faced was that he had no permanent power base. Indeed, he lacked even the temporary support he might have hoped the crisis would attract. Though a seasoned politician – before becoming Prime Minister he had held cabinet office seven times, most recently as Daladier's Minister of Finance – he was essentially a loner and, by virtue of his opinions, something of an outsider. His disapproval of the Munich agreement in 1938 had severed his ties with Flandin's moderate conservative group, to which he had belonged until then. His enthusiasm for the war had alienated those further to the right. Daladier and his radicals now resented his rise at their expense. In fact, he owed his vote of confidence from the deputies largely to the generous intervention of the Socialist Léon Blum. Yet in the vote itself those who favoured his appointment outnumbered those who abstained or opposed it only by one. Edouard Herriot, the Speaker of the Chamber, was heard to doubt if he had really achieved even this slender majority.

So Reynaud was far from being in a position to create a *Union Sacrée*, or truce between parties, of the sort France had enjoyed for much of the First World War. From the start he found himself fatally entangled in the manoeuvrings of Third Republic politicians who showed no inclination to change their usual ways. De Gaulle, who was in the gallery of the Palais-Bourbon for the debate which confirmed Reynaud in power, was horrified to find it dominated by 'the spokesmen of those groups or men who considered themselves injured by the new coalition. The danger in which the country stood, the necessity of a national effort, the co-operation of the free world, were mentioned only to adorn claims and complaints.' For fear of further offending those on the right, Reynaud did not dare to appoint too many Socialists to his cabinet; in particular, he shunned Léon Blum who, as leader of two Front Populaire governments, was still particularly objectionable. For fear of further offending the radicals, he could get rid of the defeated and embittered Daladier only with difficulty and by degrees. While Prime Minister, Daladier had served as both his own Minister for Foreign Affairs and his own Minister of War and National Defence. He managed to hang on to the War Ministry until Reynaud's first reshuffle, when he was moved back to Foreign Affairs and Reynaud himself took over the War Ministry; a second reshuffle removed him from the government altogether.

Politicians had earned the Third Republic the contemptuous nickname of the *République des camarades* (Republic of Cronies) by such games of musical chairs. Forced to continue playing them by the fragility of his hold on power, Reynaud actually managed to weaken his position by opening the door to those who lacked his own resolve that the fight be carried on to its bitter end. It is true that his first reshuffle, on 18 May, promoted Georges Mandel to the Ministry of the Interior and thus put at his side a determined ally whose early career as Clemenceau's aide also linked him with the glories of the past. By the same token, a second reshuffle on 5 June brought in de Gaulle (newly promoted to the rank of general)* as Under-Secretary of State for War and the staunchly militant Yvon Delbos as Minister of Education. Yet the first reshuffle had also replaced Gamelin with the more emphatically defeatist Weygand as Supreme Commander. The second promoted Paul Baudouin, a long-time advocate of the need for an armistice, and appointed new members who agreed with him.

By far the most significant change came on 18 May, when Reynaud made Pétain his Deputy Prime Minister, praising him – in the same speech which reminded people that Weygand had been Foch's right-hand man – as 'the man who knows how a French victory can come out of a cataclysm'. The praise of both men was singularly wide of the mark and Reynaud himself would declare in his memoirs that he had made a fundamental mistake. The depths of Weygand's defeatism may not have been known to him until it was too late. But, from his position on the sidelines as France's ambassador to Franco's Spain, Pétain had made his views clear to anyone who cared to listen. Since the outset he had thought France's involvement in the war a mistake, even if she should be victorious. The early successes of the German invasion made him fear that France faced losses too great to sustain. By the time he returned from Madrid to Paris he was all but convinced that France would lose and so should end the fighting as quickly as she could. Yet Reynaud had not been simply panicked by the pressure of events into appointing Pétain: he had been wooing him at least since early April. And, though Pétain would represent himself as having returned to the centre of public life only in response to a national emergency, he seems to have agreed in principle that he would serve under Reynaud by the beginning of May, before the Germans had even invaded.

Historians have probably puzzled too much over Reynaud's decision and exaggerated how mistaken it was. In fact, it would have

---

* For whatever reason, he still preferred to style himself colonel when he went into exile.

been surprising if he had not brought Pétain into the government and failure to do so might even have accelerated his own and France's fall. Pétain was by then aged 84 and starting to show it. Contemporaries duly admired his snow-white moustache, clear complexion and dignified bearing – all the attributes that made them call him a man of marble – but they also noted his growing deafness. Insiders whispered that he was going senile too, and spoke knowingly of his 'daily hour of lucidity': they pointed to his habit of throwing irrelevant remarks into the conversation, of wandering remorselessly from the point in question and of falling asleep in public. Yet he was still a hero to a nation otherwise deeply divided in its political views. The right admired him for his belief in the old-school discipline which had made France glorious, the left for the humanity which had tempered his generalship. It was inevitable that Reynaud should have felt his untarnished presence – and perhaps merely his presence rather than his advice – necessary to the credibility of a government struggling, with the weakest of mandates, to handle a rapidly growing crisis.

The reputation Pétain enjoyed was undoubtedly balm to a man, proud and scornful beneath his apparent modesty, whose career in the First World War had both unexpectedly rewarded him late in life and then deprived him of ultimate command. He turned sometimes a blind and sometimes an enigmatic eye to the backstairs intrigues which, since the outbreak of war and even before, had been promoting him as France's best hope. He neither compromised nor committed himself. He did not publicly encourage the deputies who greeted Reynaud's appointment as Prime Minister with the prophecy that Pétain would soon replace him and bring an end to the fighting. He replied to Reynaud's overtures in April by saying that he would serve only as a military adviser. In short, he behaved like that most seductive and dangerous of animals: the man of political ambition who professes to be, and convinces the public he is, above ambition and above politics. He did not enter the government until leaflets were already circulating on the streets with this slogan beneath his photograph: 'Yesterday, a great soldier! . . . Today, a great diplomat! . . . Tomorrow? . . .' And, when he did enter, the veteran right-winger Charles Maurras greeted the news in his journal, *L'Action Française*, with one word: '*Enfin*'. At last.

Pétain's influence proved decisive and disastrous. He immediately established himself as the rallying-point – though hardly the most effective spokesman – for the *mous* (or doves) in their quarrel with the *durs* (or hawks) like Mandel, Delbos and de Gaulle who supported Reynaud. The rift in the government emerged during the build-up to the Dunkirk evacuation at the end of May and, as it grew wider in June, the weight of opinion moved steadily towards the doves. At its first meeting in Bordeaux on 15 June two-thirds of the cabinet supported a proposal by Camille Chautemps, a former Prime Minister with an unusually well-developed gift for compromise, that France send out unofficial feelers through a neutral party to find out if the Reich would be ready to offer an armistice on 'honourable' terms.

Yet even before this, on 13 June, Reynaud had been reduced to asking Churchill if Britain would be willing to release France from her treaty obligations so that she could negotiate a separate peace. The various forms in which the inquiry was recorded do not make it clear if it was practical or hypothetical. Reynaud may have been hoping for an emphatically negative response which would strengthen his hand against the *mous*. If so, he was outmanoeuvred by Baudouin, who contrived to interpret the essence of Churchill's reply, *'Je comprends que vous allez demander l'armistice'*, not as 'I understand that you are going to ask for an armistice' but as 'I understand that you should ask for an armistice'.*

Reynaud himself reassured an alarmed de Gaulle that he had made the inquiry just to shock the British into sending more help. If this was the case, it was still a sorry comment on the level to which Franco-British relations had sunk. Only a month before, the omens had seemed promising. Churchill and Reynaud already respected one another before they came into office and, by what looked like an amazing piece of luck, the usually fragile ability of the British and the French to co-operate was due to be tested at one of the few points in history when the Prime Minister of Britain was a francophile and the Prime Minister of France an anglophile.

It did not withstand the test, though Churchill and Reynaud remained on cordial terms. Traditional suspicions were reawakened, voiced and encouraged in France by the *mous*, who numbered anglo-

---

* 'Tell them my French is not as bad as all that,' Churchill protested. Unfortunately it often was. After Churchill had brushed aside his interpreter and broken into French at one meeting, Reynaud absentmindedly turned to his own interpreter and murmured: *'Traduction?'* ('Translation?').

phobia among their grounds for disliking the war. Dunkirk fed their scepticism of Britain's real value as an ally. The sacrifice of French lives in defending the rear of the British Expeditionary Force and the British failure to evacuate French soldiers from the beaches during the first days of the retreat added new bitterness. It was not assuaged by Churchill's belated insistence that British and French troops henceforward be evacuated *bras dessus, bras dessous,* arm in arm. The French could, and did, still point to the disparity between the numbers of British and French finally rescued – 227,000 as against 110,000 – and to the 30,000 or more French soldiers left in the lurch.

They remained disappointed, suspicious or angry at Britain's failure to commit its full resources, particularly the RAF, to their defence. At Briare on 11 June Churchill insisted that the British needed to reserve twenty-five fighter squadrons to preserve 'our chance of life'. When he tried to reinvigorate Pétain by a tactful reference to the Allies' reversal of their difficulties during Ludendorff's offensive in March 1918, the Marshal (according to de Gaulle) angrily reminded him that at Amiens he had sent forty divisions to help the British: 'Today we're the ones getting smashed to pieces. Where are your forty divisions?' The long-nursed grievance against Britain was still on his mind when he sought to account for France's defeat in one of his early radio broadcasts, on 20 June: 'In May 1918 we had eighty-five British divisions; in May 1940 there were only ten.'

By this time, de Gaulle lamented, 'strategic unity between London and Paris was practically broken'. Always far from being identical, British and French perceptions of their respective national interests now differed radically. Believing that France would inevitably be defeated, Britain sought to delay her fall in order to prepare its own defence and to minimize the advantage to Germany: hence the overriding concern that the French navy should not fall into German hands, the first question Churchill raised when Reynaud broached the issue of a separate peace on 13 June. As for the French, or at any rate the *mous* in the government, they were not convinced by Churchill's repeated declarations of Britain's resolve to fight on regardless: Pétain, Anthony Eden noted, was 'mockingly incredulous'. 'You have no army,' the Marshal told Churchill's liaison officer, General Spears. 'What could you achieve where the French army has failed?' If France could be crushed so quickly, then Britain would either capitulate or be defeated with equal speed. Weygand claimed that, once his army had been beaten, Britain would not wait a week before negotiating with the Reich and that its neck would be 'wrung like a chicken'.*

These considerations alone guaranteed the failure of the last, quixotic attempt to rescue the Franco-British alliance and prevent France seeking an armistice. It was Jean Monnet of the French Economic Mission in London, with the French ambassador and an official of the British Foreign Office, who originated the idea of an 'indissoluble union' between the two peoples: joining their governments, resources, liabilities and, above all, their destinies.† They put it to de Gaulle when he arrived in London on 16 June. Though he had no difficulty foreseeing a host of practical objections, particularly to handling so grand and complex a plan through a simple exchange of notes, he thought it 'a manifestation of solidarity which might take on a real significance'. Churchill agreed and before the day was over de Gaulle was able to phone Reynaud in Bordeaux with the text of a proposed declaration of union.

The French Prime Minister returned – 'transfigured with joy', noted General Spears – to the cabinet meeting then in progress and to final disillusionment. Pétain dismissed the union as marriage with a corpse. Chautemps or the Marshal's supporter Jean Ybarnégaray (the record of these eleventh-hour deliberations is not clear) said it would reduce France to the status of a British dominion: 'Better to be a Nazi province. At least we know what that means.' Reynaud retorted that he preferred to collaborate with his allies rather than his enemies, but the meeting returned to Chautemps' proposal for finding out what terms Germany might dictate to France – the slippery slope, as Churchill had called it, on which it was impossible to stop.

So the scheme for Franco-British union was buried in the same grave as all the other schemes by which Reynaud had sought to resist the growing clamour for an armistice. On the same day it was conceived and died, President Roosevelt turned down a desperate appeal for immediate help from the United States. Before that, Reynaud had taken seriously a proposal for creating a Breton redoubt: the govern-

---

* Mandel attributed the phrase to him, though Weygand disowned it (and much else) when he gave evidence at Pétain's trial in 1945. Churchill made his famous riposte, 'Some chicken! Some neck!', in the House of Commons on 30 December 1941.

† After the war Monnet took a leading part in founding the European Community, being proclaimed by the council of its heads of government the first (and still the only) 'Honorary Citizen of Europe'.

ment and what remained of the army would withdraw to the Breton peninsula, which with British naval support could be held long enough to allow a more calculated retreat into exile, perhaps to one of France's north African territories. He had sent de Gaulle, and Churchill had dispatched General Sir Alan Brooke, to assess the position in Rennes before the speed of events pushed the plan aside.

The idea of north Africa as the base for a government and army continuing the fight from exile had been voiced even earlier (Reynaud had indicated his support for it by the end of May) and it remained practicable until the last moment. Yet it was discredited by Pétain himself in an unusually eloquent speech at the cabinet meeting on 13 June. He began by casting a sceptical eye on the dying plan for a Breton redoubt. A redoubt in mainland France, he argued, would not really be secure and, besides, could be created only with help from British reinforcements. He then turned his attention to north Africa. To form a government in exile outside mainland France would simply be to abandon the country to the invaders. He himself would always stay 'among the French people to share their sorrows and their miseries'.

It was a curious stance for a one-time advocate of strategic with-drawal to adopt, but it was immensely effective. In fact, Pétain had transformed the rhetoric and logic of debate about the honourable course for any future government. Those who remained in France, whatever the circumstances, were patriots; those who left were cowards and deserters. So the nineteen deputies and one senator who took advantage of the offer to sail for Casablanca on board the *Massilia* on 21 June were merely the victims of a shabby political trick to vilify their reputations. They included Mandel, Delbos and the former Prime Minister Daladier; all were arrested on one pretext or another after they arrived in north Africa.* De Gaulle, who slipped virtually unnoticed on to General Spears' plane for London on 17 June, was tried and condemned to death in his absence. Again and again in the months and years to come the underlying rationale of Pétain's government was simply this: it was legitimate, it was patri-otic, it was the guardian of France's honour not because of what it did or did not do but because of where it was.

By the time of the cabinet meeting at Bordeaux on 16 June Pétain and his supporters were firmly in the ascendant. In a gesture of

---

* See Chapter 6 for Mandel's fate.

deliberate strength he read out a draft letter of resignation, declaring himself unwilling to continue in a government which further delayed bringing about an immediate end to hostilities. After Churchill and de Gaulle's proposal for Franco-British union had been brushed aside and Chautemps' proposal for inquiring about an armistice revived, Reynaud had no options left. He tendered his resignation to President Lebrun, in no doubt as to who would succeed him but nonetheless looking like a man from whom a great burden had been lifted. Late that evening Lebrun asked Pétain to form a new government. Modest and unprepared as ever, the Marshal promptly took a list of proposed cabinet members from his pocket.

WHEN CHURCHILL, VISITING the French government in Paris on 16 May, looked out of the windows of the Foreign Office on the Quai d'Orsay, he could see black smoke rising in the courtyard. Some of it was drifting along the river to the Palais-Bourbon, seat of the Chamber of Deputies and the National Assembly, where politicians would soon hear the official announcement that Pétain had been recalled from Madrid to serve at Reynaud's side. The Germans had crossed the Meuse and the way to Paris lay open. Ministry officials had been ordered to destroy government documents and, after rejecting the idea of throwing them into the Seine, had soaked their green folders in petrol and made a bonfire. The politicians and civil servants were getting ready to leave.

So the smoke warned the people of Paris that not just their army but also their government was being routed. It tempted them to flee as well. So, too, did the scenes witnessed by the American writer Clare Boothe Luce at the Gare du Nord and the Gare de l'Est, where refugees from Belgium, Holland and Luxembourg were pouring in every day:

> They came off the trains with their bewildered faces, white faces, bloody faces, faces beaten out of human shape by the Niagaras of human tears that had flowed down them. . . . With bicycles and bundles and battered suitcases, holding twisted bird-cages, babies, and dogs in stiff arms, or holding one another up, they came and came and came.

On 10 May, the first day of the German offensive, about 25,000 Luxembourgeois had fled down the road which led through Esch-sur-Alzette to France. One way or another, about two million

Belgian refugees would cross the French border before the fighting was over.

At first they were received hospitably. But when King Leopold ordered his army to surrender on 28 May – an order given, in Reynaud's angry words, 'without a thought or a word for the French or British troops who went to the aid of his country in response to his agonized appeal' – the tide of public feeling turned against Belgium. Until the authorities brought in severe penalties for such behaviour, the French threw Belgian refugees out of the houses where they had been welcomed, burned the carts in which they had carried their goods, shouted *salauds* (bastards) at them in the streets, and attacked them in the railway stations and on the roads.

By the time the Belgians surrendered the French themselves were on the move. *L'exode* – the exodus – had begun. 'Somewhere in the north of France', wrote Saint-Exupéry, who was serving as a pilot, 'a boot had scattered an ant-hill, and the ants were on the march. Laboriously. Without panic. Without hope. Without despair. On the march as if in duty bound.' The French, of course, had traditionally been among the most stay-at-home people in Europe, sentimentally loyal to the native soil of their *pays*, fiercely attached to their domestic comforts and reluctant to leave home even to go on holiday, much less to emigrate. The First World War had unsettled their habits, and the paid holidays introduced by Blum's Front Populaire government in the mid-1930s had encouraged working people from the towns to sample the delights of the countryside: 1940 completed the change with sudden violence. By June, historians have variously estimated, between six and ten million of the country's forty million inhabitants had left their homes.

The exodus started in the regions directly in or threatened by the enemy line of advance. In central Paris, which normally had a population approaching three million, there were only about 800,000 people to see the German army arrive on 14 June; in affluent *arrondissements* only about a quarter of the population, and in poor ones only about a half, remained. 'Shops shut,' noted one Parisian who had refused to leave:

> The odd passer-by. The Rue de Châteaudun deserted. Same thing around the Opéra, the Avenue de l'Opéra, and the streets off it. All buildings have their doors closed. . . . The *grands boulevards* in the direction of the Madeleine, on the far side from the corner of the Rue Drouot, as far

as the eye could carry, absolutely deserted, all the shops closed. And the silence!

Another witness, who had stayed behind in her flat with her husband, remembered that even the clock over the Renault factory had been allowed to run down:

> We stared so long into the distance that the angle of the fingers, marking twenty past eight, seemed to be engraved on my brain. The only living thing we could see was a little grey dog which walked interminably round a tree on the pavement beneath us. All day long it walked in circles round the tree. From time to time one of us went down to comfort it, but it ran away, only to come back when we had gone.

It was the end of the first week in July before the population reached a million again.

At Evreux in Normandy the population sank from about 20,000 to less than 200 by 11 June, after the Germans had overrun nearby Rouen, and was still only half its normal level a month later. By mid-June the number of inhabitants left at Chartres, in the Beauce, had dropped from about 23,000 to about 800; at Troyes, capital of the Champagne region, it had dropped from 58,000 to just thirty. Such places, a British journalist noted, took on a 'naked and bruised' look. Tame birds freed from their cages flew aimlessly about; lost or abandoned dogs roamed the streets. Most pathetic of all were the stragglers too old or too ill to keep up with the exodus: 'A man came by with his head down, wheeling a sick woman in a handcart. They didn't give us a glance, as though no man's hand could help them.'

The depopulation of the island of Sein was particularly dramatic. A bleak slab of rock off the western tip of Brittany near Audierne and Pont-Croix, it usually sheltered about 1,100 people, mostly fishing families, though in 1940 many of the men were already away on military service. The Germans did not reach Sein until July but by then the islanders had taken communal action. On 24 and 25 June two small fleets of fishing boats had put to sea with 133 men aged from 14 to 51 – virtually all the able-bodied males from the island. Each took a little food and a litre of wine, whatever money their families had been able to muster and a hunting rifle, if they owned one. They docked at Falmouth and de Gaulle welcomed them in London as early recruits to the Free French. 'The island of Sein stands watch duty for France,' he exclaimed.

Some pilots made the trip across the Channel as well. The Swiss and Spanish borders began to attract people eager to leave the country, especially Jews and political exiles from Germany and Central Europe. But most people could not leave France and did not want to, however fearful they may have been of staying in their homes as the invaders approached. Some fled towards Brittany: there were more than 400,000 refugees on the road leading from Paris to Quimper and another 80,000 crowding into Laval in the Mayenne, which had been designated a receiving point for people from the Aisne. Most refugees headed south, hoping that the Loire would form a trench line, as the Somme and the Marne had done in the First World War, or that in time of hardship and danger life in the country would prove easier than life in the towns and cities. And even when these illusions had been exploded they kept on going in greater and greater numbers, propelled by what Saint-Exupéry called a 'crazy contagion'.

So, as the north and east emptied, towns and cities further south were glutted with refugees. The mayor of Beaune-la-Rolande, on the way to the Loire crossing at Orléans, found himself faced with the task of receiving 7,000 or 8,000 refugees. As the exodus rolled on, about 200,000 people were sleeping rough in the streets and public gardens of Limoges. In Bordeaux the pre-war population more than doubled to 600,000. The population of Brive-la-Gaillarde in the Corrèze grew from 30,000 to 100,000, of Cahors in the Lot from 13,000 to between 60,000 and 70,000. Pau, in the foothills of the Pyrénées, had been a major centre for refugees during the First World War; in 1940 it had to deal with an influx of well over 100,000 homeless people.

The chaos was made worse by lack of official planning for such a contingency, despite the example of the First World War. Mayors and gendarmes who might have been in a position to check the impulse to flee in fact stimulated it and sometimes led the flight themselves. Saint-Exupéry and a fellow-airman tried to dissuade a group of villagers near Laon from taking to the road, but the mayor had told them to go and so they insisted. He described a scene that was being repeated all over the country:

All the stables, all the sheds, all the barns and garages had vomited into the narrow streets a most extraordinary collection of contrivances. There were new motor-cars, and there were ancient farm carts that for half a century had stood untouched under layers of dust. There were hay wains and lorries, carry-alls and tumbrils. . . . Every box on wheels had been dug up and was now laden with the treasures of the home. From door to vehicle, wrapped in bedsheets sagging with hernias, the treasures were being piled in.

One woman planning to take her children and her sister-in-law's family, seven passengers in all, did not even know how to drive: 'She won't have gone three miles before running into half a dozen cars, stripping her gears, and blowing out her tyres.'

Inexperienced drivers were not the only hazard on the road. Cars ran out of petrol or broke down or got stuck in ditches when the sound of approaching Stukas made them swerve for cover. Weighed down with people and possessions, farm carts broke wheels or axles. There were traffic jams, pile-ups and arguments. Some people simply got lost. Others had to abandon their vehicles, with most of the possessions they had thought precious enough to bring, and join those already trudging along on foot with overloaded prams or bicycles. They got used to sleeping on the floors of churches, in disused buildings and in the open. They began to run short of food, despite the efforts of overwhelmed local authorities. Even water could run dangerously low: in several places there were reports of canny locals standing at the roadside selling it by the bottle and the glass.

The railway stations presented a similar picture. On 11 May, the day after the Reich began its western offensive, a Paris newspaper reported 'an atmosphere of total calm' at the city's main stations. In the next month it evaporated. People of all classes jostled together, waiting for trains whose timetables lost a little more meaning with each day that passed. By 10 June a foreign journalist found about 20,000 people waiting outside the Gare d'Austerlitz. 'I have now been standing wedged in this seething mass for over three hours,' he continued. 'A woman standing near us has fainted. Two *agents* force their way through, and carry her off over the heads of the crowd. Children are crying all round, and the many babies in arms look like being crushed to death.' The crowds outside the Gare Montparnasse, hoping to leave for Brittany, filled the Place de Rennes and backed all the way up the boulevard to the church of Saint-François-Xavier, almost a kilometre away. A woman gave birth on the pavement.

Things were even worse inside the stations. The fiction of reserved seats had long since collapsed as people broke the seals on the carriages and squeezed themselves into any available space. Trains had begun to make shorter and shorter journeys, so that they could return more quickly to clear the waiting masses, and then to run to unannounced destinations. And once passengers tried to change from main to branch lines they were often forced, like the drivers of elegant Hispano-Suizas on the roads, to leave their luggage behind and descend to hitching lifts on carts or just walking.

The man of letters Marcel Jouhandeau observed from the window of his home in Paris a scene which was being repeated among refugees throughout the country:

> Suddenly a wagon stops and the whole procession is blocked: a woman stands in the middle of valises and a moving farmyard. She shouts that she has lost her little Louise, and everybody in her group turns back toward Neuilly, calling Louise as horses whinny and horns are tooted; stray farm dogs throw themselves at the gates of houses along the street as they let off a death howl.

The danger of families getting split up was greater in the railway stations and trains than on the roads. Parents lost touch with their children in the crush or entrusted them to strangers rather than give up the chance of getting them on the couple of remaining seats which might take them to safety. The Red Cross and other agencies reunited some 90,000 children with their families but the process – like the larger process of recovering from the shock of invasion and conquest – was often slow and painful. For months afterwards the columns of classified advertisements in local papers were littered with attempts to trace the missing: 'Madame Cissé, refugeed in Loupiac-de-Cadillac, seeks her three children, Hélène, Simone and Jean – lost at Saint-Pierre-des-Corps, 15 June. Box number . . .'; 'Their mother has lost Marc, Luc, Jean, Marie-Françoise, Michel, on 17 June. They were left with the luggage at Poitiers station. Write to her as soon as possible at La Tremblade.'

Only a few weeks before, this human flotsam and jetsam had been an apparently calm and stable society. Now ordinary people mixed in common desperation with soldiers fleeing battle and the inmates of prisons and lunatic asylums whom the German troops released as they advanced. The exodus became a major impediment to the operations of the already disorganized Allied armies which, like the civilian authorities, had not planned for such a contingency. As early as 20 May General Ironside, Chief of the Imperial General Staff, found himself badly delayed by an 'indescribable mass' when he attempted the 20-kilometre journey from Wahagnies to Lens, between Lille and Arras. He viewed the women with prams and the children sitting on top of farm carts with a mixture of gruff compassion and the soldier's exasperated eye: 'Poor devils. It was a horrible sight and it blocked the roads.' 'One's eyes', General Brooke lamented, 'rest incessantly on terrified and miserable humanity cluttering the lines of communications on which all hope of possible security rests.'

In many cases the exodus was not just a threat to military tactics: it was the final blow to the morale of troops whose resolve was ready to crumble. Saint-Exupéry's friend Léon Werth (himself the author of a pacificist novel about the First World War) told of a group of artillery men sent north to defend a position which had in fact already been overrun by the Germans. They found themselves confronting the enemy across a road packed with refugees. Instead of encouraging their fellow-countrymen, or just scattering out of the way, the refugees jeered at them for trying to keep on fighting, even jeered at them for not being able to find the war they were supposed to be fighting. The soldiers eventually agreed to forget their orders. When they turned their lorry round and headed south again, they took some of the refugees with them, including a woman in labour and a woman dying from a car accident. As Saint-Exupéry put it, they had decided to join the peace.

WHILE FRANCE FELL the radio broadcast dance music and out-of-date communiqués. The same failure by officialdom to give people clear guidance as to what they were best advised to do also deprived them of reliable information as to what was really happening. So they fell back on word of mouth, and the phrase on everybody's lips was *on dit que* . . . (it's being said that . . .). People exchanged gossip, embellished it, exaggerated it and helped it further on its way. Rumour quickly became the common currency of the invasion, as it would remain during the Occupation.

The Comte de Paris, son of the exiled Duc de Guise and pretender to the French throne, would soon head a fascist puppet monarchy. People were saying that in Paris by April, before the invasion. The Communists had seized Paris and installed one of their leaders (some said Maurice Thorez and some Jacques Duclos) in the Palais de l'Elysée. That story was circulated widely enough for General Weygand to present it as fact to the cabinet when it met near Tours on 13 June; Mandel disproved it by a simple phonecall to Roger Langeron, *préfet* of police in Paris. It is hard to tell whether Weygand had believed it himself or had just been exploiting fear of Bolshevism to help pave the way for an armistice with the Reich.

Rumour creates an atmosphere which is both credulous and cynical, making people eager to believe anything they hear, however fantastic, but at the same time reluctant to believe anything, however well authenticated. So there is no means of knowing in what spirit the French really received all the other *bobards* (tall stories) which drifted on the wind, informing them, among other things, that: the United States had entered the war; Russia had declared war on Germany and Italy; Russian planes had set fire to Berlin; Gamelin had shot himself, been shot by a Communist, been shot by the French authorities, or been put in jail; General Corap had killed himself; the Russian and British navies were blockading Hamburg; the British were shooting their way through French lines to get to the coast; the British had landed again at Dunkirk and Boulogne; the Pope had committed suicide; Hitler had already invaded Britain; and the armistice had been signed three days ago.

The last story was at least plausible, as for that matter was the story about General Corap, the French commander who had the bad luck to bear the brunt of Rommel's attack. Yet, even when they are wild and perhaps particularly when they are wild, rumours reveal a lot about those who circulate them. The rumours about the advancing enemy hold particular interest. The Germans cut off boys' hands, people said, so they could not grow up to fight. And when they occupied houses, they did not just loot and vandalize them but left their excrement behind as well. Such stories were not specifically anti-Nazi: the French in 1940 showed themselves quite as ignorant of Nazism as did the British. They were anti-*boche*, reviving rumours or propaganda from the First World War and beyond, eventually reaching back into age-old memories of the invading barbarian tribes who had swept across the Rhine as the Roman hold on Gaul weakened. Neville Lytton, an English artist who witnessed the fall of France, happily related these tales in language that makes their provenance abundantly clear. The 'strange and barbarous' habit of leaving excrement behind as a calling card, he told an English audience, 'has been practised by the Germans in the last three wars: in the last war we used to call it "the mark of the beast". I know of no other race which indulges in such practices.'

Yet in the popular imagination the German soldiers were not just shaggy and uncivilized brutes. They were also cunning supermen. They marched twice as fast as French troops, striding through the ripening cornfields stripped to the waist in the hot sun. They used refugees as a human shield, driving them ahead of their own convoys. And their planes swooped on the columns, bombing, strafing and killing innocent civilians as they fled their homes. That, at least, is what everyone said and believed in France at the time, though historians now agree that, even though such attacks did sometimes occur, they were not widespread or the result of Luftwaffe policy. Saint-Exupéry, whose work as a reconnaissance pilot made him a valuable witness, saw Stukas giving the columns a 'nip in the hock' as a sheepdog might to hurry a flock of sheep along, but no more. The Germans did not need to create panic among the refugees, since that had already taken hold. Yet the refugees themselves felt frightened and vulnerable to attack from the skies: that is why they piled mattresses on their cars and carts, sometimes three deep. The Stuka had done its work of demoralization even more effectively than its inventor had foreseen.

In other ways, too, the rumour-mill credited the Germans with more power and guile than they actually possessed. People were sure they had a fifth column. The term was made all the more sinister and persuasive by the fact that it had been coined during the Spanish Civil War only a few years before, when General Mola claimed that, as well as the four columns laying siege to Madrid, he had a fifth inside the city. A child had died after eating poisoned sweets distributed among refugees at the Gare d'Austerlitz in Paris. Booby-trapped watches, pencils and trinkets had been left lying about for people to pick up. Enemy agents had prepared secret petrol dumps in France to fuel the Panzers, and were busy disseminating false orders to French troops and guiding German bombers to their targets. The Meuse bridges had not been blown up in the face of the advancing enemy because fifth-columnists disguised as priests and farmers had shot the French soldiers charged with the task in the back. Reynaud himself appeared to lend his authority to the last story by promising punishment for the 'unbelievable' mistakes which had led to the fall of Sedan.

The famous legend of paratroopers disguised as nuns – betrayed, in some versions, by the hob-nailed boots visible below their habits – was endorsed by the Dutch Foreign Minister when explaining the fall of his country at a press conference in Paris on 16 May. It had no more basis in fact than most of the other rumours, or the widespread belief that the exodus itself had been set in motion by the whisperings of fifth-columnists and German agents posing as beggars, blind men, wounded French soldiers and, inevitably, nuns. This story proved equally convenient to the Nazi propaganda machine, seeking to magnify German strength, and to French officialdom, seeking to minimize its own responsibility in stimulating the panic.

Belief in a fifth column also suited the mood of people increasingly inclined not just to fear their uniformed enemy but to look sideways at each other as well. Spy mania flourished. It had begun with the outbreak of war when, for example, Neville Lytton had been treated as a suspicious character for sketching a view of a château which included a railway line in the background. By June 1940 any stranger to the neighbourhood might be a German soldier in disguise or a German sympathizer at his task of sabotage and disinformation. Foreigners – exiled victims or opponents of Nazism, Belgian refugees, downed British airmen – made obvious targets, but in a land of the uprooted and the homeless few people were safe from sudden suspicion or hysterical accusation. Mandel's Ministry of the Interior boasted of the number of cafés and restaurants it inspected and doubtful characters it questioned: 62,000 people, of whom only 500 were arrested and interned, 334 of them foreigners. At the local level, French soldiers on a train managed to persuade themselves that a journalist from *The New York Times* was a German parachutist. While the gendarmes stood helplessly by, he needed help from three more level-headed army doctors to make his escape. Cycling through a strange village, the correspondent of *Le Figaro* found himself surrounded by an angry mob from which he was rescued only by the mayor. Not everyone was so lucky. Twenty-two aliens rounded up by the authorities in Abbeville, including a group of Belgians, were shot out of hand.

'Had there been treachery?' Simone de Beauvoir asked herself as the Panzer divisions came crashing over the French border: 'No other explanation seemed plausible'. Others were quick to agree. Clare Boothe Luce recorded a conversation she had at the Gare du Nord in mid-May:

An old Red Cross nurse, a Frenchwoman with a white face and staring eyes, put down the bowl of broth she was ladling out to the refugees and came over to me and took my arm in tense fingers.

'Madame,' she said, 'you are an American?'

I said: 'Yes,' and she went on: 'Then you must tell me the truth: *qui nous a trahi*? Who has betrayed us?'

'That was the first time I heard the word *trahi* in Paris,' Luce added. 'At first it was no more than a whisper, like the little winds that come in the dim days before the hurricane . . . . And then the whisper became a great wail that swept through France, a great wail of the damned: *Trahi . . . trahi . . .*'. Neville Lytton noticed that retreating soldiers had chalked on the back of their vehicles the slogan *Vendu pas vaincu*, betrayed not beaten.

German agents could be blamed, of course, and the British and the Belgians too. But even that was not enough to explain what had happened. The French must also have been betrayed by the French. In describing the mood of 1940 and the time that followed they themselves came to speak of *la psychologie du rachat*, the mentality of atonement. This is not quite accurate since, though there was near-universal agreement that the country had been betrayed from within, nobody actually offered to stand up in public and say *mea culpa*. Instead, people blamed each other. 'No attempt to discriminate, to discover political motive-patterns,' Arthur Koestler noted: 'everything is *merde* [crap] and *pourriture* [corruption], one ubiquitous, all-embracing conspiracy of betrayal.'

The historian H.R. Kedward has described this seemingly endless chain of recrimination in all its unhappy complexities. Soldiers of the line blamed their commanders and their commanders blamed the politicians. Right-wing politicians blamed left-wing politicians and vice versa. Pétain and his circle blamed the Communists, the Freemasons and Blum's Front Populaire. The Front Populaire blamed the army. The Communists blamed the French fascists. The fascists blamed the Jews. And, if none of these targets was satisfying, people in the street could always blame the whole system of *papier timbré*, or red tape, which had apparently both held together and finally strangled the Third Republic.

All this was hardly surprising in a society already split by political differences when it went to war and then suffering the trauma of sudden defeat. The peculiar tragedy of France in 1940 was that finger-pointing was not just a brief hysterical outburst, like the vogue

for atrocity stories about the advancing enemy. It was institutionalized by the choice of Pétain as leader. In him and in the men he chose
to serve him, the French found a government which, for all its
rhetoric of unity and renewal, depended at root on finding scapegoats. Its characteristic policies would be denunciation and the
witch-hunt. And so the history of the Occupation, which began with
the humiliation of the French by the Germans in 1940, would
develop into the humiliation – and soon afterwards the persecution – of the French by the French.

In the meantime, the impulse to point the finger of blame at their
neighbours helped to change the view the French took of their
invaders. National self-criticism and fear or hatred of the enemy
cannot easily co-exist. If France had fallen because of its internal
weakness, then perhaps the soldiers of the Reich were not barbarians
or supermen after all. This belief, and all the attendant atrocity
stories it generated, had been formed when those soldiers had just
been anonymous, sometimes unseen, figures behind the sound of
distant guns or inside the cockpits of fighters and tanks. Once the
first wave of the advance was over it was time for the French to take
a second look, still nervous but now hopeful, at the enemy moving
among them in plain view.

The Reich's propaganda machine understood this impulse well,
just as it understood the need of the defeated to find scapegoats for
their plight. In the latter months of 1939 German planes had already
been dropping crudely coloured strip cartoons on France. One
showed a pipe-smoking British soldier and his shorter, mustachioed
French colleague shaking hands and agreeing to jump together into
a swimming pool filled with blood: only the Frenchman jumps in,
while his ally walks away smirking. In 1940 Paul Ferdonnet, the
French traitor who broadcast to his countrymen, was speaking of *les
sales anglais* (the dirty British) rather than *les sales boches* and denouncing the Jews as a 'cursed race . . . which takes, amid the horror of
war, a savage joy in destroying Christian civilization'.

When the ordinary Wehrmacht soldiers themselves got the chance
to speak to the people they had conquered, they ventured a few
words of reassurance in the babytalk version of their own language
that people adopt in such circumstances: *Krieg nicht gut, Krieg kaput gut*.
French-speakers could offer something a bit more sophisticated:
'You poor French, you've been dragged into a disastrous war by a
government of scoundrels in the pay of England', or 'It's the English

and the Jews who've brought you to this sorry pass'. *'Populations aban-données,'* said the placatory slogan on the posters they put up, *'faites confiance au soldat allemand!'*: 'Abandoned populations, put your trust in the German soldier!' It was as if the French were a nation of deserted children in need of protection. And, indeed, the picture accompany-ing the slogan shows a young boy, smiling and eating a piece of bread, in the arms of a friendly Wehrmacht trooper. They are watched by two young girls, still doubtful but also longing to join in the happy scene.

It was an expressive image for people's attitude to the invaders. There might have been atrocities in the heat of battle – refugees strafed or prisoners shot – but the Germans did not cut off children's hands. Far from it. In other invaded countries they might have stopped passers-by in the street to demand their watches and jewel-lery, but in France they bought even the food and drink which they could just as easily have plundered. Jean Bruller (later to become a Resistance writer under the pseudonym of Vercors) remembered a shopkeeper shouting to her neighbours 'They're paying!' and waving a bundle of the marks which were now as good a currency as francs. 'The Germans did not stride, revolver in hand, through the streets,' Sartre wrote in his essay 'Paris Under the Occupation':

> They did not force civilians to make way for them on the pavements. They would offer their seats to old ladies on the Métro. They showed great fondness for children and would pat them on the cheek. They had been told to behave correctly and, being well-disciplined, they tried shyly and conscientiously to do so. Some of them even displayed a naïve kind-liness which could find no practical expression.

In their relief people were quick to discount not just the heated atrocity stories of the previous weeks but also the darker rumours about the true character of the Reich. When Jean Bruller tried to remind a friend of Nazi racism and the concentration camps he was dismissed: 'Propaganda! We were scared stiff when they first arrived, and look at them now! In a pacified Europe, humaneness will come out on top, you'll see. We must help them.' 'People aren't scared of them any more, not now,' said a lorry driver who gave the future Resistance leader Henri Frenay a lift. 'After all, they're humans just like us.' Troops who had just been disarmed and given chocolates when they had tried to surrender were impressed: *'Ils ne sont pas méchants, les boches, tout de même'* ('They aren't nasty, the Boches, all the same'), Arthur Koestler heard them report. They spoke for most of their nation, and the favourite words that the French found for praising their conquerors became the catchphrase of the day. *Ils sont corrects*: they behave properly.

On the whole the French were right. No military commander has an interest in letting his men run riot and, braced by special instructions from the Reich's propaganda machine, commanders in the Wehrmacht took special care to keep theirs in line. Naturally, the men were granted certain luxuries. First-class compartments, marked *Nur für Wehrmacht*, were reserved for them on trains, and in Paris they could travel free in the first-class carriages on the Métro. In major cities some restaurants were soon requisitioned as *Lokale*, or troop canteens, and some cinemas as *Soldatenkinos*: the French were excluded from them or allowed in only if they had a special permit. But, these privileges aside, the Reich required its soldiers to behave properly and courtmartialled them if they did not.

They were not even allowed to play PMU, the French state-controlled betting system, for example. When off duty, they were subject to curfews: in Paris soldiers in the ranks had to be back in barracks by eleven in the evening, non-commissioned officers by midnight and officers by one in the morning. The female military personnel officially known as Nachrichtenhelferinnen had to observe rather more rigid hours. An elaborate, though less effective, set of regulations restricted sexual contact with the defeated, in tribute to a desire not to offend the locals and a preoccupation with the dangers of venereal disease. Soldiers could not walk arm in arm with French women in public or travel with them in *vélo-taxis*, the new bicycle-taxis which began to appear on the streets of Paris. Nor, naturally, could they take French women – or indeed French men – back to their barracks. The doggedly puritanical and disciplinarian General Otto von Stülpnagel, appointed Militärsbefehlshaber (military commander-in-chief of the Occupied Zone) in October 1940, would not even allow the Nachrichtenhelferinnen to travel in official vehicles with their German boyfriends.

Not all the regulations simply expressed the concern for discipline that one would expect of any well-run army. In Paris, for example, soldiers were required to show proper reverence at the tomb of the *soldat inconnu*, the nameless victim from the field of Verdun, whereas they had been expressly forbidden to show reverence at the tomb of Poland's Unknown Soldier in Warsaw. To start with, at least, the

Germans viewed France with a respect which they did not feel for Poland or Czechoslovakia or Yugoslavia – which, in fact, they did not feel for any other nation they conquered and occupied except Greece. There, their traditional philhellenism made them visit the Parthenon in awe. In France, they paid tribute to the history and culture of the old enemy they had defeated.

At its simplest, this meant that the Germans liked French food. Stories abounded of soldiers guzzling butter straight from the packet as if it were ice-cream, scoffing whole bowls of cream, eating omelettes made with two dozen eggs and dying from a surfeit of fish. 'Nobody', Simone de Beauvoir reported, 'had ever seen people swallow such quantities of food.' In other circumstances such tales might have expressed resentment at being plundered in a time of shortage or contempt for the excesses of less cultivated foreigners. But in 1940 they were told without hostility, as reassuring proof that the invaders appreciated the *bonheur de vivre* on which the French had traditionally prided themselves: a derisory homage perhaps, says a contemporary French historian, but homage all the same.

The Germans also liked Paris. 'I'm getting ready to flatten Leningrad and Moscow without losing any peace of mind,' Hitler remarked chillingly in 1941, 'but it would have pained me greatly if I'd had to destroy Paris.' And, of course, the government's decision to declare the capital an open city had meant that, far from needing to destroy it, the German armies had been able to enter without firing a shot. They brought their cameras so that they could photograph each other standing in front of Notre-Dame and the Panthéon. They went up the Eiffel Tower, even though they had to use the stairs since evacuating French troops had put the lifts out of commission. They strolled in the sunny public gardens, chatting to the women and making affectionate noises to the babies in prams. They bought souvenirs, dirty postcards and pocket dictionaries; soon they were issued with their own special guidebook, over 100 pages of information in German about the highlights and low life of the capital. For all the world, they behaved just like tourists.

Hitler himself, normally uninterested in seeing the defeated countries whose fate he now controlled, followed in their footsteps before the end of June 1940. In his entourage he brought his architect, Albert Speer, and his favourite sculptor, Arno Breker, who had been an art student (and one of Jean Cocteau's lovers) in Montparnasse. During his few hours in the capital, glimpsed only by

the occasional startled or incredulous Parisian, he visited the Eiffel
Tower, paid homage at Napoleon's tomb in the Hôtel des Invalides,
admired the Opéra and expressed himself appalled by the ugliness of
the Sacré Coeur – one of several things which persuaded him that
Vienna was, after all, the more beautiful city. Still nursing grievances
from the previous war, he left orders for the destruction of the
statues of General Mangin, Nivelle's aide at Verdun, and Edith
Cavell, the British nurse the Germans had shot in 1915.

After him came Himmler, Goebbels (whose suspicion of the
French was in no way mollified), Goering (who loved shopping,
eating and plundering) and the Nazi theorist Alfred Rosenberg (who
established the Einsatz Reichsleiter Rosenberg to seize the art
collections, archives and libraries of Jews and other enemies of the
Reich). And after them came countless lesser officials, drawn by the
capital's reputation for culture or simply by the reputation of *Paris
bei Nacht*, enjoying *la bière et le nu* at the Folies-Bergère and the
Moulin Rouge and the Moulin de la Galette in 'doleful stupor', as an
observer put it. In reward for its services in Poland and Flanders,
General von Briesen's Thirtieth Division soon replaced General von
Studnitz's Eighty-Seventh Infantry Division, which had originally
entered the city. Briesen's first act was to ban all German troops not
under his command, but the magnetism of the city was so great that
his order went largely ignored in the rush for every conceivable military or political branch of the Reich to have offices in Paris. (They
even included the staff headquarters from which the occupied
Channel Islands were administered.) In the Wehrmacht the slogan
became *Jeder einmal in Paris* or *JEIP*: everyone should get to see Paris
once.

This friendly and admiring attitude gratified most Parisians, but
disturbed the few prescient enough to foresee dilemmas which
would typify the experience of being occupied quite as much as
hostility and savagery. 'Don't be under any illusion: these people
aren't tourists,' warned the journalist and early *résistant* Jean Texcier
in a pamphlet of 'Conseils à l'occupé' ('Advice to the Occupied') he
wrote in July: 'Take your time, ignore what they say, shun their concerts and their parades.' In his essay 'Paris Under the Occupation',
written just after Liberation, Sartre would recall the embarrassment
people had felt encountering Germans in the ordinary round of
their lives. When a soldier in Wehrmacht uniform stopped them in
the street to ask politely for directions, they had usually not been

able to muster hatred, much less show it; sometimes they had even felt an instinctive sympathy for another human being who looked lost or bewildered. However they had responded, they had still been left feeling dissatisfied with themselves. 'We could not be *natural*,' Sartre remembered.

Perhaps such niceties of conscience owe too much to hindsight coloured by the later events of the Occupation. In June 1940, after all the panic and chaos and rumours of atrocities, most people just welcomed German friendliness. It made them hope that being occupied was going to prove less of a change and less of an ordeal than they had feared. Things seemed to be getting back to normal. Nightclubs, bars and cafés took down their shutters and set about catering for their new clientele. By 20 June, only six days after the Germans had arrived and ten days after the last theatre to stay open had refunded the ticket money to the solitary playgoer who had turned up, theatres were asking actors to report for work again. Audiences could soon enjoy such trifles as Michel Duran's *Nous ne sommes pas mariés* (*We Are Not Married*), which invited them to ponder whether infidelity was better when it was conducted openly or discreetly. Sacha Guitry, France's Noël Coward, quickly returned to the boards, as did Albert Willemetz, France's Irving Berlin – some consolation, a wag pointed out, for having lost Metz. *Couturiers* opened their doors again and got ready to display winter collections for a smart set which now included a gratifying number of high-spending Germans.

The illusion of returning normality encouraged those who had fled to start making their way home. Whatever the practical difficulties of the journey, its mood was different from that of the exodus. 'I haven't seen anybody show hatred,' Simone de Beauvoir noted of people's attitude to the Germans, 'only terror among the villagers, and when the fear had dissipated, a surprised and grateful look.' She was coming back to Paris from La Pouëze, near Angers. For part of the way she got a lift from some German soldiers, who offered her food. A woman also travelling with them confirmed the Germans' goodwill, reporting that 'during the last two days the lorry drivers had been lavish with cigarettes, food and champagne. They were really kind, they did not just seem to be carrying out orders but spontaneously wanted to be helpful.' A Frenchman on his way back from Agen gave de Beauvoir a lift through the Paris suburbs:

When the car stopped by a bridge a German soldier threw us a bar of chocolate from a lorry. There were some more of them standing on the side of the road chatting very happily with some pretty girls. 'There'll be a lot of little Germans in the making,' the driver remarked to me. I've heard this phrase often, and it never carries any disapproval. 'It's human nature,' said the driver. 'You don't need to talk the same language for *that*.'

Women who associated with German troops would come to be known contemptuously as *collabos horizontales*, and in 1944 they would be forced to parade through the streets naked and shaven-headed. But people saw things differently in June 1940.

PÉTAIN'S BROADCAST FROM Bordeaux on 17 June set the seal on the mood which had begun to overtake the country after the first shock of its defeat. It was to be the first of many (he made the last on 20 August 1944) in which he would address his countrymen in terms ranging from the consolatory to the reproving. French radio, so disastrously uncommunicative during the German advance, had begun to assume the crucial role in propaganda it would maintain throughout the Occupation. The whole nation would soon be familiar with the Marshal's thin, high voice and the dry cough that regularly punctuated his words. He sounded like an old woman, said the novelist Jean Guéhenno; like 'a skeleton with a chill', said Arthur Koestler sourly.

Pétain's purpose on 17 June was to confirm the news that he had become Prime Minister on Reynaud's resignation and that he intended to seek an armistice with the Reich. The way he did so gave a foretaste not just of his policies but of the rhetoric that would characterize his regime. Announcing that he had taken over the leadership of the government, he used a phrase he would repeat at his trial in 1945: *'je fais à la France le don de ma personne pour atténuer son malheur'* ('I make a gift of myself to France to lessen her misfortune'). The apparent modesty of the words – the aged dignitary volunteering himself in a spirit of service – was contradicted by their deliberately Christ-like overtones. His decisive intervention in Reynaud's cabinet meeting on 13 June had made a virtue simply out of staying 'among the French people to share their sorrows and their miseries'. As leader, he elevated himself to the role of paschal lamb, sacrificing himself so that others might be consoled and saved: *'J'ai souffert pour vous, avec vous'* ('I have suffered for you, with you'), his last broadcast would insist.

Not everybody was won over by this aspect of Pétain's appeal and, as its essential passivity and helplessness became steadily apparent, support for him would dwindle. 'The tone of his homily turned my stomach,' Simone de Beauvoir remembered angrily. Yet she was still relieved by the second part of his message: *'il faut cesser le combat'* ('the fighting must stop'). That seemed only sensible. 'What a terrible absurdity those "delaying actions" were,' de Beauvoir exclaimed, 'in which men got killed for a mere sham of resistance!' But the precise import of Pétain's words was far from clear. Was he issuing a direct order to soldiers to lay down their weapons on the spot? Or should they continue fighting while the terms of their surrender were worked out? The ambiguity aggravated the already chaotic situation on the battlefield. Pétain, moreover, avoided the word 'armistice' in his broadcast – though he had not blushed to use it in the privacy of a cabinet meeting – and spoke merely of 'the means to bring the hostilities to an end'. Some listeners supposed he was talking about a purely military capitulation, not a political settlement. Those who did look forward to a political settlement were in the event disappointed that its terms did not resolve the problem of France's two million prisoners-of-war.

At the time few people were inclined to inspect the nuances of Pétain's language. Anyway, the general burden of his message was clear enough: France had lost and the time had come to say so publicly. *'Il fallait en finir'* ('Somebody had to end it'), most people agreed, though the truth held particular anguish for professional soldiers. The most aggrieved were those confronting the Italians, who had made virtually no headway in their attack on France, let alone taken a significant part in her defeat. Arthur Koestler was laughed at when he suggested that Mussolini might ask for Nice and Savoy: 'Never on your life. We'll kick him in the pants.' On all fronts officers as well as men debated whether to continue fighting until the matter had been taken out of their hands by a formal surrender document or armistice, to give themselves up to the enemy, to withdraw in good order, or just to flee singly. In places not immediately threatened by the German advance, soldiers often chose to drift quietly away, as much to avoid the red tape of demobilization as anything else. By 19 June, Arthur Koestler learned, so many men had gone missing from the barracks in Périgueux that the officers had given up holding a roll-call: 'Every evening a few do not return from the town. Whoever has his family or a girl somewhere near beats it.' *'Nous sommes en pleine pagaille,'* one of those who stayed behind told him contentedly: 'We're in a complete mess.' *Pagaille*, Koestler added, was the word he heard most often on the soldiers' lips.

Other divisions closer to the German front sometimes decided to keep up the fight, though the main result at Romans-sur-Isère was a violent quarrel between Jean Bruller's colonel and the mayor, who accused him of just trying to earn last-minute promotion. Reservists belonging to the 227th Infantry Regiment went on defending Toul until 23 June, when Colonel Marcouire marched his men in column to offer their surrender. While he did so, a local girl was already flirting with one of the victors. A German officer who spoke French congratulated the colonel and his men on their gallant resistance and gave them permission to bury their dead with proper military honours. Then the French officers were taken, as prisoners, to the infirmary in the barracks at neighbouring Ecrouves, where Marcouire awarded them the Croix de Guerre. There were not enough insignia to go round.

Throughout the country soldiers were embarking on the melancholy rituals which accompany defeat. 'France has given in,' wrote one of the cadets defending the bridges at Saumur after hearing Pétain's broadcast. 'Everyone is weeping. You cannot imagine the despair all of us here have been thrown into.' A few days later the cadets fell back to the park of the château at Chavigny, on the fringes of the forest of Fontevraud, and there at midday on 22 June Major Launay proffered their formal surrender. Meanwhile Colonel Michon, who had led the defence, was heading south with about 100 cadets guarding the Cavalry School's precious flag.

The same concern moved Henri Frenay and his fellow-officers serving on the canal linking the Marne and the Rhine:

> Our flags must not fall into the hands of the enemy. We had been taught that. We gathered them and lit a fire. As the name of each unit was called, an officer would step forward and throw in its standard or its colours. What else was there left to do except, once again, try in vain to hold back our tears?

Performed in a landscape dotted with the graves of the dead from the First World War as well as those killed in the recent fighting, the ceremony contrasted sharply with the behaviour of his troops when Frenay negotiated their surrender a few days later:

> Then I saw our men, who had fought so well right up to the last moment, throw down their weapons, cast away their equipment and join together dancing on the road and in the clearings. Forgotten were the disaster, the surrender, self-respect, the dignity which the defeated should maintain in the presence of the victor. No, I wasn't wrong: in the looks of the young German soldiers who passed I read astonishment and contempt.

Frenay was probably one of only a few who bothered to pay attention to the look of astonishment and contempt the victors gave them: what the French themselves call *le temps des autruches* (the time of the ostriches) had started. As the Occupation wore on they would be forced not just to notice it but to get used to it as well.

2

Vichy and the New European Order

Today it is no longer the time for public opinion, often
worried because it is ill-informed, to weigh our chances,
calculate our risks or judge our actions. You, the French
people, must follow me without reservation on the paths
of honour and national interest.

Pétain, broadcast of 15 May 1941

Old age is a shipwreck. That we might be spared nothing,
the old age of Marshal Pétain was to identify itself with the
shipwreck of France.

De Gaulle, *Mémoires de guerre:
l'appel, 1940–42* (1954)

FRANCE HAD BEEN thoroughly beaten. Britain would soon be
beaten too. Then the war would end and the New European
Order which the Reich sought to impose would become an established fact. So the only sensible course for France was to arrange an
armistice as quickly as possible, in order to avoid *polonisation* – the
fate Poland suffered under direct military rule – and instead preserve
a national government. By this means she would rescue from her
defeat on the battlefield as much of her sovereignty as possible. The
achievement could then be consolidated in the permanent peace
treaty which would no doubt soon follow.

This was the logic animating Pétain and the men he brought to
power. Most people agreed with it, when the pressure of events and
the chaos of daily living allowed them time or energy to contemplate
what the future might hold. With the benefit of hindsight, historians
can easily point to all the miscalculations it involved. They know

Britain did not follow France into defeat or capitulation, they know the futility of reaching paper agreements with the Reich and they know the agenda which the Reich would formulate for its New European Order in the years to come. So they call France's attitude defeatism. People had a different name for it in 1940: they called it realism. Its arguments were persuasive – even across the Channel, for all Churchill's defiant rhetoric. In France herself they seemed unshakeable. In June 1940 she was, to borrow the hyperbole of the day, a nation of forty million *pétainistes*.

During his last days in power Reynaud – one of the few politicians who did not hesitate to call the dominant attitude of the time defeatist rather than realist – had wanted to sack General Weygand and replace him with the Commander of the Second Army, General Charles Huntziger. The sheer speed of events and his weakening hold over even his own cabinet had prevented him, so a different, and sorrier, duty awaited Huntziger. On 20 June he set out from Bordeaux, where the government was still staying after its flight from the capital, as leader of the delegation charged with arranging the armistice. They headed back to Paris with little idea of how the Germans would receive them. Their only brief was to resist any attempt to occupy all metropolitan France, or take over her overseas territories, or control her fleet.

In the event they were successful, or rather lucky, since the Reich did not make strenuous demands on any of these counts. Huntziger could report to Pétain via Weygand that its terms were 'harsh but not dishonouring'. Nobody in the new government was surprised by the Reich's harshness and everybody was determined to find respect for France's honour in any scraps of consolation the Reich might offer. Even the most questionable clause in the armistice, which required France to hand over German anti-Nazi refugees on her soil, was conceded after the briefest of protests and the weakest of reassurances as to how it would be applied. The French were in no position to bargain and the Germans presented their terms for signature, not negotiation. Despite Pétain's assurance in his broadcast of 17 June that it would be reached 'between soldiers . . . and in the spirit of honour', the armistice was not a diplomatic agreement: it was a *diktat*.

Hitler himself made this clear on 21 June, and he chose the spot to do so with careful symbolism. Without being told their final destination, Huntziger and his delegation were taken from Paris to the *wagon-lit* in the forest clearing at Rethondes where the Germans had surrendered to Marshal Foch in November 1918. Army engineers had towed the carriage from the museum built to house it to the siding where it had originally stood. The American journalist William L. Shirer was among those who witnessed the arrival of Hitler and an entourage which included Goering, Ribbentrop and Hess. He remembered the Führer surveying the scene and reading the inscription condemning 'the criminal pride of the German Empire' with a look of 'hate, scorn, revenge, triumph'.

Hitler stayed only to hear the preamble to the armistice read out before departing to the sound of the German national anthem, *Deutschland über Alles*, and the Horst Wessel song. General Wilhelm Keitel, Chief of the German High Command, presented the terms themselves and added his signature to Huntziger's on the document the next day. Its twenty-second article stipulated that the ceasefire would come into force six hours after France had reached a similar agreement with the Italian government. This was done in Rome on the evening of 24 June, and so hostilities between France and Germany formally ended soon after midnight with the blowing of bugles and the firing of three ceremonial cannon shots. Announcing the news in an early-morning broadcast, Hitler called for Germans to hang out flags for the next ten days and ring their church bells for the next seven days in celebration. Meanwhile troops towed away the *wagon-lit* from Rethondes, blew up the slab with its offensive inscription and razed the entire site except for the statue of Marshal Foch. France and Germany had fought in 1870 and again in 1914–18. Now, the gesture said, the cycle of humiliation and revenge had been ended by the permanent triumph of the Third Reich.

ECHOES OF THE Treaty of Versailles ran insistently and deliberately through the conditions of the armistice. It was only to be expected that France should be forced to disband and demobilize most of the armed forces she had fielded. But the size of the army she was allowed to retain was set at 100,000 men: exactly the same figure, as Keitel was at pains to point out, that France and her allies had allowed Germany in 1919. Of these, only 3,678 could be officers; the rest were to be given a *congé d'armistice*, or armistice leave, until a permanent peace treaty had been agreed. France and her allies had required Germany to pay reparations after the First World War. Now

Germany made France take on the cost of being occupied. The payments, which began in August but were backdated to June, were first set at 20 million marks a day, or 400 million francs at a crippling exchange rate of twenty to one; they were lowered to 300 million francs between May 1941 and November 1942 but then raised to 500 million until the end of the Occupation. Nor could they be avoided in the way Germany had avoided paying most of the reparations due after the First World War. In all, France ended up paying nearly 60 per cent of her national income to the Reich.

Such harsh terms were in keeping with the calculated melodrama of the ceremony surrounding the signature of the armistice. So was Article Ten, which stipulated that French citizens who continued to fight in alliance with any foreign state at war with Germany would be treated as *francs-tireurs*, or mavericks unprotected by the Geneva Convention. And so was Article Nineteen, which provided for the immediate release of all German prisoners but left French ones in German hands until a permanent peace treaty was agreed. Most sinister of all was the preamble which, though not a binding part of the document, spoke of France being required to help in the fight against Britain. The Reich was as exacting in its determination to reap the benefits of victory as it was in its determination to savour revenge.

Historians have not been slow to make this point. Yet they have sometimes overlooked the equally striking fact that the Reich chose to be lenient in the central conditions of the armistice most apparent to ordinary French people. Huntziger and his delegation had, after all, sat down at the table in the *wagon-lit* with virtually no cards in their hands, and they could have been told that France was to suffer the same fate as Poland. In fact, they put their signatures to a document which relieved such anxieties. Hungry though he may have been for revenge, Hitler had also calculated how far he could afford to push his defeated enemy, even an enemy as thoroughly defeated as France. His concern was that too much harshness would provoke the French government to opt for defiant exile in Britain or France's overseas territories.* In fact, Pétain's regime never had the slightest inclination

---

* There is no real evidence for the theory adopted by some historians that in framing the armistice, as in ordering his tanks to halt before Dunkirk, Hitler was trying to send reassuring signals to Britain: to build a 'golden bridge' which might tempt Churchill and his cabinet to bargain with the Reich.

to make such a move, since it saw remaining in France as fundamental to its claim to legitimacy. But in the circumstances Hitler's
fear was understandable, and it made him willing to offer concessions, particularly when they did not damage the Reich's interests.

So France kept her empire, her fleet and the illusion of her
national sovereignty. Article Three of the armistice acknowledged
Pétain's government as the government of all metropolitan France,
as well as her overseas territories. The Reich even undertook to
smooth the way should it decide to return to Paris, which of course
it sensibly did not. Yet the article also went on to make it clear that in
roughly the northern two-thirds of the mainland Pétain and his
cabinet governed in name only, entirely subservient to 'the rights of
the occupying power'. And experience would show just how limited
their power was in the remaining southern third of France, even
before the Reich used the Allied landings in north Africa as a pretext
for extending total occupation to the whole of the country in
November 1942.

Before that date the two areas were known respectively as the *zone
occupée* and the *zone libre*, until a German decree of December 1940
insisted that the second term be replaced by the less loaded *zone non
occupée*. The French soon nicknamed them the *zone O* and *zone Nono*.
A map attached to the armistice document marked the boundary
between them with a line which headed north-west from Geneva
and the Swiss border to Dôle, then ran west through Chalon-
sur-Saône, Moulins and Vierzon, and swung south to pass east of
Tours, Poitiers and Angoulême. It reached the Spanish frontier near
Saint-Jean-Pied-de-Port at the foot of the pass of Roncesvalles. This
course did not immediately suggest a careful policy at work. Its
broad outline did not respect the integrity of France's departments,
and at many points its local windings cut towns and villages in two.
The line did not even correspond to the German front line in June
1940 but signalled, on the one hand, a withdrawal from parts of the
Auvergne and the regions round Lyon and Grenoble and, on the
other, an advance down the Atlantic coast.

So why did the Reich draw the line where it did? Why, indeed, did
it bother to draw a line at all instead of imposing total occupation on
the whole of France in June 1940? Part of the answer is that, since
the speed and completeness of their victory had surprised even the
conquerors themselves, the arrangements they first imposed were
rough and ready. The details did not greatly matter because the

Reich's position of strength meant it did not need to feel bound by them, let alone by the precise language of the armistice document. The very confidence with which it moved south in November 1942, and the lack of resistance it met, proved that. In terms of local detail, the decision to withdraw from Lyon might have looked odd, but did not actually reduce the aid the city's factories gave to the German war machine. Leaving the Southern Zone in contact with the Swiss border was certainly a blunder, but its effect could at least be mitigated by sabotaging the railway line.

In broader terms, the Reich did not occupy the whole of France in June 1940 because it did not need to. It could achieve its immediate goals more easily and more cheaply. In the zone which it directly occupied the Reich had Paris. It had the Atlantic and Channel coastlines, useful both as a possible jumping-off point for an invasion of Britain and, as later events made necessary, a bulwark against Allied attack from the sea. It had secured part of the border with Spain, which, given General Franco's canny stance toward the combatants in the war, had to be regarded as a potentially hostile country. It controlled, moreover, 67 per cent of France's population, 66 per cent of her cultivated land, 70 per cent of her potatoes, milk, butter and meat, 97 per cent of her fishing and more than 75 per cent of her industry. The Southern Zone, granted at least on paper to Pétain and his government, was poorer and less productive, superior only in wine, fruit and, by a quirk of geology, bauxite mines yielding aluminium.

Moreover, the mere existence of the Southern Zone served the interests of the Reich. To start with, at least, it made those who advocated a defiant government in exile less credible. It encouraged the French to rally round the national government which had miraculously survived the disaster. Thus, on the political level, Hitler's fears of effective opposition inside France were stilled. On a practical level, the national government and its sovereignty were tolerated by the Germans as devices for getting the French to do their dirty work for them – a sensible and thrifty policy for an occupying power to adopt, saving money, manpower and excessive damage to its reputation. The French, or at least those who served Pétain's government, were caught in a vice which would close ever more tightly around them. Given a degree of apparent sovereignty, they found that often the only way to assert it was to volunteer for the dirty work rather than leaving the invaders to do it for themselves.

Realization of this predicament, this fundamental flaw in the status accorded Pétain and his regime, would cause honest people to reject the armistice and all it implied and turn instead to resistance. That process took time, however, as any process which requires difficult and dangerous decisions is bound to do. Meanwhile, the warning was already written into the map of France which the armistice had established. The meandering course of the *ligne de demarcation* between the zones did not trace a boundary between different bureaucratic arrangements. It marked a frontier as absolute as any dividing foreign countries: a major barrier to the movement of people, the ordinary business of communication and the operations of commerce.

Indeed, in the early days after the armistice was signed it amounted to a virtually impenetrable barrier. Even those returning refugees who were allowed to cross – and by no means all of them were – had to wait at least twenty-four hours. Post was let through only in small quantities and personal correspondence was not allowed until September 1940. Even then it was restricted to printed postcards, thirteen lines long, on which the sender could tick or cross out words and fill in blanks, a series of cryptic options powerfully evoking the sort of news the French had for each other in the autumn of 1940:

> Date . . .
> . . . in good health . . . tired . . . slightly, seriously ill, wounded . . . killed.
> . . . prisoner . . . died. . . . without news of . . . .
> The family . . . is well . . . in need of supplies . . . of money . . . news, luggage . . . has returned to. . . . is working in . . . will go back to school at . . . is being put up at . . . is going to. . . .
> Best wishes. Love . . .
> Signature

These cards were replaced with blank ones allowing seven lines of writing in May 1941 and then with ordinary postcards the following September, but it was not until several months after the Germans had moved south and eradicated the distinction between the zones that a normal postal system was resumed.

While the demarcation line stood people needed a *laissez-passer*, or *Ausweis*, to cross. Like so many of the ordinary transactions of life under the Occupation, trying to get one meant first a queue and then a battle with red tape, even for those who lived in a community cut in two by the line. Others could apply on the grounds of needing to attend the funeral of a close relative, for example, or to travel south for health reasons. But *laissez-passers* were never issued as a right, only as a privilege. They could be withheld from officials like the *préfets* of departments and even the politicians in Pétain's government. Admiral Darlan was for a long time the only minister to possess a permanent *laissez-passer* allowing him to cross between the zones whenever he liked, while Xavier Vallat, Commissioner of Jewish Affairs, was specifically denied one. On being appointed Minister of Education, Jérôme Carcopino had to wait seventeen days to get the *laissez-passer* he needed to travel south and take up his post.

The flow of goods between the zones was disrupted in a similar fashion, so that even Paris in the richer Occupied Zone suffered shortages of what had to be regarded as imports rather than, as before the Occupation, the customary tribute of the southern provinces. Sartre, one of the few writers to challenge the myth of the capital's resilience and vitality, wrote in his essay 'Paris Under the Occupation' of its 'languid existence', dependent on the weekly quota of trucks and lorries that the Germans allowed to enter:

> Paris would grow peaked and yawn with hunger under the empty sky. Cut off from the rest of the world, fed only through pity or for some ulterior motive, the town led a purely abstract and symbolic life. Dozens of times during those four years, on seeing bottles of Saint-Emilion or Meursault wine stacked in grocery-shop windows, Parisians would hurry up to find, below the display, a notice saying, 'All these bottles are dummies'. Paris, too, was a dummy.

To the French, then, the demarcation line itself was a major impediment to ordinary life. To the Germans it was another means of control. General Karl Heinrich von Stülpnagel, chairman of the German delegation to the Franco-German armistice commission, described it to General Huntziger as 'a bit we have put in the horse's mouth. If France rears, we will tighten the curb. We will loosen it to the extent that France is amenable.' That is why, though they moved into the Southern Zone in November 1942, the Germans did not abolish the line until February 1943, when they judged that Pétain's government deserved a reward for introducing the forced labour scheme. Indeed, the demarcation line epitomized how power really worked during the Occupation. The bilingual signs at the crossing-points, saying *überschreiten verboten* and *passage interdit*, suggested Franco-

German co-operation. Yet it was the Germans who made, and changed according to whim, the rules determining who and what managed to cross and with what ease or difficulty.

THE CONCESSION WHICH allowed France to keep her own national government actually served the interests of the Reich as much as the interests of France. Indeed, it served the interests of the Reich at France's expense. The control France was granted over her navy also proved a Greek gift. But, while it took months if not years for the flaws vitiating Pétain's regime to be made plain to the majority of people, the fate of the navy was played out quickly and spectacularly in the weeks following 22 June.

The navy had been the best equipped of the armed forces when war broke out, and it had emerged virtually unscathed from the defeat which had devastated the army and the airforce. So it enjoyed immense political and military significance at the time the armistice was agreed and signed. By gaining control of it, the Reich could give a material boost to its plans for invading Britain and an extra flourish to its symbolic humiliation of France. By keeping control of it, the French government could console itself with at least one tangible power to set beside the long list of powers that existed merely on paper. As for the British, when Reynaud dared to broach the possibility of an armistice to Churchill in mid-June, their first thoughts had been of the French navy. All parties, then, agreed that control of the navy and the use to which it was put were critical factors in the puzzling and volatile situation brought about by France's defeat.

Yet, when it addressed the future of the French navy in Article Eight of the armistice document, the Reich did so in terms glowing with magnanimity. The French navy would remain the French navy. To be sure, all ships except those safeguarding French interests in her overseas territories would have to return to their peacetime bases and be demobilized and disarmed, but the Reich 'solemnly' disavowed any intention of appropriating them to the German war effort. It even went on, without prompting, to state 'solemnly and formally' that no further claim would be made on the navy in any permanent Franco-German peace treaty. Such reassuring language does not appear elsewhere in a document whose characteristic phrasing is terse and dictatorial.

On the face of it these terms seemed almost too good to be true. Certainly de Gaulle, broadcasting from London before he had the full text of the armistice to hand, took it for granted that France must have been forced into total surrender of the navy. For all its determination to find the terms offered by the Reich honourable, Pétain's government remained anxious and suspicious, if only because even the briefest look at the map reminded it that several of the home ports to which French ships had to return lay inside the Occupied Zone: Brest in Brittany, for example, was the traditional base of the Atlantic fleet. Yet the French were reassured by the intervention of the Italians, which relaxed the terms to allow the navy to base itself in Mediterranean ports like Toulon, well outside the Occupied Zone, or on the north African coast. Darlan – sole Admiral of the Fleet since June 1939 and Commander-in-Chief of the navy since a few weeks before the outbreak of war – set about confirming these arrangements while repeating his assurance to the British that he would never let his vessels fall into German hands.

So it looked as if Darlan could congratulate himself on steering a middle course between the two warring powers. And surely this achievement was a good augury for a fledgling government whose wisest path lay in staying as neutral as circumstances allowed, placating both its former enemy and its former ally? But in fact the anxiety felt by the British government had not been stilled. Even before the fall of Reynaud, much less the signing of the armistice, it had prepared Operation Catapult, which looked squarely at the possibility of destroying the French navy if that should prove necessary to prevent its abuse by the French or appropriation by the Germans. In the wake of 22 June, when Churchill denounced the armistice and the government which had signed it, and Pétain replied in 'saddened amazement' that it was not Churchill's business to judge the interests or honour of France, not only trust but even basic communication broke down. Ignorant of the modification which Italy had insinuated into Article Eight, Britain had nothing to rely on except promises from Darlan and Hitler. Darlan's word was not enough. As for Hitler's, Churchill exclaimed rhetorically, 'What is the value of that? Ask half a dozen countries.'

He gave Operation Catapult the go-ahead on 2 July. Admiral Sir James Somerville led Force H from Gibraltar to Mers-el-Kébir, the port of Oran where a major part of the French fleet lay under the command of Admiral Marcel Gensoul. The next morning

Somerville presented the British ultimatum: the French could join Force H on the spot, set sail with reduced crews for British ports, take refuge in the neutral waters of the United States or the West Indies, or scuttle their ships. Otherwise the British would attack. Gensoul could not get in touch with Admiral Darlan and, when he did speak with one of Darlan's subordinates, he chose to abbreviate the list of options which had been presented to him, paring it down to the stark choice between sailing to Britain or facing attack. Mers-el-Kébir was fated to end, as it had begun, in 'a tragedy of non-communication'. But non-communication hardly mattered any longer and, for all the muddle, Gensoul's answer to Somerville was doubtless what Darlan would have ordered him to say. It reiterated that French vessels would never be allowed to fall intact into German hands but insisted that they would also resist any show of force by the British.

Taking Gensoul's response as final, Force H opened fire shortly before six o'clock that evening. Lasting less than twenty minutes, the action was not a battle but a massacre: the French ships, at anchor or in some cases already laid up, were in no position to manoeuvre, much less to defend themselves. Only one, the battlecruiser *Strasbourg*, managed to escape from the harbour and head for Toulon. About 370 French sailors were wounded and 1,147 killed; another 150 died when the British returned on 6 July to complete the job. In parallel actions on 3 July the British took over French ships berthed at Alexandria and at several ports in Britain, including Plymouth and Portsmouth. The *Richelieu*, the most up-to-date battleship the French navy boasted, was struck from the air at Dakar in Senegal on 8 July.

When Churchill came to write his history of the Second World War he called the launching of the attack at Mers-el-Kébir 'a hateful decision, the most unnatural and painful in which I have ever been concerned'. Yet he could not wish it unmade. By eliminating the better part of the French navy he had deprived the Reich of a potential asset – which it might have found irrresistible – in any attack on Britain. Of equal importance was the message he had sent Hitler, Pétain, the French, the doubting element of the British population and the doubters in his own cabinet, a message which he had been struggling with some frustration to get across: he had no intention of suing for peace. After Mers-el-Kébir no observer could doubt his, and Britain's, determination.

And, almost miraculously, he had achieved these goals without permanently alienating the exiled de Gaulle and knocking the fragile Free French movement on the head. The General himself had never been under any illusion about Britain's ruthlessness in protecting its interests at the expense of friends or allies. His next broadcast to France anticipated Churchill's choice of adjective in calling Mers-el-Kébir 'hateful' – it was an *'odieuse tragédie'* – but still insisted that 'Our two ancient nations, our two great nations remain bound to one another. They will either go down together or together they will win.'

Churchill may well have judged Britain's immediate interest and, indeed, the long-term interest of Europe correctly, but for France the immediate consequences were disastrous. Never secure, the Franco-British alliance had already been on the point of breaking down even before Reynaud's government fell in June. After the armistice Churchill and Pétain had descended into mutual recrimination. Mers-el-Kébir completed the process so dramatically that the decision to break off diplomatic relations with Britain on 5 July surprised nobody. Nor was it surprising that Pétain's government should have meditated reprisals against the British. Inevitably Darlan was their chief advocate. On 14 July he persuaded Pétain to authorize an air strike against Gibraltar, though Paul Baudouin, now the Minister for Foreign Affairs, induced the Marshal to change his mind – never a difficult thing to achieve. Churchill and de Gaulle's continuing denunciation of the French government encouraged Darlan to revive his proposal, and the botched Anglo-Gaullist raid on Dakar in September allowed him to carry the day.

The raid on Gibraltar, made on 25 September, might have been modest but it was enough to perpetuate the cycle of violence between former allies and pave the way for Franco-British conflict in Syria the following year. Mers-el-Kébir had begun what amounted to a *de facto* war between France and Britain. That war has generally been forgotten and perhaps rightly so, since it consisted largely of a sea blockade of France established by the British and, where possible, evaded by the French. In the enlarging theatre of the Second World War it was little more than a sideshow. Yet its domestic consequences in France, and particularly in the claustrophobic circles of Pétain's administration, were profound. Mers-el-Kébir had made it possible for people to view Britain, not Germany, as their enemy.

'I declare war on Britain,' proclaimed the right-winger Pierre Costantini in a memorable explosion: 'It's what France must do now.

It's what Europe must do now. We can't wait any longer.' Starting in November 1940, Radio-Paris and the daily papers ran a competition inviting their audience to identify the authors of anglophobic quotations such as: 'Impious England, fatal executioner of all that France held divine, murdered grace with Mary, Queen of Scots, inspiration with Joan of Arc, genius with Napoleon.' The answer was Alexandre Dumas; other sources pillaged for quotation included Bertrand du Guesclin (the Breton opponent of England in the Hundred Years War), Saint-Simon (the chronicler of Louis XIV's court), Napoleon, Balzac, Victor Hugo, Edward VII and George Bernard Shaw. Perhaps most tellingly of all, the weekly magazine *Gringoire* – which also thought it timely to reprint an article by Henri Béraud called 'Should England Be Reduced to Slavery?' – published an epitaph on Franco-British relations in the form of this epitaph for an imaginary French sailor:

> Here lies Leading Seaman Jean-Yves.
> Wounded at Dunkirk on 30 May 1940
> protecting the evacuation of the British.
> Killed at Mers-el-Kébir on 3 July 1940
> by the British.

On the face of it, such reactions are easy to dismiss as mere extremism or German propaganda. Radio stations and the press in the Occupied Zone were effectively under German control. Though published in the Southern Zone, where German pressure was indirect, *Gringoire* already had a long pre-war record as an organ of the Catholic Right and would elect to cease publication in the build-up to the D-Day landings; Béraud was condemned to death, though not executed, for collaboration later in 1944. As for Costantini, he went on to found a collaborationist movement, the Ligue Française, but escaped the fate of men like Béraud by being, in the words of one historian, 'charitably admitted to an asylum after the war'.

The anglophobia of men like Costantini and Béraud had found a voice in France before the war: Béraud's article, 'Should England Be Reduced to Slavery?' had originally appeared in 1935. And it had certainly been echoed – and sometimes, indeed, been funded as well – by the Reich's propaganda machine. Yet it had remained marginal. Now, in the summer of 1940, it struck a more resonant chord than the vague rhetoric that de Gaulle mustered. The names of Mary, Queen of Scots, Joan of Arc and Napoleon were (and are) etched deep in the French memory. They added authority and potency to the more recent names of Dunkirk and Mers-el-Kébir. The resentment which broke to the surface answered a widespread public need. Nor did it die with the events of 1940: even some French who welcomed the reversal of German fortunes in north Africa in 1942 and Normandy in 1944 still took care to speak, not of *les anglais* or even *les Alliés*, but of *les américains*. Being forced to live with an occupier one apparently has to appease makes it satisfying to vent frustration in vilifying a supposed ally who has yet again proved treacherous.

Translated into policy, this impulse helped to shape the direction Pétain's government took, or perhaps it just made it easier for the government to take the direction that in any event it found desirable. Once Britain had been identified as an enemy it became tempting to court the approval, if not the friendship, of the Reich. And, of course, the refusal of the French fleet to join the British at Mers el Kébir had helped *rapprochement* by stilling at least some of Hitler's suspicions: his fear, for example, that there had been a secret agreement between the quiescent, stay-at-home Pétain and the exiled, defiant de Gaulle. The proof of France's real relations with Britain did not incline him to make further concessions – the relaxation in the terms of Article Eight was the last France would get for some considerable time – but it changed his public style from rituals of vengeance to gestures of respect.

This shift in alignment is marked in the careers of the politicians who flourished under Pétain's patronage. One was Admiral François Darlan. At first glance, he was merely a victim of Mers-el-Kébir: the commander whose word had been doubted by his former ally, the admiral who had lost his fleet. Yet he also found a personal opportunity in the disaster. A time-serving politician with (according to one contemporary) 'all the bad qualities of Talleyrand', he had already switched his allegiance at a critical point in the fall of Reynaud's government and the fall of France. Now he could voice with passionate conviction a dislike of the British which had been simmering at least since George VI's coronation in 1937, when he had been humiliated to find himself placed behind Siam and Ecuador in diplomatic ranking. So, having refused the chance to take his fleet to Britain and eclipse de Gaulle as leader of the nascent Free French, he rose instead to become Pétain's deputy. In Churchill's elegiac words, 'he went forward through two years of worrying and ignominious office to a violent death, a dishonoured grave and a name long to be execrated by the French navy and the nation he had hitherto served so well'.

Darlan became Pétain's deputy in February 1941; he met his death by assassination in Algiers in December 1942, shortly after a final attempt to switch sides and reach an agreement with the Allies. His predecessor as Pétain's deputy, and his successor too, was Pierre Laval. Like the Admiral, he was both a sincere time-server and a sincere anglophobe who found in Mers-el-Kébir the chance to assert his voice and to claim power. On 4 July he told a meeting of senators:

> France has never had and never will have a more inveterate enemy than Great Britain. Our whole history bears witness to that. We have been nothing but toys in the hands of England, who has exploited us to ensure her own safety. Today we are at the bottom of the abyss where she has led us. . . . I see only one way to restore France . . . to the position to which she is entitled: namely, to ally ourselves resolutely with Germany and to confront England together.

Though his conclusion belonged peculiarly to the mood of 1940, his opening sentences could have been spoken by any number of politicians on any number of occasions in French history. Yet this occasion was of particular importance. Laval spoke at Vichy, where Pétain's government had finally taken refuge after leaving Bordeaux. In venting his dislike of Britain and promoting his vision of France as Germany's ally, he aimed to destroy the Third Republic: to destroy, that is to say, the last vestiges of democracy which the armistice had left his country.

WHEN PRESIDENT ALBERT LEBRUN asked Pétain to replace Reynaud as Prime Minister on 17 June, the Marshal surprised him by producing on the spot a list of the cabinet ministers he intended to appoint. If further confirmation were needed that, for all his protestations of being above politics and beyond the desire for power, Pétain was the willing, though slightly forgetful, candidate of a faction which had actively sought Reynaud's downfall, he went on to surprise Lebrun again by showing his unfamiliarity with some of the names on his own list. One name, however, which he knew perfectly well was that of Pierre Laval. Everybody in politics knew Laval. He had entered the Chamber of Deputies as long ago as 1914, when he had been 31, and the Senate in 1927. After first holding government office in 1925, he had gone on to serve twice as Prime Minister in the rapidly shifting administrations which characterized the Third Republic in the 1930s.

Pétain's list proposed Laval as Minister of Justice rather than Minister for Foreign Affairs, the post he had hoped for. His reputation, it had been judged, would have made him harmful to relations with Britain which, though soured, had then still not been entirely abandoned. The coveted job went to Paul Baudouin. Laval refused the Ministry of Justice and briefly contented himself with the behind-the-scenes manoeuvring that was second nature to him. As a result, he entered the cabinet as a minister of state on 23 June, the day after the armistice was signed, and became Deputy Prime Minister on 27 June. The following December he was ousted from government altogether in Pétain's only dramatic assertion of control over his own appointments. But when he returned in April 1942, thanks partly to pressure from the Germans, he did so with increased power: he brought his own favourites and protégés with him, and he assumed the title of Prime Minister which Pétain had hitherto reserved to himself. He served in that capacity, as well as in that of Minister for Foreign Affairs and Minister of the Interior, until the chaos of August 1944, when Pétain's government lost whatever slender claim to legitimacy it had ever possessed.

The ups and downs of Laval's career during the Occupation were typical of his entire career in politics. And ups and downs in his relations with Pétain were particularly to be expected. It would be hard to imagine two men more sharply contrasting, at least in their public images. The only apparent bond between them was that both were rural and working-class in origin and that both chose to stress the fact, Pétain citing his humble farming background in the Pas-de-Calais and Laval his roots in a little town in the Auvergne. 'I am a man of the soil, a member of a true peasant family,' he liked to boast. His Auvergnat accent earned him one of several, usually unflattering, nicknames he attracted during the course of his career: *le Bougnat*, the coal merchant, from the Parisian belief that all coal merchants came from the Auvergne.

Any resemblance between Laval and Pétain ended there. The public did not give Pétain nicknames: except for a stubborn minority of unbelievers, they called him *le Maréchal*. To most French people in 1940 and still to many even at the time of his public disgrace and trial in 1944, he looked the embodiment of dignity, rectitude and grandfatherly benevolence. Laval, on the other hand, looked like a rogue. Even the white cravat he had affected as his personal trademark since his early days at the bar lent him an air not of distinction but of gangsterism. Small and sallow, he had a ferrety face, bad teeth and fingers stained by chain-smoking. According to many people, he acted like a rogue as well. They cited his history of changing political allegiance. He had first made his reputation as a lawyer defending trades unionists and strikers, then entered politics as a Socialist. During the First World War his pacifism had won him a place on the *Carnet B*, or list of unreliable politicians, and another nickname, *Pierre Loin-du-Front*, literally Pierre Far-from-the-Front, the equivalent of handing him a white feather. Yet he had tempered principle by declining military service (not mandatory for deputies) on the grounds of varicose veins and by making clear his admiration for Clemenceau. After the war he had sat in the Chamber of Deputies and the Senate as an independent and had given his support to right-wing parties.

Distrust of Laval was increased by the fortune he had contrived to amass along the way and the obvious pleasure he took in owning a château, a newspaper and other business interests in his native province. In France (as in other nations) the stereotype of the peasant can imply rough and ready integrity or it can carry suggestions of miserliness, hard bargaining and shady dealing. Few people doubted which sort of peasant Laval was. Edouard Herriot, President of the Chamber of Deputies, certainly did not: according to him, Laval was 'one of those people who buy a garage and exchange it for a building, which he exchanges for a farm, which he exchanges for a collection of paintings. And each time he keeps a car, an apartment, a cow, or a Rembrandt.' So the French also called *Pierre Loin-du-Front* and *le Bougnat* by another, more enduring nickname: *le Maquignon*, the horse-trader or shady operator.

On the face of it, then, a politician of Laval's character and reputation had little to commend him to Pétain, especially in a crucial position of trust as Pétain's deputy and *dauphin*, or acknowledged successor. A youthful pacifist and evader of military service, he was bound to disappoint an old soldier who looked in his political subordinates for the same qualities he had expected of his staff officers. A political operator who liked playing his cards close to his chest, he was bound to annoy a tidy-minded man who delighted in written reports. Even his chain-smoking irritated the Marshal, who prided himself on his spartan habits and allowed himself only the occasional after-dinner cigar. Laval knew this perfectly well and delighted in it: he used to boast that, when he wished to make sure that Pétain signed a particular document or consented to a particular proposal, he had only to blow smoke in his direction to make him hastily agree. The two men endured each other only with reluctance and out of necessity. To Pétain, or so he claimed, Laval was a tool made useful and, as it proved, indispensable by the difficulties of the time. To Laval, or so he claimed, Pétain was merely an old fool who made an impressive figurehead. 'Who's talking about work?' he retorted when it was objected that the Marshal was too senile to do a leader's work. 'We need a flag. A flag doesn't do any work. You stand in its shade.'

The question of whether Pétain was using Laval or vice versa would dissolve into something approaching mutual recrimination at their trials after Liberation. Then each man, previously eager to claim he had wielded the real power, became understandably eager to disown it. During the Occupation itself the French public answered the question by keeping a lurking respect, or at least pity, for Pétain because of his First World War record and reserving its growing distrust and eventually its hatred for Laval. He vied with Raphaël Alibert, Minister of Justice until February 1941, and Bernard Ménétrel, Pétain's personal doctor and factotum, for the title of *éminence grise*, responsible for all the mistakes committed in the Marshal's name. Laval knew what they said. He was used to being distrusted, he was used to being hated, he could even put up with being demonized. It seems in some obscure way to have consoled him, perhaps given him a perverse pleasure. To Laval, who took pride in being a wondrous necessary man, anything – even being a necessary evil – was better than being thought unnecessary.

And in 1940 people did not just accept his presence in the government as necessary. They welcomed it. Pétain had dignity, integrity and all the reassuring qualities written in his record. Yet his age and his seeming aloofness from the day-to-day business of politics left him looking less than ideally equipped to handle tough negotiations with the Germans by himself. Who better to serve the Marshal in that capacity than Laval the horse-trader? And who better than the Marshal to make sure that Laval's horse-trading served honourable interests? The very differences between the two allowed an anxious public to greet them as a dream ticket. Pétain lectured reassuringly on the radio about the domestic state of France, while Laval – willing to get his hands dirty, but this time in a good cause – handled foreign relations by sitting down at the bargaining table with the Reich.

Besides, for all its apparent opportunism, Laval's career still showed an ideological coherence that gave him the necessary credentials to win respect in Pétain's regime. His support and then abandonment of Socialism had left him, like so many others of his generation whose views had described a similar curve, strongly anti-Bolshevik. And distrust or open hatred of the Soviet Union abroad and Communists at home was perhaps the deepest bond uniting the Vichy regime, whose members otherwise showed wide differences in their degrees of sympathy for fascist ideology or Hitler's Reich. Indeed, their anti-Bolshevism was the strongest appeal which the men of Vichy held for conservative middle-class opinion. 'Better Hitler than Stalin', many of the French (like many of the British) had comforted themselves by saying as they had watched Hitler's rise to power in the 1930s. And, looking at their own country after the success of the Front Populaire in the 1936 elections, they had said: 'Better Hitler than Blum'. Such views were consolatory in 1940: despite his pact with Stalin, Hitler was still a bulwark against the threat of Bolshevism from the east, and the presence of the Germans in France promised tough measures against its domestic counterpart.

Moreover, Laval's early pacifism had – like the pacificism of countless others of his generation – made him an appeaser in the 1930s. Already a believer in cordial relations with Germany, he had during his second stint as Prime Minister pursued an agreement with Mussolini to the detriment of Franco-Soviet and Franco-British relations. Appeasement had looked discredited with the outbreak of war in 1939, yet with the fall of France it easily reconstituted itself as realism. And realism, of course, had always been the watchword of Laval's career. He was still defending it from his prison cell in 1945:

> It has been said that I lacked idealism, doubtless because I believed and still do believe that, while politics must not neglect the imponderables, it must be based upon realities, especially in the foreign field. Regimes follow one another and revolutions take place, but geography remains unchanged. We will be neighbours of Germany for ever.

Though he would largely be identified with the conduct of foreign affairs – if that term could still be used to embrace France's relations with the Reich – Laval began his services to Pétain on the domestic front. He led the attack on the Third Republic, whose very constitution had brought him and Pétain to power. This in itself was a popular and timely move. The Third Republic, unhappy and unstable child of the conflicts of 1870, had never attracted many admirers, and by the summer of 1940 it had no real defenders left. In the public mind it was associated not with effective action but with *papier timbré* and idle debate which had made France into *la France babillarde*, a nation of chatterers. The administrations which succeeded each other with bewildering speed had been tainted by croneyism and scandals like the Stavisky affair.*

On 6 February 1934 discontent with the Republic had brought the right-wing *ligues*, led by Colonel de la Roque of the Croix du Feu, out on the streets in riots which conjured up memories of General Boulanger's near *coup d'état* in 1888. Edouard Daladier's government was frightened out of office after only eight days, something of a record for brevity even by the standards of the Republic. By then not just right-wing leaguers but a growing section of the ordinary middle classes had come to see the Republic as the formal embodiment of all those tendencies which they deplored: secularism, Freemasonry, dilution of the national character by 'foreign', especially Jewish, influences. The triumph of Blum's Front Populaire in 1936 moved the spectre of Bolshevism higher up on the vague but emotive list of grievances.

In 1940 the temptation to blame these forces for humiliation at the hands of the Germans was irresistible. When Pétain told his fellow-countrymen in his broadcast of 25 June that he too 'hated the lies which have done you so much damage', everyone knew that he was not referring to the inadequacy of recent military communiqués but indicting the whole direction in which the Republic had taken French society. Henri Frenay heard a representative voice of support on his way home by train from Lyon to Sainte-Maxime just after the armistice had been signed. It belonged to an old gentleman, a retired officer wearing the rosette of the Légion d'honneur, who told the stranger opposite him in the carriage that 'what had happened served the French right. According to him, it was all the fault of the Republic, the Jews, the Freemasons, the schoolteachers,

---

* In January 1934 the swindler Sacha (Serge Alexandre) Stavisky supposedly shot himself rather than give himself up to the police. Laval was just one of many politicians whom the press linked with the affair, though he managed to clear his name.

the parliamentary deputies.' Frenay added: 'I even thought I could tell that, to a certain extent, our defeat secretly pleased the old soldier. Doubtless, in his eyes it confirmed sentiments he had always held.'

Laval's denunciations were the public equivalent of the private grumbling by the man in the railway carriage. And, like the man in the railway carriage, he spoke with a vehemence that came from personal resentment. In this, he was typical of those who surrounded Pétain. On the whole, they were not drawn from the fascist sympathizers or ideologues who included men like Pierre Costantini or (to cite more formidable figures) the *cagoulard* Eugène Deloncle* and Jacques Doriot, leader of the fascist Parti Populaire Français. Until its very last days in power, when it was quite openly scraping the bottom of the barrel, Pétain's regime found scarcely more room for such people than the Third Republic had. They stayed in Paris, courting the attention of the German ambassador Otto Abetz and being encouraged, funded, exploited and quietly despised by the occupiers.

Most of those called to serve Pétain were of a different stripe: good '6 February men' or mainstream Republican politicians, but in either case men whose hopes and careers had been thwarted by the triumph of Blum's Front Populaire in 1936. Laval, excluded from government after his second term as Prime Minister had ended in failure early that year, was their most prominent representative. His presence, more than anyone else's, helped to justify the sneer of *revenants* (ghosts) directed at the new government and the nickname it would earn as the *régime des recalés*: the regime of rejects.

The National Assembly, Laval is supposed to have said, 'vomited me out. Now I shall vomit it out.' He may well have done so, since he was nothing if not open in his rancour. He certainly made it plain that he did not want to adjust Third Republic politics to the circumstances of the Occupation: he wanted 'to destroy the whole set-up'. The arts of bullying and cajoling that he had always commanded were lent additional weight by the authority of Pétain and the newly agreed armistice, and by the tragedy of Mers-el-Kébir and the threat of German displeasure. Meeting at Vichy on 9 July, their numbers depleted by the defiant spirits who had been rash enough to set sail

---

* The Cagoule (Hood) was a secret society credited with infiltrating the army and carrying out political assassinations.

for Casablanca on the *Massilia,* first the deputies and then the senators voted in favour of revising the 1875 constitution. Only three
deputies dissented; the solitary opponent in the Senate was,
appropriately enough, Lafayette's great-grandson. The next day
Laval, brandishing a letter of authorization from Pétain, persuaded
the parliamentarians meeting together as the National Assembly to
turn their powers over to the Marshal, including the power to dictate
a new constitution by personal decree. The motion was passed by
569 votes to 80.

After Laval had so enthusiastically supplied the weapon and the
parliamentarians had so obligingly agreed to mass suicide, it was left
to Pétain only to sign the death certificate. The same evening he
issued three decrees: the first declared him Head of State rather than
President, the second assigned him total power and the third
adjourned the Chamber and the Senate indefinitely. 'And that',
crowed Laval, 'is how you overthrow the Republic.' Wags said that
the white cravat he customarily wore was that day made from the
white flag of its surrender. After an unstable and unpopular life of
nearly seventy years, the Third Republic had gone to its death with
such indecent haste that nobody seems to have bothered to inform
Albert Lebrun officially that he was no longer President and that
there was no longer a Republic to be President of. He quietly packed
his bags and retired into private life.

Hitler had begun by regarding Pétain's government with suspicion, and he would often be exasperated by it during the Occupation.
But in the reassuring aftermath of Mers-el-Kébir he chose to set his
seal of approval on the terms by which it had reconstituted itself. On
his way to see General Franco near the Spanish frontier he stopped
to meet Laval at the old town of Montoire, north of Tours. As on
future occasions, Laval was acting as the advance guard in high-level
contact with the Reich. Two days later, on 24 October, Hitler paused
at Montoire on his return journey to meet Pétain himself. The photo
of them shaking hands made a memorable image of the friendly relations between the two leaders and of the status Pétain's government
now enjoyed.

To many of the French it was reassuring, coming as it did only
four months after their defeat on the battlefield and their further
humiliation at Rethondes. The spectacle of the two old soldiers
together – both, of course, wore uniform for the occasion – implied
an equality between former enemies now allied in mutual respect.

Further comfort could be taken from the fact that Pétain was a Marshal while Hitler had been just a corporal in the previous war. Some such reflection might even have passed through Pétain's mind, since he was always quick to find solace for his ego. Yet he also understood the anxieties that Montoire might provoke and he set about stilling them in his radio talk of 30 October by emphasizing that he had gone willingly to meet Hitler: 'I did not yield to any *diktat*, any pressure from him.'

It was an ominous, though unremarked, sign of the way things would go under the Occupation that one of the first German words to gain currency in French should have been *diktat* – the very word, incidentally, which the Germans had used for the Treaty of Versailles. Pétain's reassurance, however, was quite true. And Hitler, who had already got most of what he wanted at Rethondes and believed he could take the rest without further parley, made no more demands on the French at Montoire. He viewed the meeting with Pétain largely as an exercise in public relations; it was his encounter with Franco which had really mattered as an occasion for diplomatic bargaining.

The French, however, had hoped to negotiate some relaxation in the terms of the armistice: reducing the costs of the Occupation, loosening the stranglehold of the demarcation line and getting back some of their prisoners-of-war. They had been disappointed, but of this depressing augury Pétain's broadcast understandably made no mention. Instead, he referred only briefly to such problems, postponing their solution to an unspecified point in the future. As for his present understanding with Hitler: 'Collaboration between our two countries was envisaged. I agreed to it in principle. The practical details can be discussed at a later date.'

'Collaboration': a mundane technical term had begun a career which would make it the most highly charged word in the political vocabulary of the Occupation. The Germans themselves had already used it in Article Three of the armistice, where the French government was required to order its administration to 'collaborate' with the German military authorities in the Occupied Zone. In this context its meaning was clear and unsurprising. Yet Pétain had picked it up and used it again in a revealingly imprecise way; when it came to phrasing policy he was always happier with generalities than with details. Such an approach can have diplomatic advantages. On this occasion, the Germans seem to have been led to hope that 'collaboration' implied active French help in the war against Britain, which in the event they never got.

Yet Pétain clearly meant to do more than throw sand in the Germans' eyes or confirm to Hitler and his own fellow-countrymen that he had read the armistice. In a crucial passage of his broadcast he made the word fundamental to the goals he proposed: 'It is in a spirit of honour and in order to preserve the unity of France – a unity which has lasted for ten centuries – within the New European Order which is being built, that I today embark on the path of collaboration.' Somewhere inside this sonorous rhetoric, throbbing with patriotic emotion, collaboration was being commended as the logical refinement of the realism which had helped bring him to power in the summer months.

Pétain's supporters liked to call it *collaboration à raison*, but it implied something more than collaboration on the grounds of common sense. Grudging acceptance of the German presence might ensure survival and hence be a suitable posture for a caretaker government to adopt. But Pétain did not see himself as a caretaker. Even his intervention at the Bordeaux cabinet meeting on 13 June, which had affirmed his intention of staying in France to share, Christ-like, in her suffering, had also declared that the fruit of this suffering would be a national renaissance. As Head of State he aimed to revive the country in the long term as well as to ensure its survival in the short term. The very language of his 30 October broadcast, and all the other talks in which he sought to maintain a dialogue with the French, was meant to inspire hope for the future as well as stoical endurance of the present. And in that process, clearly, he did not regard the German presence just as a hardship and collaboration just as a necessity. The Germans were an example and a stimulus: winning their respect by becoming more like them was an opportunity to be embraced.

P ÉTAIN'S GOVERNMENT HAD been born of makeshift and panic, and it would end in disarray and disgrace. From the start even the limited and reasonable goals it could have set itself would have been hard to achieve, given the restraints dictated by the armistice and the increasingly harsh reality of the occupiers' power. As it was, the spectacle of its powerlessness soon turned the brief popularity it enjoyed into public disappointment, distrust and contempt. Yet to its ministers and servants the view looked very different in the summer and autumn of 1940. They saw the public relief which had greeted Pétain's assumption of power, the apparent respect with which the occupiers treated him, the ease with which he had sent the last representatives of the Third Republic packing and the fact that, constitutionally, he now enjoyed more power than any leader of France since Louis XIV. These heady considerations tempted them to regard their tenure as permanent – secure in the shadow of the Thousand-Year Reich – and, at the least promising moment in her history, to embark on a campaign for the regeneration of France. The attempt made their failure all the more absurd, but also all the more sinister.

Absurdity was inherent from the start when the government, ending its flight from the invaders, decided to make Vichy its capital. The armistice acknowledged its right to return to Paris yet, for all his publicly proclaimed confidence in himself and his agreement with the Germans, Pétain always showed deep distrust at the idea of venturing into the Occupied Zone. When Hitler, in one of his benignly theatrical gestures, arranged for the ashes of *l'Aiglon* – Napoleon's son, the Duc de Reichstadt – to be returned from Vienna and interred at Les Invalides in December, Pétain gave lasting offence by his failure to attend the ceremony. He did not visit Paris until April 1944, only weeks before D-Day, and then he spoke of himself as a prisoner of the Germans. Various factors ruled out cities in the Southern Zone which might otherwise have been candidates for the seat of government. Lyon was the stronghold of Edouard Herriot, its mayor as well as President of the Chamber of Deputies, and Toulouse was the stronghold of the Sarraut family, all of them rivals too powerful to have as hosts. Marseille was too close to north Africa and Perpignan too close to the Spanish frontier, locations which could have fuelled the Germans' fear that the government had half a mind to go into exile or, indeed, could have made it easy for dissenting members to defect.

But Vichy? The place had neither historical resonance nor geographical convenience. It was, and is, an insignificant little spa town in the Auvergne, the French equivalent of Tunbridge Wells but Tunbridge Wells relocated somewhere in the Northumbrian National Park. Its population of 25,000 was swollen each summer by the visitors who came to take the waters and gamble in the casinos. Yet it was acceptable because it lay far from any of France's borders and outside the sphere of influence exercised by any leading politician – even Laval, who had hoped the government would prolong a temporary stop at Clermont-Ferrand, where he owned the local newspaper and printing press. But, above all, Vichy fitted the bill simply because it could offer enough hotel beds to accommodate a government.

The Pavillon Sévigné, named after the eighteenth-century letter-writer who had come to take the cure, became Pétain's official residence. In practice, however, he used it only for ceremonial occasions and lived in a modest suite at the Hôtel du Parc, where he also kept his office and the room used for meetings of his *petit conseil*, or inner cabinet. Each day he would emerge from the hotel to stroll in the tree-lined park, acknowledging the salute from his guard of honour and the respectful cheers from onlookers who came to get a glimpse of him. On Sundays, when he was more punctilious in his attendance at Mass than he ever had been in private life, he was greeted at the church door by priests and by schoolchildren who sang inspiring songs in his praise. In the evenings – and the evenings proved long at Vichy – the main pastimes were gossip and bridge.

These rituals came as a welcome relief to an elderly leader who had been forced to put up with cramped and unsuitable accommodation in his migration from Paris to the Loire valley, Bordeaux and Clermont-Ferrand. Yet the sedate unreality of Vichy struck an ominous note from the start. Even Albert Lebrun had his doubts when he arrived there with his retinue: 'Everyone will say we're a casino government,' he exclaimed. 'Everyone will say, "They're only here for the season".' As an epitaph on the Vichy government, his words are still hard to beat, and they were particularly apt coming as they did from a man who would shortly be expelled from office by a hasty vote taken in the town's Grand Casino. Such comic-opera touches were all of a piece with a regime which was forced to check with the occupiers the appointments it announced with such a fanfare of sovereign independence, and which was even reduced to appointing an ambassador to half its own territory.*

These realities did not deter the Vichy government from embarking on the campaign it called the *révolution nationale*, though the Marshal himself, who had originally called it a *renaissance*, still pre-

---

* The post, technically General Delegate of the French Government to the Occupied Territories, was first held by General de la Laurencie, later an opponent of Vichy. He was replaced by Fernand de Brinon in December 1940.

ferred to avoid the explosive noun *révolution* and think of it as the *redressement national* or *rénovation française*. Its character was announced in the decrees he signed on the evening of the day the National Assembly gave him a free hand in the fate of his country. He did not style himself President but Head of State and the state he governed was no longer *la République française* but simply *la France*. The decrees he signed, moreover, began 'Nous, Philippe Pétain . . .', a revealing habit which made the novelist Céline dub him *Philippe le Dernier* (Philip the Last) and others *Philippe le Gaga*.

In fact, *pétainisme* – which depended on personality as much as ideology – combined the paraphernalia of absolute monarchy, fascist dictatorship and saint's cult in more or less equal parts. Pétain himself was promoted as the object of national veneration. Buildings, squares, streets and even natural features were renamed in his honour: the Aiguille de Chamonix in the Savoie became the Aiguille Maréchal Pétain and, in reverential allusion to the insignia of oak leaves on his marshal's kepi, an old oak in the forest of Tronçais, near Vichy, was dedicated as the Chêne Pétain in his presence. At the ceremony he modestly remarked: 'Two hundred and seventy years old. I'm overwhelmed. I'll never catch up with it!' *Résistants*, more eager to attack Pétain the symbol than Pétain the man, later blew up the tree.

In his official portrait he wore his marshal's uniform and organized his features – the famous clear blue eyes and trim white moustache – into a paternal look which blended benevolence with sternness. It gazed on the French from public buildings (where it was required to be displayed), posters on walls (where it was accompanied by the slogan '*Je fais à la France le don de ma personne*'), postcards and stamps. In their homes people made little shrines in his honour, often featuring the busts of him which the factories turned out by the thousand. The regime found its anthem in a sickly little song especially written by André Montagnard:

> *Maréchal, nous voilà!*
> *Devant toi, le sauveur de la France.*
> *Nous jurons, nous, les gars,*
> *De servir et de suivre tes pars.*

'Marshal, here we are before you, France's saviour. We, your men, we swear to serve you and follow in your footsteps.' The refrain ran: 'For Pétain is France, and France is Pétain.'

His daily walk and weekly visit to Mass were just local versions of larger tours, always confined to the Southern Zone, providing the occasion for displays of popular feeling which, though sincere, were also carefully orchestrated. The crowds shouted '*Vive le Maréchal!*' and sang Montagnard's song or one of the countless others written in his praise. Officials greeted him by swearing flowery oaths of loyalty which, like all such oaths under the Vichy government, were to Pétain himself, not the state. A typical one began: 'Marshal, I firmly believe in the truths you are teaching, since you can deceive neither yourself nor the people . . .'. Reports of these events were monitored with equal care by the Agence Française de l'Information de Presse, as l'Agence Havas became after it had been taken over. It proved particularly sensitive to any reminder, however well-intended, of the Marshal's age, much less the suggestion that he might be too feeble for his great task:

> In referring to the Head of State the expression 'old gentleman' must be avoided, even when preceded by a well-disposed adjective like 'illustrious' or 'valiant'. Terms which evoke his military past such as 'illustrious warrior' or 'valiant soldier' should be used as little as possible, though in certain circumstances it is permitted to employ the term 'victor of Verdun'. On the other hand, frequent mention should be made of the Marshal's moral and physical vigour, his generous disposition, his lucidity, and the interest he takes in every problem. Such qualities do not have to be directly described, but should be shown in action, as if incidentally. For example:
> 'The Marshal came forward with a quick and decisive step.'
> 'He takes the liveliest interest in explanations which are given to him.'
> 'He welcomes the delegations with warmth and consideration.'

Children always have a prominent role to play in the iconography that dictators create for themselves, just as education in the literal as well as the wider sense of the term figures high on their list of pre-occupations. Pétain and those immediately round him had long viewed the state-funded primary school system with particular suspicion: it had weakened traditional ideas of service and patriotism, actively promoting the moral rot which had undermined France. Now was the time to change all that, first by teaching children proper respect for their leader from the earliest age. In the Southern Zone all classrooms displayed the Marshal's portrait. 'There was this horrible coloured print,' wrote Jean Guéhenno: 'That man with seven stars,* sometimes covered with paper pellets, who, like God the Father, presided over our work.' Schoolchildren began their day by singing '*Maréchal, nous voilà*'. In civics lessons they read pamphlets culled from his speeches to the nation. At Christmas they were 'encouraged' – a euphemism for 'required' – to send cards, messages and drawings to their leader; two million arrived at Vichy for Christmas 1940, so officials claimed. In the form reply that the Marshal sent the children he professed pleasure at the care they had taken and admired their skill at drawing. Subsequent replies to those children who continued to write to their leader congratulated them on having profited from his advice and urged them to stay loyal to him, obey their parents and teachers, work hard, and carry out the daily tasks assigned to them.

Not only children were subject to indoctrination in the Pétain cult, since to the Marshal, as to the invading German armies in the summer of 1940, the whole defeated nation was a nation of children in need of a father to reassure, guide and discipline them. When youngsters left school, or approached the school-leaving age, they became candidates for youth organizations. The Germans regarded such groups with suspicion, approving regimentation in principle but fearing that in France it could easily be adapted to subversive uses and foster resistance as much as collaboration. In the Occupied Zone they frowned on the Boy Scouts and tolerated other societies only with reluctance. Vichy had no such qualms. Youth affairs were placed in the charge first of Jean Ybarnégaray as Minister for Youth, the Family and Sport (itself a revealing collocation) and then, after September 1940, of the Minister of Education. With their encouragement more than sixty organizations had sprung up in the Southern Zone by March 1941.

The first was the Compagnons de France for youths aged 15 to 20, subsidized by Vichy and praised by Pétain but banned from the Occupied Zone by the Germans, attacked by the Paris collaborators for its supposedly Gaullist elements and eventually persecuted by the Milice. But by far the most important, if only because it was mandatory for young men, was the Chantiers de Jeunesse, a substitute for the military service which had vanished with the truncation of the French army into *l'armée de l'armistice*. The *Jeunes de France* or just *Jeunes*

---

* Worn on a marshal's sleeve. Seven stars, in red, white and blue, became one of the emblems of the regime.

(motto '*Toujours Prêts*': 'Always Ready') were called up for a five-month regimen which mixed military and scouting values, stressing physical exercise, hygiene, community life and rural skills: all the ingredients of Vichy's recipe for *formation virile*, or manly training.

Among the adult population, the most fertile group for regimentation were the veterans. In the 1920s and 1930s the *mutilés, gueules cassées* and other soldiers from the First World War had been a highly visible presence, honoured at 14 July parades and active, through the leadership of men like André Maginot, in asserting their right to proper pensions and in championing the need for proper defence against Germany. Now their ranks were swelled by the bewildered and frustrated soldiers defeated and then discharged after the armistice. The Germans tolerated existing veterans' organizations in the Occupied Zone but did not permit new ones. Vichy, however, founded the Légion Française des Combattants almost as soon as it came to power, with Pétain as its honorary leader, and the following spring it widened eligibility for membership to all men in the Southern Zone over the age of 20.

The take-up was gratifyingly large. The Légion appealed to the multitude of Pétain's admirers who, in the early stages of the Occupation, still believed that under his leadership France would arise renewed, cleansed and even strengthened after her defeat. Rather than appearing collaborationist, except in the most prudent sense, the Légion seemed impeccably patriotic and immaculately respectable. Membership of it was always an advantage, and often virtually a necessary qualification, in getting public jobs, offices and privileges. Jean Guéhenno's diary vividly evokes the workings of the Légion at the local level in a description of a ceremony held in August 1942. The town's pharmacist presided, proudly taking his revenge for never having wielded any influence before in his life. The others present included the mayor (anxious not to endanger his Légion d'honneur), the schoolteacher (scared of losing his job), civic employees and businessmen, even an old man who worried that if he insulted the pharmacist by not attending he would not get proper treatment the next time he fell ill.

The Légion disclaimed any political purpose. Officially it existed to foster friendship between ex-soldiers, help prisoners-of-war and their families, and honour the memory of fallen comrades. Yet its support of *pétainisme* was written into its oath of allegiance, if only by the firm reference to the state of affairs existing after the armistice as a 'peace' and not just a suspension of hostilities. Everything Vichy authorized claimed not to be political. In fact, everything it did proved divisively so. While the Compagnons de France were suspected of Gaullist tendencies from the start and the Chantiers de Jeunesse slowly fell apart through defections to the Resistance, the Légion trod a path towards ideological collaboration which caused members to feud with each other or leave its ranks. In Nice, where Joseph Darnand was the local leader, the Légion denounced Jews, Communists and Freemasons. The campaign stepped up in January 1942 when Darnand created an inner circle, the Service d'Ordre Légionnaire, dedicated to promoting the National Revolution and rooting out its enemies more vigorously. It appealed not so much to bourgeois notables as to ideologues and toughs. And from the SOL evolved the Milice, more damning to Vichy's reputation than any other group it smiled on.

Whatever the differing ideologies or fates of these organizations, they all testified to a love of regimentation. When he travelled down from Paris to the Southern Zone for the first time in July 1942, Jean Guéhenno found it 'a strange land, a sort of principality where everyone, from children of six upwards, regimented into groups from *Jeunesses* to *Anciens Combattants*, wearing Francisques or symbols of the Légion, seemed to be in uniform. Where is France?' The answer, as he knew all too well, was that Republican France had gone, even its symbols replaced by the symbol of the Francisque, which combined a Frankish double-bladed battleaxe and a marshal's baton. It appeared on the medal which Pétain created and on Vichy coinage, potent testimony to a belief in discipline and its enforcement. Liberty had been replaced by loyalty to the group, equality by the hierarchy of ranks inside the group, fraternity by unquestioning obedience to the leader.

The slogan which actually replaced *Liberté, Egalité, Fraternité* was *Travail, Famille, Patrie*: Work, Family, Homeland. Both Pétain and Laval were proud of their peasant origins. Though Laval was too cynical to concern himself with the National Revolution – negotiation with the Germans was more his line anyway – Pétain was determined it should reflect the values he took from his background. His vision of an ideal France, respectfully ordered under proper authority, was laced with rural nostalgia. When they were not parading in uniforms or attending Mass, its patriotic subjects (not citizens) belonged in the fields working hard and uncomplainingly to support their families. '*Labourage et pâturage sont les deux mamelles de France,*' proclaimed the motto on Vichy banknotes, quoting Henri IV's finance minister, Sully: 'Ploughing and sowing are the two udders of France.' Yet it was not so much the time of Henri IV that this fondness for an agrarian society invoked as that of Louis XIV. The Marshal liked implicitly to compare himself with the Sun King, whose reign he viewed as the last point in history where there had been a contented peasantry untouched by revolutionary and republican discontents, its mind untroubled by notions of Socialist class struggle or capitalist competition.

This vision had little relevance to the realities of France past or present. The *charte paysanne*, or peasants' charter, of December 1940 and the work of Pierre Caziot, Minister of Agriculture until the spring of 1942, introduced some useful reforms which had been demanded before the war: making it easier to unite scattered plots of land into one farm, for example, to rebuild farmhouses and to ensure that the son who wanted to farm the land inherited the property. Yet the unmistakable tendency of Vichy's agricultural policy – as indeed of its policy in business and industry – led in fact to corporatism and state management rather than peasant co-operation or independence. And neither corporatism and state management nor rural nostalgia answered the urgent problems of the Occupation, when almost half a million farmworkers remained prisoners-of-war and those who were still on their farms were struggling with the rising price of fertilizers and a shortage of fuel to run their machinery.

The failure of the National Revolution in this respect was symptomatic of a general failure which soon led the French to delight in mocking distortions of *Travail, Famille, Patrie*: *Trahison, Famine, Prison* (Treason, Hunger, Prison), *Tracas, Famine, Patrouilles* (Bother, Hunger, Surveillance) or, a Gaullist slogan, *Travail: Introuvable. Famille: Dispersée. Patrie: Humiliée* (Work: Unobtainable. Family: Scattered. Country: Humiliated). Even the most predictable of Pétain's attempts to reach back into pre-republican and pre-revolutionary history for safe national rallying cries provoked the same dissent. Defending Verdun, he had quoted Joan of Arc to good effect: '*Courage, on les aura!*' Now he invoked her again as 'the heroine of national unity' and declared her feast day, 11 May, a public holiday as an alternative to 14 July and 11 November, both embarrassing for their links with, respectively, the Revolution and the end of the First World War.

Joan of Arc seemed ideally suited to his purposes: a military leader who had rallied a dispirited nation, a name synonymous with French resentment of the English who had burned her at the stake, a national saint recently canonized by the Church, even (because of the voices she had heard) the patron saint of radio, the very medium which Pétain cultivated so assiduously. And yet she held other resonances which the French were quick to note. 'How dare he do this!' exclaimed the Communist journal *L'Humanité* at Pétain's attempt to appropriate her memory: 'Joan of Arc put herself at the head of an army to drive out the invader.' Joan's defiance could equally well serve as an emblem of resistance, as it did in Claude Vermorel's play *Jeanne avec nous*, staged in 1942. Its portrayal of the English as the enemies of France satisfied the official mood and the censorship of the time, but Vermorel and his audience also found a different contemporary parallel in a story of brutal invaders aided by traitors and collaborators. The poster giving the text of de Gaulle's first broadcast from London was headed by words often, though wrongly, attributed to her: '*La France a perdu une bataille! Mais la France n'a pas perdu la guerre!*' ('France has lost a battle! But France has not lost the war!'). The Free French adopted as their emblem the double-barred cross of Lorraine, her native province.

Even the Reich, which destroyed statues of Joan in the Occupied Zone, claimed her memory when it licensed a propaganda poster showing her ghost hovering over Rouen (where she had been executed) after it had been bombed by the Allies. 'Murderers always return to the scenes of their crime,' said the caption. Some historians have concluded that Joan, *une sainte pour tous*, was a figure sufficiently ambivalent to be claimed by all sides during the Occupation.* Yet the national unity which Joan supposedly embodied and to which Pétain appealed did not exist. Defeat on the battlefield, coming hard on the turbulence of the 1930s, had shattered it. Nor was Pétain really trying to restore it. Speaking the lofty language of patriotism, despising the petty rivalries of politics, his regime was in fact sectarian from the very start. Far from being all-embracing, the France that Pétain personified was narrow, defined by what it excluded.

The Vichy government institutionalized the impulse to find scape-

---

* They make the same point about Joan's admirer, the poet Charles Péguy, who could be remembered either for his Catholicism and heroic death in the First World War or for his Socialism and support of Dreyfus, but rarely on both counts at the same time.

goats which had gripped the French in the first shock of defeat. The impulse had its origins in the tensions of pre-war France – when the right-wing *Gringoire* had delighted in listing the Jews included in Blum's Front Populaire government – and it would have survived the summer of 1940 anyway. The Paris collaborators certainly kept it alive, their vengeful and triumphalist spirit aptly expressed in the name of the weekly *Au pilori*: *To the Pillory*. The magazine specialized in personal denunciations, and its name was only just metaphorical. It helped to fuel the mood in which Marx Dormoy, who had stood up to the Cagoule when he served in the Front Populaire government, was assassinated in 1941 by Eugène Deloncle's *cagoulards* under their new name of the Mouvement Social Révolutionnaire. Robert Brasillach hailed the killing as 'the only act of justice carried out since the armistice' in the most trenchant of the collaborationist magazines, *Je suis partout*. Its name means 'I am everywhere' but those not gripped by its fervour took to calling it *Je chie partout*: 'I shit everywhere'.

The rhetoric of denunciation was already moving hand in hand with violence towards that grim settling of accounts which would almost tear France apart during the latter years of the Occupation. By then, the Vichy government would look increasingly like a helpless witness to the spectacle of violence, wringing its hands in timid outrage. Yet it had taken the initiative in urging the downward spiral on its course. It had thrived on private denunciation and it had refined public hysteria into the official machinery of persecution. Its most obvious targets were those in public life whom it blamed for the disaster of 1940, and its chosen weapon was the show trial. At Riom, near Vichy, in the spring of 1941 a High Court specially created to investigate the origins of France's defeat heard indictments against Gamelin, Daladier, Blum, Jean Zay and other politicians, particularly those from the Front Populaire. Their presence among the accused showed that the trial was directed against those who had opposed Munich and advocated war as much as those who had failed France's armed forces. And the specific terms of the indictments were even more revealing: in Blum's case, they extended to his introduction of a forty-hour working week and paid annual holidays.

Pétain himself had publicly declared his belief in the guilt of the accused even before the trial began. Yet they were still able to launch a defence vigorous enough to embarrass the government, Daladier proving particularly effective in attacking Pétain's own record on national defence before the war. Vichy was forced to suspend the proceedings and abandon the attempt to impose its selective and partisan reading of history in the name of patriotism and national unity. But its failure did not help the defendants, who remained in prison, still vulnerable to the hostility of the Germans and their own countrymen. And it did not prompt Vichy to change its policy. Witch-hunting, a vital part of the public mood which had brought it to power, had become an essential part of its working methods.

At the abortive Riom trial Léon Blum was, in effect, accused of having been a politician of the Third Republic and, worse than that, a Socialist politician of the Third Republic. He was also a Jew, as neither his enemies at Vichy nor his prosecutors at Riom forgot for a moment. His co-defendant Jean Zay was in an even less fortunate position: a politician of the Third Republic and a Socialist, partly Jewish, he was also a Freemason.* The categories of those whom Vichy began by blaming and ended by persecuting frequently over-lapped and interlocked. In the minds of the persecutors, of course, this merely confirmed their belief that they were dealing with a common tendency, a Hydra whose many heads sprang from the same body. Servants of the secular state, opponents of Munich, Socialists, Jews, Freemasons, Communists, teachers, even jazz musi-cians: the details of the indictments against these groups or particu-lar individuals mattered less than the simple satisfaction of finding vague, sinister connections among enemies. It was expressed in ugly jargon – 'Judaeo-Bolshevism' or 'the Jewish-Marxist plutocratic alliance' or, later, 'Judaeo-Gaullism' – labelling what was at best suspect and at worst disloyal, but at any rate not truly French.

Take, for instance, the case against the Freemasons, already elabo-rated in France as in other western European countries virtually since the inception of Freemasonry itself. In the specially charged atmosphere of the Occupation, the leading anti-Mason was Bernard Faÿ, honoured by Vichy and made the head of an agency in Paris devoted to helping the Germans root out secret societies. The Freemasons, it appeared, were enemies of the Church, buttresses of the Third Republic and warmongers who had urged France into the disaster of 1940. So were the Jews of course. Thus it is no surprise to

---

* See Chapter 6 for Zay's eventual fate.

find the Masons themselves accused of *philosémitisme* (Jew-loving), as well as secret plotting, the very crime which, historically, anti-semitic hysteria has laid at the door of the Jews.

Indeed, Pétain himself seems to have thought them morally more culpable than the Jews: 'A Jew cannot help his origins, but a Freemason has chosen to become one.' Freemasonry, he told Faÿ, was the chief cause of France's suffering: it had lied to the French and taught them the habit of lying. In the name of such logic, 60,000 Freemasons or ex-Freemasons were investigated and 14,000 of them dismissed from public posts. They included more than a thousand teachers; all other teachers were required to sign documents renouncing their connection with Freemasonry. 'Oh, what stupidity!' exclaimed Jean Guéhenno in his diary after reluctantly complying. Worse than stupidity: 989 Masons were eventually sent to the camps, where 549 of them died.

Though it may be misleading to separate the treatment of any particular group from the general picture, it is nevertheless instructive to examine how the Vichy government spent its early months in office assembling the machinery of persecution against the Jews. Its first concern, inevitably, was with the foreign-born Jews whom France had admitted in the 1930s. Many of them were refugees from Nazism and by 1940 they amounted to perhaps 200,000 of France's Jewish population of between 300,000 and 350,000. A disproportionate number were now in the Southern Zone since they had, understandably, been among the first to flee the German advance for what they supposed to be a place of greater safety. On 17 July 1940, just five days after it assumed power, Vichy promulgated a law restricting entry into public service to those born of French fathers; it was followed in August and September by similar laws affecting the medical and legal professions. On 22 July a commission was set up to review all naturalizations granted since 1927 (when the criteria had been relaxed) and to strip 'undesirables' of their citizenship; about 6,000 of the 15,000 people who fell victim to its work were Jewish. On 4 October *préfets* were authorized to intern foreign Jews in special camps or force them to live in remote areas under police surveillance.

Though foreign Jews had been objects of the hostility reserved for immigrants since before the war, they were not – even in the earliest days of Vichy power – the only target. On 27 August the repeal of the *loi Marchandeau*, an executive order of 1939 which had outlawed press attacks on ethnic or religious groups, declared open season for anti-semitism. On 3 October the government issued its first *statut des Juifs*, setting forth its definition of Jewishness and excluding those defined in this fashion from the higher levels of public service and from professions, such as teaching and the media, deemed to influence public opinion. Vichy consolidated this first phase of its activity in March 1941 by creating a special department for Jewish affairs, the Commissariat Général aux Questions Juives.

After the war those who had served the Vichy government would claim that it had acted in response to German pressure or that it had acted first in order to prevent the Germans imposing harsher measures. In a striking image André Lavagne, chief of Pétain's civilian staff, compared Vichy strategy to the firefighters' practice of 'lighting small fires [*contrefeux*] to save the forest'. Actually it took its first anti-semitic steps not in forced acquiescence to the philosophy of the Reich but in a spirit of independent zeal. Of German pressure during the opening months of the Occupation there is no evidence whatsoever, except in the matter of establishing the Commissariat Général aux Questions Juives. But there is abundant testimony to the anti-semitic atmosphere of Vichy, in which (for example) a senior official could lecture the Protestant leader Pastor Marc Boegner on the need for 'collective punishment' of the Jews. And revealingly, the man Vichy appointed as first Commissioner-General for Jewish Affairs, Xavier Vallat, had impeccably anti-semitic qualifications but (like many of his colleagues at Vichy) no pro-German sympathies. He was a fierce believer in French independence, by which he meant that France should handle its own 'Jewish problem' in its own anti-semitic way. His record of conflict with representatives of the Reich was one of the reasons he was sacked in March 1942.

Nor could Vichy claim that in the Occupied Zone the Germans were setting a stiff pace it felt obliged to keep up with. Indeed, many Jews whose instinctive fear of Nazism had made them flee south longed to return to Paris, where they now believed they would fare better. The Germans, after all, had more urgent matters to keep them busy. They did not establish their Judenreferat, or police branch for Jewish affairs, until 12 August, or issue their equivalent of Vichy's first *statut des Juifs*, defining who was Jewish, until 27 September, three months after they had overrun France and only a week before Vichy acted.

Vichy's statute did not echo the German statute or try to modify its terms. It embodied its own brand of anti-semitism, broadly compatible with the Reich's, of course, but different in detail. The crucial differences, moreover, identify Vichy's anti-semitic policy as harsher than the policy the Germans began by adopting in the Occupied Zone. The German ordinance defined Jewishness by religious practice; the Vichy statute spoke more broadly of race. The German ordinance defined Jews as people having more than two Jewish grandparents who had observed Jewish religious practices. The Vichy statute included people with only two grandparents who had been Jewish by race, if they themselves were also married to a Jew. In other words, somebody who did not count as a Jew in the Occupied Zone could count, and suffer, as a Jew in the Southern Zone.

The German ordinance also banned Jews who had fled to the Southern Zone from returning to the Occupied Zone. The provision could not easily be enforced to start with, since the census for identifying Jews was only then being compiled, but it highlighted an immediate conflict of interest between the Reich and Vichy on the 'Jewish problem', whatever broad agreement of principle may have existed. Not yet committed to a policy of extermination, nor yet in a position to organize mass deportation from France, the Reich simply wanted to get rid of as many Jews as possible from the territory it controlled. Far from planning to make the Southern Zone *Judenrein* (purified of Jews), it welcomed the convenience of using the Southern Zone as a dumping-ground. Indeed, Otto Abetz, the German ambassador in Paris, had been eager for the September ordinance to begin this process, after first stripping the Jews of their property. But that, of course, was the last thing the anti-semites of Vichy wanted to see happen.

The pattern which emerges from a comparison between the Germans' stance and Vichy's stance towards the Jews in 1940 is thus one of broad agreement in principle and local disagreement in practice.* Vichy was at one with the Reich in its belief that there was a 'Jewish problem' and in its approach to it. Vichy, however, had its own brand of anti-semitism just as, in practical terms, its immediate

---

* Vichy's policy toward blacks was also influenced by French tradition, though in this case the tradition was one of assimilation. It joined the Reich in viewing 'Negro culture' as contributing to modern decadence and it enforced German measures against *gens de couleur* but, in contrast to the matter of the Jews, took no independent steps of its own. The cabinet even included Henri Lémery, a Martinique lawyer and friend of Pétain, as Minister for the Colonies until September 1940.

goals did not square with those of the Germans in the Occupied Zone. The pattern is worth stressing, if only because it helps to define the relations between Vichy and the Reich, the National Revolution and Nazism, in general terms as well.

Vichy was not run by pro-Nazi ideologues eager to do the Reich's bidding; nor was it run by scared men forced against their patriotic inclinations to obey the Reich's commands. Its National Revolution was home-grown, rooted in French soil and carried out by people who believed, or could easily persuade themselves, that they served the best interests of France. Their local loyalties guaranteed that relations with the Reich would include suspicion and conflict, considerably more suspicion and conflict than anyone in Vichy foresaw in 1940. Yet the National Revolution was also, if not fascist, close enough to being fascist to tempt its architects into believing it would win France the respect of the Reich and, with that respect, a worthy place in the New European Order. And this ambition guaranteed tragedy on a scale which the men at Vichy did not glimpse until it was too late for them to do anything other than avert their eyes from it.

'BETTER TO BE a Nazi province', a member of Reynaud's cabinet had said at its last meeting on 16 June, dismissing the proposal for Anglo-French union: 'At least we know what that means.' In retrospect his ignorant confidence sounds chilling. And not just in retrospect: by 1940 there was already enough warning of the extent to which Hitler owed his success to colleagues, rivals and enemies who had thought they could understand his motives, accommodate themselves to his goals and even profit by hitching their star to the bandwagon of his ambitions. As for Vichy's hopes, Admiral Darlan presented them in their clearest form to the occupiers in July 1941. In effect, he suggested that France be released from the armistice to resume normal relations with Germany. Should defence of her imperial interests lead her into conflict with Britain and the United States, Germany would guarantee her pre-war borders. Unsurprisingly, the Reich showed no enthusiasm for the proposal.

So what did the Reich mean to do with France? What would have happened if the New European Order had been established and the Reich had gone on to last for a thousand years? The short answer is that the grandeur of Nazi rhetoric concealed vagueness about anything except the most immediate plans. Hitler certainly raised the question of what the long-term fate of the French should be: 'Can we absorb them with advantage – do they by blood belong to our race?' But he never reached a precise answer, and seems to have admitted as much to Admiral Raeder. Would France be integrated into the New European Order or would she just be crushed? That, Hitler hinted to Raeder, belonged in the ultimate category of state secrets: the category reserved for matters he had not yet had time to think about. 'One must put the French on ice,' wrote Goebbels in his wartime diary, putting the most charitable construction on his Führer's lack of ideas. 'The longer one leaves them hanging in the air the readier they will be to submit.'

Of course, Hitler knew perfectly well why he had invaded France in the first place, and he had several reasons for congratulating himself on the success of his calculated gamble. German national pride had been restored by avenging defeat in the First World War and reversing the *diktats* of Versailles. As for the military position, the Reich had gone most of the way towards securing its western flank by eliminating the possibility of attack from the land by Britain as well as France. Yet this flank would not be completely secure until Britain was neutralized, and Hitler's indecisiveness in moving toward this goal showed how short-term his thinking had been. Unable to launch a convincing diplomatic initiative yet reluctant to launch a full-scale assault, he did scarcely more than toy with Operation *Seelöwe* (Sea Lion) while the moment of advantage passed. Goering's Luftwaffe failed to gain air superiority over Britain in the summer of 1940 and by autumn the weather in the Channel could no longer be relied on: the invasion plan was shelved, nominally until the following spring but never really to be taken up again.

In France he demonstrated that knowing why to invade a country and knowing how to invade it are not the same thing as knowing what to do with it once it has been invaded. France, it turned out, had fallen victim not to a master plan but to short-term expedients which grew increasingly desperate and increasingly brutal in the course of the Occupation. Most were at root economic. The armistice agreement forced France to pay for the cost of being occupied. Apart from confirming the Reich's desire to settle old scores, the demand showed its habit of falling back on greed when vision failed. 'The collaboration of *Messieurs les français* I see in only one light,' Goering told his colleagues with characteristically oafish frankness in August 1942: 'let them deliver whatever they can until they can't deliver any more.' '*Ils sont corrects*' ('They behave properly'), the French had said of the Germans in 1940; soon they were saying, '*Ils nous prennent tout*' ('They're taking everything from us'). And greed remained the guiding motive long after it had provoked a revulsion of feeling among the French which made the whole business of occupying France harder and harder to sustain. To the administrators of the Reich, France was above all a source of booty: food, resources, goods and art treasures from the start, and afterwards people, whether as workers or as candidates for extermination.

The same hasty and short-term approach was written into the sometimes erratic, sometimes arbitrary course of the demarcation line across France, ignoring established bureaucratic boundaries, chopping towns or villages in two. It was made even more obvious by the finer detail of the map which the Reich imposed, for the arrangements did not just divide the country into the Occupied Zone and the Southern Zone, the one controlled from Paris and the other, supposedly, from Vichy. They went much further, chopping France up into additional smaller units, satisfying the military convenience of the moment effectively enough but suggesting a lack of any larger political strategy.

In the south, strips along the frontier facing the Alps were put under the control not of Vichy but of the Italians, as a sop to Mussolini. After the Germans moved south in November 1942 the Italian Zone was extended towards the Rhône, so that it consisted of eight departments: Alpes-Maritimes, Basses-Alpes, Hautes-Alpes, Savoie, Haute-Savoie, Isère, Drôme and Var. In the north and east a line as tight as the main demarcation line itself followed the Somme and the Saint-Quentin Canal, swung south at Sainte-Menethould for Saint-Dizier, and joined the Marne and the Saône. It separated a *zone réservée* from the main Occupied Zone, fifteen departments subject to differing sorts of special status. The region stretching east to Charleville-Mézières was the *zone interdite*, sealed off even from ministers of the Vichy government until Pierre Pucheu, Minister of the Interior, was allowed to visit it in September 1941. In the northern corner the coal-rich departments of the Pas-de-Calais and the Nord were declared a *zone rattachée*, directly controlled by the German High Command in Brussels. Their coastal strip formed a high-security *zone rouge*, later extended along the Channel and down the Atlantic coast to the Spanish frontier in order to meet the threat of Allied landings.

This complex network of administrative and military arrangements reflected the Reich's love of administering through parallel, overlapping and sometimes even competing agencies. And, like every other aspect of their conduct as occupiers, it expressed a sensible belief that the best way to rule a conquered nation is to divide it. The same pragmatism led the Reich to create the Volksdeutsche Sprachgemeinschaft Nordfrankreich (German-language Community of Northern France), made up of *émigrés* from pre-1914 German Poland who wanted to recover German citizenship. The same pragmatism led it to smile on separatist tendencies in Brittany where, though not authorized, Le Parti National Breton was among the handful of political parties to be tolerated in the Occupied Zone.

Larger policy goals were clearly at work only in shaping the fate of Alsace and the eastern part of Lorraine: the three departments of the Bas-Rhin, Haut-Rhin and Moselle. In the 1930s Hitler had repeatedly denied having any designs on them, and they were not mentioned in the armistice agreement. Yet the memory of Versailles and of disputes reaching back to 1870 and beyond made them too tempting to resist. The Reich annexed them directly to its own territory in deed, though not in word. Customs controls were set up on the old frontier by the middle of July 1940 and in September two Gauleiters, or provincial governors, were appointed to establish German sovereignty. (A Gauleiter for Luxembourg was appointed at the same time.) Vichy protested in private and in vain against this violation of both the armistice and international law, but now the Vosges once more marked France's eastern border, as they had in 1914.

People who had fled Alsace and Lorraine during *l'exode* could return only if they had been resident since before 1918. All Jews, some of whose families had been rooted there since the Middle Ages, were barred from returning home – though, ironically, in the later phases of its campaign of persecution the Reich would take steps to retrieve them from the Southern Zone. In addition, the Gauleiters expelled more than 100,000 Jews, post-1918 residents and people foolhardy enough still to regard themselves as French who had stayed at home during *l'exode*. The majority of the Jews resettled themselves in the Dordogne. The faculty of the University of Strasbourg went into exile at Clermont-Ferrand, a popular centre for the refugees, where the Germans harassed it first with demands for the return of the university's great collection of German medieval manuscripts and later with arrest and deportation.

Those left in the communities thus purified were treated as citizens of the Reich, declared 'racial Germans' in the official jargon. Posters on office walls proclaimed: '*Morgens grüsse ich dem Führer. Und Abends danke ich dem Führer*' ('In the morning I salute the Führer. And in the evening I thank him'). In the spring of 1941 service in the Arbeitsdienst, the Reich Labour Service, was made compulsory for men and women between the ages of 17 and 25. The following year all boys were required to join the Hitler Youth. Men of the age for military service, exempted since October 1940 from the *armée de l'armistice* and the Chantiers de Jeunesse, were conscripted into the armies of the Reich from August 1942 onwards. By 1944 the Germans were calling up boys as young as 16. Of 200,000 *malgré-nous* (against-our-wills), as they came to be called, about 10,000 were seriously wounded, 22,000 reported missing in action and 25,000 killed. The survivors included fourteen Alsatians, mostly aged between 17 and 19, serving in the Das Reich Division of the SS who were tried after the war for their part in the massacre at Oradour-sur-Glane, near Limoges, in June 1944.

Culturally, the people of Alsace and Lorraine were subjected to a rigorous campaign of Germanization. The wearing of the beret, traditional symbol of Frenchness, was banned. So was the speaking of French in schools, churches and shops, where the currency was marks, not francs. Though the names 'Alsace' and 'Lorraine' themselves survived, they were replaced whenever possible by Oberrhein or sometimes Elsass for the Haut-Rhin, and Westmark (or West Frontier) for the Germanized part of Lorraine. The name of Strasbourg was changed to Strassburg, Mulhouse to Mülhaussen, Saverne to Zabern, Ribeauvillé to Rappoltsweiler and Château-Salins to Salzburg. Even Alsatian place names needed changing: Obernai became Oberrennheim and Riquewihr, Reichenweiher. In Strasbourg the Place de Broglie was renamed the Adolf Hitler Platz and in Mulhouse, to the amusement of the locals, the Rue du Sauvage became the Adolf Hitler Strasse. Throughout the region the *mairie* was relabelled the Bürgermeisteramt and the school the Volksschule. Even people's surnames were Germanized: Dupont became Brückner, Rochet Roth, Flajeolet Bohn and so on.

Long before such measures provoked resistance, the Germans betrayed doubts about their success in, for example, their use of the term *das alt' Reich* for pre-war Germany as distinct from its less securely loyal territory. Predictably, the eventual remedy proposed was the forcible transfer of populations: moving people of German stock to Saxony or Pomerania or occupied Poland and replacing them with more reliably German people from the Tyrol or evacuees from Bessarabia and Bukovina, both conceded to the Soviet sphere of influence as a result of the Hitler-Stalin pact.

Similar ideas for the rest of France included annexing more of its north and east to create an enlarged Reich, with Alsace and Lorraine closer to its heartland than its border, and combining French Flanders with Belgium and Holland to form a German protectorate. Hitler himself liked to remember that 'a large portion of German history took place in the old kingdom of Burgundy, and that this land is therefore age-old German soil, which the French stole from us in times of our weakness'. So Burgundy could be made into an SS state or simply integrated into the Reich. Either way, exulted Goebbels, whose propaganda claimed that the Germans were lineal descendants of the Dukes of Burgundy, 'we will win a territory superior in beauty and riches to almost any other German province'.

Such proposals were never more than dreams which the Reich did not live to realize. Yet, like the network of zones it actually established, they made one thing very clear. Vichy spoke of national interest, national unity, national revival: it looked to the day when a renewed and cleansed France would be written into the map of Europe which the Reich was busy creating. The Reich, pausing occasionally in its brutal practicality to indulge in fitful visions of the future, had other ideas. France had already been chopped into convenient pieces. In the short run she would be plundered. In the long run, Goebbels foresaw the day when she would be reduced to the size she had been in 1500, before Louis XIV consolidated her power and confirmed her identity as a nation state. Her name would virtually have disappeared from the map.

PART II

The Shameful Peace

Long live the shameful peace!

Jean Cocteau

I will corrupt the countries I occupy.

Adolf Hitler

3

Are You in Order?

I have been receiving politicians, town councillors, *préfets*, magistrates. Out of fifty of these dignitaries, forty-nine have asked me for special permissions of one sort or another, or for petrol coupons – and the fiftieth spoke of France.

Otto Abetz, June 1940

To tell the truth, it is through the privations it brings, and through them only, or almost only, that the majority will be affected by the defeat. Less sugar in their coffee and less coffee in their cup: that's what they will notice.

André Gide, *Journal*, 13 July 1940

'*ETES-VOUS EN RÈGLE?*' asked the posters on a thousand walls: 'Are your papers in order?' At least, that is how the slogan translates most idiomatically into English, but in its literal meaning it asked a broader and more sinister question: 'Are you in order?' However little status the Reich might have planned to give France in the New European Order, it certainly meant to bring the French into line as thoroughly as it could. Even the French clock had to be brought into line: one of the Reich's first acts, apparently the very first change it officially imposed on its new conquest, was to make French time synchronize with German time by putting it forward an hour. So, as autumn turned to winter in 1940, the unnaturally late darkness in the mornings was among the first and most expressive harbingers of the mood of life under the Occupation. The older generation still remembers it as one of the details typifying the grimness of the times.

Yet that grimness was not the grimness of order: few, if any, periods in modern French history have seen less order, legally, socially or morally, than the years 1940 to 1944. Those among the French who were rash enough to believe that the Stukas and Panzers storming into their country in June 1940 had brought with them the promise of salutary discipline soon learned better from the stream of decrees spewing forth from the Militärbefehlshaber (military commander-in-chief), the Kommandantur (military headquarters) and all the other German agencies establishing themselves in Paris, and from the slightly blurred carbon copies of these expedients produced by Vichy. This was no antidote to the despised bureaucracy of the Third Republic but bureaucracy run rampant: intricate, muddled and muddling, eventually unworkable. However patiently people queued (and queuing was, above all, what the Occupation required of people), they stood less and less chance of getting what they were queuing for.

The new regulations were not made unworkable by resistance, much less by the Resistance. Few people were thinking of resistance in the summer of 1940, and when the Resistance did effectively come into being the best goal it could set itself was to help deliver the *coup de grâce* to a system which already showed every sign of falling apart. The regulations were made unworkable first and foremost by the profound disorder of the society on which they were imposed, the disorder following the national catastrophe France had undergone in the summer of 1940. All the Reich and Vichy could achieve – all they ever did achieve, really, as administrators – was to add *papier timbré* to the underlying chaos. The chaos adjusted, accommodated itself to the red tape, and finally triumphed.

AFTER THE INITIAL panic of the invasion and the exodus, when the armistice had been signed and the reassuring tones of Marshal Pétain had been heard over the airwaves, 'France went in search of France', or so the historian Henri Amouroux has written. But it was not that simple. Dislocation was not a brief nightmare of June 1940 but a prolonged ordeal which defined the Occupation for most communities and, indeed, touched the lives of most people in one fashion or another. Few families were fully reunited in their homes.

The homes themselves might have been damaged or looted or taken over by the Germans. As for the families, many children were still missing after those muddled and makeshift journeys by road or rail. For months to come the classified columns of the papers mournfully detailed their names, ages, appearances, distinctive luggage, the places they had last been seen and their home addresses. Missing, too, were the 90,000 or so servicemen killed in the fighting. Another 200,000 had been wounded and nearly two million taken prisoner: some were released and some managed to escape in the prevailing muddle but most, about one and a half million, were deported to Stalags (or, if they were officers, Oflags) in Germany. It took a long time to establish the fate of all these casualties of war. The first official lists did not appear until more than a month after the armistice, and they were not sufficiently full or accurate to prevent anxious relatives from besieging the Ministry of Pensions and the special information centre set up in the Archives Nationales in Paris with inquiries.

Families who had not lost a child or a soldier might still be displaced, and fated to remain so for the rest of the Occupation. The demarcation line made the journey home difficult or impossible even for those with energy, money and a safe home to return to, let alone for those who had ended the exodus in hastily organized refugee centres like the one at Beaune-la-Rolande or just living rough in cities like Limoges or Bordeaux. Jews who had fled south, only to form doubts about the goodwill of the Vichy regime, found themselves stranded by the Reich's decree forbidding their return to the Occupied Zone. The more affluent took refuge in the friendlier atmosphere of the Italian Zone, where the pre-war population of perhaps 15,000 to 20,000 Jews had increased to 30,000 or even 50,000 by 1943 – at any rate, increased so dramatically that anti-semites took to calling Cannes 'Kahn'. Other Jews joined the first wave of a growing illegal traffic to neutral Switzerland, Spain and Andorra, taking a boat across Lac Léman by night or making the rugged climb over the Pyrénées. And, of course, the Reich's *de facto* annexation of Alsace and Lorraine soon added the 100,000 'undesirables' it expelled to those already banned from their native provinces.

It is hardly surprising that the American writer Gertrude Stein, who fled her Paris flat with her companion Alice B. Toklas for Culoz, near Annecy, should have found herself far from alone in her plight: an expatriate leading an insecure and increasingly dangerous life in an unfamiliar part of her adopted country. The little town was now home to other Americans, Poles and Belgians, as well as Alsatians, Lorrainers and French Jews. 'Everybody is a refugee,' she remarked with relief. All that Culoz needed to make it a perfect microcosm of wartime France was perhaps a German Jewish *émigré* from before the war, or a Republican in exile after defeat in the Spanish Civil War, or a downed Allied airman in hiding, or one of the soldiers from the British Expeditionary Force stranded after being left behind in the evacuations of 1940.

The statistics which historians have pieced together for the cities of the north and north-east, included in the Occupied Zone, show the other side of the coin. Evreux in Normandy has already been mentioned as an example of depopulation. Less than 200 of its pre-war 20,000 inhabitants had still been there on 11 June 1940, just after nearby Rouen had been taken. By 18 June, the day after Pétain announced his intention of seeking an armistice, there were scarcely more than that. By the end of the month, a good week after the armistice had been signed, there were still only about 6,800 people And even by the middle of July, when Pétain declared himself Head of State, only half the population of Evreux was back home again.

That was not normality returning slowly: it was the first warning that normality would not and could not return under the new status quo. Paris told the same story, despite the conspiracy of German propaganda and perverse national pride to congratulate the capital on how quickly it got down to business as usual, how easily it went back to living with its distinctive flair. The pre-war population of three million had sunk to a mere 800,000 people by the time the Germans first came marching down the Champs Elysées and took until the first week in July to creep back over a million again. A month later it had scarcely increased.

Inevitably, many who belonged to what the French call *le tout Paris* – the rich and fashionable circle which had helped to give the city its pre-war reputation – had gone for good. Coco Chanel stayed behind to indulge in anti-semitic diatribes at dinner parties given by newly popular hosts of the day like Fernand de Brinon, the ambassador from Vichy, or Otto Abetz, the suavely francophile ambassador appointed by the Reich. But the Duke and Duchess of Windsor had left their house in the Boulevard Suchet near the Bois de Boulogne and taken to the road, grumbling at British diplomats' failure to give them VIP treatment, on a journey which would take them via Spain to diplomatic quarantine in the Bahamas. The Aga

Khan, Daisy Fellowes (said to be world's most beautifully dressed woman), the American heiress Peggy Guggenheim and other darlings of the international set had fled.

Collaborationist writers like Pierre Drieu la Rochelle, Lucien Rebatet and Jean Luchaire were there to set the tone in journalism and letters, joined by Robert Brasillach when his stint as prisoner-of-war was over. Simone de Beauvoir made her way back after the exodus; Sartre escaped from his prisoner-of-war camp on the Luxembourg border in March 1941 and Albert Camus arrived later in the Occupation to add lustre to the growing reputation of their circle at the Café Flore in Saint-Germain-des-Prés. Picasso refused to abandon his studio despite invitations from across the Atlantic. The careers of Cocteau and the dancer Serge Lifar, actors like Sacha Guitry and Arletty, and entertainers like Maurice Chevalier, Suzy Solidor and Mistanguett all flourished. Jean-Louis Barrault, Simone Signoret, Charles Trenet and Edith Piaf, with her protégé Yves Montand, were among the rising new stars. Yet James Joyce had gone to Switzerland, and Maurois and Nabokov to America, along with the film directors René Clair and Jean Renoir, the painter Fernand Léger and the composer Darius Milhaud. Apart from Gertrude Stein, exiles in the Southern Zone included Aragon and Malraux, Chagall and Matisse, who retreated to a Provençal village to produce paintings which were, said Aragon, 'like a great banner unfurled'.

During the exodus itself the poorer people of Paris had, of necessity, stayed put in larger numbers. About half of them had remained, as compared with only a quarter of their affluent neighbours. Yet the gaps in their *arrondissements*, less conspicuous than those in the fashionable set, proved equally damaging, equally demoralizing: a family lacked a breadwinner, a block of flats a *concierge*, a workshop a vital employee, a *quartier* a shop on which it had relied. In such a state did Paris and the rest of the Occupied Zone come to terms with the fact of the German presence.

They did so under the first round of restraints which ushered in the new order. People were forbidden to show hostility to German soldiers, hide weapons, help soldiers of any sort except the Germans, help those trying to flee to the Southern Zone, help escaped prisoners-of-war, communicate with countries hostile to the Reich, or listen to foreign propaganda, particularly from the radio stations of hostile or neutral countries. (The terms of the last injunction officially deprived them of nourishment not just from the BBC in London but, equally important, from Swiss radio.) The list of thou-shalt-nots steadily lengthened as the occupiers' grip grew at once more thorough and more nervous: people could not keep radio transmitters, take photos out of doors, gather in crowds or assemblies without special permission, parade in the streets, or display insignia or flags of any kind.

Such measures were, after all, only to be expected of any occupying power, and particularly of one which began its rule by making so conspicuous a point of correctness in its own behaviour. Besides, in 1940 few people felt any inclination to do most of the things they were banned from doing – except, perhaps, listening to radio stations that did more than repeat German propaganda. Their lives were more directly affected by the curfew. In Paris it ran from eleven o'clock at night, soon relaxed to midnight, until six in the morning. But since the Germans saw the curfew, like the demarcation line, as a means of political and psychological control and not just as a security device, they periodically brought its starting time forward in reprisal for public acts of disobedience.

Jean Guéhenno's diary caught the atmosphere of one evening in December 1941 when the curfew had started at five o'clock:

> It is 6.30 p.m. and I'm watching night fall. No noise, not even a whisper. That's Paris!
>
> Behind their windows ('Thoughout the curfew, windows must be kept closed,' the authorities order), the people in the house opposite are watching the street like me. We make signs to each other. Prison solidarity. But suddenly, from an inner courtyard somewhere near the end of the street, the noise of a bugle rings out: some Paris urchin thumbing his nose at servitude.

Usually the silence that followed the curfew was broken only by the Germans. The sound of their hob-nailed boots as they patrolled the streets in units of five grew so familiar it came as a surprise to learn, at Liberation, that American soldiers wore rubber soles. Ninetta Jucker, an Englishwoman who spent the Occupation in Paris, listed the other noises which punctuated nights in the capital:

> Rifle shots; the sudden pepper of a machine-gun – or could it be the firing squad? – the rush past of a powerful car (someone being swept away by the Gestapo perhaps) and towards the early morning, singing . . . on

command. One could hear the order given a second before the marching song burst forth, rhythmic and in tune.

Even the normal curfew hour of midnight still meant that plays, films and concerts had to be over by eleven, before the Métro trains stopped running.* The last Métro, indeed, became something of an institution in its own right, with performers and audiences crammed together in the deliberately festive mood people sometimes adopt to put up with irritating restraints which have grown familiar. Like the early nightfall and the knowledge that any sound in the street at night came from the occupiers, it typified the Occupation in the memories of those who lived through it.

YET PEOPLE RESIGNED to observing the curfew and largely uninterested in tuning their radios to London or Switzerland were still far from satisfying the letter of the new law. To be properly in order, they had to get papers – by queuing, of course, and from French, not German, officialdom. And they had to carry their papers with them at all times, producing them on demand for any inquisitive official, who was more likely to be a French gendarme or *fonctionnaire* (civil servant) than a German soldier.

The *carte d'identité* was the most basic, and the one already most familiar to the French. Like a passport, it carried a photograph and all the personal details in which bureaucrats customarily take an interest – full name, nationality, profession, date of birth, place of birth, physical appearance, distinguishing marks, home address – together with stamps and signatures from the Préfecture de Police. But that was not the only document officialdom demanded, even for those who had no need to go in search of the elusive *Ausweis* or *laissez-passer* for crossing the demarcation line. Men of an age for military service had to prove they were not deserters or escaped prisoners-of-war by carrying either proof of exemption from conscription or, more usually, their *fiche* (or *feuille*) *de démobilisation*. After the Service du Travail Obligatoire, the forced labour scheme, had been introduced, men in the relevant age groups who remained behind in France needed to prove they were in a reserved

---

* As it was, Henry de Montherlant's play *La Reine morte*, one of the great critical successes of the Occupation, was so long that performances had to start in the afternoon.

occupation, had a disqualifying illness or had been wounded in the campaign of 1939–40.

All these papers were essential: the lack of them could, at best, provoke embarrassing inquiry and, at worst, land someone in prison or drive them into hiding. Yet none dominated people's lives as completely as the ration card (*carte d'alimentation*) and its accompanying coloured stamps, which the French called *tickets*.* Of course, food restrictions had been in force since the outbreak of war. The authorities had issued bread tickets and banned the sale of meat, sugar and alcohol on certain days of the week; luxury chocolate had disappeared from the market. Yet, like the rest of the phoney war, these measures had seemed no more than a temporary annoyance, and sometimes not even that. On a restricted day an American journalist could still find a Paris restaurant offering a choice between seven kinds of oysters and six or seven kinds of fish, including *bouillabaisse*, followed by rabbit, chicken or curry, and fruit salad, pineapple with kirsch or *soufflé à la liqueur*. 'Thanks to a couple of fairly decent wines,' he reported, 'we managed to get this sort of thing down.'

The Occupation changed all that. It made the French realize that, despite their national pride in the richness of their land, they had in fact grown to rely on imports, particularly from their territories across the Mediterranean in north Africa, now dangerously dependent on the whim of both the German and the British navies. Worse than that, the German invasion had damaged the harvest, the displacement of people had left shops without suppliers and farms without labourers, and the demarcation line had disrupted the normal traffic in goods between the largely agrarian south and the industrial north. And then, of course, there were the Germans. The original invading army, with its love of French food that gratified French national pride and its appetite for wolfing down omelettes made with two dozen eggs, soon looked mild by comparison with the Germans who followed. Once the occupying force had settled in, it requisitioned food and other goods for its own support and unleashed on the market soldiers made rich by the official exchange rate between the franc and the mark. Not just their pockets but the warehouses of their official purchasing agencies were soon crammed with luxury goods, a term which quickly came to embrace things

---

* Originally an English word. The British chose to use a French word, *coupon*.

like wine and tobacco which the French had taken for granted before the war.

A popular joke told of two Frenchmen who disguised themselves as Wehrmacht officers but were quickly unmasked because they were not carrying suitcases. It hardly exaggerated. Photos of German officers leaving France when their tour of duty ended show them followed, like explorers, by trains of local bearers carrying their booty. The policy of plunder intensified as the Reich grew increasingly desperate to prop up its own failing economy and its faltering armies on the Eastern Front. France was slowly being bled dry by the outflow not just of meat and drink, fuel and leather, but of wax, frying pans, playing cards, axe handles, perfume and a host of other goods as well. Parisians, at least, had got the point as early as December 1940. When Hitler shipped back the Duc de Reichstadt's remains for solemn burial in Les Invalides, people said they would have preferred coal rather than ashes.

The more stringent system of food rationing introduced at the beginning of August 1940 required people first to register with the authorities, then to register with their usual baker, butcher and so forth, and then regularly to collect the *tickets* issued by their local *mairie*. Janet Teissier du Cros, a Scot who stayed in France throughout the Occupation, described the frustrations of the process as she encountered it in Paris:

> You took your place in the long queue that overflowed from our local food-office, and streamed along the pavement with no protection from the rain. During the long wait, as the queue moved forward inch by inch, conversation was soon joined with the other grumbling women. We all spoke our opinion without restraint and I never even attempted to conceal the fact of my origins for it only made them more friendly. When at last my turn came and I was inside the building, going from counter to counter, from queue to queue, for the various cards, I was always in a fever lest some mistake be made and I come away with less than my due.

'How I hated the women behind the counters!' she added. 'They were most of them tasting power for the first time in their lives; they were also certainly as underfed and overworked as the rest of us; but I took no account of that.' The camaraderie of fellow-sufferers in the queue, as in the last Métro, and its antithesis, the hatred of officials, and not just of German officials: the mood of the Occupation was taking shape.

The bureaucratic maze was made necessary by the complex set of categories into which the population was divided for its food entitlements. Category A embraced most adults, defined as between 21 and 70. They received the standard ration but farmworkers (Category C, for *Cultivateurs*) and manual workers (Category T, *Travailleurs*) got extra allowances of bread and milk. Children under 3 were in Category E (*Enfants*), getting more milk and less bread than adults. Older children, in Category J (*Jeunes*), were divided into J1s (3 to 6), J2s (6 to 13) and J3s (13 to 21). Those of school age got biscuits containing protein supplements, pink vitamin pills and the dubious delights of drinks like Banania and Phoscao instead of coffee. J3s got extra milk and bread, in effect promoting them to the status of those in Categories C and T. People over 70, in Category V (*Vieux*), were not thought to need milk.

The list of rationed goods began with obvious staples like bread and sugar, and quickly extended to meat, milk, butter, cheese, eggs, fats, oil, coffee and fish – the last made scarce, even in coastal areas, by the petrol shortage which hampered fishing boats. Then the list lengthened remorselessly to include wine, salt and potatoes, for example, and widened to embrace other necessities of life like soap, clothing and tobacco. The quantities allotted did not just differ from category to category and from region to region: they changed from month to month as the Occupation wore on, usually diminishing. So did the availability of food, whether it was rationed or, like seasonal fruit and vegetables, still unrationed. All these variables make generalization about how badly people actually fared almost meaningless, though statisticians have estimated that the average daily intake by adults during the Occupation sank to something between 1,200 and 1,500 calories a day, half or only slightly better than half the generous 2,500 calories the French had been in the habit of consuming before the war. This put France almost at the bottom of the table of western European countries: only Italy fared worse. In eastern Europe even the people of Romania, Bulgaria, Hungary and Bohemia-Moravia were eating better.

In France the authorities admitted the urgency of the situation from the start, not just by the stringency of the rationing system itself but by the increasingly desperate additional measures they promoted. Big cities like Paris opened *rescos*, a word which combined *restau*, the slang abbreviation of *restaurant*, with *rescousse* (help or rescue), to label what were in effect soup kitchens. The Vichy regime encouraged *jardins ouvriers*, or urban vegetable gardens, in a defeatist echo of the British 'Dig for Victory' campaign. It extolled the virtues of thrift by encouraging people to forage for acorns and chestnuts and setting its Boy Scout army, the Chantiers de Jeunesse, to work making charcoal for fuel. And Vichy joined the Germans in attacking waste, particularly in the form of the *doryphore*, or Colorado beetle, which had recently migrated across the Atlantic. The campaign against the *doryphore* had children and their teachers deserting their classrooms for the fields during school hours to pick the beetles from the potato plants and drown them in bottles of water.

When the inadequacy of these feeble though much-publicized remedies grew apparent, the rationing system steadily came to rely on official substitutes for substances which France could no longer import or manufacture for herself: chicory or roasted acorns instead of coffee, for example, and saccharine or worse instead of sugar. People called these substitutes *ersatz* – a word, like *blitz* and *diktat*, which the Reich gave to the languages of Europe. The other word for them was *national*. So, in addition to her *révolution nationale*, France had her *café national*, *sucre national* and *tabac national*. There was even a 'national suit' for men, which could be bought on presenting the appropriate clothing coupons and two worn-out suits. The entertainer René Paul won ready laughter with a song claiming that the trousers turned into short trousers when it rained.

Adults in Paris began the Occupation by having to make do with 350 grams of bread a day, 350 grams of meat a week, and 500 grams of sugar, 300 grams of coffee and 140 grams of cheese a month. The diary of the young Micheline Bood helps to bring these figures to life by showing how a reasonably well-off family could still manage to eat. In her household, lunch on Saturday consisted of beans, two slices of sausage for each person and some cheese, while dinner was soup, chestnuts and more cheese. Sunday brought bean salad, boiled beef and a dessert made of chestnuts for lunch, then soup, beans and jam for dinner. Monday's lunch was an egg for each person with vermicelli, followed by jam, and Monday's dinner was beans, bean soup and jam again. And so on through the pinched and dreary week.

The relative absence of meat, the lack of variety, the sinister recurrence of beans, jam and chestnuts all tell their own story, even though Micheline Bood was inexact about the amounts of food served. The official rationing quotas are exact, and they show Parisians getting less and less. By 1943 the daily allowance of bread was down from 350 to 180 grams and the weekly allowance of meat down from 350 to 90 grams plus, grumbled one sufferer, 'an occasional distribution of sausages that exuded a sinister liquid when fried, or some equally disquieting galantine'. The monthly sugar ration stood at only 390 grams, while coffee and cheese (now fatless) were in equally short supply. Potatoes and macaroni could be found only occasionally and eggs – the adult allowance was one or two a month – were usually unavailable. Milk could be bought only for children, and their supply ran out the next year.

By 1944 everybody's diet had got even worse. People said that the meat ration was so small it could be wrapped up in a Métro ticket. A hostess making a special effort to entertain friends to dinner might risk making a potato pie with an egg in it and boiled carrots with a dab of butter on top. Carrots now appeared in all sorts of guises. In restaurant menus, *potage paysanne* meant carrots and water, *filet de boeuf garni* meant very little meat and a lot of carrots, and *macédoine de légumes* meant mainly carrots. Swedes, traditionally despised and grown only for cattle fodder, became a staple in kitchens with near-empty cupboards. Often they were the only available substitute for potatoes. Even an Englishwoman like Ninetta Jucker, used to them from school meals in Britain, found them disgusting: 'great knotty roots which rent the bowels and filled the hospitals with appendicitis cases and ulcerated stomachs'. Afterwards the French would say that getting them to eat swedes, let alone queue to buy them, was the greatest victory the Germans had achieved. (And, rather than bringing relief from deprivation, the Allied landings and Liberation wreaked havoc with fragile systems of supply and so pushed the food shortage further into crisis.)

The lack of other goods and services increased the hardships suffered by Parisians. Transport was a problem from the start. Before the war the city had about 350,000 parking spaces. By the winter of 1940 the Franco-German Service Public set up in the Préfecture de Police had issued permits for only 7,000 private cars. The privilege was restricted to people in certain occupations, such as doctors, midwives, firemen and nightworkers, though others who cultivated friendly relations with the Germans (notoriously, Sacha Guitry) were quick to use their influence. Even they could not drive on Sundays, when traffic on the streets was exclusively German.

On other days they had to battle with the acute shortage of petrol – which, of course, the Germans eagerly requisitioned, together with unlicensed private cars laid up from before the Occupation. Some drivers turned to the *voiture à gazogène*. A German invention marketed in France by the Société Imbert, it replaced the petrol tank with a natural gas-cylinder, standing about a metre high, on the back or side of the vehicle. The cylinder needed replacing every 40 kilometres and new ones were obtainable only from special depots, so many *gazogènes* were simply wood-burning; the disadvantage was that drivers had to wait for the stove on the back to heat up before the vehicle would start.

Though traffic had not vanished from the streets of Paris, the change was eerie to anyone who remembered the city before the war. An observer who conducted his own amateur survey toward the end of 1943 counted, during a ten-minute period near midday on the Place de la Bourse, just three cars, a motorbike and a horse-drawn cab. 'As silent as the country!' he marvelled. His fellow-Parisians were taking the Métro, where ticket sales rose dramatically in spite of the interruptions which more and more often plagued its service. And, like the rest of the French, they were riding bicycles. The number of bicycle thefts shot up in the early months of the Occupation. By the time it ended Paris alone had two million bicycles, more than three-quarters of them newly acquired, even though they cost almost as much as a car had done before the war. In Paris and other large cities, they were adapted to make *vélo-taxis*, bicycle-powered rickshaws which could carry one or two passengers, easier to keep on the road than carriages with horses needing hay. There was an official scale of charges like the one for pre-war taxis. The more adventurous drivers plied their trade even in the most fashionable spots (like the racecourse at Auteuil), where they took German passengers as well as French, and blazoned their carriages with eye-catching names: *A la grâce de Dieu, Les Turfistes, Pourquoi pas moi?, Securité – confort – rapidité, Les Temps modernes, La Belle Equipe.**

Vélo-taxis took parcels as well as passengers, but for most heavy chores people had to rely on their own initiative and muscle: hitching a home-made trailer on the back of their bicycle, getting out the

---

* 'With the Grace of God', 'The Racegoers', 'Why Not Me?', 'Safety – Comfort – Speed', 'Modern Times', 'The Great Team'. The last two names echoed the titles of films popular in the pre-war years: Chaplin's *Modern Times* and Julien Duvivier's *La Belle Equipe*, starring Jean Gabin, had both been released in 1936.

pram or cart that had already seen service in the exodus and the journey home. Simone de Beauvoir hired a barrow when she needed to move from one to another of the Paris hotels where she and her circle liked to live:

> I had never put too high a value on the respect of others, yet even so, before the Occupation I should never have dreamed of getting between the shafts. But at present few people could afford the luxury of caring what others said about them, and I was not one of the lucky ones. . . . I light-heartedly dragged my suitcases and bundles of books across Paris. No one found this an odd sight, and even in Saint-Germain I would not have been embarrassed to meet people who knew me. One managed as best one could.

It was not only the Germans who always had suitcases: even on their normal daily round, most people carried something or pushed something or pulled something in which to put food or any other scarce household item they might be lucky enough to snap up.

Not everything people needed could be found or carried. Fuel for heating grew scarce as the mild summer of 1940 gave way in Paris to the first of the unusually cold winters that made life under the Occupation harder to endure. Otto von Stülpnagel, the new military commander-in-chief of the Occupied Zone, might have set an admirable example of German correctness in refusing to heat his headquarters in the Hôtel Majestic rather than requisition precious French coal. But that was no consolation to people who knew that for one reason or another – requisitioning by Germans less correct than Stülpnagel, the exclusion of the coalfields of the Pas-de-Calais and the Nord from the rest of the Occupied Zone, the barriers against imports – their country now had only about a third of the coal and a tenth of the oil supplies it had enjoyed before the war. Nor were they consoled by Colette's serene recommendation of the heat-generating properties of gold jewellery. They dampened old newspapers, filled old cardboard boxes with ashes or sawdust, used anything that promised to keep a dying fire alight for a little longer. And even Colette took her own most drastic advice: go to bed whenever you can. Yet still, as Jean Guéhenno grumbled to his diary, 'you get so cold you can't think of anything else'.

The electricity supply grew more and more uncertain – and, despite German claims, by no means always because of Allied bombing raids. At first people turned to makeshift contrivances in which they could take a certain good-humoured pride: hairdressers used pedal-powered generators to run their dryers and photographers posed their studio portraits out of doors. Then the Métro service started to fail more and more often. Cinemas and theatres were limited to afternoon shows. At home, where food could be cooked during only a few hours of the day, people returned to using candles. By the end of the Occupation, some plays were being performed by candlelight. Lightbulbs had long since been in short supply: to buy a new one, people had to take their old one back to the shop with them. Now there was a candle shortage as well.

On the whole people fared better in rural areas than in great cities like Paris. In the countryside, people were better placed to produce for themselves, exchange with their neighbours, forage for food or fuel and, of course, to conceal produce from requisitioning. Yet even this pattern does not apply universally to hardship made diverse and unpredictable by local circumstances. The rich agricultural land of the Lyonnais, for example, helped to buffer France's second city from the suffering experienced by Parisians in the winter of 1940–1. Yet when suffering came to Lyon, in the spring of 1941, it came as harshly as it did anywhere else. Meat was available only twice a week and in small quantities; butter, fat, potatoes and even skimmed milk were hard to find; pasta and rice were unobtainable. The bread, which everywhere lent itself to adulteration, contained more bran and coarse rye than wheat flour.

They were eating better than that in many country areas, and might be eating still better towards the end of the Occupation, when the same chaos that brought an acute shortage of supplies to the cities could effectively end the Germans' ability to requisition local produce. Yet some country people – on the Côte d'Azur, for example, where much of the land was poor – suffered as much as their urban fellows. 'It's really a *famine*,' Roger Martin du Gard reported to Gide from Nice in June 1943:

> People feel they're going to starve. Nothing on the market – absolutely *nothing*. And every day we go back, we queue in front of the empty stalls from seven in the morning until midday, in the hope that a basket of beetroot for cattle might turn up at last and we might be able to buy a bit. We see a few handfuls of pasta and split peas which the Préfecture distributes when there's been nothing on the market for three or four days in a row (and these are taken *out of the reserve supply for next winter*). The bread is a gluey paste, inedible. A little meat every twelve or fifteen days: the ration

for two people is just one thin slice. . . . And that's for fifteen days! *One* egg between two people every six or seven weeks! No oil, no fat. At the end of the month we throw our unused coupons away. Not the slightest sign of vegetables, not the slightest sign of fruit.

One thing was clear. Wherever they might live, it was always difficult and often impossible for anyone, except perhaps a baby, to survive on the rations officially allowed them, much less the amounts of these rations that they could actually find at the market. People took special care to see their ration cards were in order and that they were issued their full entitlement of coupons. They got used to queuing patiently, at first for several hours during the normal shopping day and then from the early hours of the morning. Finally, if they lived in a city, they slipped a fee to the *concierge* of a building near the market so that they could sleep overnight in the porch, the lobby or the cellar and be first in line when the curfew ended.* When they finally got served, they made sure that the shopkeeper did not try to palm them off with old or rotting items from his stock: pasta swarming with maggots, for instance. They paid higher and higher prices from incomes that remained fixed at their 1940 level: by the end of the Occupation people were spending about 70 per cent of their budget just on food. In many households a pair of scales stood on the dinner table so that portions could be minutely weighed before they were served. And still there was not enough.

B Y 1942 THE mortality rate in Paris was 40 per cent higher than it had been in the years 1932–8; deaths from tuberculosis among the elderly and young had doubled. In the poorer districts of the city adolescent girls growing up between 1935 and 1944 were 11 centimetres shorter, and boys 7 centimetres shorter, than their predecessors. A generation developed bad teeth. Adults lost anything between 4 and 8 kilos. The whites of people's eyes grew dull and their complexions turned grey or sallow. Skin became dry and cracked, and joints stiff and painful from oedema, the pathological accumulation of fluid in tissue spaces. Vitamin deficiencies caused boils, at

---

* A cartoon by André François showed a queue at a building site where work has not progressed beyond the ground floor. The man at the head of the queue is whispering to his neighbour, 'Apparently there's going to be a *charcuterie* in the building.'

first on the hands and feet but spreading to the face and the rest of the body. In winter chilblains grew so large and persistent that they could make fingernails and toenails drop off. Minor infectious diseases were rife and, naturally, they ran a longer course than in well-nourished people. Overeating when the opportunity presented itself was, after all, only the other side of the same coin as deprivation, so the occasional bout of indulgence induced what the French call *une crise de foie*.

The psychological effects of malnutrition are subtler, less noted by the sufferers themselves and less susceptible to scientific survey. They include tiredness and problems with the short-term memory. These symptoms cast considerable light on the mood of a country, already demoralized by its defeat, which some observers have found unaccountably and even shamefully passive in the face of the growing indignities of the Occupation. Yet the chief effect of being unsure of one's next meal and of being naggingly hungry in the longer term is that one gets overwhelmingly preoccupied with food. Ignoring the complaints of the stomach while searching for food in the market, remembering past meals which have satisfied or fantasizing about future ones that will again satisfy the appetite while trying to put up with the inferior menu which the present day offers: such activities quickly blot out other considerations. They become more pressing than thoughts of past defeat or future resistance, infinitely more pressing than the abstract rhetoric of politics. Surviving from day to day is what matters.

In retrospect this would seem, to many of those who did manage to survive, the real humiliation of being occupied: they had thought of themselves and their stomachs when they should have been thinking of France. At the time hunger and shortage seemed a challenge and people were proud of rising to meet it. The French have a verb, *se débrouiller*, and a corresponding noun, *débrouillardise*, which like all the words for things most cherished by the speakers of a particular language are multiple and elusive in their meaning. *Se débrouiller* means, approximately, 'to manage', 'to get by', 'to fend for oneself', 'to look out for oneself', in certain contexts 'to wangle' or 'to weasel out of'. *Débrouillardise* is thus an admirable resourcefulness. Together these terms have generated a slang idiom, *le système D*. It serves as watchword for a society which has, at different points in its past, variously prided itself on peasant independence and republican individualism but always on its knack of simultaneously subverting and accommodating itself to officialdom. The Occupation was the golden age of *le système D*.

'One managed as best one could,' Simone de Beauvoir wrote by way of explaining her undignified appearance between the shafts of a barrow. People managed as best they could at the dinner table too. They copied their government in devising *ersatz* or *national* substitutes for foods which had grown scarce. For coffee they were driven to experiment with chestnuts, chick peas, dried apples and lupin seeds. When they got fed up with running the water three or four times over the same few spoonfuls of tea leaves, they turned to lime-tree leaves, apple skins or dried carrot tops. Sugar could be replaced by liquorice or boiled pumpkin, though everyone agreed that using grape juice instead of sugar to make *raisiné* jam produced appalling results. So did most home experiments in baking bread with buckwheat, millet flour, chestnuts, oil cake, bean flour or even potatoes. 'Well, if the war lasts till 1970 I expect we'll find that good!' joked one guest at a particularly unpalatable meal.

The *tabac national* which contained – indeed, soon largely consisted of – dried grass and herbs gave the cue to smokers. They bought hand-rolling machines and mixed their own substitutes: oak leaves with camomile and peppermint or other kitchen herbs, perhaps, or lettuce leaves or beetroot leaves or corn silk or even Jerusalem artichokes. Every smoker had a special recipe to swear by, though none refused the chance of smoking real tobacco on the increasingly rare occasions when it presented itself. To combat the clothing shortage, women made themselves turbans or hats with extravagant decorations of artificial flowers and fruit, which had the advantage of concealing the lack of a proper perm. But no Sunday inventor or seamstress could do anything about the scarcity of leather. People had to depend on the ingenuity of manufacturers, who supplied shoes with soles of compressed paper or wood. Too flimsy in winter, the paper soles were less popular than the wooden ones, which were hinged to make them more comfortable, though the hinges easily collected loose pebbles. About twenty-four million pairs were sold during the Occupation and, as Maurice Chevalier celebrated in the song 'La Symphonie des semelles de bois', the pavements rang again to the sound of clogs.

The meat shortage was the most galling of all. In Paris some people who lived in flats took to keeping guinea pigs, and respectable folk could sometimes be observed braining the pigeons in the public parks. They meditated even more desperate expedients: in October 1941 the authorities found it necessary to publish warnings that it was unsafe to use cats in stews. In the country, of course, people could more easily rear their own chickens, pigs and rabbits, as well as grow their own vegetables. So city-dwellers found the Occupation a convenient time to remember their rural ties, and from 1941 people in the country were officially allowed to send them *colis familiaux*, or family parcels. Thirteen and a half million of them passed through the strictly supervised postal system in 1942 alone.

They did not always arrive in an appetizing condition, as Simone de Beauvoir discovered with the meat she got a friend to send from Anjou. The beef had to be soaked in vinegar and boiled for hours; a joint of pork had white maggots in it, but she and Sartre cooked it anyway. Sartre was usually oblivious to what he ate but even he found the state of a rabbit so revolting he insisted on throwing it in the dustbin – an action whose difficulty can really be appreciated, perhaps, only by someone who has lived through such times of hardship. City-dwellers who lacked obliging friends or relatives in the country set out at weekends on expeditions, returning with meat or sacks of produce slung over their shoulders. Such forays became so regular a custom that the train services from Paris were nicknamed after vegetables: the *train des haricots*, the *train des pommes de terre* and so on.

Money changed hands less and less frequently in these transactions between country and city, and in all the other dealings by which people sought to fend for themselves. As people usually do in times of growing scarcity accompanied by growing regulation, the French reverted to an economy of barter. A city-dweller setting out for the country in search of meat or vegetables, home-made soap or eggs, would take not cash but something precious like real coffee or real cigarettes which country people were less likely to be able to grow, make or find in their own communities. Meanwhile, country people and city people were bartering freely among themselves. In Culoz even Gertrude Stein, a temporary resident who grew and reared nothing for herself, found she could still join in the system: a neighbour who lacked milk to fatten her pig agreed to take Stein's dishwater in return for guaranteeing Stein the right to buy eggs. If she had still been living in Paris, she might instead have collected cigarette ends and used them to establish a privileged arrangement with her butcher or baker.

Exchanging waste matter for a place near the head of the queue might have been a bizarre transaction, but it was still more direct than the complicated chain of bartering which the need for even a simple commodity could often demand. 'You have to buy what you do not want to buy in order to buy what you do want to buy,' Stein herself explained oracularly. Alfred Fabre-Luce was more specific: 'Whoever wants tobacco brings a chicken, and whoever wants a bag of raisins trades a cheese.' Nor did the chain have to consist only of commodities, since services and ration coupons had their exchange value as well. A doctor would supply medical advice, or a plumber would mend a tap, in return for the food they wanted or for food that could be swapped for the food they wanted. Non-smokers would contrive to register for the tobacco ration. People who made their own bread at home would prize their unused bread coupons as highly as they prized their cash.

Such trading in ration coupons was, of course, illegal. The inadequacy of official rations and the need for *débrouillardise* meant that sooner or later everyone broke the law, in however minor or innocent a fashion. *Le système D* merged inevitably with the *marché gris*, and the grey market shaded inevitably into the black market, the *marché noir*. But where exactly did such distinctions lie? And, besides, did they matter any more? Maybe the extra coupons people acquired under the counter were actually stolen or forged. But they still worked, since shopkeepers would usually take anything but the grossest forgeries, and the goods they made it possible to buy were often necessary for survival. Maybe people had to go to a black-market operator to get something, like coffee or a proper joint of meat, which had now become a luxury. But surely there was nothing wrong with that in times when governments themselves had made the whole notion of law at best nonsensical?

In fact, nothing showed the nonsensicality of the law more clearly than the attitude the authorities adopted to the black market itself. The Germans, of course, condemned it and tried to punish it. Yet they themselves had virtually summoned it into existence in the first place through Goering's policy of hiring buyers to supply the German purchasing agencies. This German black market had an official life from late 1942 until the spring of 1943 but a much longer unofficial one as an example to the French of the advantages of the *système D*.

Vichy, like the collaborationist writers in the Paris papers, joined the Germans in condemning the black market; the Milice originally put it high on their list of targets. Yet by the spring of 1942 Vichy was already exempting minor personal infringements of the law from prosecution. It had been preceded by the Church in the person of Monsignor Suhard, Cardinal-Archbishop of Paris, who by December 1941 had agreed to wink at 'modest' black-market operations. Even the Resistance, which condemned the black market and seems to have been far more effective in stamping it out than either the Germans or the Vichy regime had been in the rural areas it came to control by the end of the Occupation, was not free from hypocrisy and equivocation. After all, how else could *résistants* on the run or 'living off the land' manage to survive without illicit supplies of food, 'liberated' through theft, forgery or the obliging mechanisms of the black market?

Most ordinary people seem to have reached some form of rough and ready compromise with their conscience or their reluctance to think of themselves as criminal. A resident of Culoz explained to Gertrude Stein how the compromise usually worked: 'to find something is one thing, to indulge in black traffic is quite another thing'. In explanation she added that 'to find is when you find a small amount any day at a reasonable price which will just augment your diet and keep you healthy. Black traffic is when you pay a very large sum for a large amount of food, that is the difference.' To buy for a reasonable price what you needed for yourself and your family, even perhaps to buy a little more to have something left over for bartering or an even rainier day: that was just 'finding', that was acceptable, that was *marché gris*, not *marché noir*.

It was a paper-thin distinction. What counted as a reasonable price when all prices were rapidly inflating, and what counted as a reasonable amount when nobody knew what shortages tomorrow might bring? But the Occupation was not a time for niceties of definition. People could even take a certain relish in their dealings with small-time black marketeers like Maria de la Baraquette, a Cévenol woman who emerged every so often from the woods with a sack on her shoulder:

> She would come into your kitchen, casting a wary look behind her, plunge her hand into the sack and produce a lump of butter wrapped in a sheet of writing-paper, or half a dozen eggs and a small piece of bacon. . . . Sometimes there had been a clandestine kill . . . and she would have in her

sack a hind- or fore-quarter of mutton. On these occasions, delightfully steeped in secrecy, she would not even expose the contents of the sack but would plunge in a sun-baked arm that tapered off in a long wicked-looking knife and would hack off blindly whatever cared to come.

Every village had its Maria de la Baraquette. They were often people who had not shown much concern for legal niceties before the Occupation, and even then the law might well have turned a blind eye to them. Some, at least, of the locals who brought illicit tobacco, silk stockings, olive oil and coffee over the Pyrénées from Spain and Andorra had pre-war experience in the trade as well. Now they could be seen as romantic outlaws, particularly since they also took downed Allied airmen, SOE agents, *résistants* and victims of persecution out of the country, though for a stiff price. Even the smugglers of tobacco from Belgium, where it was cheaper, could be greeted with a wry shrug: 'as long as a blade of grass remains in Belgium,' people said, 'our sister France shall not lack tobacco'.

The criminals from the *milieu* (underworld) in cities like Paris and Marseille, who took to the black market as enthusiastically as American gangsters had during Prohibition, were harder to swallow. Yet the middle-class conscience is always resourceful in persuading itself it can touch pitch without being defiled. All its agility is put to the test by the suburban doctor and his family with whom the young hero stays in François Maspero's novel about the Occupation, *Le Sourire du chat*:

> It would seem that for the last four years the energies of his entire family have been concentrated on food and the means of acquiring it. 'One more the Jerries won't get', the head of the family sighs victoriously as he polishes off an unctuous dish of sweetbreads or an exotic guinea fowl which cost its weight in gold and was procured through the combined efforts of a network of priceless connections. And victory is exactly what is reflected in his triumphant gaze. This is a daily battle, it's war, real war, the only one worth fighting, with its tight spots and moments of heroism. He conducts his resistance activities on the black market in perfect good faith.

Everybody needed the black market, as all the authorities tacitly admitted; nobody liked a real black marketeer. Hardship and the commitment to the *système D* might have called such profiteers into existence and guaranteed that they should prosper, yet they were still the easiest of villains to hate. Maspero's satire at the expense of his suburban black-market customers in *Le Sourire du chat* needs to be set beside Jean Dutourd's portrait of the Poissonard family in another novel, *Au bon beurre*. The title comes from the name of the shop in Paris where the Poissonards sell milk, butter, cheese and so forth, but in French the idiom *faire son beurre*, literally 'to make one's butter', means 'to feather one's nest'. And behind the name Poissonard itself lurks the idiom *être comme un poisson dans l'eau*, literally 'to be like a fish in water', though the English would say 'to be in one's element' or, vulgarly, 'to be like a pig in clover'. The Poissonards live up to these allusions by exploiting every opportunity to thrive at the expense of their neighbours. They charge outrageous prices, water the milk they sell, buy goods from the Germans, denounce an escaped prisoner-of-war, help a Jew evade the authorities but only for money, before becoming Gaullist at the last moment and welcoming Liberation. In short, they are what the diarist Jean Galtier-Boissière with his usual irony called *girouettes*: weathercocks.

Dutourd's comedy of small-time profiteering should in turn be set beside real-life cases, at once disturbing and pathetic, like that of Maurice Sachs. Before the war he had published studies of Gide and the Communist leader Thorez; his theatrical ambitions had introduced him to Cocteau's circle. In his early thirties at the time of the invasion, he was working for Radio-Mondial in Paris. Returning after the exodus and re-establishing himself there in January 1941, he found the black market in full swing. Everybody, he quickly saw, except a few aristocrats, priests and academics had a hand in it. Even teenage crooks were selling ration coupons, though the most successful black marketeers were the accredited buyers for the Germans. Sachs' posthumously published memoir of the years 1940–2, *La Chasse à courre*, reproduces fragments of some typical phone conversations:

> 'Hello, darling. Listen, I've got three tons of sugar at sixty francs a kilo.'
> 'Oh, I've got 100 litres of oil.'
> 'Hello, old chap, I need five tons of copper. Absolutely definite, it's for the Germans.'
> 'Do you need rice by any chance?'
> 'I might. . . . How much is it?'

Doubly offensive to the ideology of the day as a homosexual and a Jew, Sachs stood in particular need of mastering the art of *débrouil-*

lardise. So what else could he do but join in? He rented a fashionable flat overlooking the Seine and dealt in gold and jewellery – a shrewd choice, since many of the rich were finding it wise to convert their wealth into forms that could easily be hidden or transported. Among his specialities were gold wafers in the shape of visiting cards for those planning to leave the country. His motley list of suppliers included a Dutch stamp-dealer, a Belgian banker, a goldsmith, two brothers who smuggled gold from the Southern Zone (where it was 40 per cent cheaper), professional gamblers, criminals with the proceeds from robberies, ladies selling off their family jewels, and a pseudo-Marquis, 'astonishingly stupid, oozing phoneyness from every pore, but candid about his newly acquired depravity as a businessman'.

The French police took no interest in him; the German authorities might have done, but Sachs found a protector in the Gestapo. His main problem came from his own miscalculations of the market itself, which left him with a string of angry creditors. He was briefly reduced to making nocturnal expeditions out of Paris in search of meat to sell before leaving the capital altogether. He resurfaced in November 1942 among French workers at a factory in Hamburg. The Gestapo may have planted him there from the start; at any rate, he was soon informing on fellow-workers with anti-Nazi sympathies, dealings in the black market or plans to escape. A year later he fell foul of his masters and was thrown in prison. Doubts obscure the end of a life already fast receding into the shadows. Some acquaintances even thought they saw Sachs again on the streets of Paris after the war; another account has him being lynched by fellow-prisoners. It seems most likely that he was shot by the SS when they evacuated the prison in April 1945.

THOUGH HE BELONGED entirely to his times, Maurice Sachs and his 'cowardly war' (as he himself called it) were not typical. Few people followed the *système D* to such extremes, enjoying his brief hour in the sun and suffering his squalid fate. Most people survived. They took care to stay *en règle* when they could, but not out of respect for the law. Law, regulation, bureaucracy and officialdom were forces to outwit – forces it had become a matter of pride to outwit – in the daily battle to keep fed, clothed and warm. And so they managed not just to survive but to survive in better shape than their liberators had expected. Or so, at least, the correspondent for *Time* magazine claimed when he reported from Paris in 1944:

> Americans who entered Paris last week were amazed. They expected to find Parisians starved, tattered, numb from oppression. They looked the same as they did before the Occupation. The women had smart clothes and cosmetics, the children were tubby and well-fed. The truth seemed that the Nazis entered Paris as a moonstruck lout courting a handsome woman. Paris had smiled grimly.

For all its exaggeration – plenty of women had neither smart clothes nor make-up, and plenty of children were neither tubby nor well-fed – what *Time* said cannot be discounted entirely. Sartre was just one of many Parisians made aware that they did not quite correspond to the 'pathetic image' British and American troops had formed in advance of their arrival. The care Parisian women had taken to keep up their reputation for being *chic* was particularly striking, even to such level-headed observers as Janet Teissier du Cros, who confessed to feeling dowdy by comparison, and Simone de Beauvoir, puritanically defiant in her shabbiness. When the leather shortage forced them to wear a modified version of clogs, women had made thicker and thicker wooden soles the fashion of the day. When the hairdressers could no longer be relied on to perm their hair and the clothing shortage forced them to make their hats out of old scraps at home, they had devised the turban and headgear of such extravagant floral decoration that it attracted good-humoured mockery on the Métro. Their inventiveness, the magazine *Comoedia* claimed after the event, had represented 'a victory for French ingenuity, a victory for Parisian taste'.

In a similar spirit the young of both sexes – the J3 generation – had created their own youth cult. From as early as the winter of 1940–1, and in much greater numbers by the spring of 1942, they had become *zazous*. The boys wore long hair greased with oil, long jackets, high collars and drainpipe trousers; the girls wore jackets with padded shoulders, short pleated skirts and striped stockings; both affected dark glasses, chunky unpolished shoes and umbrellas kept furled even when it was raining. They listened to jazz – *le swing*, Django Reinhardt and the Hot Club de France – and shocked their elders by being the first generation to *tutoyer* them, to use the familiar *tu* rather than the respectful *vous*. Such insolent decadence provoked the same disapproval as the various post-war youth cults which were the natural successors of the *zazous*, starting with the *éxistentialistes* in the cafés and bars of Saint-Germain-des-Prés. In particular, the Germans frowned on the *zazous'* love of jazz, that product of inferior negroid culture, and the Vichy regime deplored their rejection of its uniforms. Abel Bonnard, Vichy Minister of Education, denounced them as 'the last remnants of an individualist society'; gangs of youths from the fascist Parti Populaire Français waylaid them in the streets and forcibly shaved their heads.

After Liberation such things would be remembered with pride by the *zazous* and even their elders. Like the fashion for floral hats and thick-soled shoes, the cult had demonstrated something reassuring about France: a resilience that had gone beyond the ability to gather food for the table, an individualism that had mocked the efforts of Vichy and the Reich to keep everything *en règle*, a cultural flair that had made the occupiers look lumpen. And had not these things been a form of resistance: innate, spontaneous, but unmistakable? Johnny Hess, the singer who claimed to have started the *zazou* cult and even invented its name, liked to remember that groups chanting *judéo-gaulliste* had tried to disrupt his concerts. Lise Deharme, poet and hostess to a Surrealist salon, put the case on behalf of fashionable women:

> Yes, Parisian women, true Parisian women, were supremely elegant for four years, with the elegance of a racehorse and not of a horse pulling a hearse. With a tear in their eye but a smile on their lips, beautiful, well made-up, incredibly discreet and insolent in their impeccable suits, yes, they exasperated the Germans. The beauty of their hair, their complexion, their teeth, their slimness contrasting with the fat hideousness of those trouts wrapped in grey, yes, that got on the Germans' nerves. These Parisian women were part of the Resistance.

Not the least extraordinary thing about this tribute is that *Les Lettres françaises*, where it appeared, was a Communist journal. Its easy self-congratulation smacks altogether too much of Maspero's doctor in *Le Sourire du chat* pointing to the meat on his Sunday dinner table as a triumph of anti-German activity. Both comments reflect the change in national mood which caused *girouettes* eager in 1940 to denounce their own government, the war, the British, the Jews, the Freemasons, anyone except the Germans, to have become by 1944 every bit as eager to claim kinship with, indeed virtual membership of, the Resistance. And both express the myths with which the

French sought to heal their pride. Yet neither Deharme nor Maspero's doctor shed light on the psychological pressures of the Occupation, let alone on how people might have felt about their behaviour later.

Janet Teissier du Cros does. Though Scottish by birth and French only by marriage, she had suffered with the French throughout the Occupation, and so earned the right to speak as one of them. On first seeing her liberators, she was struck by their healthy pink-and-white complexions and the contrast with her own sallow appearance. Yet at the same time she was aware that the marks of her own deprivation were slight, and she felt obscurely ashamed. She knew perfectly well this was unreasonable, since she had done nothing disgraceful but had lived by the exacting requirements of a Scots-bred conscience. Nevertheless the shame was there and could not easily be argued away.

Survivor guilt affects people this way: it makes them ashamed of having survived ordeals that others did not, and it makes them ashamed of how they survived. Janet Teissier du Cros feared that the pangs of deprivation and the successful practice of the *système D* had together blunted the 'finer feelings':

> We were all of us driven to some form of dishonest practice. It was no small hardship having to throw our moral scruples to the winds and settle down to a dishonest way of life, in full view of the children and in contradiction to all we were striving to teach them. Not but what my practical Scotch mind made a clear distinction between what is immoral and what is merely illegal; but such distinctions are not easy to explain to a child. Besides, there was a haunting feeling that this was the thin end of a wedge and, as such, not a good thing for the nation.

She was not alone in the fear that, by the very ways in which they survived, the French had been, if not destroying, then at least betraying something in themselves, something in France. Another shrewd but sympathetic foreign observer, Ninetta Jucker, agreed in remembering 'a pall of egotism . . . smothering charity and the sense of civil obligation': 'You could not so much as buy a cabbage or get on a bus without sensing the general hostility, thinly veiled by an appearance of manners which shattered nerves made little effort to sustain.'

Nor was the fear just retrospective, the sort of scruple through which the guilt of the survivor could emerge once the ordeal was safely over. It surfaced during the Occupation itself in the disgust with what was happening. Paul Léautaud, for example, gave way to it in his diary in December 1942. 'How many people', he asked, 'notice the collapse of France, think about it, are affected by it, are interested in it, except just as a spectacle?'

> You have only to look at them in the Métro, listen to them talking just about food, young boys and girls, fooling around, laughing, cuddling, kissing, or look at them in the never-ending queues at the cinemas on the Avenue d'Orléans for the rubbish you see there, which the public has come to need, and I mean need. For them nothing is happening, and they are too stupid and too ignorant to take an interest in anything with a political, a European aspect.

He could understand writers continuing to write as though things were normal, but 'these employees, shopkeepers, labourers with their trivial distractions, who seem interested only in themselves! They eat, they do their work, they sleep, and that's it.'

In its way, of course, this jaundiced outburst is as extreme as Deharme's burbling praise of Parisian women. Yet, if anything, it gains rather than loses authority from Léautaud's pro-German standpoint: in his eyes the French, by their self-absorption and their trivial distractions, were failing a high destiny, not of resisting but of cultivating the virtues of their conquerors. French disgust with the French could make strange bedfellows during the Occupation. Micheline Bood, the young girl whose weekly menu has already been cited, confided to her diary in 1941: 'It is terrible to say so but I have reached the point when I find the French no longer men: I am renouncing my country, I no longer want to be French! . . . Nobody has ever seen people so conquered as the French are.' André Gide was also asking himself if he was still proud of his country, and he could find no more reassuring an answer:

> At times France seems so unfamiliar that one suspects one was mistaken about her in the first place. She seems to have set about renouncing her best and rarest qualities, her virtues, one after another, or relinquishing them like useless luxury goods or like belongings which, in time of hardship, cost too much to look after. France now is no longer France.

It takes a great deal to make the French ashamed of being French. Even the defeat of 1940 had not quite managed to do that, however deep the crisis of national self-esteem and however loud the clamour of mutual recrimination it had provoked. But the years that followed did. They created a sense of disgrace more subtle yet far more disturbing than anything that had happened on the battlefield. It was at once national and personal. It reached into the minutiae of daily life, where people detected self-absorption, indifference to each other and small dishonesties grown habitual not just in their neighbours or fellow-passengers on the Métro but eventually in themselves as well. When Jean Guéhenno grumbled about being so cold he could think of nothing else, he was not just talking about the state of his toes: he was worrying about a loss of moral perspective and where it might lead him. And for those who lacked his imagination or conscience, the loss of moral perspective and its results were written unmistakably large in the official life of their nation.

When he came to publish his diaries, Gide added a stern footnote to his conclusion that France in 1941 had ceased to be France: 'I refer, of course, to the France of Vichy.' As well as originating so many of the dilemmas which pervaded French life, the Vichy regime became the public example of their shameful consequences. To some, indeed, it became the precedent which justified pursuing those consequences to their shabbiest ends. And nothing it did was more profoundly corrupting than its practice of claiming to represent, indeed to safeguard, the soul of the entire nation – Pétain is France and France is Pétain – while in fact institutionalizing its most divisive tendencies. Vichy gave the cue to ordinary people, the people waiting in the queues and the people eating swedes and the people getting through their day feeling hungry. Deprivation had sharpened resentments they already felt, resentments which dated back beyond the disaster of 1940 to the turmoil of the interwar years. Now they were invited to confuse prejudice, grievance and envy with patriotism, even patriotic duty.

'In times like these, to eat well and to eat a lot gives a feeling of power.' So Ernst Jünger, novelist and German officer, wrote in the curiously dispassionate diary he kept of his time in Paris. His point may be obvious, an appropriately lazy thought to help the digestion of the good meal he had just enjoyed, but it should not be overlooked. It was, after all, ever-present in the minds of the French throughout the Occupation. To understand where power and powerlessness lay they had only to compare what they had on their plates with what the Germans had on theirs. Yet the immediate result of the comparison was not the simple anger of French have-nots against German haves, not yet a feeling which would fuel resistance on any scale. The French grumbled and told each other jokes, reaffirming behind the occupiers' backs their prejudice that the Germans had always been a greedy, gluttonous, boorish lot. But what else could they do? Things were as they were and nobody should be surprised at Germans behaving like Germans.

By the terrible logic of the Occupation, the French who went hungry kept most of their anger for the French who ate well. On a rare visit to the sort of restaurant where Ernst Jünger regularly dined, Galtier-Boissière noted the Germans there only in passing. There was nothing remarkable in the sight of them drinking champagne and tucking into forbidden beefsteaks imperfectly concealed under token fried eggs. His attention focused on his fellow-countrymen: 'The best wines flowing. The filthy rich come out on top in the New Order. If you're loaded, really loaded, you can always fill yourself up to here, while housewives spend hours queueing in the snow to get swedes.' Nor were these filthy rich just the traditionally privileged and well-heeled. They were largely *arrivistes*: time-servers and opportunists enjoying the spoils of a victory won not against a foreign enemy on the battlefield but at the expense of their neighbours by lack of scruple.

The have-nots, which meant most of the French, did not have to visit expensive restaurants to find such filthy rich to despise, such *arrivistes* to resent. They could find them in profiteering shopkeepers who, like the Poissonards, charged ridiculous prices or tried to fob them off with unsaleable goods. They could find them in the ostentatiously successful black marketeers on whom they periodically had to depend. And at a time when even the smallest grudge could flourish unchecked, they could find them in the *fonctionnaires* who issued their ration cards and *tickets* even though they knew perfectly well that, for all their new-found power, these officials probably ate no better than the rest.

Such anger could also be sparked off when people from the cities went out into the country to buy and to barter. In theory, such occasions should simply have been tributes to French resilience and the *système D* in action: determined to fend for themselves, town and country got together and made unofficial arrangements to their mutual benefit. In fact, they could revive age-old tensions in a society which, while taking pride in the richness of its soil and paying tribute to the virtues of those who worked it, had also spawned cities whose inhabitants looked on their rural cousins with contempt – or so the country people themselves had complained. Now, city people grumbled in their turn that peasants seized the chance to take their revenge and bore out all the worst alleged of them: they were indifferent to the suffering in the cities, they overcharged ruthlessly, they preferred to supply black marketeers rather than people honestly in need.

For a government which proclaimed its dedication to national unity and its belief in an agrarian ideal, Vichy reacted to this reawakened friction in a way that betrayed its real character. It exploited it by blaming *la cupidité paysanne* – rural stinginess – when it was forced to reduce the rations on which city-dwellers were, to a greater degree, forced to survive. That, when it came to it, was preferable to blaming the German plunder that Vichy was virtually powerless to check. And, naturally, the German propaganda machine was happy to endorse an explanation which served the interests of the Reich so conveniently. Anger directed not against the Germans but against other French people, anger given official sanction by the Vichy government, anger serving the German policy of dividing its conquest in order to rule it: it would be hard to find a clearer paradigm than this antagonism between the country and the city for the internal damage France agreed to inflict on herself.

WORSE DAMAGE WAS being done; more bitter divisions were being opened. They stemmed from the word 'collaboration', prosaically introduced into the armistice agreement by the Reich and given the stamp of authority but no more precise definition in Pétain's broadcasts. In seeking to trace its convoluted meanings historians nowadays often begin by distinguishing between 'collaborationism' and simple 'collaboration'. By 'collaborationism' they mean collaboration from ideological sympathy.

Like all the countries the Reich occupied – like all the countries of Europe, in fact – France had her fascists and pro-Nazis ready to welcome the Reich, to applaud its acts and to urge its policies forward. Such ideologues could boast with Robert Brasillach: '*Nous ne sommes pas des convertis.*' They were believers before the fact of the Occupation, not converts after it. Journalists like Brasillach, Drieu la Rochelle and Lucien Rebatet – the so-called *ubiquistes* ('everywhere-ists') of *Je suis partout* – and Jean Luchaire of *Les Nouveaux Temps* dominated a Paris press which was often German-funded and German-inspired and always German-censored. The voices of Jean Hérold-Paquis and Philippe Henriot dominated the airwaves of Radio-Paris and Radio-Vichy: Paquis with his cry of '*Car, comme Carthage, l'Angleterre sera détruite*' ('Since, like Carthage, England shall be destroyed'), and Henriot with an insinuating rhetoric which, thought Gertrude Stein, did more than any other single factor 'to turn Frenchman against Frenchman'.*

Collaborationist organizations or political parties (if the term still had any meaning) were equally easy to identify since they existed only because the Reich licensed or at least agreed to tolerate them. Despite the different shadings of opinion, they shared obvious common ingredients: a journal of their own, a taste for totalitarian and revolutionary rhetoric, a leader who modelled himself on Hitler, Mussolini or Franco, and, of course, German money. The two most prominent – indeed, the only two of consequence – were the Parti Populaire Français founded and led by Jacques Doriot, a renegade Communist, and the Rassemblement National Populaire founded and led by Marcel Déat, a renegade Socialist. Other organizations, which their historian Pascal Ory aptly calls *groupuscules*, included: the Francistes, or Chemises Bleues, of Marcel Bucard, with his rallying-cry of 'Follow the leader who has never made a mistake'; the Ligue Française of Pierre Costantini, who had single-handedly declared war on Britain after Mers-el-Kébir; and the cultural Groupe Collaboration of the essayist Alphonse de Châteaubriant, apparently determined to rival Pétain in the senile grandeur of his oratory.

It is revealing that even so short an approved list should extend to the marginal and the eccentric. Collaborationists were guaranteed their brief hour in the sun: access to print and the airwaves, the right to hold parades and wear uniforms apeing those of the occupiers. And then, in the months before and after Liberation, they became targets for a different kind of publicity, in the vengeance of *résistants* and the justice of the courts. Even today their names still feature prominently in studies of collaboration in general rather than just collaborationism in particular. Yet they, and indeed collaborationism itself, were less important than all this attention would suggest.

---

* See Chapter 6 for Henriot's assassination in 1944.

Not even the best-known organizations were large. Déat's Rassemblement National Populaire might have boasted of 500,000 adherents in June 1941, but historians estimate it probably had only about 20,000 (largely drawn from the urban working class), and they stress that its influence was limited to the years 1941–2. Doriot's Parti Populaire Français was longer-lived but, despite its grand claims, probably no bigger. And neither organization, nor any of the other collaborationists, was taken seriously by the Germans, if being taken seriously implies being regarded as partners or potential partners rather than convenient tools. Far from encouraging a unified collaborationist movement, the Reich stirred the rivalries which the various movements and leaders were adept at brewing for themselves. It was, moreover, a point of policy to compromise rather than foster their relations with French public opinion since (as Bertram M. Gordon has pointed out) 'the more compromised they were, the more dependent upon Hitler's aid and the more likely they were to fight by his side to the end'.

Relations with Vichy were no happier. In the collaborationists' eyes Pétain was too mild to command more than brief or provisional respect. Vichy's nostalgia for the appeasement of 1938, anger at the war of 1939–40, anglophobia, anti-Bolshevism, anti-semitism, love of discipline and order might all have been promising, but these ingredients never coalesced into a coherent ideology, much less an ideology stern enough to satisfy collaborationist requirements. So the collaborationists were as likely to chide or attack Vichy as to applaud it, even though many of them still nursed hopes of advancement at court. For its part, Vichy was in practice content to cold-shoulder them until the last year of its life, when it took Henriot, Déat and (most damagingly) Joseph Darnand, organizer of the Milice, into its ranks. Even these appointments, though they further corrupted the regime's policies, were less an ideological shift than an admission that Vichy itself had by then been marginalized.

Until that time Vichy had been dominated by *collaboration à raison*, the realism of 1940 which said that Germany's victory in Europe had to be accepted. As with so many self-proclaimed realists, their realism involved more than bowing reluctantly to the facts: it welcomed the facts as moral proofs. 'France cannot resist' turned into 'France should not resist', 'France has lost' into 'France was wrong'. The example of collaboration in this spirit held far more subtle yet more tempting dangers than anything the heated rhetoric of the collaborationists could offer. It did not just tell public servants and those in charge of business and industry that it was their duty to get back to work as usual, that getting things back to normal was a patriotic and not a political act. It told them that they were still being patriotic if the restored normality incorporated the German indictment of what had been wrong in the first place, if they actively collaborated with German goals.

This is one reason why French industrialists turned their factories over to the service of the German war machine and purged their workforces of people they had regarded as troublesome even before the war but could now denounce as traitors jeopardizing the emerging Franco-German accord. This is one reason why French bureaucrats traced undesirables of whatever hue, French gendarmes arrested them and French judges handed them over to the occupiers. 'I saw matters only as a business leader,' the Lyonnais lorry-manufacturer Marius Berliet would tell the court which tried him after the war, just as René Bousquet, Vichy chief of police, would insist he had wanted only what was in the best interests of his gendarmerie. But it is just one reason, and by itself it might not have empowered Vichy to lead the way in compliance as effectively as it did in the early years of the Occupation. As it was, the overt political message was accompanied by sub-texts plain enough to be understood and vulgar enough to appeal. The first said simply: 'stick with the winners if you want to stay safe and survive'. And the second said: 'stick with the winners if you want to do well for yourself'.

A belief in the coincidence of national interest and self-interest was written into Vichy from the start by the combination of Pétain and Laval, *le Maréchal* and *le Maquignon*, which gave the regime its distinctive character. Pétain spoke of France and her honour. Laval spoke in metaphors of gambling. 'Me, what can I tell you? I'm playing the game as if the Germans were the winners': that might have been said in confidence to friends but in fact Laval's opportunism was an open secret. Parisians could regularly observe its rewards when, amidst public hardship, he dined with lavish self-satisfaction at Maxim's. Nor was Laval unique, or even unusual, at Vichy. Abel Bonnard, the last of a rapid series of Ministers of Education, was notorious for high living; when the time came for him to flee Vichy he needed a whole convoy of vehicles to carry his booty. Ambassador Fernand de Brinon – whom even Bonnard thought 'a creature of the shadows, very silent and very dangerous' – was in the habit of embezzling official funds and selling the precious *laissez-passers* of which he had a generous allotment.

Actually, Bonnard and de Brinon had credentials which linked them more closely to collaborationism than most Vichy ministers: before the war both had been granted audiences with Hitler, and de Brinon's admiring accounts had been translated into German. Bonnard wrote for *Je suis partout* in the early years of the Occupation. Yet in the atmosphere of Vichy, self-interest flourished happily beside conviction or apparent conviction and could easily triumph over it if the need arose. It arose, of course, when the Germans stopped looking like the winners. By 1942 the Reich no longer seemed quite as invincible as it had in 1940 and the time could seem right for a little hedging of bets.

The Allied landings in north Africa in November 1942 prompted two highly public defections. The first defector was Admiral Darlan, willing to temper the anglophobia which had made him pass intelligence about British naval movements in the Mediterranean to the Germans, and the belief in Franco-German accord which, during his time in office as Pétain's deputy, had made him pursue the vision of France and Germany as peacetime allies. Happening to be in Algiers for family reasons when the landings took place, he negotiated an armistice and went over to the Allies. His example was followed by Pierre Pucheu, a former Vichy Minister of the Interior who had played a murky role in selecting the hostages executed by the Germans at Châteaubriant in October 1941.* By early 1942 he was already in touch with the Resistance, interpreting his government's policy to Henri Frenay: 'It was essential to be in the victor's camp and for the moment they believed in a German victory. If victory changed camps, then so would they.' In May 1943 he turned up in Casablanca. In the event, neither *girouette* profited from his change of heart. Darlan relieved both Vichy and the Free French of further embarrassment by getting himself assassinated in December 1942. Pucheu was tried and executed in March 1944, the first official victim of the *épuration*, or purge of collaborators. Yet the damage had been done. 'Where on earth are we heading', asked the comedian René Lefèvre, 'if we can't trust our traitors any more?'

In fact, the self-interest so nakedly exposed in Darlan's last manoeuvrings had all along been a more palpable force than ideo-

* See Chapter 5.

logy, not just among the *collaborateurs à raison* of Vichy but among the collaborationists of Paris as well. The tone of their journalism might have been set by Brasillach, fervent and willing, even perversely eager, to die for his beliefs when Liberation came. But more typical of those who fed the hungry presses was the journalist who wrote as 'Bénédix' in Charles Dieudonné's *La France au travail*, an exercise in Nazi populism flung together by a team of right-wingers, ex-Communists and hacks to try and attract Communist readers. It rushed into print at the end of June 1940 but failed the next year.

Jean Galtier-Boissière bumped into Bénédix in a Paris restaurant only a month after the Germans had arrived. He dimly remembered the man, though his memory needed jogging, as a scribbler who had worked for Doriot but had later hawked around the Paris magazines an exposé of what really went on behind the scenes in Doriot's movement. Galtier-Boissière himself had rejected it on behalf of *Le Canard enchaîné* because it stank of personal resentment: it read, he recalled, like the work of a dismissed servant. Once worn and plodding, Bénédix was now expensively turned out, ordering extra food and drinking champagne without thought of regulations or *tickets*. He could hardly wait to boast of his good fortune in having his proposal for a comments column snapped up by the Germans: 'At last I can express myself freely.' To Galtier-Boissière's distaste he went on to sketch out his plans: 'And the Yids aren't going to get away with pulling the wool over my eyes! At last we're going to strangle all those bastards!' The two Jewish friends accompanying Galtier-Boissière sat pale and silent during the exchange. It ended with Bénédix blithely insisting they should lunch together soon: 'I'll pay, old boy. Oh, yes! I'll pay, word of honour!'

The same ethos made it only fitting that Marcel Déat's Rassemblement National Populaire should be given for its headquarters the Paris flat confiscated from Georges Mandel, Reynaud's former Minister of the Interior, Blum's colleague in the Front Populaire and long-time target of the anti-semitic Right. The collaborationists had other enemies and victims in their sights, and would extend their list as the Occupation wore on, but Jews were always the most satisfying. It was easy not just to defame, humiliate and persecute them but, thanks to the laws providing for the 'Aryanization' of their property, to plunder them as well. In July 1944 Marcel Bucard, the Franciste leader who never made a mistake, was arrested at a Parisian jeweller's shop owned by a Jew while making what was euphemistically called a *perquisition*, literally a search but really a robbery. Gendarmes shot the tyres of the Delage in which he tried to make his getaway and threw him in the Santé prison.

The only curious thing was that Bucard had been arrested at all. It was even rumoured that the incident provoked a hasty cabinet meeting at Vichy, though this seems unlikely given the graver matters Pétain and Laval had to worry about by July 1944. As it was, the German ambassador Abetz, Bucard's local protector, soon called at the Santé and engineered his release. Right up to the last days of the Occupation – indeed, with particular ferocity during its last days – German protection offered a cloak for collaborationist movements to join the occupiers in looting and to pursue their own private vendettas. Their rank and file seamlessly overlapped with people who may have worked for German purchasing agencies or called themselves *administrateurs des biens juifs* or even occasionally risen to the dignity of wearing a German uniform but who were simply gangsters, rooted in the underworld.

Lyon, for example, boasted among the opportunists who flourished in its *milieu* Francis André, who already had a record for burglary, a history as a paid informer for Doriot's PPF and, because of his deformities, the sinister nickname of *Gueule tordue*: Twisted Face or Ugly Mug. From 1943 onwards he embarked on a career as informer and all-purpose thug for the Germans. Recruiting a gang of fellow-criminals from Montluc prison, he specialized in tracking down saboteurs and in hunting Jews for a bounty and the chance to loot their property. 'There are a lot of people who're going to sleep at nights when I'm gone,' he told the court which sentenced him to death in 1946.

The most notorious gangster of the Occupation was Henri Laffont (or Lafont), born Henri Chamberlin, already known as a petty criminal before the war. Within a month of the German invasion he secured the approval of the Abwehr (German Military Intelligence) in forming what became known, from its Paris address, as the Gestapo of the Rue Lauriston. The gang eventually numbered more than 100 men, including a former police inspector, Pierre Bonny (or Bony), and criminals whom Laffont allegedly hand-picked with German help from Fresnes prison. Among the rivals with whom it engaged in internecine warfare were the so-called Neuilly Gestapo run by Frédéric Martin, better known as Rudy de Mérode, and the gang run by Georges Delfanne, better known as Christian

Masuy, a Belgian who had been working for the Germans since before the Occupation.

Liberation completed the exposure of men like Laffont: his trial documented the cold-bath torture of suspects in the Rue Lauriston, the fortune piled up in his suburban home at Neuilly, the familiarity with the good and the great which had permitted him to address Laval, for example, as *tu* rather than *vous*. It was easy to be shocked by such details then, less comforting to be reminded how easy it had been even for those who lacked Laffont's contacts or his monstrous daring to venture at least a short distance down the path he had blazed. Everyone, however humble, knew something about a friend or neighbour or acquaintance, even if it was just gossip and rumour: a question mark about the purity of their race or the colour of their opinions or the probity of their conduct. Such crumbs had value. And if they had any doubt about how to use such knowledge (most did not), people needed only to turn to the obliging pages of *Au pilori*:

> Many readers ask us to which organization they should address them-selves in order to point out the occult activities or frauds of the Jews. It is sufficient to post a letter or a simple signed note to the Commissariat Général aux Questions Juives, or failing that, to the offices of our paper for forwarding.

The word the French use for denunciation or laying information with the authorities is *délation*. During the Occupation they also had a phrase, *'j'irai le dire à la Kommandantur'*: 'I'll go and tell the Germans about it'. It came from the title of an article by the poet Robert Desnos published in *Aujourd'hui* in September 1940, when Henri Jeanson's editorship seemed to guarantee it some freedom of opinion.* It bravely appealed to people's 'sense of dignity' to stop them denouncing one another. The appeal failed but the phrase stuck. According to the Abwehr officer Hermann Bickler, the Germans needed 32,000 *indicateurs* (informers) – what the French colloquially call *indics* or *mouches*. They found them, and more, without difficulty. As for *corbeaux*, or writers of poison-pen letters, rumour said that by 1942 their work was pouring into the Paris Kommandantur at the rate of 1,500 letters a day.

Jews were the favourite target. From private citizens to the Kommandantur or the Commissariat Général aux Questions Juives,

---

* Desnos was deported in 1944 and died in a concentration camp in 1945.

from minor officials to senior officials, from senior officials to government ministers, scribbled with a semi-literate hand or typed on expensive stationery, the letters use the same formulae: 'I believe it my duty to let you know that . . .', 'I respectfully draw your attention to the following facts . . .'. Many add that they seek only the public good and hate denunciation. Business rivalry, envy between neighbours and personal spite show all too plainly through their threadbare language:

> I am a furrier at 3, Rue du Maréchal Joffre in Cahors. A Frenchwoman, born in Cahors, I find it absolutely impossible to get work since I am being squeezed out by the large numbers of Jews working at full capacity for the firm called Marie-Antoinette Auweill. . . .

> I have the honour to draw to your attention, for whatever useful purposes it may serve, that an apartment at 57 bis Boulevard Rochechouart, belonging to the Jew Gresalmer, contains very fine furniture. . . .

> Since you are taking care of Jews, and if your campaign is not just a vain word, then have a look at the kind of life led by the girl M. A., formerly a dancer, now living at 31 Boulevard de Strasbourg, not wearing a star.* This creature, for whom being Jewish is not enough, debauches the husbands of proper Frenchwomen, and you may well have an idea what she is living off. Defend women against Jewishness – that will be your best publicity, and you will return a French husband to his wife. . . .

> I take the liberty of addressing you to ask you if you can protect Christian families against the activities of scheming Jews. In our town many Christian homes have been destroyed by Jews who have found it profitable to snatch fathers away from their children.
>   It is not for me to expose the misfortunes of others, but I take the liberty of bringing our case to your attention. My husband, the shipowner Michel C., aged 57, a veteran of 14–18, after an exemplary life devoted to working hard to bring up his six children, has been distracted from his duties by a Jewess of notoriously bad morals, engaged in prostitution. . . .

Some writers were anonymous, or used manifestly false names, or signed themselves 'a good Frenchman', 'a loyal Frenchman' or 'Long Live Pétain'. The authorities soon outlawed such communication. Anyway, most writers were quite willing to identify themselves, even to use letterhead stationery and vaunt their credentials, though

---

* A yellow star: see Chapter 4.

sometimes – in the case of employees informing on their bosses, for example – they thought it prudent to ask that their names be kept out of any investigation.

Even the close and friendly atmosphere of the Café Flore in Saint-Germain-des-Prés, the haunt of artists and writers who included Sartre and his circle, was infected by fear of the *mouche* and the *corbeau*. Germans blundered in only by mistake and the silence that greeted them soon persuaded them to leave. Yet, surprisingly, the regulars included two *collabo* journalists – obvious soulmates of Bénédix – who talked in strident voices about what they would like to see happen to the Jews. Simone de Beauvoir found herself overhearing what they said without shock, since they seemed so like characters from 'a farce for the simple-minded' that she had to remind herself: 'It was their very nullity that made them dangerous.' None of the other customers spoke to them except a man claiming to be Laval's private secretary, whose eyes continually checked what was going on around him. There were ostentatiously bored and listless young men who hung around, and an oddly dressed old lady who spent a suspicious amount of time in the lavatory. Perhaps she was listening to conversations on the public phone and writing reports. The proprietor broke the glass of the phone cubicle to remind people to guard their tongues, but nobody ever really knew who had been responsible for the absences from their circle – the regulars who had disappeared and whom people no longer felt comfortable talking about.

Yet perhaps the most striking testimony to the extent of denunciation came from the Germans themselves, surprised at how ready the French were to betray each other. It suited their purposes, of course, and they encouraged it without scruple, but it altered their view of the people they had conquered. While he watched his troops dancing with joy after their surrender in 1940, Henri Frenay had noted the astonishment and contempt on the faces of the Germans. In the first days of the Occupation a group of German soldiers driving down the Avenue de la Bourdonnais in Paris shouted to some giggling French girls who had turned out to see them: *'Unverschämt!'* ('Shameless!'). Serious-minded Germans took to asking their French acquaintance why Parisians had so little pride. They were surprised because they had not expected the French to behave like that. For all their willingness to lecture France on her lack of discipline and her decadence, they also had a respect for her culture, her history and her traditions. The slightly awed look captured in photographs of the young Wehrmacht soldiers touring the monuments of Paris reflects it at its most naïve. Now denunciation deepened the contempt the Germans had begun to feel in 1940 – and so helped pave the way for greater brutality.

Contempt was also the dominant note in Henri-Georges Clouzot's controversial film *Le Corbeau*, made in 1943 for a German-backed production company. It depicts a small provincial town torn apart by anonymous letters: everybody, it seems, has something to hide and everybody has a motive for vilifying their neighbours. *Le Corbeau* has been attacked as anti-French propaganda, praised as the authentic voice of the French cinema and simply rejected as unacceptably sharp satire. Yet its theme had already been anticipated in real life by the dog-eat-dog spread of denunciation. *Indics* and *corbeaux*, who began by attacking the obviously vulnerable and the obviously undesirable, soon turned their attention to those who continued to eat well. And so collaborators, or those widely assumed to be *collabos*, themselves became targets even within the first year of the Occupation.

Sacha Guitry, impresario and playwright as well as actor, had been quick to reopen his Paris theatre, eager to dine with the occupiers in the best restaurants, proud to acquire a licence to continue driving his Hispano-Suiza on the streets of Paris. According to *Au pilori* and *France au travail*, the paper where Bénédix had found his niche, Guitry's mother was a Russian Jew and he privately boasted of deceiving the Germans about his racial origins. *Au pilori* even dug up Guitry's youthful friendship with Georges Mandel. He had to produce the usual documents establishing his ancestry: birth certificates, baptismal records and marriage certificates. With his usual flair he even added a letter from the Chief Rabbi of France attesting that he was Aryan. Charles Trenet, *le fou chantant* who entertained Wehrmacht officers at the Folies and the Gaieté Parisienne with songs that included the Vichyite 'Terre', had to rebut the charge that his name was an anagram of the Jewish-sounding Netter. Serge Lifar, director of the ballet company at the Opéra, had an embarrassing interview with the authorities because his name, spelled backwards, formed Rafil.

It was not just entertainers, artists and high-society figures, always tempting fodder for the rumour-mill, who were denounced. Slowly, the cancer spread back through the body of France towards the head where it had started in the first place. Victor Barthélemy, a Corsican and secretary of Doriot's Parti Populaire Français, had to deny he was Jewish; the accusation sprang from the assumption that names beginning 'Bar-' and 'Ben-' were Hebrew in origin. De Brinon (who really was married to a Jew, though he lived apart from her most of the time) was said to be a friend of the Jews. Otto Abetz was said to be a Freemason, even though he persecuted Freemasons; so were two of his staff at the embassy, Rudolf Rahn and Dr Ernst Achenbach. For good measure Rebatet decided that Achenbach also had Jewish grandparents. Captain Paul Sézille of the Institut des Etudes des Questions Juives, an anti-semitic propaganda organization inspired and controlled by the Germans, was an ardent believer in the widespread rumour that Laval himself was Jewish.

Surely denunciation could reach no higher? It could in the mind of Céline, the loosest cannon among the collaborationists, at once the most lucid and the most crazed of all the Nazi sympathizers in French intellectual life. He was acclaimed virtually as a prophet for the anti-semitic pamphlets he had written before the war, 'Bagatelles pour un massacre' and 'L'Ecole des cadavres'. To them he added 'Les Beaux Draps' in 1941. Yet otherwise Céline wrote little during the Occupation, and never for German pay. He was not in the Reich's – or anyone else's – control, though Abetz, Achenbach and Dr Karl Epting of the Deutsche Institut in Paris unwisely attempted to cultivate him. As the Reich's fortunes waned Céline formulated the theory, and was given to arguing it at length in the most ill-chosen company, that Hitler was in fact already dead. The Führer had been replaced by a Jewish pseudo-Hitler bent on promoting the world-wide Jewish conspiracy.

FRANCE BEGAN THE Occupation under a framework of authority, French as much as German, which neither guaranteed social order nor provided moral example. Hardship bred self-interest and self-interest was spurred on by the spectacle of the few who still managed to escape hardship. Divisions multiplied, separating group from group, neighbour from neighbour and friend from friend. Eventually group came to prey on group, neighbour on neighbour, friend on friend.

This is not to suggest that most, let alone all, people followed the *collabos*, the *indics* and the *corbeaux* into the dark recesses of betrayal, any more than it could be argued that the almost universal dependence on the *système D* made the cowardly war of Maurice Sachs anything but a pathetically extreme case. Even in such times, not everyone was confronted by situations which forced them to choose dramatically between great suffering and great reward. But, in however humble a fashion, everyone still had to decide how they were going to cope with life in a fragmenting society. Above all, they had to decide how they were going to cope with occupiers whose burdensome presence was made heavier by the status it had been given by a government composed of Frenchmen.

So Sartre's worries, in his essay 'Paris Under the Occupation', about how to react when a German soldier stopped him in the street and asked politely for directions were not as fussily inconsequential as they might at first sound. They were emblematic of how the dilemmas of the Occupation presented themselves in daily life. He wrote that if he muttered an answer to the German and passed on quickly or just said he did not know – which is what he seems to have been in the habit of doing – he still did not come out of the encounter feeling at ease with himself. There were other options, of course, though he did not mention them. Misdirect the soldier, some suggested. Teenagers often made a practice of it, and some of their elders too. The French certainly took pleasure in swapping *bobards* (tall stories) like the joke about the German who asked where he could find a swimming pool and was told there was one between Calais and Dover. Shun the German altogether, Jean Texcier had advised in his early pamphlet of July 1940, 'Conseils à l'occupé' ('Advice to the Occupied'). Do not listen to him, do not talk to him, ignore him except when he asks for a light for his cigarette: 'Never, from the most primitive times, have people refused a light, not even to their deadliest enemy.'

Shunning the occupiers drew the line well short of collaboration, by any definition; in silence lay purity. If not resistance, silence was at least a first step towards resistance. It was no accident that the first literary expression of resistance, and the most enduringly popular, should have been a story suggestively called *Le Silence de la mer* ('The Silence of the Sea'), written by Jean Bruller under the pseudonym of Vercors and issued by him to inaugurate his underground press, Les Editions de Minuit, in February 1942.* In it the narrator and his

---

* Les Editions de Minuit went on to issue forty titles in twenty-five volumes. Contributors, who followed Vercors in adopting pseudonyms from French regions, included Louis Aragon, Elsa Triolet, Eluard, Mauriac, Gide and Guéhenno.

niece refuse to speak to the German officer, Ebrennac, billeted in their home. They make no objection as he comes and goes each day, they serve him coffee, they suffer his presence by their fireside, but otherwise they 'treat him as if he were a ghost' from the moment he arrives: 'The silence lengthened. It grew thicker and thicker, like morning mist. Thick and motionless. My niece's stillness, and doubtless mine too, increased it, gave it weight.'

Apart from the admiring glances he casts at the niece, Ebrennac himself behaves like the very model of a properly behaved German, and more. He takes pride in his Huguenot origins, speaks French fluently, loves French literature and frankly admires patriotism wherever he finds it. Vercors' portrait is scrupulously fair, since the occupying forces certainly included men like Ebrennac, albeit in a minority: not just self-advertising francophiles like Otto Abetz but the novelist Ernst Jünger and the liberal censor Gerhard Heller. (General Moritz von Faber du Faur, the military commander in Bordeaux, even liked to emphasize his Huguenot ancestry by styling himself Maurice Fabre du Faur.) Ebrennac is not enraged or driven to brutality by the silence which greets his courtesy. Instead, he is slowly broken down, first launching into revealing monologues about himself and, finally, suffering a crisis of conscience as he compares the dignity of his reluctant hosts with the indignities his fellow-Germans have in mind for France.

'French writers had two choices: collaboration or silence,' Vercors wrote after the war. Those writers who did effectively choose silence included Jean Galtier-Boissière and Jean Guéhenno. Galtier-Boissière, who had made his name writing for the satirical magazine *Crapouillot* before the war, flirted briefly with *Aujourd'hui* while Henri Jeanson was editor but otherwise ran a second-hand bookshop. Though he did contribute to Les Editions de Minuit near the end of the Occupation, Guéhenno returned to his former profession of teaching. Both men refused not just the cheap success of a Bénédix but also the more subtle contamination (which many others accepted) of writing books for a system policed not so much by the Germans as by a self-denying ordinance of French publishers.

Though it brought hardship, their stance was still a luxury open only to the established and the resourceful. And the diaries both men privately kept show that shunning the occupiers posed psychological difficulties, even moral dilemmas, only hinted at in Vercors' fable. Guéhenno wrestled with them in a long note addressed 'to the

German I pass in the street', which took up the same mundane example as Sartre chose. It begins with a ringing statement:

> I don't hate you, I don't hate you any more. I know that you'll never be my master. I pretend that I don't see you. I act as if you don't exist. I've promised never to speak to you. I can speak your language, but if you speak to me, I throw my arms up and pretend I don't understand.

Despite the present tense, this sounds more like a resolve for the future than a report on his normal practice. No sooner has Guéhenno put it down on paper than he admits infringing his own rule:

> The other day, though, I was on the Place du Châtelet and you came up to me. You were wandering about like any lost soldier, looking for Notre-Dame. Then I did deign to understand and, with a gesture, but without speaking, I pointed to the towers rising up into the sky on the other side of the river, big enough to blind you. You felt a fool and you blushed and I felt happy. That's what we've come to.

The admission of his pettiness carries with it an acknowledgement that there is no rule of conduct, no way of reacting to the presence of the occupiers, that feels satisfactory.

'That's what we've come to': Galtier-Boissière also understood this uncomfortable truth. His diary describes an incident when he was travelling with his wife on the Métro. A German soldier, as correct as the officer in Vercors' story but less self-assured, offered her his seat. She refused. The soldier offered the seat to Galtier-Boissière. He refused as well. 'The unlucky man didn't know how to get out of this ridiculous situation and stood in confusion by the seat nobody wanted.' It is characteristic of Galtier-Boissière that he should not merely avoid making heroic claims for himself but implicitly catch his own unease and his sense of the absurdities in which both he and the German are caught. 'Everything we did was equivocal,' wrote Sartre: 'we never quite knew whether we were doing right or doing wrong; a subtle poison corrupted even our best actions.'

4

Presence and Absence

Madame la concierge,
I am writing to you because I have nobody else. Last week
Papa was deported. Mama has been deported. I have lost
my purse. I have nothing left.
> Letter from a 7-year-old child in Drancy

As a Frenchwoman I appeal to your ministry and shout
out my indignation. Where is my husband? What has
become of my husband?
> Letter from Madame Roussetzki to Pétain

IN MAY 1940 the first real warning to Parisians of the disaster they
faced – a warning infinitely more expressive than the banal communiqués and politicians' speeches broadcast on the radio – had
been the smoke from burning official documents which drifted
down the river from the Foreign Office on the Quai d'Orsay towards
the Palais-Bourbon, seat of the Chamber of Deputies and the
National Assembly. By the time the Germans arrived on 14 June a
pall of black smoke had been hanging over the city for several days,
far denser than anything civil servants had created in their eagerness
to destroy records. It came from the oil depots of the Basse-Seine,
which retreating French troops had set alight. Rumour quickly attributed it to the Germans: rumour attributed everything unwelcome
and unexplained to the Germans. But, whatever they took the source
of the smoke to be, Parisians agreed that the unnaturally darkened
skies and streets struck a fittingly apocalyptic note for a capital city
preparing to receive its conqueror.

So darkness, which would prove one of the most common practical inconveniences of the Occupation, was also from the first its

symbol. The late daybreak on winter mornings and the power cuts which robbed homes of light: these were not just irritations or hardships that soon grew commonplace. They were identified with the Occupation on a quite elemental level. Darkness, or so people at first feared, was like the darkness which visited the people of Egypt in the Old Testament: a sign of divine disfavour, that the gods who had once smiled on the nation had now indefinitely withdrawn their protection. Later, as the Occupation appeared less a judgement, an inevitable punishment, and more a perversity to be challenged, so darkness itself came to stand for an inversion of the order of things, a violation of nature.

Most people, of course, remained unconscious of the symbolism. They did not trouble to examine the ramifications into metaphor of experiences which, after all, had their root in the gruelling practicalities of everyday life. The ramifications were no less powerful for all that. And they were made articulate – indeed, spelled out insistently – by the writings that marked the growth of resistance and, after Liberation, the stocktaking or record of what the Occupation had been like. Vercors showed real sureness of imagination in calling the series of books which issued from his underground press Les Editions de Minuit: The Midnight Press. When Jean Guéhenno published his diary of the Occupation it was natural that he should call it *Journal des années noires* (*Journal of the Dark Years*), just as it was natural that Jean Texcier should call one of his writings *Écrit dans la nuit* (*Writings in the Night*) and Henri Frenay his memoirs of the Resistance *La Nuit finira* (*The Night Will End*).

The Free French in London kept pace with Vercors by reprinting his Editions de Minuit as they appeared in France, but they retitled the series Cahiers du Silence: Notebooks from the Silence. They did so, no doubt, in tribute to Vercors' own contribution, *Le Silence de la mer*, its first and most famous volume. In that story silence is the beginning of resistance: to withhold speech is to refuse collaboration. And, as the previous chapter of this book argued, his equation struck a chord with writers like Guéhenno and Galtier-Boissière, however troubling its application might prove when transferred from the spareness of fable to the reality of ordinary encounters in the street or on the Métro. Some of the complexities attaching to silence, indeed, are already present in the fable itself. Or rather they surround it, lying tantalizingly just outside its boundaries: in the powerful yet cryptic metaphor of the title, which the text itself deliberately does little or nothing to explain, and in the obvious paradox that the integrity of silence which Vercors is concerned to assert can be asserted only by recourse to words, by writing and publishing a story about it.

Vercors himself, a committed but never simply a propagandist writer, did not brush these considerations aside as stumbling-blocks to his purpose. He was artist enough to welcome them as part of his theme. Silence may be adopted deliberately, in a fable or on the Métro, as a gesture, an action or a stance, but it remains more than just a gesture, an action or a stance and it cannot be reduced to a single meaning. To adopt the sort of paradox which forced itself on writers like Vercors, silence carries its own resonances. They ensured that silence would join darkness in the popular imagination as a dominating metaphor for the times.

Like darkness, silence began its journey into metaphor simply by being a daily fact of life. It was there, for example, in the streets emptied of their accustomed traffic, where an observer could count on the fingers of both hands the cars which passed at a once-busy time of day in a once-busy part of the capital. It was there on the winter evenings when an early curfew was imposed, like the evening in December 1941 when Guéhenno stood at his window looking out at the empty street and exchanging signs with the neighbours opposite. And, above all, it was there during the nights when the last sounds of footsteps had marked the passing of people hurrying to meet their midnight deadline, broken only by the crunch of hob-nailed boots from the German patrols and the other noises signalling that the occupiers were at their work.

Like darkness, silence began as an emptiness where something familiar had once been, something so familiar that the mind did not consciously note it until it had been taken away. Ordinary activities had stopped. Life was absent. Again like darkness, silence came increasingly to define the spaces which now belonged to fear: not just the long hours of the night when the enemy could do things made all the more frightening because they were unseen and barely heard, but also the moments during the day when neighbours did not talk about those things because they were afraid to, even with neighbours they had once trusted. Breaking such silences – even just by standing in a courtyard blowing a bugle, like the boy Guéhenno heard on the evening of the early curfew in December 1941 – came from a courage more instinctive than any formulation of principle or politics could inspire.

When Guéhenno heard the boy blow the bugle he immediately understood the sound as an act of resistance, pathetically futile in practical terms but immeasurably reassuring to the spirit. It spoke to that level of being on which everyone knew darkness and silence were provinces ruled by tyranny and fear. Yet, since paradox was of their very nature, darkness and silence were not just enemies to defy but also themselves the necessary friends of resistance, the refuges where resistance could start. The darkness which favoured the sudden arrest or the covert execution could also be the midnight in which Vercors' press did its work. The silence of people who did not trust each other enough to speak openly of atrocities could also become the silence between people who did not need to speak in order to understand each other and agree. When Sartre, so often an eloquent witness to the divisions and self-doubts which the Occupation imposed on the occupied, wanted to convey the solidarity, the sense of confident, instinctive fellowship it also inspired, he turned to an image which contrasted those years with the chattering days of republican politics: he called his essay 'The Republic of Silence'.

Previous chapters have several times mentioned another essay by Sartre, 'Paris Under the Occupation'. Like 'The Republic of Silence', it is sensitive to the symbolic dimension which the experience of being occupied assumed for those who were forced to live through it. And so, inevitably, it treats the themes of darkness and silence. But, instead of trying to decode them in detail, it implictly connects them with two concepts Sartre regarded as central to what the Occupation demanded of people and what it put them through: presence and absence. The Occupation began by demanding that people accept the fact of presence, the presence of a foreign conqueror in their midst. Yet increasingly it demanded that they also reconcile themselves to the fact of absence, or rather to a series of absences which began with the disappearance of friends, neighbours or fellow-citizens and pointed towards a vacancy of the spirit, an engulfing nothingness. It is worth taking Sartre's cue and exploring what this sense of presence and this sense of absence involved, how they combined in people's minds and what, together, they did to the French.

To SAY THAT the Occupation forced the French to adjust to the presence of Germans may sound trite. But in fact the experience was oddly elusive even at the time and almost impossible to reconstruct faithfully in retrospect. Even today, when people who are not French or did not live through the Occupation look at photos of German soldiers marching down the Champs Elysées or of Gothic-lettered German signposts outside the great landmarks of Paris, they can still feel a slight shock of disbelief. The scenes look not just unreal but almost deliberately surreal, as if the unexpected conjunction of German and French, French and German, was the result of a Dada prank and not the sober record of history.

This shock is merely a distant echo of what the French underwent in 1940: seeing a familiar landscape transformed by the addition of the unfamiliar, living among everyday sights suddenly made bizarre, no longer feeling at home in places they had known all their lives. It was not something for which even gloomy fears about the weakness of the French army in the field or political sympathy for the Third Reich could prepare the imagination. Nobody was ready for it. Naïve rumours that the advancing Germans were atrocity mongers who chopped off boys' hands or supermen who marched bare-chested through the ripening corn, and the equally naïve belief which soon took hold that the Germans were after all immaculately correct, testified to more than a lack of political education. They were reminders that, to many of the French, the Germans – old neighbours, old enemies, already encountered twice before on the battlefield in the memory of some still alive in 1940 – remained unfathomably alien. From some rural areas came reports of locals mistaking German troops for British, so little did they know about German uniforms or the German language.

They learned to tune their eyes and ears to the detailed forms this new presence took, not just moving beyond the elementary ignorance which could confuse German with British but soon being able to tell the difference between all the various types of German who now flooded into their country. They knew whether this soldier belonged to the Wehrmacht or the SS, and hence what might be expected from him, whether that official was a security policeman or a civil administrator, and hence what might be feared from him. Such knowledge, after all, had become a basic survival skill. War, and especially conquest, make even the civilian expert in the enemy's uniforms and insignia, just as they make even the monolinguist fluent in words and phrases from the enemy's language. But where did this education start and on which aspects of the alien did it focus?

What struck people most in their first shock and what continued to hold their attention as they took in the changed landscape was the German flag. This is hardly surprising, since flags are deliberate, purpose-made emblems of group or national identity and war always intensifies the emotive significance they carry. As France fell, Henri Frenay had stood at attention while his fellow-officers burnt their regimental flags to prevent them falling into German hands. Wishing to reassure the French that their honour was still intact, Pétain had fallen back on one of those figures of speech so clichéd that the mind hardly registers it as metaphoric language: 'Our flag remains unstained', he had insisted in his broadcast of 23 June 1940. Even as he spoke, reality was busy contradicting his metaphor. Few regimes in history have been more preoccupied with their own emblems than the Third Reich, and probably none has shown more skill in exploiting the effect of its banners and flags, more determination in imposing them on the territories it conquered. On becoming Chancellor in 1933 Hitler had replaced the flag of the Weimar Republic – horizontal bands of black, red and gold – with the bolder, ideologically charged emblem of National Socialism: a black swastika, asserting the German people's supposedly Aryan origins, in a white circle against a red background.

This *Blutfahne* (blood banner) was the flag which troops immediately hoisted over the Hôtel de Ville on entering Paris. Soon afterwards they climbed the stairs of the Eiffel Tower – evacuating French forces had spiked the machinery of the lifts – to fly a huge flag from the top, where all Paris could see it. In fact, it was so large that the wind tore it and a smaller flag had to be put in its place. Other gestures proved more successful, most famously the banner spread across the façade of the Palais-Bourbon, until only a few weeks before the home of the Third Republic's fragile democracy but now the offices of the Kommandant von Gross-Paris.* DEUTSCHLAND SIEGT AN ALLEN FRONTEN, it proclaimed in aggressive capitals 13 metres high: 'GERMANY IS VICTORIOUS ON ALL FRONTS'. Above the slogan was the V-sign which in 1940 still referred to German victory and had not yet effectively been appropriated by Britain and the Reich's other enemies.

So the French were confronted with the public symbolism of the Occupation before they had the chance to digest its mundane real-

---

* The administrative region embracing the then departments of the Seine, Seine-et-Marne and Seine-et-Oise as well as the capital itself.

ities. Most memoirs by writers who lived in Paris or visited it mention the banner on the Palais-Bourbon, and virtually all of them dwell on the red-and-white flags with their black swastikas flying from the other public buildings which the proliferating agencies of the Reich rushed to make their headquarters. Indeed, such descriptions became what analysts of rhetoric call *topoi*, or stock themes, of Occupation literature. They crystallized the writer's reaction to the whole experience of being defeated and subjugated. Janet Teissier du Cros at first lived in the Southern Zone and so did not see the flags of Paris without advance warning of their presence. It did not diminish their impact. In particular, her attention was caught by the Palais du Luxembourg, where the Senate had met in pre-war days:

> This building was occupied by the German air force, and an enormous Nazi flag had been hoisted over it, the first I had seen. It floated there in all its hideous symbolism, against the luminous changing sky of the Ile de France. White hoardings had been put up to prevent the Paris population from coming within bomb-throwing distance, and German sentries with closed hostile faces were mounting guard.

The same building and the same flag held Simone de Beauvoir's attention in 1944. After news of the Allied landings came she made a practice of looking at the Palais every day, to check if the swastika still flew over it.

Each day, Henri Frenay wrote, he suffered *'un sentiment de viol'* – 'a feeling of rape' – as he walked the streets of Paris, and the feeling was never more acute than when he came down the Champs Elysées into the Place de la Concorde. The Hôtel Crillon and the Admiralty, then headquarters of the Kriegsmarine, or German navy, 'were topped with immense flags bearing swastikas. In front of the doors sentries stood frozen like stone statues or hammered the pavement with their slow march, twenty metres to the right and twenty metres to the left.' The flag on the terrace of the Admiralty prompted André Labarthe to a meditation which pushed the *topos* to its extreme, in the essay 'Paris interdit' which appeared in *La France libre*, the journal he edited from London:

> The Place de la Concorde. In that spacious square, wide open to the sky – in that vast expanse with the obelisk planted in the middle – the flag is tiny, it hardly exists at all. And yet everything the eye can see, the stones, the monuments, the colonnades, even the trees in the gardens, seem to

shrink into the background because of it, as if time had suddenly been halted. The flag is sole master. What we have before us is not a theatrical setting, a view of some foreign capital, or a corner of a dead town – it is something very distressing. It is a place which has been branded. The monuments are reduced to mere outlines.

Paris, Sartre said, had been reduced to a sham: it was like the empty bottles of wine displayed in the windows of shops which could no longer manage to stock the real thing. Labarthe is reaching the same conclusion, though his metaphors take him by a different route. 'The flag', he writes, 'is sole master', and one notes that the flag does not just represent or symbolize mastery: it is mastery. Though tiny in relation to the scale of the buildings around it, just as the regime and the historical moment it belongs to are tiny in relation to the scale of the institutions and the history those buildings embody, it dwarfs them. Indeed, it nullifies them completely. It leaves France and everything she had been – the real France – drained of her identity, an insubstantial outline, as much a dummy as the wine bottle in the window.

The city, Labarthe also writes, had been *marquée*: branded. The melodramatic word underlines the fact that all these descriptions of the flag depend, at some level, on a metaphor of unnatural assault or violation. To Frenay the flags which meet his gaze every day contribute to 'a feeling of rape' – a very common metaphor (and, of course, not always a metaphor) for the sufferings of the defeated and occupied. Janet Teissier du Cros invokes the idea of violation only in the most discreet way. She merely notes without comment that the German flag, with its bold design and violent colours, floats against a background of 'the luminous changing sky of the Ile de France': the very sky, in other words, which had for so long been celebrated by painters and poets who found in its mercurial subtlety a reflection of the French character, the spirit of the nation.

Despite their differing tones, then, all these passages make the same point about the German presence, other than the obvious and explicit one that the Germans were masters determined to make the most public display of their mastery. The German presence in France was unnatural; the Germans never belonged. Reduced to these terms, the descriptions convey both the writers' initial shock at the arrival of the victors and their slowly accumulated outrage at the indignities forced on the occupied. And perhaps they contain as well the nourishing hope that, for all the Reich's propaganda about its thousand-year life, it will by its very character be only a temporary suspension of the natural order of things.

All these points, and particularly the last, were well to the fore in a memorable photo in Labarthe's *La France libre* which showed a bull-necked German officer browsing at one of the bookstalls by the Seine under the quizzical gaze of an elegantly bearded Frenchman. The caption read: '*L'Allemand profane les Quais de la Seine, qui appartenaient naguère aux poètes et aux rêveurs*' ('The German profanes the quays of the Seine, which were formerly the haunt of poets and dreamers'). Actually, 'profanes' is a deliberately bland translation of *profaner*, a verb whose wide and forceful meanings can variously be rendered as 'to desecrate', 'to defile', 'to debase' and 'to violate'. Sartre cannot have been the only person later to smile ruefully at the crudity of this item. Of course, some of the Germans in France did have bull necks and no doubt their close military haircuts accentuated this unattractive feature. Certainly the French often made mocking jokes about bull necks, delighting in those cases where reality conformed to the brutish stereotype they expected to see. But no, not all the occupiers had bull necks, any more than all the customers of the *bouquinistes* by the Seine in pre-war days had been poets and dreamers. The confrontation between German and French did not always look or feel quite the way *La France libre* wanted to portray it, though this was also the way the French often chose to remember it afterwards. In fact it had not been nearly as dramatically satisfying, nearly as clear-cut.

Obviously Janet Teissier du Cros, Henri Frenay and André Labarthe do not avoid the danger into which *La France libre* fell either. But the first two were writing after the event, and Labarthe was writing from London after a brief clandestine visit to Paris. Nothing betrays their distance from their subject more clearly than the decision all three share, the decision which actually defines the literary *topos* they use: to portray the German presence almost exclusively through the public symbols the Reich itself proffered so insistently, to focus on the flags rather than the troops who marched under their colours. In Labarthe's account the Place de la Concorde appears to be empty; indeed, any sign of life in it would destroy the literary effect he is so obviously striving to create. German soldiers appear in the scenes Janet Teissier du Cros and Frenay describe, but only as embellishments to the depersonalized symbol of the flag:

those sentries with 'closed hostile faces', standing 'frozen like stone statues' or pounding the pavement with their goose-stepping, are observed no more clearly than the bull-necked officer in *La France libre*.

Surely this cannot have been how people viewed the Germans during the Occupation itself? Surely such crude stereotyping could not have survived the forced intimacy which four years, even four years of suffering and fear, had brought? Inevitably, the written record of people's immediate impressions is scanty by comparison to the flood of reminiscence, and even the diaries and other contemporary accounts which do survive can seem oddly uninformative. The pressure of historic events might make people feel the need to put down their reactions but, by its nature, does not usually prompt more than jotting. Sustained description, deliberate meditation and the literary *topoi* constructed from them come only in safety or in leisure after the event. There was little place for them during the Occupation and none at all during the volatile early days when the public mood had just switched from fearing the Germans as epitomes of barbarism to admiring them as models of correctness.

So it is no use looking for set-pieces which dwell on how writers first reacted to German troops in the knowledge that Germany was going to be their master for the indefinite future. Instead one finds, for example, the following:

> We drove around Paris for curiosity's sake. There were a few people about in the Latin quarter, a few tarts sitting around tables at the Capoulade with German officers, a few more pedestrians on the Boulevard Saint-Germain, but along the Rue de Rivoli and on the Place de la Concorde there were only an occasional German or two and the great red flags, astonishing at first glance, with their black swastikas floating over the centre of the town.

This is Maurice Sachs, not yet embarked on his career as black marketeer and informer, describing what he found when he got back to Paris immediately after the exodus. It comes from *La Chasse à courre* (*The Hunting*), the memoir of the Occupation he broke off in 1942. To judge from the flatness of its tone, *La Chasse à courre* is a lightly reworked version of a journal, or perhaps just notes, kept on the spot as events in his cowardly war unfolded.

This flatness of tone, which makes the passage so disappointing to start with, is in fact a guarantee of its authenticity. The red flags with their black swastikas dominate Sachs' impressions, if anything can be said to dominate an account so little sorted or contrived, but not in the way André Labarthe made them dominate his evocation of the Place de la Concorde. 'Astonishing at first glance', they are seen only in the distance and out of the corner of the eye, as something the eye will need to register again and again – but always, one suspects, obliquely and from a distance – before the mind can get over its first numbness. The soldiers in the middle ground of the scene are neither stereotyped nor individualized. They are 'an occasional German or two', which is about as inexpressive as descriptive language can get, and they are officers sitting around café tables with tarts. No closed hostile faces, no sentries like stone statues, no goose-stepping march, not a jackboot in sight: just ordinary soldiers (they could belong to any nation) relaxing in the way soldiers do after an easy victory.

Untrustworthy though he may have been in almost every other respect, the witness Sachs bears to the mood of the summer and autumn of 1940 agrees with the handful of other references which make up the unvarnished contemporary record. Galtier-Boissière set down his first impressions of occupied Paris in the sparest of catalogues. The swastika flags on the public buildings were at the top of the list, of course, followed by 'the busloads of soldiers; the groups of tourists in *feldgrau* being shown round by a guide who used to sell dirty postcards'. Then he added a few observations that mark the first real stirrings of curiosity. The gendarmes were quick to salute the Germans. All the Germans got their photos taken in front of the tomb of the Unknown Soldier. There was less formal distance between the officers and ranks in the German army than in the French: in the Place de l'Etoile (nowadays officially the Place Charles-de-Gaulle) he saw a captain strolling about with two privates.

Most observers did not get even this far. Paul Léautaud, who had insisted on staying in Paris while others fled, saw his first German in the form of a trooper being shown by a gendarme how to use the public phone by the entrance to the Jardin du Luxembourg. 'It didn't affect me at all,' he insisted in his diary: 'I didn't even stop to look at him.' 'It doesn't shatter me,' claimed the dance-band leader Georges van Parys, only three days after the capital had been occupied: 'To be in Paris with them neither surprises me nor makes me uneasy.' André Thérive told of a friend whose reaction on first seeing German soldiers was to ask a gendarme who they were, explaining afterwards, 'I thought they might be Dutch.'

The refugees who had flooded into France in 1940 certainly included Dutch troops, but this mistake did not stem from the simple ignorance that led some country people to take German soldiers for British. Shock takes many forms. When it does not make people seem casual and matter-of-fact, as Sachs and Galtier-Boissière do, it can cause a blank indifference, or denial. Adults can often pass this state off as insouciance or bravado, like the wit among the crowd of onlookers when the Germans first came marching down the Champs Elysées: 'Now I see where we went wrong. We've taken too many prisoners.' Children reveal it more nakedly. Ninetta Jucker knew a small boy who insisted the flag on the top of the Eiffel Tower was still really the *tricolore*, though the blue could not be made out from ground level.

By its very nature, this sort of shock could not last long. What succeeded it was by and large equally uncommunicative, so Jean Guéhenno was breaking with the practice of both his own journal and other journals when he wrote this apostrophe to the soldier he met in the street:

> What on earth do you look like in your green uniform, in our streets, our squares? A soldier in Paris, a soldier in France, is blue or yellow. You are too buttoned-up. And those elegant gloves you wear? You are too proper. And that dagger of yours? And your revolver? Executioner in gloves. And your boots? How many pairs of shoes they would make for those who now go barefoot. . . .
>
> I look you over from head to foot. Your uniform is a little crumpled these days and rather worn at the knees and elbows. In your middle, over your navel and on your belt-buckle, is this inscription, which I always decipher with the same surprise: *Gott mit uns* [God with us]. . . . I must be dreaming. *Gott mit uns!* I wonder who this God is who is with you. Funny God.

Guéhenno wrote these words in February 1943 – that is, after nearly three years of adjustment to the German presence – and he wrote them in the course of formulating his resolve to shun the Germans altogether.

Like that resolve, the passage betrays a disjunction between the reality of the German presence he found on the street and the idea of it he recreated in the privacy of his diary. Indeed, the passage lives precisely at the point of their disjunction. On the one hand, it comes directly, even urgently, from all the small daily experiences his journal elsewhere records, but on the other it pulls away from them towards abstraction. The German he describes is not an individual but a representative, an all-purpose identikit German, and the address he delivers is purely of the imagination. This in itself is enough to give what he writes all those attributes of the set-piece – the studied rhetorical devices and the insistently polemical purpose – which link it more closely with post-Occupation writing than with the scattered comments in earlier diaries.

Yet abstraction does not triumph entirely: the actuality of the Occupation is still too strong to allow him the easy refuge of just addressing and demolishing symbols. The French eye which had begun merely by noting the astonishing sight of Nazi flags in the distance or seeing the Germans as undifferentiated figures in the middle ground had absorbed quite a lot between 1940 and 1943. Of course, what it picked up was still by definition only the knowledge that comes from the eye. If nothing else, the passage stands as a reminder of how little contact most people had, or needed to have, with their occupiers: largely a matter of those trivial occasions, when a soldier asked for directions or offered his seat on the Métro, which Guéhenno and others agonized about. So the German he describes is still very much a spectacle to be observed and deciphered, definitely not someone to be approached, much less someone he has in any meaningful sense come to know.

His eye has taught him, for example, the falsity of the original impression Parisians had received. The troops who first entered the city had been a specially chosen 'chorus line' (as people came to call it) designed to impress by their appearance and their behaviour. Three years on, they look shabby or, worse, hypocritical in the elegance that belies their savagery: executioners in gloves. Nor is the reference to the revolver merely a melodramatic flourish in the writing: originally discreet in their display of weaponry, the Germans were sometimes allowed out only in armed groups by 1943. Guéhenno's eye has grown familiar with mundane technical details as well. It has dwelt on the *feldgrau* – literally, of course, a 'field-grey' but really a muddy green – which distinguished Wehrmacht or regular army soldiers from the élite Allgemeine-SS, who wore black, and Waffen-SS, whose uniforms combined black and green. It has noted the ceremonial chained dagger worn at the waist, which distinguished Wehrmacht officers from the men they commanded. It has even taken the care to read and ponder the motto on the Wehrmacht belt-buckle. (If the soldier Guéhenno had in his mind's eye had been SS, the motto would have read: 'Our Honour is Our Loyalty'.)

By 1943, then, inspection of the Germans had become particular enough to differentiate the obvious categories their uniforms announced. The popular slang in which the Occupation was so fertile had already found appropriate nicknames for them. The Feldgendarmerie (military police) were *bouledogues* (bulldogs), because of the metal plaques and chains they wore round their necks, or *têtes de veau primées* (prize calf's heads). The jawbreakingly named Nachrichtenhelferinnen, women auxiliaries operating wirelesses, telegraph systems and phone switchboards, whom the Germans had taken to calling Blitzmädchen, were known as *souris grises* (grey mice) because of the grey uniforms which attracted unflattering comment from admirers of Parisian women's fashions. German civilian officials and diplomats were *faisans dorés* (golden pheasants), a nickname borrowed directly from German slang; it originally referred to their golden-brown uniforms but, in French, also mocked the elaborate insignia, buttons and braid they sported.

Such nicknames demythologized the Germans as much as particularizing them. So, too, did the all-embracing names people had taken to calling their occupiers. In 1940 the common terms had been *les boches* and *les chleuhs*, the French equivalents of the English Huns or Krauts. *Les chleuhs* – taken from 'Shluh' (as the English language spells it), the Berber dialect spoken in Morocco and Mauritania – associated the enemy with barbarism. So did *les boches*, like Huns a propaganda term from the First World War. Distantly derived from *les alboches*, it lent itself to a simple pun, *les sales boches* (dirty Huns), from which the French could derive apparently endless delight.

But *chleuh* and *boche* fell out of fashion in the aftermath of defeat. Their disappearance from print was, of course, a result of censorship, for the Germans were prickly enough about the names they were called to make long-suffering journalists joke that one day the word *vandalisme* would be banned out of respect for the Germanic tribe it referred to. Their disappearance from speech was a tribute to people's determination to forget propaganda about atrocities and take their occupiers' correctness at face value. *Chleuh* would later regain its currency in France but *boche* lived mainly on the lips of the Free French abroad, and when the French who had stayed behind heard it from them again after Liberation, it had a dated ring. By then *les boches*, like *les prussiens*, evoked the conflicts of a past age rather than the corrosive realities of the Occupation.

The term which defeat first ushered in was *ces messieurs*: these gentlemen or, more likely, those gentlemen. Formal to the point of caution, it had the discreet advantage of suggesting, according to the circumstances and the speaker, either servility or irony. In the slang which in turn succeeded *ces messieurs* formality shaded into familiarity, carrying all the nuances of acceptance or resistance that went with it. Often the Germans became simply *les autres*. This deliberately bland usage gave subversive meaning to Sartre's famous aphorism in *Huis clos* (1944), '*l'enfer, c'est les Autres*', which otherwise innocuously translates as 'Hell is other people'.

Other terms had more specific connotations. *Les fritz* and *les fridolins*, from the familiar forms of German Christian names, were inoffensive, jocular and almost friendly – in British terms, more like Jerries than Krauts. The French could, in the right circumstances, venture *fritz* and *fridolin* to a German's face, but never *boche* or *chleuh*. *Les doryphores*, adopted in mocking response to the German obsession with stamping out the Colorado beetle, belonged to the hostile language the occupied devised among themselves to refer to their occupiers. It gave an ironic twist to the injunction shouted from official posters throughout the Occupation, '*Luttez contre les doryphores*': 'Fight the Colorado beetle'.

For most people the typical German – the figure whom the very word *occupant* conjured up in the mind – was the Wehrmacht soldier, and the salient feature of the Wehrmacht soldier was the muddy green colour of his uniform. In 'Conseils à l'occupé' Jean Texcier proposed that, by analogy with *doryphores*, the Germans should be called *sauterelles vertes* (green locusts) because they arrived in swarms, darkening the sky and covering the ground: 'Brace yourself. They'll end up by wearing out their mandibles.' The suggestion never took on, but other nicknames playing on the idea of green did. The occupiers were *haricots verts* (green beans, as Americans would say), which was innocuous in its humour, and *race verte*, much more pointed in its mockery of the Nazi obsession with race, and satisfying in that the words could be formed by defacing letters in the *Rauchen verboten* (No Smoking) signs plastered on railway and Métro carriages. By such small, encoded gestures – coining slang, making jokes, defacing a German poster, scribbling a V-sign on a wall – did private resentment slowly blossom into resistance.

Guéhenno's apostrophe to his imaginary occupier disdains colloquialisms. In fact, its formal rhetoric, its distance from the street, is one of the things that obviously impoverishes it. Yet he too remains preoccupied with German *feldgrau*, simply with its colour: 'A soldier in Paris, a soldier in France, is blue or yellow.' (Blue and *réséda* were, of course, the traditional colours of the French army.) Less shockingly violent than the red, white and black of the *Blutfahne*, Wehrmacht green still clashed, subtly and pervasively, with how things were supposed to look. In *Le Caporal épinglé* Jacques Perret claimed that, though intended as camouflage, it never blended because nowhere in France had nature made greens of so sickening a shade. In doing so, of course, he combined two common but powerful ideas: that the difference between German and French was, aesthetically, a contrast between crudity and subtlety, and that the German presence was inherently a violation of nature.

Yet, for all its neatness, Perret's remark still sounds strained. Guéhenno was more honest. 'A soldier in Paris, a soldier in France, is blue or yellow': this effectively conveys a quite primitive outrage. And it determinedly reads the juxtaposition of the German soldier with the French background not as making the whole scene look surreal but as making the German look absurd, though without knowing he looks absurd. Where post-Occupation writing remembered the German presence as horrible and denounced it, writing from the time itself often portrayed it as silly and mocked it, albeit in private. Here this laughter behind the hand saves what Guéhenno writes from rhetorical excess. More generally, it was one of the strengths of the French: there was hope for people who could laugh at executioners because they affected elegant gloves or turn a campaign against a potato pest to their own private amusement.

Yet, just as Guéhenno's resolve to shun the Germans altogether signalled its unworkability more or less on the spot, here his outrage and mockery deflate themselves even as they are expressed. Or, at least, they contain the seeds of self-mockery and even a sense of impotence. However long his eye might continue to insist that the German does not fit in, and however ridiculous that might make the German appear, there is after all – as Guéhenno obviously knows full well – no law of nature which says that soldiers should be blue or yellow rather than green. Such things belong to the realm of the arbitrary. The natural order, which had not stopped the Germans coming in the first place, offered no assurance that they would go away again.

And so the alien presence, increasingly hated and feared in private, could seem so permanent that, in the public places where daily life went on, it was taken for granted. It grew almost invisible. Even the *feldgrau* uniforms, target of popular slang and Guéhenno's rhetoric, became – as Sartre wrote – just 'a pale, dull green, unobtrusive stain, which the eye almost expected to find among the dark clothes of the civilians'. Sartre ended 'Paris Under the Occupation' with a story, plausible even if apocryphal, of a Wehrmacht trooper who had hidden in a cellar while Paris was liberated but was eventually forced out of his refuge by hunger. He found that he could steal a bike and cycle down the Champs Elysées without anybody stopping him: 'Passers-by had got so used to the sight that *they did not see him.*'*

The familiarity which had rendered the once glaring stain almost inconspicuous was already written into the language. Slang might have come up with terms like *haricots verts* or *doryphores*, but in practice people did not necessarily use them when they talked among themselves about the Germans. People called the occupiers *ils*: they. *Ils* are not us and are different from us and we don't like them. But they are so ever-present, so powerful a force in our lives that we don't even need a specific label for them to make it clear who we're talking about. In short, *ils* was the word the French had already used for the governments they had lived under before the Occupation – and it remains the word they use today.

A S THEY ADJUSTED to the German presence – at first shocking but eventually, though hated, so familiar as to go almost unnoticed – people also had to come to terms with the fact of absence. The battle of 1940 had already left its lists of the missing: soldiers killed or taken prisoner, deserters who had made themselves scarce, civilians who had fled in the exodus and not returned home. To them were added others, whose abrupt departure signalled not just the despair of 1940 but the terror of the years to follow. Fifteen Parisians

---

* Sartre's italics.

killed themselves on 14 June, the day the Germans entered the capital; they included Thierry de Martel, a well-known surgeon in the military hospital at Neuilly. Arthur Koestler dedicated his memoir, *The Scum of the Earth*, to the memory of six exiled German writers who had taken their lives when France fell. The list was headed by the Marxist critic Walter Benjamin, turned back at the Spanish border, and Albert Einstein's nephew Carl, author of a book on African sculpture, who drowned himself in the river Oloron in the Pyrénées.

Absence and disappearance were not just accidents of warfare but an essential part of the policy adopted by the occupiers and by Vichy. They happened both literally, in brutal fact, and metaphorically, in a cultural agenda which sought to excise even the famous dead from the public memory. In Paris the Théâtre Sarah-Bernhardt expunged the name of the Jewish actress and called itself the Théâtre de la Cité. The publishing house of Calmann-Lévy, which had issued the work of Flaubert, Dumas and George Sand, changed its name to Les Editions Balzac. The *Liste Otto* banned both the living and the dead, from Britain and Germany as well as France: Shakespeare and Virginia Woolf, Stefan Zweig and Erich-Maria Remarque, Bertolt Brecht and Thomas Mann, along with Aragon, Giradoux, Maurois, Malraux and even, though he was a supporter of Vichy, Paul Claudel.* Biographies of Jews could not be published and, wherever possible, works by Jewish artists were suppressed. Mendelssohn's music might have been too well-loved to be denied a hearing, but Ibert and Milhaud could be silenced without difficulty.

In schools the standard history textbook universally known as 'Mallet and Isaac', in fact largely the work of Jules Isaac, became simply 'Mallet'. Anthologies containing poems by Heine had those items pasted over with white bits of paper, or were reprinted with his name left out: in France he became *poète anonyme*, as he had already been *unbekannter Dichter* in Germany for several years. The bully-boys could be relied on to silence a figure like André Gide, once respected as a mentor of the young but now blamed for fostering decadence

---

* Named after Otto Abetz, the list was prefaced by a statement of compliance from French publishers, stressing their eagerness 'to withdraw from sale those books which have systematically poisoned our public opinion; more particularly the publications by political refugees and Jewish authors'. In practice, censorship was in the hands of a liberal francophile, Gerhard Heller of the Referat Schriftum (Publication Section) of the Propagandstaffel.

in pre-war France. Threats from Darnand's Service d'Ordre Légionnaire made him cancel a rare public appearance – a lecture in Nice on the poet Henri Michaux – in the spring of 1941. Gide was left to protest unconvincingly to his diary that what he would have said had not been important enough to justify taking a stand against the mood of the times.

Paris, Sartre wrote in a fine oxymoron, 'was peopled by the absent'. The streets, empty of traffic during the day and empty of innocent pedestrians during the curfew, spoke of more than emergencies, shortages and restrictions. They spoke of absences which eventually touched ordinary families and ordinary communities as thoroughly as the losses of 1940 had done. Simone de Beauvoir described how friends from among the circle at the Café Flore vanished:

> One morning we heard that Sonia had just been arrested; she had apparently been the victim of another woman's jealousy; at any rate, someone had denounced her. She sent a message . . . asking for a pullover and some silk stockings to be sent on; no more requests came after that. The blonde Czech girl who lived with Jausion vanished. A few days afterwards, when Bella was asleep in her boyfriend's arms, the Gestapo knocked on their door at dawn and took her away too. One of her friends was living with a well-off young man who wanted to marry her; she was denounced by her future father-in-law. We didn't know much about the camps, but the way these gay and beautiful girls simply vanished into the blue, without a word, was terrifying enough. Jausion and his friends still came to the Flore, and even went on sitting at the same table, where they talked among themselves in an agitated, hectic sort of way. But there was no mark on the red banquette to indicate the empty place at their side. This was what seemed to me the most unbearable thing about any absence: that it was, precisely, a *nothingness*.

'All around us, people seemed to be quietly swallowed up,' Sartre confirmed. 'What's more, we talked about it very little.'

Galtier-Boissière cryptically noted such events in his diary, particularly during the black year of 1942. On 25 February, for example: 'Michel informs me of the arrest of his niece Marie-Claude, such a charming woman, daughter of Lucien Vogel and widow of Vaillaint-Couturier.' Paul Vaillant-Couturier, Communist politician and editor of *L'Humanité*, had died in 1937. Marie-Claude, so Galtier-Boissière eventually heard after Liberation, died in

Ravensbruck nursing a fellow-prisoner with typhoid. On 20 March 1942 he noted:

> Jean Dumaine has been arrested as he was getting on the Monte-Carlo express with a Jew he was helping to escape into the *zone libre*. He had a big sum of money on him, and the stamps he used in making false passports for his friends.
>
> The news was brought by his secretary Thérèse. She had been confronted with him by the Gestapo, because she had lent him her own *Ausweis*. She was at a complete loss what to say without making things worse for him. Jean looked as if he'd been beaten up.

In the event, Thérèse served three weeks in prison; her father, who took what Galtier-Boissière laconically called 'the right side', hoped the sentence would teach her the proper way to behave. Dumaine, who had worked with Galtier-Boissière on the pre-war magazine *Crapouillot*, was released after six months' internment, first in prison and then in a camp. One of the men held with him had committed suicide before his eyes.

Sartre's essay 'Paris Under the Occupation' remembered in detail how bystanders like himself usually learned that someone had disappeared:

> One day you might phone a friend and the phone would ring for a long time in an empty flat. You would go round and ring the doorbell, but no-one would answer it. If the *concierge* forced the door, you would find two chairs standing close together in the hall with the fag-ends of German cigarettes on the floor between their legs. If the wife or mother of the man who had vanished had been present at his arrest, she would tell you that he had been taken away by very polite Germans, like those who asked the way in the street. And when she went to ask what had happened to them at the offices in the Avenue Foch or the Rue des Saussaies she would be politely received and sent away with comforting words.

No. 11 Rue des Saussaies, just round the corner from the Palais de l'Elysée, was the Gestapo headquarters. The Gestapo had additional offices in the Avenue Foch, at the other end of the Champs Elysées and on the way to the Bois de Boulogne. Everyone knew that. Indeed, rather than saying that someone had been picked up by the Gestapo, people would often just say they had been taken to the

Avenue Foch or Rue des Saussaies – the latter address being already familiar because No. 11 had been headquarters of the Sûreté Nationale, the French CID, before the Occupation.

At least, this is how people spoke at the time and how the French still commonly remember the machinery which persecuted them. Always wary of German words, the French language adopted only the most common ones during the Occupation, like *diktat, Ausweis, feldgrau* and *ersatz*. But it quickly adopted *la Gestapo*. Parisians spoke of the *Rue des Saussaies* or the *Avenue Foch*, and a few ironists were in the habit of referring to *la Geste* – in allusion to the medieval poems which had celebrated heroic deeds – but otherwise the language developed no colourful or universal nicknames of its own, no equivalent of *souris grise* or *faisan doré*. The Gestapo remained *la Gestapo*.

The German word *Gestapo*, of course, was simply an abbreviation of Geheime Staats Polizei, or Secret State Police, the organization founded in 1933 by Goering and soon controlled by Himmler. Yet by the time of the Occupation the Gestapo was only one of many agencies which handled security work in the baroque structure of the Reich. Like the Sicherheitsdienst or SD, it was a division of the Reichssicherheitshauptamt or RHSA, the SS-controlled security service whose growth in power had marked the increasing control of National Socialist Party loyalists. Despite its dominance, the RHSA in turn still shared its work with other security services, such as the Feldgendarmerie and the Abwehr (both part of the Wehrmacht), and the agencies specially dedicated to anti-Jewish measures. And it operated through terror squads other than the Gestapo *per se* – such as the Kommando der SIPO und SD or KDS, generally known as the Einsatzkommando, the special police unit formed in the Southern Zone after it had been taken over in November 1942.

The French never troubled to master the intricacies of this bureaucratic maze. One term, *la Gestapo*, was enough to label those who arrested people and made them vanish: it served as a synonym for everything people feared. The very imprecision was expressive, like the vaguely generalizing *ils* which lumped all the occupiers together under one pronoun. It paid tribute to the least seen, the least known, the most elusive aspect of *ils* – the hardest to reconcile with the usually unthreatening face of the Wehrmacht soldier who asked for directions in the street, or even the polite faces of those who answered callers' questions in the Rue des Saussaies.

Ninetta Jucker saw the hidden face of the occupiers in December

To remind Parisians of their power, the occupiers staged a parade –
complete with military band – down the Champs Elysées each day

Paul Reynaud, Prime Minister as France fell in 1940.
On either side of him stand (*left*) General Maxime Weygand and Paul Baudouin
and (*right*) Marshal Pétain, whose appointment decisively strengthened
the voice of the *mous*, or doves, advocating an armistice

Pétain shakes hands with Hitler at Montoire in October 1940.
The gesture symbolized the 'path of collaboration' to which the
Vichy regime committed France

Maréchal, nous voilà! Busts of Pétain on the production line at the Musée National
Paris, 1943. By then the Marshal's popularity had begun to wane but his image wa
still displayed in private houses as well as, by law, in public buildings

ortages of food and other items which had once been common made people queue
or hours in response to even the vaguest rumour of fresh supplies. Here Parisians
wait outside a funeral parlour in the hope of being able to buy milk

A *vélo-taxi*, or rickshaw, and a horse-drawn cab in Paris in 1941.
The shortage of petrol and the scarcity of permits to drive motor vehicles
brought makeshift expedients, old and new, on to the streets

A gendarme directs traffic at the Rond-Point of the Champs Elysées.
The presence of the occupiers, with their German signs and swastika flags,
could make the most familiar scene look alien

'*L'Allemand profane les Quais de la Seine qui appartenaient naguère aux poètes et aux rêveurs*', said the caption when this photo appeared in *La France libre*: 'The German profanes the quays of the Seine, which were formerly the haunt of poets and dreamers.'

A Jew wears the yellow star in Paris. In the Occupied Zone the star was made mandatory for all Jews over the age of 6 in June 1942

Resistance began with words: a selection of the underground journals which took on a critical function in a time of official propaganda, censorship and rumour

Maquisards being trained in the Haute-Loire. The instructor holds a Sten gun, the most common weapon which the British supplied: cheap, light and easy to disassemble into parts that could be concealed, but also prone to misfire and jam. Like so many photographs of the Maquis in action, this scene may well have been posed, or re-staged, after Liberation

Local people return to Falaise in Normandy, where the German defence created one of the most savage battles in the campaign following D-Day

A collaborator is arrested after the liberation of the town of Laval in 1944

A *collabo horizontale* after ritual punishment, in Gisors

Pierre Laval argues with his accusers and judges at his trial in October 1945

De Gaulle leads the parade from the Arc de Triomphe to Notre-Dame
on 26 August 1944, the day after Paris had been liberated

1940. British by birth, though married to an Italian, she was called in to answer questions from two German officers, 'one young and disagreeable, obviously of the Nazi school; the other considerably older'. Her account did not specify, and perhaps she never learned, their rank or affiliation. In any event, she was able to satisfy her interrogators, and evidence from her doctor of her ill health ensured that she avoided internment. But the episode had begun disconcertingly enough, with a ring at the doorbell of her Paris flat in the early morning, which she answered, still in her dressing-gown, expecting to find the *concierge* with the morning paper:

> To my surprise I saw a sergeant of the Garde Mobile, who immediately addressed me by my name. His manner was so amiable and conciliatory that I felt no misgiving and asked him blankly to step inside. Looking rather embarrassed, he explained that he had orders to accompany me to the *mairie* of the Seventh Arrondissement.

The sergeant drank a cup of coffee and – on learning she had a baby, not mentioned in the paperwork he had been supplied with – let her send out to get some food for it, as well as consulting with her husband and summoning her doctor to her side.

Democracy, people joked nervously, is 'a system under which when they ring your bell in the early morning it's the milk'. But the persecutor who rang your bell in the early morning, the official with the power to make you disappear, might well turn out to be a gendarme in a uniform familiar from republican times before the Occupation. And the ordeal of confronting the hidden face of the Germans might happen not in the Rue des Saussaies but in the local *mairie*. That was how the collaboration which the Vichy government had embarked on worked in practice. Indeed, that was how it had always been meant to work: according to the perverse logic of Vichy, a gendarme rather than an agent of *la Gestapo* standing on the doorstep was living proof that French sovereignty was still being preserved.

As pursuit of the Reich's various enemies grew more determined with the passage of time, and raids in the night or the early morning gave way to daytime arrests, so the involvement of the French in the persecution of the French grew yet more visible, yet more public. Ninetta Jucker, again, made an eloquent witness to the sort of scene people grew almost accustomed to:

Once, in 1944, as I was coming home from market with the child, we found a knot of people standing at the entrance to our road. Two German soldiers armed with *mitraillettes* [sub-machine guns] were watching a house. It was lunchtime and the inhabitants of the street were wondering anxiously whether to hurry home or pretend they were just passing by. A woman said to me: *Dépechez vous, madame. Ce n'est pas rassurant* [Don't hang about. This doesn't look good].

I seized the child by the arm and began to run. The German soldiers signalled to us with their guns to be quick. 'What's happening, Mother?' said the little boy. *Une méchanceté?*

A wickedness? Yes, indeed. From the terrace of our flat I looked down into the street which backed the building under watch. Presently a police van drew up and one after another the blue-coated *flics* jumped out and ran into the house. I turned away.

Nobody seemed to know, or to have tried to find out, who the fugitive was or why the authorities were after him. A gendarme lent him his coat to help him escape, but both were caught and shot.

This brave gesture is just one reminder that by no means all servants of the state were comfortable with the role Pétain and Vichy had assigned them. It is a reminder, too, of the risks run by those who chose to resist it. But the real damage had been done. Gendarmes, in particular, were fatally linked in the public mind with the occupiers who made people disappear and created the atmosphere of fear which made it difficult, if not dangerous, to talk about the disappearances. They had become part of the undifferentiated *ils* – literally so in the naïve perceptions of a child like Ninetta Jucker's young son. He recognized ordinary Germans in their *feldgrau* well enough to shrink from them. When he was on a visit to the aquarium, a passing soldier tried to pick him up so he could see the fish better, but the boy turned white and looked as if he might be sick. 'His misery was so apparent', his mother remembered, 'that the soldier put him down gently and walked away.' When Liberation came and the soldiers in *feldgrau* left, he asked his parents in puzzlement why the gendarmes in their blue uniforms had not gone with them.

THE OCCUPIERS USED French officials, particularly the French police, right up to the last days when desperation forced them to rely more and more on the SS under one or other of its names and guises (like the Einsatzkommando, which gave Klaus Barbie his authority in Lyon). And even then they swallowed their inherent distrust of collaborationist organizations and called on Darnand's Milice. They did not do so just to save manpower, though that grew an increasingly urgent consideration as the invasion of Russia began soaking up the Reich's resources. Nor did they do so just to maintain a show of legitimacy – of France acting in her own best interests, which of course included Franco-German co-operation – though that, too, was something they were always careful to bear in mind.

The occupiers used the French against the French because they judged *Tarnungszwecken* (camouflage) essential to their policy. Camouflage demanded that an official wearing a French rather than a German uniform ring the doorbell whenever possible and, indeed, carry out as many as possible of the sordid acts in the bureaucracy of repression and persecution. Camouflage also shaped the distinctive vocabulary of the Reich which the philologist Victor Klemperer has ironically called LTI: *Lingua Tertii Imperii*. As well as including its predictable share of abusive terms for its enemies, internal and external, LTI was from the start rich in euphemisms, the linguistic equivalents of camouflage, for describing its own acts. Hitler, for example, preferred to call the financial burden the Reich imposed on defeated nations not *Besatzungskosten* (occupation costs) but *Aufbaukosten* (rebuilding costs). When the occupiers began taking and executing hostages in reprisal for acts of resistance – as Hitler ordered them to do in September 1941 – they called the reprisals *Vergeltungssanktionen* (retaliatory measures) and the hostages themselves *Sühnepersonen* (expiators). General Karl Heinrich von Stülpnagel – who would succeed his cousin Otto as the Militärbefehlshaber, or military commander-in-chief, in February 1942 – specifically forbade the word *otages* (hostages) in official communiqués addressed to the French.

The policy of mass deportation and extermination to which the Reich committed itself was, in every sense, conceived as a policy of stealth. The undesirables and enemies of the Reich who were its victims would not have public trials or executions or any chance of being acknowledged as martyrs. They would disappear, said General Keitel's decrees of 7 and 12 December 1941, *bei Nacht und Nebel*: under cover of night and fog. If nothing else, uncertainty about their fate was essential to the intimidation which would allow the work to continue. So 'deportation' was labelled *Abwanderung* (migration), *Evakuierung* (evacuation), *Umsiedlung* (resettlement) and, closer to the reality but still not that close, *Verschickung zur Zwangsarbeit* (sending away for forced labour). Lengthy questioning at the Nuremberg trials confirmed that victims marked for *Sonderbehandlung* (special treatment) were in fact under sentence of death. Even the Reich's name for its policy of genocide – *die Endlösung*, the Final Solution – was itself the final euphemism.

Yet, at a certain point, the attempt at secrecy was bound to fail. Rendering people invisible *en masse* became itself a public event. Indeed, even the preliminary stages of rendering them invisible had the paradoxical effect of drawing attention to the victims, making them highly visible. The fate of the Jews in France during the Occupation enacted these paradoxes with particular clarity. To say that is not to prejudge who knew about the death camps, or what they knew, or when and how they came to know it. No generalization can address itself adequately to those questions and, besides, the detail of their answers matters much less than a more obvious truth. People saw enough to know that something very bad was going on, something the occupiers wanted to hide.

At first, conditions looked ideal for the Reich. It had not just defeated France but had also secured a willing partner in the processes of camouflage and intimidation. The Vichy regime rushed its anti-semitic measures into effect during the first months of its life, more than keeping pace with the steps the Germans took in the Occupied Zone. By October 1940, when Vichy published its first *statut des Juifs*, Jews were defined, required to register and excluded from public service and the professions. The repeal of the *loi Marchandeau* meant they could be vilified freely in the press, which did not hesitate to exercise this privilege. With Jews very much in mind, the status of foreign-born citizens naturalized since 1927 was being reviewed. Jews who were still foreign citizens could be kept under police surveillance or interned, and both Vichy in the Southern Zone and the Reich in the Occupied Zone were looking round for ways of ridding their territory of as many of them as possible. If Jews were not being rigorously persecuted by the standards which would soon prevail, they were already being marginalized.

There was no sign of public opposition to what was happening, or even widespread unease at the direction in which events were heading. 'The violent nature of this campaign, right from the start, was something I found terrifying,' Simone de Beauvoir would later write: 'Where would they draw the line?' She and the other writers of diaries or memoirs whom this chapter has quoted belonged, by definition, to a minority and were acutely conscious of their near-isolation. Yet the rhetoric of the *collabo* press in Paris did not quite express the general mood either. Vichy, which at this time certainly had its finger on the pulse of the nation, did not go in for such excesses in its own pronouncements. Under Xavier Vallat, even Vichy's Commissariat Général aux Questions Juives kept its distance from aggressively propagandist displays like 'Le Juif et la France', the German-funded exhibition which opened in Paris in September 1941: it went on to tour cities in the Occupied Zone but not the Southern Zone.

Many people, perhaps even most people, were indifferent. In the autumn of 1940 they had other things to think about; later they could find little room for fellow-feeling or concern for the public good in their own struggle to survive. What happened to the Jews was a secondary matter: it was beyond their immediate affairs, it belonged to that realm of the 'political' which they could no longer control or even bring themselves to follow with much interest. And when they did pay attention, they were inclined to agree with the measures Vichy and the occupiers had taken, even to welcome them, since the measures satisfied the taste for finding scapegoats which the humiliation of defeat had left. Above all, the first stage of anti-semitic policy corresponded – as, indeed, it was deliberately designed to correspond – to popular impressions of the Jews in France.

Whatever else people thought about Jews, they believed that there were a lot of them and that their numbers were mostly made up of recently arrived immigrants. Historians now estimate that France in fact had a population of somewhere between 300,000 and 350,000 Jews in 1939. This figure, amounting to less than 1 per cent of the total population, meant she had more Jews than any other western European country, occupied or not. But it was still smaller than most people assumed, and it was dramatically smaller than the estimates on which the Reich proceeded. The Reich began by assuming a figure of 800,000, while the Wannsee Conference which committed it to the Final Solution in January 1942 put the surviving number of Jews in France and her north African territories at a grotesquely exaggerated 865,000.

In particular, the French joined the Reich in a wildly distorted belief that the overwhelming majority of Jews in France were recent arrivals, and they allowed their stereotype of the immigrant to dictate their stereotype of the Jew. Historians now estimate that Jewish immigrants numbered 200,000 at most (30,000–50,000 of them exiles from Germany and Austria) out of a total immigrant population of three million. But that was not how people saw the matter. In 1941, for example, the right-winger Charles Maurras passed on to Xavier Vallat reports that Bourbon l'Archambault in the Allier was being flooded by foreign Jews. Yet Vallat's own investigation established that the village, which normally boasted 2,784 inhabitants, had received 362 refugees; of them only thirty-one were Jewish and of these in turn only five were foreigners. The Reich's miscalculations operated on a grander scale. It pressed Vichy to revoke the citizenship of foreigners naturalized between 1927 and 1940 in the hope of netting an extra 50,000 Jews; in fact, only about 24,000 seem to have fallen into this category.

The popular idiom of the day distinguished between the two groups by calling native-born Jews *Israélites* and foreign-born Jews, naturalized or not, *Juifs*. The first term was polite; the second was not. The *Israélites* were 'assimilated'. They were far from universally tolerated: the abuse hurled at politicians like Blum and Mandel before the war showed the risks run by those who put their heads too far above the parapet, particularly in a controversial cause. But by and large, they were sufficiently accepted for people to underestimate their numbers, if not to forget their existence entirely. Until special attention was drawn to them, many *Israélites* could pass almost unnoticed by their neighbours or, when noticed, be regarded as not really Jewish. The *Juifs*, on the other hand, were 'unassimilated'. At least in the popular imagination, they were distinctive in their religion and their culture, perhaps even their language and their physical appearance.

Hardline anti-semites charged them with spreading global conspiracies or introducing subversive ideas even before the war, of course. (In France, as in the rest of Europe, the older anti-semitic stereotype of the Jew as the capitalist running the banks and the arms industries had been joined by the newer stereotype of the Jew as the factory-worker spreading Bolshevism in the workplace.) During the Occupation such people were quick to allege that the *Juifs* ran the black market, or cleared off to Cannes to enjoy a life of idle luxury, or stirred up trouble in the factories harnessed to the German war machine, or were behind any sign of disorder which threatened the new status quo. The inconsistency in the catalogue of accusations, particularly the inconsistency between the Jew as capitalist parasite and the Jew as revolutionary agitator, did not greatly matter to the mood of a public in whom a certain degree of unthinking anti-semitism was already endemic and could survive the most urgent call for examination.*

Yet behind most, if not all, of these attacks lay much deeper, traditional suspicions of the immigrant which have always been the obverse face of French national pride, the belief in the unique character of France. In time of peace, the *Juifs* usurped jobs and houses from the native French; they endangered what was truly French about France, if only with the threat of dilution. During the Occupation, they were convenient sacrificial victims to offer up to the occupiers – at least, so long as nobody bothered to ask or to spell out exactly what fate the victims might eventually meet. The *Juifs* did not belong to the France it was sworn to protect, said Vichy. And good riddance to them, added its supporters.

In such a spirit did France open the door to persecution. After the first round of anti-semitic measures in 1940 the Jews were pushed further and further towards the fringes of society and beyond without, in any sense, their eventual destination being specified. Jewish businesses were required to declare their net worth. Then Jewish businesses and property were 'Aryanized' – that is to say, confiscated and placed in the hands of trustees, or receivers, who were thus given the most blatant opportunities for greed and corruption. Jews could not change their address without notifying the police, or travel outside the area where they lived without special permission. They were banned from cafés, restaurants, theatres, cinemas, concerts, music halls, markets, fairs, museums, libraries, historic monuments, public parks and gardens, sporting events, camping grounds and swimming pools. They could not use public phones, which had signs saying *Accès interdit aux Juifs* on them. Their private phones were disconnected, a rule from which even Jewish doctors could not easily get themselves exempted. Their radios were confiscated and they could keep their bicycles only with special per-

---

* Unthinking and hence undeclared anti-semitism persisted, for example, in the Resistance and the Free French in London, and certainly did so within SOE. Peter Churchill, an SOE agent, was able to write in *Duel of Wits* (1953) of a Jewish Resistance colleague whom he disliked as 'this son of Israel' and 'Suss [*sic*]'.

mission. In the Paris Métro they had to travel in the last carriage. Throughout the Occupied Zone they were required to keep an earlier curfew than other people, and they could not go into non-Jewish shops except between three and four in the afternoon, when shortages meant that most goods had already been snapped up by earlier customers.

'The Jews and their property are excluded from ordinary laws and rights,' announced the Einsatz Reichsleiter Rosenberg in November 1941, brushing aside protests from Vichy at its plundering of Jewish libraries, archives and art collections. In other words, even before the internments were stepped up and the deportations begun in earnest, the Jews were being treated as if they did not exist. Though still present, they were less and less visible, already being made absent. Janet Teissier du Cros gives a vignette of the shadowy, fugitive existence they were forced to lead in her description of an old lady who had chosen to go shopping at the wrong – the forbidden – time of day.

> She came humbly up and stood hesitating on the edge of the pavement. Jews were not allowed to stand in queues. What they were supposed to do I never discovered. But the moment the people in the queue saw her they signed to her to join us. Secretly and rapidly, as in the game of hunt-the-slipper, she was passed up till she stood at the head of the queue. I am glad to say that not one voice was raised in protest, the policeman standing near turned his head away, and that she got her cabbage before any of us.

Like Ninetta Jucker's account of the gendarme giving his coat to the hunted man, this vignette suggests a covert popular sympathy for the persecuted. It also raises an obvious question: how did Janet Teissier du Cros and the other people know the old lady was a Jew? The answer, of course, is that they knew because she was wearing a yellow star. The ordinance requiring it in the Occupied Zone was issued on 29 May 1942, to come into effect on 7 June. The star itself, a piece of yellow cloth about the size of a hand, had the word *Juif* or *Juive* printed across it in black letters. All Jews over the age of 6 had to wear it sewn firmly on their clothing over the region of their heart. They had to buy three stars each from their local police office, and the purchase was deducted from their clothing coupons.

The logic behind the imposition of the star was simple: to discriminate against people, let alone persecute them, you first have to be able to identify them. The Reich knew this well. It had first run into the issue in France with its difficulties enforcing the clause in its ordinance of September 1940 forbidding Jews to cross from the Southern Zone into the Occupied Zone. The clause was plainly unworkable unless the authorities could easily establish who was Jewish. All the absurd and complex definitions of Jewishness that Vichy and the Reich adopted, and all the crazed pseudo-scientists who claimed expertise in spotting Jews, were of no use without a system of registration.* This had been put in hand without delay and so, for example, the dying Henri Bergson had shuffled through the streets of Paris in his carpet slippers to declare himself 'Academic. Philosopher. Nobel Prize winner. Jew.' In Paris itself the tally had been greatly aided by the efficiency of André Tulard, a police official whose immaculate files were regularly updated and even colour-coded to distinguish French from foreign Jews. They were among the most useful instruments of persecution the French put at the disposal of their occupiers.

They helped, for example, in the next logical step after registration, which was to require all Jews in the Occupied Zone to have the word *Juif* or *Juive* stamped on their *cartes d'identité*. This enabled any official to identify on the spot Jews trying to infringe any of the restrictions that hemmed their lives, whether by using a public phone or travelling between the zones. It was only a short step further to require the yellow star. And yet the imposition of the star was more than a bureaucratic expedient. It served other purposes, not the least of which was to keep up the policy of harassing the Jews with regulations and restrictions at every point. It was meant not just to identify but to humiliate, and it worked. Paul Léautaud's diary for 14 June 1942 records the case of a 12-year-old boy who killed himself by jumping out of a window rather than undergo the ordeal of wearing the star. Jacques Adler – once a victim and now a historian of what happened to the Jews of Paris – has testified how greatly the star increased the sense of isolation felt particularly in the immigrant communities.

Nor was the star introduced only with the effect on those who

---

* Probably the most powerful French expert on Jewishness was Georges Montandon, author of *Comment reconnaître le Juif?* and head of the propaganda institute which succeeded Paul Sézille's Institut des Etudes des Questions Juives. Bonnard, the Vichy Minister of Education, considered appointing him to a newly established chair of Racial Studies at the Sorbonne. The Commissariat Général aux Questions Juives called Montandon in to adjudicate in cases of doubt. He was killed by *résistants* in 1944.

wore it in mind. It was meant to make a spectacle of Jews in the eyes of non-Jews. Hitlerian doctrine, of course, did not look any more leniently on the 'assimilated' Jew than it did on the 'unassimilated' Jew: indeed, the more 'assimilated' the Jew, the more insidious was the threat he posed. It was vital – as an exercise in public education, one might say – to flush out the 'assimilated' Jews as thoroughly as possible: in French terms, to brand the *Israélites* once and for all as *Juifs*. And so at a critical point the policy of making Jews invisible, first marginalizing them and then making them disappear altogether *bei Nacht und Nebel*, required they be made highly visible: exposed to the popular gaze and submitted to the popular judgement.

Even before the risks this entailed became fully apparent, the occupiers encountered another, purely technical difficulty. Using Tulard's filing system, they had estimated the number of Jews in Paris and its suburbs who had to wear yellow stars at 100, 455. Yet by 7 June, the day the ordinance came into force, stars had been issued to only 83,000 people. The shortfall of nearly 20 per cent owed nothing to a lack of official co-operation from the French authorities, though it does suggest that some Jews, at least, simply ignored the new regulation. The letters of denunciation flooding into the Kommandantur and the Commissariat Général aux Questions Juives were certainly thick with stories of Jews failing to wear their stars, while Simone de Beauvoir could not remember seeing anyone wearing one in the neighbourhoods of Montparnasse and Saint-Germain-des-Prés.

Eichmann's protégé Theodor Dannecker, head of the Juden-referat of the SD in Paris, also worried that Jews were escaping illegally to the Southern Zone and was not satisfied by reassurances from Vichy. Stricter controls would be needed if Berlin's orders were to be fulfilled. His determination is in itself a reminder of how far the Reich's policy had moved since the first days of the Occupation, when it had been content if Jews landed up in other people's territory: now it wanted to cage them more and more tightly. And it introduced another note which would be heard again and again from the Reich's administrators as the Final Solution got underway. They had begun by overestimating the numbers of Jews, and they had compounded the error by overestimating what even the most efficient bureaucracy could achieve. Increasingly they were consumed with desperate, panicky haste and with continual frustration at failing to meet their deadlines, achieve their quotas, fill the cattle cars bound for the east.

Nevertheless, 83,000 people wearing yellow stars on the streets of Paris and its suburbs alone made an impact. 'The abundance of Jews on the Paris pavements has opened the eyes of the most blind,' exulted *Paris-Midi* on 8 June. Even an ideological *collabo* like Robert Brasillach, who approved of the star, was surprised at how many people wore it. The sheer number was part of Hitler's point: there are more Jews than you thought, the infection has spread more widely than you realized. But not everyone took it that way; some took it very differently. This is the German officer Ernst Jünger writing in his diary for 8 June:

> In the Rue Royale I encountered for the first time in my life the yellow star, worn by three young girls who passed close by me, arms linked. . . . In the afternoon I saw the star again far more frequently. I consider that this is a date which will leave a deep mark, at the personal level too. A sight like this cannot but provoke a reaction. I was immediately ashamed to be in uniform.

And this is Janet Teissier du Cros, recalling the first time she saw the star being worn:

> It was not till he was close upon us that I saw the man. He was little and elderly, with bowed shoulders and poorly dressed. I doubt whether I would have noticed him at all if it had not been for the sinister distinguishing mark on his left breast, the yellow star with *Juif* printed across it. . . . I stopped dead in my tracks, stunned. He passed us by without looking at us, but it was a full minute before I recovered the use of my legs. In all my life I have never felt so deeply humiliated.

Neither writer can be offered as a 'typical' witness, though it may be that in some elemental way everyone senses that branding can stigmatize the onlooker as well as the victim. And Jünger was certainly right in his instinct that the imposition of the star would leave a deep mark. In fact, it was the first anti-semitic measure of the Occupation to provoke spontaneous protest, however scattered. In solidarity some non-Jews took to wearing yellow stars; forty such cases, all of young people, came to the attention of Helmut Knochen, the SS officer who commanded the Sicherheitsdienst in Paris. Others wore yellow flowers, yellow handkerchiefs or pieces of yellow paper with *Auvergnat*, *Goy* or just their own Christian names written on them. In Paris some students sported badges reading *Juif*, allegedly an acronym for 'Jeunesse Universitaire Intellectuelle Française'. Such ridicule was quickly suppressed. But for the first time the Jews, so long abused or regarded with indifference, became objects of pity.

As the reactions of Jünger and Teissier du Cros suggest, pity concentrated largely on the young girls and the old men forced to wear the star: the two images which the stereotyping of latent anti-semitism and active xenophobia had least prepared people to see. Jewish children, of course, were victims of playground bullying. 'It was terrible,' one remembered. 'Every recreation, every day after school, the other children would taunt me; I couldn't bear it, I fought to the death.' But in the eyes of most adults such children bore so little resemblance to what they thought they feared or hated in Jews that the yellow star looked grotesque on them, even heart-rending. It did so on the elderly as well, particularly on the men who combined it with medals from the First World War. The reminder of their patriotic service came as a salutary shock to people inclined to imagine Jews as inherently foreign, ill-disposed or disloyal to France. The Germans banned the wearing of medals with the star as 'inappropriate', but wits had already labelled the star *Pour le sémite* in mocking allusion to *Pour le mérite*, the Prussian Order of Merit.

'A large part of the population shows little or no understanding of this distinctive emblem,' Knochen complained. Vichy agreed with his judgement and Vichy, though losing popular support, was always closer to the mood of the French than the Reich was or thought it had need to be. Vichy had never used language as violently anti-semitic as the Nazi propagandists or the Paris *collabos*, and it objected to the yellow star on the same grounds: not because it was anti-semitic but because it was the wrong note for anti-semitism to strike in France. Its stand was no more dignified than it was principled: Vichy politicians were reduced to using their influence to get exemptions granted to individual Jews in the Occupied Zone, like Bergson's widow, and in December to decreeing that Jews in the Southern Zone should have their *cartes d'identité* and other personal documents stamped *Juif* or *Juive*. But, in one of its few outright disagreements with the Reich's policy towards the Jews and its only act of refusal, it did not adopt the star in the Southern Zone.

When it came to internment and deportation, Vichy's reaction was its customary one of compliance. It had assumed the power to intern foreign Jews in its first wave of anti-semitic measures in 1940. The facilities already existed in the camps set up before the Occupation to house political undesirables: citizens of the Reich (who of course included many anti-Nazis and Jews), Communists whose patriotism had been rendered suspect by the Soviet Union's pact with the Reich, and Spanish Republicans who had fled after their defeat in the Civil War. The importance of the last group explains why the Pyrénées and their foothills should have made convenient locations for notorious camps like Le Vernet (in the valley of the Ariège south of Toulouse) and Gurs (in the Oloron valley). As a result of Vichy's measures the number of camps in the Southern Zone rose to more than thirty. Their fluctuating population, sometimes swollen by a new influx, sometimes reduced by the work of charity and relief organizations, stood at about 17,000 by the end of 1941. Eleven thousand of them were Jews.

It goes without saying that the conditions in which these prisoners lived were appalling, even according to a report Vichy itself had commissioned in April 1941. The sick might have to stagger, or be carried, 150 metres to the nearest lavatory. Even the healthy might lack underclothing or shoes, or be reduced to wearing garments pieced together from old blankets. With no better protection, without heating or even glazed windows in the huts where they slept, they might have to endure 20 degrees of frost. Medical attention was primitive, disease was rife and beatings were common. The cemetery at Gurs holds the bodies of more than 1,100 people, twenty of them Spanish and the rest Jewish. As for Le Vernet, Arthur Koestler – an inmate from October 1939 to January 1940 and on his way to becoming an expert on European prison conditions – wrote: 'In Liberal-Centigrade, Vernet was the zero-point of infamy; measured in Dachau-Fahrenheit it was still thirty-two degrees above zero.'

In the Occupied Zone it was German policy to hold Jews in three camps, all under French administration: at Beaune-la-Rolande and Pithiviers, both deep in the countryside of the Loiret, and at Drancy, on the outskirts of Paris. Together they held well over 7,000 prisoners by the end of 1941. All were adult men, most were foreign and most came from Paris. Those at Beaune-la-Rolande and Pithiviers had been interned in the first mass *rafle*, or round-up, on 14 May. Drancy had been opened for the 4,000 or more men who fell victim to a second *rafle* in the eleventh *arrondissement* on 20 August. An unfinished housing estate near Le Bourget airport, it was almost entirely lacking in electricity, water and toilets. One latrine in the courtyard served the whole complex. Prisoners slept fifty to a room, on bunk beds or planks, eventually just on straw. The authorities turned away relatives who tried to bring the prisoners food, and starvation and disease set in by September. When people began dying, their cause of death was described as *misère physiologique*. More than 900 – most of them French Jews, some of them veterans – were released in October, mainly to avoid further scandal. The population again increased when a party of Jewish hostages, taken in reprisal for resistance activity, was moved from Compiègne in the middle of March 1942.

By then the reputation of the place was so bad that prisoners who had escaped from Beaune-la-Rolande or Pithiviers would sometimes voluntarily return to those camps rather than run the risk of being arrested and sent to Drancy. Its real function was declared only a few days later. On 27 March 1942 gendarmes loaded the first train with prisoners and accompanied them to Novéant on the Moselle, the border with the annexed territory of Alsace and Lorraine, from which they continued east under German guard to Auschwitz. Of the 1,112 Jews – French as well as foreign – who made the first journey, one escaped *en route* and only twenty others returned. By the time the last train had left for Auschwitz on 17 August 1944, on the eve of the liberation of Paris, 76,000 Jews had been deported from France and the overwhelming majority of them had passed through Drancy. Only about 2,500, or 3 per cent, of the deportees survived.

The year when the deportations started, 1942, also marked their peak: its total of about 42,500 victims almost halved in 1943 and halved again in 1944. Dannecker was eager to meet Berlin's most exacting demands, even to make extravagant promises of his own. Vichy provided willing partners in Darquier de Pellepoix, Vallat's successor at the Commissariat Général aux Questions Juives, and René Bousquet, the civil servant and former *préfet* of the Marne whom Laval had appointed chief of the national police.* Dannecker, Darquier and Bousquet served together on the committee which planned the *grand rafle* of July 1942, originally designed to take place simultaneously in several cities of the Occupied Zone but in practice limited almost entirely to Paris. There it called for so many police-

---

* Bousquet was assassinated in June 1993 while awaiting trial for crimes against humanity.

men – about 9,000, divided into more than 1,500 teams – that students from the police academy had to be roped in to help.

They went to work at four o'clock in the morning on 16 July and finished the bulk of the operation the following day. By then twenty-four people had been killed resisting arrest and more than a hundred had killed themselves, sometimes in response to advance warning from well-disposed policemen. Some had died in the most public fashion, like the women clutching their babies who had thrown themselves from upper windows. In all 12,762 people had been arrested in Paris. Another 122 had been seized elsewhere, largely in the Gironde and its neighbouring departments, and about 840 fugitives were picked up by the end of August. The total was reached by seizing some French as well as foreign Jews, as in the previous *rafles*, but this time the victims were not just grown men: they included 5,919 women and 4,115 children below the age of 16. Whole families had been taken.

Those arrested in the Gironde and its region were taken to the camp at Mérignac, in the suburbs of Bordeaux.* In Paris the police took their prisoners first to their local *mairie* and then to the Vel d'Hiv, an indoor sports stadium used for winter cycle races, where some of them languished for days without even rudimentary facilities. Then they were transferred to Beaune-la-Rolande, Pithiviers, Compiègne and Drancy. Almost all the victims eventually made their way through Drancy, the waiting-room for Auschwitz. The first train, with the customary shipment of about 1,000 people on board, left on 19 July.

The round-up had been codenamed *vent printanier*, or spring wind, and the label is just one proof of the delays which had bedevilled its planning. The last had been caused by the need to avoid the embarrassment of carrying it out on 14 July, the greatest festival in France's republican calendar. Nor had delays been the only problem. Berlin had hoped to deport 100,000 Jews by the end of the year. Dannecker had set himself a target of 40,000 in the first three months of concentrated work. It proved wildly unrealistic, despite the relaxation of virtually all the criteria of eligibility first proposed for deportees. The age limits, originally set at 19 and 40, were broad-

---

* The Vichy secretary-general in the Gironde in charge of the round-ups and deportations was Maurice Papon, after the war Préfet de Police for Paris, Gaullist politician and a minister in Raymond Barre's cabinet. He was indicted for crimes against humanity in September 1996.

ened to 16 and 50; then healthy 15-year-olds were included, together with women up to 55 and men up to 60. The exemption of pregnant women, nursing mothers and men or women married to non-Jews was apparently forgotten. So was the plan to target only stateless Jews and Jews from Germany, Austria, Poland, Czechoslovakia and the Soviet Union, and to avoid Jews from neutral countries or countries allied with the West. And yet the *grand rafle* still succeeded in netting only a little more than half the 22,000 people Dannecker had aimed for that month.

That made Vichy's co-operation in the process not just of internment but of deportation all the more necessary. Indeed, Dannecker was already touring the camps of the Southern Zone on 16 July, leaving supervision of the *rafle* in Paris to a deputy, Heinz Röthke. There he selected for deportation about 4,700 foreign Jews, mainly exiles from the Reich; the first of them, from Gurs and the transit centre at Les Milles near Aix-en-Provence, were sent to Drancy on 5 August. They were joined not just by the other designated prisoners from the camps but also by 6,594 people arrested in *rafles* in the Southern Zone towards the end of the month.

Vichy had stated its attitude to deportation in a cautious document of 26 June – so cautious, indeed, that it avoided using the term 'deportation' altogether and instead spoke of 'measures of constraint'. It acknowledged that the 'Jewish problem' had been handled in a severe fashion in Germany but warned: 'French opinion would have difficulty accepting identical measures in France, where the problem has never been as acute.' When deportation was mentioned by name at a cabinet meeting of 3 July, Laval had insisted on the need to distinguish in the Southern Zone between French Jews and foreign Jews, especially those from the territory of the Reich itself. The remark hinted at a sliding scale of expendability which, in its full extent, attached no value at all to German Jews, little or none to other foreign Jews, some unspecified value to French Jews, and sentimental value to Jewish war veterans. Apologists would later represent this as a canny line of defence which required Vichy to light small blazes to contain the forest fire: sacrificing the foreign Jews, beginning with the German Jews, in the hope of saving native ones.

Such an interpretation conveniently overlooks the basic facts of Vichy's position. Far from challenging the Reich's policy of deportation, it never even quibbled with the scale or the schedule of the deportations proposed. It did not intervene to help the French Jews seized in the Occupied Zone, or to protect the prisoners in its own internment camps. In short, as Asher Cohen and other recent historians have been quick to argue, it complied with what it knew very well was only the first step in a campaign which the Reich had every intention of prosecuting with extreme vigour. And its manner of doing so was hardly that of reluctant or fearful concession. In distinguishing between expendable and non-expendable Jews, for example, Laval did not sound like a man forced against principle into distasteful expedients. He spoke of the French Jews as *Juifs français*, denying them the term *Israélites* and conceding the very label which was a licence for their persecution. As for the German Jews, they were *déchets*: refuse.

The deportations from the Southern Zone underlined all those reasons for profound disquiet which the *grand rafle* itself had already given, had already made public, on a grand scale. The victims might be shunted to the Vel d'Hiv, where photographs were not allowed, and then to Drancy, where people in the apartment blocks overlooking the camp did not dare to talk among themselves about what was going on, and then to an unnamed destination in the east. But amid the night and fog certain things could be clearly seen, and they confirmed the worst fears which the imposition of the yellow star had aroused. It was known that the victims could include French as well as foreign Jews, and that fact alone could give pause for thought to those who had gone along with anti-semitic measures in the vague belief that the Jews were just unwelcome foreigners, rather than neighbours whose Jewishness had gone unremarked a few years before. It was known that young children, the most pitied victims of the yellow star, were among not just those arrested but those deported as well. Indeed, this fact received considerable publicity since they were herded on the eastbound trains only in the face of Eichmann's hesitation and at Laval's insistence.

Laval explained his extraordinary intervention as a desire to keep families together rather than leave children stranded in France without their parents. Few historians can accept this at face value, though most agree that in fact Laval was probably also demonstrating his ignorance of the fate that awaited the children at Auschwitz – his ignorance, indeed, of Auschwitz and the whole policy of genocide to which the Reich was committed. He was not a passionate anti-semite driven by ideological hatred but an opportunist driven by ambition. If he had been privy to the Final Solution, he would have taken care to keep silent about the children. Yet his ignorance, like that of all the others who later protested their ignorance of the Holocaust, was increasingly just technical and the result of choice. The deportation of children, and of the sick and the old, did not square with the Reich's camouflage talk of labour camps. And if resettlement rather than forced labour was the goal, then surely the Reich owed him and he owed the French some details? It was not enough to talk vaguely, as Laval did, of the Reich's intention to establish a Jewish state somewhere in eastern Europe. But he chose not to inquire further because it was easier not to know. It was easier to go along with the general drift of what the occupiers were doing and, by his enthusiasm in the matter of the children, score a few points which might be to his advantage in a future round of bargaining.

Not everyone could bring themselves to choose such ignorance. And, though they might have lacked precise answers to their questions, those who did not choose it also had to add Vichy's complicity in what the Reich was doing to their most urgent concerns. This complicity, announced from the start of the Vichy regime and reaffirmed by Laval's contribution to the *grand rafle*, was seen in its simplest and most painful form in the street scenes when French policemen, not Germans, had taken Jews from their houses in Paris. Madame Rado, arrested with her four children at her home in the Rue du Faubourg Saint-Antoine, remembered the shame she had felt at being watched by the crowds who had gathered. She did not know what they were thinking: 'Their expressions were empty, apparently indifferent.' In (ironically enough) the Place Voltaire one woman shouted, 'Well done! Well done! They can all go to hell.' A man standing next to her said, 'After them, it'll be us. Poor people.'

Two voices: one of unquenched hatred, the other of troubled compassion. The first voice had already been heard many times during the Occupation and its cry would continue. But the second voice had begun to make itself heard more and more loudly. It was heard, for example, from churchmen such as Cardinal Gerlier of Lyon, the only cardinal in the Southern Zone and a man hitherto ready, like many French Catholics, to agree with Vichy on the existence of a 'Jewish problem'. Archbishop Saliège of Toulouse spoke out with particular vigour. His pastoral letter, read out on Sunday 23 August in all the churches of his archdiocese, said in part: 'You cannot do whatever you wish against these men, against these women, against these fathers and mothers. They are part of mankind. They are our brothers.' Such protest marked a turning-point in the reactions of the Catholic establishment and its attitude to the regime which had courted its approval. Catholic families, schools and organizations like Père Chaillet's l'Amitié Chrétienne began to hide and shelter potential victims, joining Protestants swayed by memories of the persecution their own sect had suffered in earlier centuries. Pastor Marc Boegner, president of the National Protestant Federation, had already attacked the *statut des Juifs* in a public letter of March 1941; now he denounced the *rafles* in a statement read from Protestant pulpits in September.

The public mood was changing, and not the least significant part of the change was in the mood of the Jews themselves. They had begun the Occupation divided in reality as in public perception, with 'assimilated' *Israélites* distant and often aloof from 'unassimilated' *Juifs*. They had been demoralized by the machinery of discrimination and persecution which isolated them, made them almost absent from the places they lived in. Now, as the threat of absence became brutally literal, their choices were more sharply defined, more urgent even than for other people in France. The differing fates or courses of action open to them are epitomized in the three-part dedication to the history book Jacques Adler has written about experiences he himself survived. The first part of the dedication is to his father, murdered in Birkenau, and the second is to the French who saved his mother and sister. The third is to his Jewish comrades in the Resistance.

PART III

Resistance and Liberation

If you succeed, you're a hero; if you fail, you're a *couillon* [arsehole].
De Gaulle, making his tank attack at Montcornet
in May 1940

5

Living in Fear, Living in Hope

We have lived in fear, now we shall live in hope.
Tristan Bernard to his wife as they were arrested
in the *grand rafle*

THE FIFTEEN OR SO months from the autumn of 1941 to the end
of 1942 were a special period. They marked a turning-point in
the Occupation, a change which many of those who lived through it
felt vibrantly on the pulse and which most historians now label as
decisive. In the aftermath of 1940 the popular mood remained
defeatist and for the most part compliant. For a long time France,
which had been frighteningly easy to conquer, proved quite as
easy to occupy. During the first year of the Occupation, the
Kommandant von Gross-Paris had at his disposal only two
high-ranking specialists and five or six inspectors to supervise the
French police in his region. Indeed, the Germans were able to hold
and administer the whole country with a mere 30,000 men, a ratio of
only one soldier or official to every 1,000 French people. But in the
autumn of 1941 the atmosphere began to change and occupation
stopped being so easy for the conquerors.

It was not that people began to feel discontent: they had felt that
ever since the occupiers had first arrived. It was rather that discontent was transposed into a new and active key. Inconvenience,
hardship and a sense of humiliation had been present from the start,
but they had been so taken for granted – in some cases, even perversely welcomed – that they were virtually subsumed into the dreary
round of ordinary life. Now, at last, they took on the status of grievances: things to resent, things to protest, even things to hope to
change. And the critical point about this list of verbs is that, in

however timid and fragile a form, hope had begun to re-enter the national vocabulary. France was coming out of her depression.

Though the summer of 1942 saw the first and largest wave of deportations, the suffering of the Jews did not bring about this change alone. It was not even the main factor in a process that was already well under way. What happened to the Jews never dictated the popular mood in France during the Occupation: it was always at best something of only secondary importance, to opponents and supporters of the new status quo alike. And by itself the spectacle of the Jews being rounded up and herded on to the east-bound trains, and of the Vichy government's compliance with these measures, might merely have depressed even further those still inclined to care, those not taken in by the propaganda and those not just absorbed in the business of day-to-day survival.

There were other factors at work on both the domestic and the international front, conspiring together to challenge the assumptions which had created the passivity of 1940. Events inside France exploded the hope that the Germans would prove 'correct' in their Occupation, and that Pétain and his ministers could or would protect the French when correctness came to an end. Events outside France undermined the belief, until then axiomatic, that Hitler's armies were invincible. The Reich, it emerged, was at once more brutal in its treatment of the French and less certain of victory on all fronts than people had at first supposed.

THE STRONGEST ARGUMENT which the realists of 1940, who saw no alternative to the path of collaboration, had on their side was the international picture which the fall of France had created. If France herself could be defeated, and defeated so easily and so quickly, then surely Britain could not be far behind? Her surrender would come in a matter of weeks, thought men like Pétain and Weygand, seeking to assuage hurt pride by predicting the humiliation of an ally they had never really trusted.

Britain's survival in the summer and autumn of 1940 did not entirely confound the realists. It could easily be attributed more to Hitler's lack of interest in pushing ahead with plans for a cross-Channel invasion than to the new determination Churchill's leadership had brought to Britain's war against the Reich. The timetable for Britain's withdrawal from the battlefield might have been extended, and so the terms Churchill could hope to negotiate with Germany might have improved, but nothing else had changed. Those who wished could still argue that Britain had as bad a record as France in making military preparations and almost as bad a record in summoning up the stomach for a fight. Many in France held to this view, and more clung to their ingrained suspicion of their neighbour across the Channel. After all, Britain still could not be relied on to prosecute any cause but its own. Britain was still *la perfide Albion*, with a centuries-old reputation for reneging on international proclamations, commitments and treaties whenever it proved expedient.

In practical terms, moreover, Britain still stood alone. Despite the example of the First World War, when British and French generals – Pétain among them – had spent months quite openly waiting for the Americans to arrive, the prospect of American intervention in the European catastrophe of 1940 seemed remote and unlikely. Reynaud's last-minute appeal to President Roosevelt before his fall from power had been the gesture of a man ready to grasp at straws, and its rejection had surprised nobody. Since the First World War the mood of the American people had sunk into a wary isolationism which it took all Roosevelt's obstinate energy to overcome. When the United States did finally enter the war in December 1941, the decision was triggered not by events in Europe but by the Japanese attack on Pearl Harbor: first and foremost, it signalled the opening of a Pacific theatre. Hitler's declaration of war on the United States, which his treaty obligations to Japan did not demand, reflected his confidence that the Americans would not greatly affect the course of events in Europe. And, however rash such confidence would come to look, others shared it at the time. In France, the enlargement of the conflict might have confirmed some in their hope that the fall of France had ended a battle rather than the war, but the clash of arms remained too distant and too faint to bring any dramatic change.

The bleakness of their perspective left people acquiescent in their fate. The future, for those who could bring themselves to contemplate it rather than immersing themselves in the difficulties of their present lives, seemed to hold a New European Order which left the map of nations permanently redrawn. Only a few events seemed to relieve the prevailing gloom, and the hopes they inspired for the most part turned out to be short-lived. The Italian invasion of Greece in the autumn of 1940 offered a particularly sad example. The setbacks which the Italians met provoked glee in France: 'If you want to visit Italy, join the Greek army.' But the joke said more about the low regard the French had for Italian soldiers, and the resentment left smouldering by the concessions accorded Mussolini in the 1940 armistice, than it did about any real belief that the power of the Axis was beginning to fail.

In any event, the Reich easily confirmed its reputation by mopping up Greece the following spring, and Yugoslavia too. In Greece the 'heroic madness' of resistance made itself felt almost immediately, in defiant gestures like the removal of the swastika flag from the Acropolis only days after it had first been flown there. In Yugoslavia the new puppet Croat state almost immediately drove the Serbs into the arms of the nationalist Chetniks and Tito's Partisans. But in France, as she neared the first anniversary of her defeat, there was as yet no answering spirit.

Hitler's invasion of the Soviet Union proved a different matter. The Soviet Union had been the wild card in the pack which the democracies of western Europe had shuffled as they moved clumsily and unenthusiastically towards war in 1939. It remained at once a potent yet ambiguous force, a state newly constituted and barely understood, an international power as yet untested, whether as enemy or ally. Perhaps the Soviet Union was Europe's best hope of checking the rise of Hitler's Reich? Or perhaps, as the embodiment of Bolshevism, it was the real enemy to be feared, and perhaps Hitler's Reich was the best bulwark against it? Britain and France had debated these questions, and struggled with all the divisive ideological ramifications they suggested, in the pre-war years. The outbreak of war did nothing to end a debate which would continue to muddle popular opinion and blunt international policy.

Hitler cut through such questions by regarding the Soviet Union as the greatest prize his ambition could propose. Most historians would probably agree that, had he pursued his goal directly and unleashed his armies on the Eastern Front immediately after conquering Poland, France and Britain might well have stood aside – just as, for all practical purposes, they had already done when Poland was invaded. The history of the war, the Reich and Europe would then have proceeded along radically different lines. But, perhaps because of the very importance he attached to it, Hitler had not pursued his ambition so directly. Instead, he had relied on the pact with Stalin forged in August 1939 to secure his Eastern Front and, after Poland, had turned his attention to France.

When the Reich's attack on the Soviet Union did finally come in June 1941, nobody in France or Britain doubted its importance. At the very least, it redrew the battle lines of Europe in the most dramatic way. Nor did people need to wait for the difficulties which the German campaign encountered to suspect that this time the Reich might have bitten off more than it could chew. The suspicion was not stilled by early German successes, and it was confirmed by the reverses Germany met towards the close of 1942 and by Field Marshal Paulus' humiliating surrender at Stalingrad in early 1943. Doubt had come early and easily to the French in particular, from the memory of their own military past. If conquering Russia was the supreme test of a daring leader and his previously invincible army, had not even Napoleon and his *Grande Armée* failed the test?

'*Je souhaite la victoire de l'Allemagne*,' Laval told his radio audience on 22 June 1942, the first anniversary of Germany's attack on the Soviet Union: 'I am hoping for a German victory because, without it, tomorrow Bolshevism will set in everywhere.' Lucien Rebatet voiced the same hope, in almost identical language, in his memoir *Les Décombres* (*The Ruins*), published that October: 'I hope for a German victory because the war they are waging is also *my* war, our war.' But Rebatet belonged to the collaborationist set in Paris, which never hesitated to use its privilege of extreme utterance, while Laval spoke for a regime normally careful to keep its rhetoric fuzzy. Privately he justified his bluntness in characteristic terms. He was busy negotiating the release of French prisoners-of-war and wanted to improve his bargaining position with the Germans: 'a phrase like that can bring back 100,000 prisoners', he claimed at the time. (He later raised the number to an even less plausible 200,000.) People might soon forget the occasion for Laval's speech, and his apparent motive for making it, but the words themselves lodged in the public memory. They did more than anything else he said during his time in power – even his public insistence that the Jewish children snatched up in the *grand rafle* be deported with their parents – to ensure he was executed after Liberation.

The intensity of the dislike Laval provoked has helped to obscure the two most salient points about what he actually said. The first is that he phrased his statement of support as a hope or a wish for German victory. In June 1940, or even June 1941, he would have taken German victory for granted: that assumption was fundamental to the realism, the *collaboration à raison*, on which he and fellow-politicians at Vichy had staked their careers. It was thanks to the Russian campaign, even before the siege of Stalingrad had begun, that his belief in German victory had been qualified into mere hope. The second point is that Laval went on, specifically and immediately, to link his hope for German victory to the Reich's role as the declared enemy of Bolshevism throughout Europe.

The impact of the Russian campaign, not just on far-away battlefields but on political alignments inside France herself, was immense. In a sense, it simplified matters. It brought about, or restored, what most people saw as the real situation which the Nazi-Soviet pact between 1939 and 1941 had muddled. Hitler's international appeal had always lain partly, if not chiefly, in his anti-Bolshevism during a period when Bolshevism was seen not just as a system governing the Soviet state but as a domestic threat inside the nations of western Europe. Even those not attracted by Nazism on other grounds could find this aspect of Hitler's policy enough to make him tolerable, in fact distinctly useful. Whatever doubts it might have inspired in purely strategic terms, the German invasion of the Soviet Union was welcomed by the Vichyite Right as strengthening its ideological position. Publicly and dramatically, it emphasized the safest and most broadly acceptable ground of common cause with the Reich.

The Vichy regime lost no time in capitalizing on the advantage it had been handed and in commending Hitler as the leader of an anti-Bolshevik crusade prosecuted on the international scene as well as on the home front. The benign portrait of Pétain soon appeared on posters urging the French to fight alongside Hitler's armies on the Eastern Front. The campaign was organized by the Légion des Volontaires Français contre le Bolchevisme, as it was called in the Occupied Zone, or the Légion Tricolore, as it was known in the Southern Zone. Hitler gave it his approval, though the conditions he attached also betrayed how unwelcome he found the idea of French troops taking any real part in what he hoped would be a quick victory: the initiative for recruitment had to come from approved political parties in France; the recruits could not number more than 15,000; and Vichy could not ask for any favours in return. The last condition shrewdly forestalled exactly what Vichy had in mind, eager as it always was to find a bargaining counter that might be used to reduce the bill for the Occupation or get back some of the prisoners-of-war from Germany.

The implicit rebuff stopped Vichy from giving the Légion official status, but it did not stop politicians proffering their blessing. Laval took his place on the platform with Marcel Déat, leader of the Rassemblement National Populaire, at a ceremony in Versailles honouring the first batch of recruits on 27 August. Both were wounded by a would-be assassin's bullets during the proceedings. The warning did not deter other collaborationists from rushing to embrace the Légion. Eugène Deloncle, *cagoulard* and bomber of Paris synagogues, campaigned on its behalf in the capital; Joseph Darnand, future leader of the Milice, headed its office in Nice. Déat's rival demagogue, Jacques Doriot of the Parti Populaire Français, actually volunteered for duty in the Soviet Union – enhancing his prestige while weakening his effectiveness by his absence, and so inadvertently serving the German design that he be kept on the back burner as a potential counter to Laval's influence, should one be needed. The Légion's committee of honour was stuffed with other familiar names from the Right: the journalist Jean Luchaire, for example, and dotty old Alphonse de Châteaubriant of Groupe Collaboration. The presence of two Abels – Abel Hermant and Abel Bonnard – prompted the journalist and *résistant* Jean Paulhan to ask, in a bitter quatrain, just what the Cains were doing?

Yet for all the support, the propaganda and the impressive roster of names, the Légion pursued a career as miserably ineffective as all the other military and para-military organizations owing their existence to German and Vichyite patronage. It never even began to come near its recruiting target. Barely 3,000 men had come forward by the end of August, and a sizeable number of them proved unfit for service. Those who did pass the test – idealists, adventurers, crackpots, men desperate for bed and board at any price – were sent to Germany for training. There they signed a modified oath of allegiance to the Führer and donned German *feldgrau*, though in concession to national sensibilities they were allowed to wear French *réséda* while home on leave. At the Eastern Front they were used as cannon-fodder in battles which had an unquenchable appetite for cannon-fodder. In July 1944 those who had managed to survive were regrouped into a special division of the Waffen-SS, the Charlemagne, whose remnants were among the troops defending Hitler's bunker in Berlin during the last days of the Reich in April and May 1945.

Long before this story had dragged its way to a conclusion, even before German reverses on the Eastern Front had made an impact on French opinion, there were signs that Hitler's invasion of the Soviet Union would not benefit the Vichy regime as it had hoped. It was inevitable, of course, that Vichy's stock should have declined from its peak in June 1940 as the hollowness of the hopes and claims that had brought it to power was exposed. Many events – indeed, virtually all the major events of the Occupation – conspired in that direction, not least the continuing revelation of Vichy's powerless complicity in whatever the occupiers decided to impose on France or do to her people. But, by raising doubts about the invincibility of the Reich, the campaign on the Eastern Front would increasingly deprive Vichy of its most potent rationale: stick with the winners.

By August 1941 Pétain was already detecting an 'ill wind'. On the radio he warned: 'Anxiety is spreading, doubt is taking hold. The authority of my government is being challenged, its orders are often being carried out badly.' Privately he complained to his court biographer René Benjamin: 'The French people have forsaken me.' The melodramatic extravagance and the readiness to identify himself with Joan of Arc – or Christ – betray a monstrous egotism. But his vanity made Pétain quick to detect any flagging in his popularity, and gave him a prescience which Laval, for all his boasted realism, did not possess. Vichy's reputation had embarked on the downward path which would reach its next significant trough at the end of 1942. In November that year, at the very time when the siege of Stalingrad was getting under way and Anglo-Gaullist troops were scoring their first successes in north Africa, the occupiers were able to cross the demarcation line and take over the Southern Zone without the least show of resistance from Vichy.

In fact, the real beneficiary of Hitler's Soviet campaign was not Vichy and the Right but the far Left. Until Hitler's invasion of the Soviet Union, the French Communist Party had for several years been – in a sense like the Soviet Union itself – a sleeping giant. In its case, though, inactivity stemmed from the confusion into which the gyrations of world politicians had thrown it. From 1936 until 1939 the Party had taken a clear-cut stance based on its anti-fascism: supporting increased military expenditure to further the international struggle, advocating intervention on behalf of the Republicans against Franco in the Spanish Civil War and, uniquely among French political parties, voting solidly against the Munich agreement with Hitler. But Stalin's pact with Hitler had baffled it and thwarted its energy.

At least officially, the Party applauded the pact, as it was obliged to applaud all the foreign policies of the Soviet Union, including the invasion of Finland shortly afterwards. Its support gave the advantage to its opponents. Within a month of the pact, it was banned; during the phoney war its publications were suppressed, its elected deputies unseated, and its officials and militants harassed or arrested. For many of the French, such persecution had the double advantage of being both a revenge on long-distrusted political enemies and a distraction from the real issues posed by the outbreak of war with the Reich. In fact, the Party's structure and psychology enabled it to survive such attacks and adapt to clandestine existence. Yet it could not escape the ideological quandary into which it had been plunged. The unexpected *rapprochement* between Bolshevism and Nazism on the international scene robbed its arguments of coherence and threatened the loyalty of its supporters. It was left denouncing the Franco-British declaration of war in 1939 as a quarrel between capitalist and imperialist powers, a war of others, only to issue a belated call for the people of Paris to be armed in self-defence when France was invaded the following year.

The Occupation further compounded its problems, not least by adding the occupiers and Vichy to the list of enemies already determined to extinguish it. The Germans, of course, were not hindered by their non-aggression treaty with Stalin from harrying Bolsheviks as vigorously in France as they did in any of the other territories they controlled. More than a thousand Party members were arrested in Paris alone during the weeks following the armistice. Such persecution was one of several obvious reasons why individual Communists were among the first and sharpest critics of Pétain and the earliest active opponents of the Occupation. Yet corporately the Party was adrift, almost tongue-tied and incapable of giving clear guidance. Its predicament was aptly symbolized in the fortunes of its leader, Maurice Thorez, who had deserted from the army and taken refuge in the Soviet Union in October 1939, and in the fortunes of its newspaper, *L'Humanité*, which underwent the double humiliation of requesting and being refused permission from the occupiers to appear legally. It was no wonder that many ordinary Communist supporters should have been left every bit as demoralized as the rest of the nation.

June 1941 ended this ideological muddle. By again identifying Hitler as the enemy of the Soviet Union it clarified matters for the

Communists as much as for those on the Right, but to much greater practical effect. The Right expended itself in declarations from Laval as likely to alienate as to secure popular support and in pathetic projects like the Légion des Volontaires Français. In contrast, the released energy of the Communist Party brought real strength to the task of opposing the occupiers: ideological commitment, disciplined organization and, particularly useful, experience from the immediate past in the arts of clandestine survival. '*Luttez contre le Bolchevisme*', urged Vichy: 'Fight Bolshevism'. That slogan struck a familiar note but one which would sound increasingly irrelevant to issues in France. '*A chacun son boche*', urged the Communists: 'To each his German'. That militant threat struck a more immediate chord.

I<small>T DID</small> so because events in France herself were changing the mood of non-Communists as well as Communists, and would eventually touch some of those determined to seek refuge in being 'non-political'. In the first shock of defeat people had consoled themselves that the Germans were at least behaving correctly. Their relief had been almost hysterical, as much a symptom of desperation as the fear of atrocities which had preceded it. The German propaganda machine had adroitly fostered it. Its hollow rhetoric of respect for France's sovereignty and her traditions, even for her army and its performance in the field, was given colour at the ordinary level of life by well-briefed Wehrmacht soldiers admiring babies in the public parks and offering their seats to women on the Métro. France had been misled into war and France had been beaten, said the Germans, but in a fair fight and by a civilized enemy – almost, it would seem, by an admiring ally. And the French had eagerly accepted the propaganda because at that time the alternative was almost unthinkable.

The charade could not last forever. The illusion with which the French consoled themselves was bound to die sooner or later, and its death was bound to be a major psychological event, perhaps the major psychological event of the Occupation. It happened, of course, at different times and in different circumstances for different people, but for most it had happened before the *rafles* of 1942 got under way. They came as public confirmation of something already privately experienced and preserved in the memory as carefully as the moment when people had first seen a German soldier or a swastika flag flying from a public building.

To many Parisians, for example, the moment had come as early as December 1940 with the obscure fate of an obscure man. Jacques Bonsergent was 28 and an engineer. On 10 November 1940 he was walking with friends along the Rue du Havre, leading from the Gare Saint-Lazare to the Boulevard Haussmann. One of them, not Bonsergent, accidentally jostled some German soldiers and in the argument that followed one of them, again not Bonsergent, was foolish enough to raise his fist to a sergeant. It is not clear if any blows were actually struck. Nor is it clear why the Germans chose to arrest Bonsergent and Bonsergent alone, though he seems to have been scarcely more than a witness to a quarrel which was in itself trivial. When he appeared before a German military tribunal on 5 December he insisted on taking responsibility for the incident and received a death sentence. His appeal was turned down on 22 December and a firing squad executed him at Vincennes prison the following day.

Bonsergent was by no means the first person to be executed during the Occupation, the first civilian casualty in the war that was supposed to have ended with the June armistice. In Bordeaux on 28 August, two and a half months before the incident in the Rue du Havre, the local newspaper had reported the case of Israël Karp, a young Jew of Polish origins arrested, tried and shot for shaking a stick at a parade of German troops near the railway station. *Résistants* usually identified their first martyr as Pierre Roche, a 19-year-old Communist who cut the telephone cable between Royan and La Rochelle. He died on 7 September, after the Germans had judged the prison sentence imposed by a French court too mild. On 10 September Otto von Stülpnagel the Militärbefehlshaber, or military commander-in-chief of the Occupied Zone, officially proclaimed his intention of punishing sabotage with death. Scrutiny of the provincial press after that date reveals other deaths, usually forgotten and – since sabotage is a conveniently elastic term – sometimes provoked by small actions. Louis Lallier, a 25-year-old farmworker, was executed in Epinal on 11 September and Marcel Drossier, a mechanic, in Rennes on 12 September. A lumberjack called Hérault was executed in the department of the Oise in October. In November two men died in the Somme and another died in Bordeaux, the second execution in a city which did not then have a reputation for being particularly troublesome to the authorities.

Yet Bonsergent was the first person to die in Paris and, as rumour quickly asserted, he had died for an absurdly trivial reason. The

Germans, moreover, chose to make a public example of his fate by proclaiming it on posters stuck up on walls throughout the city. Many were torn down. A sticker warning that such vandalism would be regarded as sabotage and punished with appropriate severity did not stop people showing their feelings, nor did the use of gendarmes to guard the posters. Jean Bruller, who became the pseudonymous Vercors of *Le Silence de la mer* in 1942, was not alone in being 'transfixed' by the brutal announcement. All round him 'people stopped, read, wordlessly exchanged glances. Some of them bared their heads as if in the presence of the dead.' By the day after Christmas, he noted, the posters were 'surrounded by flowers, like so many tombs. Little flowers of every kind, mounted on pins, had been stuck on the posters during the night – real flowers and artificial ones, paper pansies, celluloid roses, small French and British flags.' In some neighbourhoods the tributes littered the pavements.

Simone de Beauvoir was quick to underline that it was not just an individual whose death people mourned, but the death of the whole illusion which had so far prevailed: 'for the first time these correct people who occupied our country were officially telling us that they had executed a Frenchman guilty of not bowing his head to them'. They mourned it again on 1 January 1941 when, via the BBC, the Gaullists in London urged people to mark the New Year by staying indoors between three and four o'clock in the afternoon. The call was widely heeded and not just in Paris, despite German arrangements to distribute free potatoes during the proscribed hour, but also in other towns and even villages throughout the Occupied Zone. André Weil-Curiel (a Socialist lawyer and one of the first agents sent by de Gaulle from London) described the scene in Quimper:

> At a quarter to three pedestrians crowded all the streets. At five to three, they had gone and, from behind the ground-floor windows on either side of the street, people signalled those still outdoors to hurry up and reminded them of the time. After three o'clock, their invitations grew more urgent and their gestures menacing. . . . And at four o'clock, like a class being let out of school, people hurried into the streets again, laughing and bumping into each other in their happiness.

So New Year's Day 1941 saw the first sign of organized public protest against the Occupation, the first stirring of the mood which emerged as a palpable force in 1942. And Vercors vividly conjured up the individual realization from which it sprang when he described how he had felt walking away from the first poster he had seen announcing Bonsergent's death, down the Boulevard Saint-Michel and past other copies of the same poster with silent crowds gathered round them: 'At the same time as pain and anger, a feeling of excitement was coursing through me, as if I had thought, curiously: "At last!" It was the first blood spilled.'

BLOOD WILL HAVE BLOOD: this terrible logic always dictated the course of events during the Occupation. So it was inevitable that the shedding of French blood by the occupiers would call forth the shedding of German blood by the occupied. The same logic meant that this response would in turn fuel an accelerating cycle of assassination and reprisal which destroyed the Germans' show of correctness and eventually went on to challenge even the Germans' claim to preside over any form of order, however brutally they sought to impose it.

Yet circumstances also guaranteed that this did not come about easily or quickly. For one thing, the mood of the French in general had to undergo further change: they might have supported a passive show of protest like the boycott of the streets on New Year's Day 1941, but that still left them a long way from supporting, or even tolerating, acts of violent resistance, much less an organized campaign of violent resistance. Nor was the problem simply one of popular opinion. That was, after all, a secondary matter to the hard core of people determined to oppose the occupiers by whatever means came to hand. Special difficulties dogged the transformation of individual outrage into even individual acts of resistance, let alone into determined group action. Indeed, those difficulties were never completely overcome. Though they might have been small in number, there were certainly *résistants* in France from the start, and so there was resistance, which grew from insignificance to play a part in how the drama of the Occupation was acted out. But building the Resistance of popular legend, an organized and unified movement, a force sufficiently large and effective to alter the fate of France: that was another matter.

For the first activists resistance began with what Jean Cassou and others have called a *refus absurde*, an absurd refusal to accept the facts of the time, an apparent denial of common sense and self-interest.

So unalterable and so overwhelming did France's plight seem, indeed, that one might almost call the refusal not just absurd but deliberately absurdist: a gesture signifying lack of harmony with a world which was itself out of harmony. Yet for some the gesture came so instinctively that they never acknowledged the armistice of 1940, never observed an interlude of peace between the war on the battlefield and the war by other means. Even as France collapsed into defeat, they were already considering how the fight could be continued on new fronts. De Gaulle – to take the most famous instance – proceeded with calm logic from investigating the possibility of a Breton redoubt and advocating the scheme for Anglo-French union to boarding General Spears' plane for London on the very day Pétain first broadcast his call for an end to the fighting. That bold decision would eventually give a man with a controversial reputation among fellow-soldiers and virtually no reputation outside the army a unique influence over events in France.

Jean Moulin, whose reputation and influence would stand second only to de Gaulle's, made his first gesture of refusal on the same day de Gaulle chose exile. A high-flying civil servant, he had been appointed a *sous-préfet* in 1925, which made him, at 26, the youngest *sous-préfet* in France; by 1940 he had become, at 41, the youngest *préfet*. The department assigned him was the Eure-et-Loir, administered from Chartres. On 17 June the newly arrived Germans required him to endorse a statement blaming the massacre of civilians at the nearby hamlet of La Taye on fleeing Senegalese troops belonging to the French army. Nazi ideology and French prejudice made the blacks serving in the north African regiments convenient scapegoats for the accidents and atrocities of war. But an inspection of the bodies convinced Moulin that they had died from artillery fire, far more likely to have come from the advancing Germans, and so he refused to put his name to the official story.

He was beaten up and thrown into a makeshift prison cell for the night. There he accepted that he had reached the limits of his endurance and that he would give in when torture resumed the next morning:

And yet I could not sign. I could not become an accomplice to this hideous plot which could have been thought up only by maddened sadists. I could not sanction this outrage against the French army and I could not dishonour myself.

Anything rather than that, anything, even death.

Death?. . . Since the outbreak of the war, like thousands of French people, I had come to terms with it. Since then, I had seen it close up many times. . . . It did not scare me.

And so he carried his original refusal to endorse German propaganda to the ultimate *refus absurde*: using some broken glass still littering the floor of his cell after a bombardment, he cut his throat. 'When one's mind is made up,' he wrote detachedly, 'it is simple to follow the demands of what one believes to be one's duty.'

Moulin survived the attempt at suicide, though his voice was left husky and his throat distinctively scarred. The Germans released him to avoid further embarrassment and Vichy's Ministry of the Interior sacked him from his post as *préfet* in November. He then went underground, making his way via Spain to London to join the Free French in October 1941. De Gaulle appointed him his delegate-general to the occupied territories – in effect, ambassador to *résistants*. On two long and dangerous missions in France, the first begun in January 1942 and the second in March 1943, Moulin did more than any other person to give resistance more than local organization and local power, linking the movements which had begun to emerge with each other and with London. His work ended abruptly with his betrayal and capture at Caluire, a suburb of Lyon, in June 1943; his death somewhere on the train journey toward further interrogation in Germany gave resistance its most honoured martyr. 'It was not he who made the regiments,' said François Mauriac when Moulin's remains were finally interred in the Panthéon in 1964, 'but it was he who made the army.'

Moulin's brand of heroism is given to few people; to the rest it remains simply a mystery to be admired. And few people had to confront a crisis of conscience as naked as the one he faced in his cell in 1940. But many were prompted less dramatically by some passing incident to the same realization that Vercors had experienced after learning the news of Bonsergent's execution. 'At last!': the moment when outrage crystallized almost involuntarily into commitment. Writings by *résistants* themselves, particularly the earliest ones whom the French honour as *résistants de la première heure*, place great emphasis on these private dramas of self-confrontation, and they show that by no means all were provoked by events as well-publicized as Bonsergent's execution.

Joseph Barthelet from Metz, who adopted the codename of Boulaya (Beard), told George Millar, a British agent working for Special Operations Executive (SOE), how 'the climax came' when some friends were arrested and he saw one of them being taken from the local jail to the Feldgendarmerie for questioning:

> I recognized him only by his hat. Only by his hat, I tell you, and because I was waiting on the roadside to see him pass. I saw his face all right, but there was no skin on it, and he could not see me. Both his poor eyes had been closed into two purple and yellow bruises.

Others found their self-defining moment triggered not by German brutality but by the behaviour of their fellow-countrymen. For Henri Frenay it was simply the look of contempt and surprise he noticed on the faces of the Germans as they watched French troops dancing with glee after they had surrendered. For Yves Farge, a journalist in Lyon and later a Maquis leader in the Savoie, the moment came as he went to work one day in June 1940:

> The trolley bus from Tassin stopped to let a German motorized column pass, and some character on the bus had the effrontery to say in a loud voice, 'At last the French are going to learn what order really is.' Then in front of the Grand Hôtel there were some women waiting to see the German officers come out. I said to one of them, 'You're too old for prostitution.' It all began in ways like that.

Popular memory now honours such men simply as patriots. Yet this entirely proper and respectful judgement does little to illuminate the combination of temperament, background and belief which made them take a stand at a time when patriotism was being claimed, and claimed as exclusive property, by virtually all shades of opinion. In fact, *résistants* came from no single political group, no single section of society, perhaps not even from any easily definable psychological category. Diversity, at once the greatest strength and the greatest weakness of resistance, was its hallmark from the start.

It comes as no surprise to find Socialists and trades unionists, in pre-war days the backbone of support for Léon Blum's Front Populaire, among the early *résistants*. The Socialist journalist Jean Texcier has already been mentioned several times in previous chapters for his 'Conseils à l'occupé' ('Advice to the Occupied'), the ironic and defiant pamphlet he had written and begun to distribute covertly in July 1940. He went on to help found Libération-Nord with Christian Pineau from the Confédération Générale du Travail, one of the largest trades union movements. Communists who had avoided the muddle afflicting their Party leadership were also drawn to resistance: Charles Tillon, the party's south-western delegate, was active in the Bordeaux region as early as June 1940. And there were even some right-wing *ligueurs* and *cagoulards* or former *cagoulards*, like Georges Loustaunau-Lacau of the group Alliance. Charles Maurras of Action Française might have thought it expedient to swallow his anti-German prejudices but others on the Right, even the extreme Right, could find their dislike of Germany or of Hitler – or, simply, of accepting the fact of defeat – unappeasable.

To some extent, these different political strands remained separate. Like naturally tended to band together with like, and resistance often perpetuated the divisions that had bedevilled the Third Republic; the relationship of Communist groups with those of other allegiances would always remain a particularly thorny issue. More generally, the task of unifying resistance – or even giving it the appearance of unity – would pose formidable difficulties. It could be undertaken at all only because some, at least, of the early groups provided the necessary example. Thrown together at a time of national crisis and forged at the most local level, they were often politically heterogeneous because they had little choice. A group like France-Liberté in Lyon, active in its opposition to the Vichy regime by late 1940, included two Communists, a supporter of the left-wing Catholic Jeune République, a former supporter of Maurras' Action Française and a Jewish refugee from Strasbourg.

Early *résistants* were equally mixed in their professions and backgrounds. They might be intellectuals and academics, like Boris Vildé, Professor Paul Rivet and their associates at the Musée de l'Homme or Jean Cassou and the other Amis d'Alain-Fournier, who had formed their groups in Paris by the end of July 1940, or François de Menthon, liberal Catholic and professor of law in Lyon, who founded Liberté. Yet they could just as easily be career army officers, like Frenay or his co-worker in Combat, Maurice Chavance, or for that matter, Loustaunau-Lacau himself. The disgust these men felt at the failure in military and political leadership since the outbreak of war could in no way be appeased by giving blind allegiance to Pétain, despite his record at Verdun. To them a soldier's task remained clear. At Brax in the Haute-Garonne an otherwise obscure colonel named

Malraison spelled it out to his junior officers just after the armistice had been declared:

A few days from now you will be demobilized, at least provisionally. While I am still your commander, let me remind you of the duty that lies ahead of you. From tomorrow, be ready for revenge. That is the goal. It is up to you to find the means. A new army will be born, weak in numbers and resources. But it must get ready for the future and its role will be vital.

Shortly afterwards many officers – including career soldiers, not just conscripts of the phoney war – were indeed given their *congés*, as the army was pared down to the token *armée de l'armistice*. Such forced disbandment might have increased their apparent helplessness but it also sharpened their sense of betrayal.

'I am going to stick my neck out and say that I believe one could resist only if one was maladjusted.' So Emmanuel d'Astier de la Vigerie, founder of Libération-Sud, would later claim. Jean Cassou, who survived imprisonment to take up resistance work in Toulouse, described himself in terms which deliberately recall the existential hero already being conceived in the writings of Sartre and Camus:

I myself had always been someone without possessions, without inheritance or title, with no fixed home, no social status, no real profession, putting on a series of masks and pretending, for the gallery, to believe in these arbitrary masks. Finally I found myself in a situation where . . . it was the norm not to give your own name, where it was the rule not to have a social position and no longer to look for one. . . . And life in prison was also to my liking, giving me the feel of being at home. At last society had found me the social position I wanted, at last it had understood me and at last I was living, adequately and harmoniously, as I wanted to live.

To someone with this sense of alienation, the *refus absurde* and its consequences came more naturally than to those at ease with themselves in society. Yet, however accurate Cassou may be in describing himself, the feelings he portrays were probably less common than the fashionable philosophy of the day liked to assume. One does not expect to find them in, for example, army officers or committed Communists or, for that matter, high-flying civil servants.

There is scarcely more point, then, in searching for a psychology common to early *résistants* than there is in searching for a common political allegiance or social background. The most, perhaps, that can be said is that since they were a minority of the French – a tiny and, as it seemed, insignificant minority – they had by definition to be people who could live with the fact, even take pride in it. Otherwise, their very differences seemed the most promising thing they had to offer. France had been too deeply at odds with herself to take a coherent stand at the outbreak of war in 1939 and, after 1940, she ran the risk of being destroyed as much by Vichy's narrow and sectarian doctrines as by foreign invaders. Now resistance might point the way to a new spirit of France.

Certainly the unpredicted alliances and the unexpected friend-ships resistance forged gave heart to *résistants* when there was little else to keep up their morale. Many took special delight in remem-bering the words of Charles Péguy, the poet who had died in the First World War: 'In wartime, he who refuses to surrender is my friend, whoever he may be, wherever he may come from and whatever party he may belong to.' As the tide of affairs began to turn, and the Germans began to lose the advantage, the sense of unlikely yet actual solidarity that *résistants* had achieved helped shape their vision of the political future after Liberation. It nourished a dream of a France emerging from the Occupation not just intact but reborn into a new sense of community and nationhood, of a France which had found herself again in the very ordeal of losing herself.

This dream, let alone its cruel disillusionment at the hands of post-war politics, still lay far in the future in the early years of the Occupation. But the problems inherent in the diversity of the *résis-tants* were already apparent. The chief and most predictable of them was inexperience. Some brought a knowledge of warfare and others a fluency with the pen; some had administrative skills and others the knack of working calmly against the grain of prevailing opinion. Yet, except for some exiles from the Spanish Civil War and from the other territories of the Reich, none had experience of resis-tance itself. After all, resistance is a task most people have to learn on the job.

Much of what it demanded could be learned and was learned, but at the price of mistakes recorded in the lists of those arrested and deported or executed. Amateurishness died hard. The most difficult thing to keep in mind was the need for security: the ability to keep secrets, to go to work unnoticed, to flourish on the margins, to survive underground. People used either to the freedom of civilian life or the discipline of army life did not easily acquire the habit of not writing things down, not keeping a regular schedule in their clandestine work, not waiting an extra five minutes at a rendezvous if the person they had arranged to meet did not turn up on time. It demanded a particular psychological balance, which did not come naturally, to remain calm and apparently unconcerned while being continually on the look-out for the black Citröens and green fedoras favoured by the Gestapo. Nor were these all the security precautions required of a full-time *résistant*. Frenay listed all the other habits which experience taught him to adopt: using not one but several *noms de guerre* (among them Francen, Molin, Maurin, Tavernier, Gervais, Lefèbre and Xaintrailles); carrying false identity papers and being ready to maintain his false identity if he were interrogated; constantly changing the places where he met fellow-*résistants*; forever checking to see if he was being followed and being ready to put on an overcoat or abandon a hat to alter the silhouette he presented; and keeping bolt-holes and retreats known only to himself.

A thousand films and novels have made these exciting ruses familiar. To many people Frenay's list reads like the very stuff of life under the Occupation. Yet he presented it partly in rebuke to all the fellow-*résistants* who had never managed or troubled to master the art of clandestine survival. 'The typical Frenchman', he concluded, 'does not have a conspiratorial temperament, and only with considerable difficulty does he acquire a conspirator's reflexes.' Sadly, the anecdotal record bears him out. One member of the cell in Paris which included Sartre and Simone de Beauvoir was in the habit of carrying his duplicating machine around the streets in full view of passers-by; another used to walk about with his briefcase stuffed full of illegal pamphlets. In Burgundy a young schoolteacher named René Laforge scribbled notes in the margin of a textbook he consulted in order to learn how to make bombs; his execution bequeathed a martyr's name to one of the more determined Maquis groups in the region. General Delestraint, the career soldier groomed by Moulin to become titular head of the Armée Secrète, found it hard to break the habit of turning up at secret assignations in his army uniform.

Delestraint's arrest in June 1943, just months after he assumed the post, was a harsh reminder of how vulnerable all resistance organizations were to infiltrators and traitors. He was betrayed to the Germans by Jean Multon (codenamed Lunel), a fellow-*résistant* captured and coerced by the Germans into touring Marseille, Toulon, Cannes, Nice, Montélimar and Lyon to point out familiar faces. His treachery – compounded, perhaps, by that of another *résistant*, René Hardy – also led to Moulin's arrest a few weeks later. Most groups, however small, could point to similar losses. Betrayal contributed quite as much as pitched battle to the high toll of martyrdom which *résistants* suffered before their struggle was over: by the time Liberation had been achieved 30,000 had been shot, 60,000 had been deported and 20,000 had disappeared.

The British agents whom SOE sent to help resistance in France were in general harsh critics of the amateurishness they found, and on no issue were they more emphatic than the lack of proper security. Too often they heard the phrase '*ça ne risque rien*' ('there's no danger in that') used to shrug off what by the standards of their own training was simple carelessness or gratuitous risk-taking. They listened with alarm as rumour and gossip broadcast cover-names to an entire neighbourhood. They watched with horror as cells conducted meetings in the same way they might have discussed the sports results in the local *café*. And, in the case of Carte, they encountered an underground group whose leader, André Girard, kept elaborate dossiers on all its members, recording not just their real names, addresses and telephone numbers but also their physical appearance, skills and, in all, sixty-one items of useful information. A briefcase containing more than 200 of these dossiers fell into the hands of the Abwehr after a courier went to sleep on a railway journey from Marseille to Paris, leaving the Germans to pick up members of Carte at their leisure.

Falling back automatically on national stereotyping, SOE agents remembered the French reputation for wearing their feelings on their sleeve and being incorrigible in their love of talk. Nor did they hesitate to draw the obvious, and condescending, conclusion: English reserve bred good agents, French openness bred bad ones. In fact Janet Teissier du Cros got much closer to the mark when she concluded that, for all their indecent haste to be rid of the Third Republic in 1940, people were more essentially republican than they realized. The political traditions of nearly a century and a half had done their work: still wedded to democratic discussion and debate, the French could not get used to the possibility that there was an informer listening in the corner or a spy working in their midst.

'What a mess!' marvelled the agent Peter Churchill. 'What a stupendous, warm-hearted bouillabaisse it all was.' Despite such amateurishness and carelessness, he had still managed to find the vital handful of colleagues he needed – vital in the quite literal sense that he could and did trust them with his life. In this way, *résistants* as well as foreign agents were confirmed in their resistance by the personal loyalties they developed. Early *résistants*, in particular, were further united by their instinctive agreement on tactics. This in itself is surprising. While still dispersed, disorganized, in touch with each other only on the smallest scale, they had in effect first to invent resistance. They had to agree what courses of action stemmed from the determination to say no, and that was not an obvious matter. 'At last!': Vercors had his moment of outrage, his moment of commitment, when he learned of Bonsergent's death, just as Yves Farge had done when he overheard the Germans being praised, or Frenay had done when he saw the contempt on the faces of the German troops. But what did they do after that? What, actually, came next?

Not violence. And not sabotage either, though minor vandalism like cutting a telephone line, slashing a tyre or defacing an official poster was always tempting. Such acts came within the elastic German definition of sabotage, but usually satisfied the psychological needs of *résistants* rather than advancing a military or even a quasi-military campaign. When it started, resistance was in no position to launch a direct assault on the occupiers or the machinery of their occupation. At its first meeting in the spring of 1941 one of the little group of amateurs which included Sartre proposed – 'with cheerful ferocity', said Simone de Beauvoir – that they organize attacks on prominent people such as Marcel Déat. His suggestion was immediately vetoed because 'none of us felt qualified to make bombs or hurl grenades'. This was true of most *résistants* and would remain so throughout the Occupation. Frenay's description of the security measures required by his life underground might feed romantic notions of what resistance was like, but his memoirs began with a necessary if distinctly unromantic reminder that by no means all *résistants* were, in the colloquial translation of the word, 'resistance fighters': 'I myself never attacked a den of collaborators or derailed trains. I never killed a German officer or Gestapo agent with my own hand.'

What Sartre, de Beauvoir and their group resolved to do instead was to gather information 'which we would then circulate in the form of a news bulletin and various pamphlets'. Frenay had done the same before them, though to much greater effect, issuing a mimeographed sheet called *Les Petites Ailes de France* (*The Little Wings of*

France) which merged with de Menthon's *Liberté* and in November 1941 became *Combat*, the change of title from stubborn hope to militancy marking the growth of its influence. The way had been led by Jean Texcier, whose first act of resistance was an act of language, the pamphlet 'Conseils à l'occupé', which was itself about the importance of acts of language. Don't listen to what the Germans have to say, he had told his fellow-countrymen, and don't talk to them, not even to give them street directions. Talk to your fellow-French, exchange information among yourselves and be sure to pass these words on. 'It is no good sending your friends to the bookshop to buy this pamphlet,' he ended with his customary cheerful irony: 'No doubt you've only got one copy of it yourself and you want to hang on to it. So make copies which your friends can copy in their turn. A good occupation for the occupied.'

A good occupation, indeed. Whatever else resistance might have lacked when it started – and in lacking numbers, experience, arms, equipment and money, it seemed to lack almost everything – it had language. And language had assumed critical power. France's collapse into defeat had been marked by her collapse into dependence on rumour running to wildness, her subjection by her subjection to propaganda and censorship from the Germans, from Vichy and from the presses they both controlled. Increasingly deprived of information quite as much as they were deprived in material terms, the French were left combining credulity and cynicism, listening to everything they could but disbelieving everything they heard. They still took the newspapers, and if anything read them more hungrily than ever, but the fashionable phrase to use when buying them from a kiosk or street vendor was '*Donnez-moi le menteur*': 'Give me the liar'.

Resistance set out to answer the hunger which neither rumour nor officialdom satisfied. It chose to make the first battle it fought a battle of language. Most of the names of the movements mentioned so far in this chapter were also the names of underground journals and, rather than being simply organs of those movements, the journals were at the start, and in a very real sense, the movements themselves. Their most tangible purpose was to provide information otherwise censored and to counter official propaganda. Effectively, the two activities were indistinguishable: merely to record the *de facto* annexation of Alsace and Lorraine and other German violations of the armistice agreement, for example, or the extent of German requisitioning, was also to protest and oppose them.

Yet the underground press also served deeper purposes. Its continual message was something the occupiers, with their own emphasis on propaganda and their strict control of the press, were never inclined to dispute: the importance of the terrain being contested, of words themselves. The underground press was self-reflexive in the same way that Texcier's pamphlet was self-reflexive. It told people that it was vital they keep on reading resistance journals rather than what the collaborationists wrote. Patriots must not read *L'Illustration* or *Gringoire*, said de Menthon's *Liberté* in June 1941; ignore *Signal* and *Gringoire*, urged d'Astier's *Libération* in August the same year. And, of course, the main action to take after reading *Liberté* or *Libération* was to distribute copies of these journals to other people. Thus did resistance consolidate loyalty and expand support.

In its concern with language the underground press created a rhetoric of resistance to counter the rhetoric of the Reich and of Vichy. From the start it relied on sayings by the great leaders of the past. 'To live defeated is to die every day,' proclaimed *Les Petites Ailes*, quoting Napoleon. 'A nation is beaten only when it has accepted that it is beaten,' proclaimed *Liberté*, quoting Foch. 'In war as in peace, those who never give up have the last word,' proclaimed *Combat*, quoting Clemenceau. The pages, and particularly the mastheads, of resistance journals were spattered with such slogans. Their effect went far beyond their generally invigorating content. Invoking the names of Napoleon, Foch and Clemenceau simultaneously challenged both the rhetoric of the Reich, which sought to lull France's national and nationalistic pride into amnesia, and the rhetoric of Vichy, which by its happy comparisons between Pétain and Louis XIV sought to blot out France's revolutionary and republican past. The battle between resistance and collaboration in the present involved – indeed, in a crucial sense it hinged on – a battle for history and the symbols history had left. Did Joan of Arc belong to Vichy or to Vichy's opponents? Was the memory of the First World War best embodied in Pétain, the Victor of Verdun, or in Clemenceau, 'The Tiger' who had withstood Ludendorff's spring offensive of 1918, and Foch, the unappeasable victor to whom the German generals had surrendered?

The whole history of the Occupation challenges any notion that words are just words and symbols just symbols, and that both are somehow separate from real action. The growth of resistance, in particular, refuted such shallow distinctions. From the start the

Occupation gave writing, printing, selling and reading the underground press the status of committed actions, and highly illegal ones at that, for they carried severe penalties. The repeated and central insistence that readers should shun the collaborationist press went hand in hand with advocating other sorts of boycott: of the anti-semitic exhibition 'Le Juif et la France', for example, and Veit Harlan's rancorous film, *Le Juif Süss,* and the Paris exhibition by Hitler's favourite sculptor Arno Breker. Boycott and sabotage, moreover, are always closely allied. Those who sold collaborationist journals should be urged to stop, said the underground press, and if encouragement or intimidation proved ineffective then their premises and kiosks should be bombed. The same logic meant that, when they did not stay away, people should disrupt showings of *Le Juif Süss* or concerts by the Berlin Philharmonic.

Symbols do not stay safe and inert on the printed page any more than words do: they too spill out on to the streets. As it grew in strength, resistance did not just remind the French of anti-collaborationist symbols from their own history or dispute with Pétain the claim of descent from Joan of Arc. It also joined other occupied countries opposed to the Reich in appropriating symbols from the enemy. So the Occupation saw, among other battles, a battle over the V-sign in France. To start with, the V-sign had been a German emblem standing for German victory. V might not begin the German word for victory (which is *Sieg*) but it is the initial letter of the word in the languages of several of those countries the Reich intended to defeat.* Besides, its very shape appealed to the penchant for aggressive emblems which had led the Reich to adopt the swastika and the lightning bolt. In this spirit, at the very peak of Nazi triumphalism, a huge V was emblazoned on the banner across the Palais-Bourbon in Paris which proclaimed 'DEUTSCHLAND SIEGT AN ALLEN FRONTEN': 'GERMANY IS VICTORIOUS ON ALL FRONTS'.

In the summer and autumn of 1941 Churchill conducted a vigorous personal campaign to invert its significance in Britain, making the V stand for German defeat and not German victory. Moreover, by converting it from a ceremonial emblem fit for banners into a gesture made with the first two fingers of the right hand, he drew on its gutter connotations of insult and defiance. These connotations

---

* The Italians, Germany's partners in the Axis, interpreted it as standing for '*Vinceremo*': 'We shall win' or 'We shall overcome'.

are unknown to the French, who make their rude gestures with the middle finger or the clenched fist. But they appreciated the significance of deriding the enemy's chosen emblems by putting them to their own uses: it was, after all, an equivalent of capturing and defacing the enemy's flag in battle. By mid-1941, with the encouragement of the underground press, they were chalking Vs on pavements, walls and military vehicles, folding their Métro tickets into Vs, breaking their matches into Vs before discarding them. And they were doing so in numbers large enough for the Germans to admit defeat, to accept that in France as in other occupied countries the V had passed from their hands into the hands of those who resisted them. Making the V-sign joined tuning into foreign radio stations and all the other apparently trivial items on the lengthening list of forbidden actions. After that, it was inevitable that the Forces Françaises de l'Interieur, the grouping which sought to unify resistance in its last phase, should add a V to the base of the double-barred cross of Lorraine to create their insignia.

For all the satisfaction it gave, the French had no need to take their symbolic gestures from the Germans by way of the British. Their own revolutionary, republican and nationalist traditions, embodied in figures like Napoleon, Foch and Clemenceau, were also marked by anniversaries and their attendant ceremonies. The two most poignant, of course, were 14 July, commemorating the storming of the Bastille, and 11 November, Armistice Day. But there were other dates too: May Day, prized by the Left which had given its support to Blum's Front Populaire before the war, and 6 September, the anniversary of the battle of the Marne, when it had been customary for the French to hang out flags in the streets to celebrate the miracle Joffre had wrought to save the country in 1914. D'Astier's *Libération* was urging them to do so again in 1941. In the Southern Zone, where Vichy tried to erase the traditional significance of May Day by celebrating it as the feast day of Philip the Apostle, many of the crowds who gathered on 1 May 1942 made their feelings clear by shouting '*Mort à Laval*' – Laval rather than Pétain always being the most despised figure of the regime. The same cry was heard again later that year when *Le Quatorze* was celebrated for the first time since 1939.

The crowds had assembled partly in response to an appeal from de Gaulle, who told them: 'We have need of our pride, our hope and our anger, and we have preserved them.' On both occasions they sang *La Marseillaise*, France's national anthem since the Revolution and the most richly emotive of all the songs expressing her capacity for pride and hope and anger. Its revolutionary origins and militant sentiments made the Vichy regime frown on it, preferring safer concoctions of its own, such as *Maréchal, nous voilà*. And when they sang *La Marseillaise* on May Day and 14 July in 1942, the crowds put particular stress on the very verse and line which Vichy found most offensive and which it had insisted be left out on the official occasions it controlled: '*Aux armes, citoyens!*' ('Citizens, to arms!').

So BLOOD WOULD have blood after all, even if eight months elapsed between Bonsergent's execution and the next phase in the cycle. The exact date was 21 August 1941 and the place was the Métro station of Barbès-Rocheouart in the Montmartre district of Paris. There, just after eight o'clock in the morning, a *résistant* fired two shots from his revolver and, with the help of three companions, made his escape among the rush-hour crowds. His victim was left dead on the floor of the carriage he had just boarded, his legs sticking out of the door. All that other Germans could do when they reached the scene was to lay the victim's cap on his stomach and carry away the corpse. Alphonse Moser, a young naval subaltern who had a desk job in the Admiralty building, was not the first German serving in the occupying forces to die by violence but he was the first to fall by public assassination.

The man who killed Moser typified the new energy which Hitler's invasion of the Soviet Union in the previous June had released into the business of resistance. Pierre Georges – then calling himself Fredo but best known by his later codename of Colonel Fabien – was only 22 but already a seasoned veteran of the International Brigades in Spain. During the Civil War he had gained experience working with explosives as well as collecting several wounds. He now belonged to the Organisation Spéciale, a militant group formed by the Communist Party from its Bataillons de la Jeunesse and the forerunner of the Francs-Tireurs et Partisans Français (French Irregulars and Partisans) or FTP. Its commitment to direct action had already been proved in the weeks before the killing at the Métro Barbès.

The cell which Fabien initiated into violence had already staged an attack with Molotov cocktails on an insulating factory in Vitry which made special parts for submarines. Shots had been fired and a pitched battle with the French workers had been averted only by well-chosen cries of '*Foutez-nous la paix!*' ('To hell with the peace!'). In the first fortnight of August two members had managed to surprise a German near the Porte d'Orléans as he emerged from a hotel used by prostitutes, still buckling up his belt. They had knifed and beaten him to death, leaving a note pinned to his body: 'Ten Nazi officers will pay for every patriot killed.' Their appetite had been sharpened when the Germans had wounded and arrested several people taking part in a Communist demonstration, which Fabien had helped to organize, at the Porte Saint-Denis and the Porte Saint-Martin on 13 August. Two demonstrators – a Frenchman, Henri Gautherot, and a Polish Jew, Szmul (or Samuel) Tyszelman – had been condemned to death for 'helping the enemy' on 15 August and executed just two days before the attack on Moser.

Fabien himself – small and thin but with an extraordinary fire burning in his eyes, a friend recalled – had no hesitation in urging the need to kill Germans. Though his comrades agreed, they were younger and lacked his experience of battle. The killing of the German near the Porte d'Orléans was only a back-street affair, after all, and they hesitated at public and declared acts of violence. Some, despite themselves, still shied away from violence altogether. One followed a German officer up a staircase at the Gare de Lyon before his nerve failed. Another stalked a German who was strolling the streets with a prostitute on his arm but could not bring himself to fire because his intended prey looked so happy and full of life; he went home 'humiliated at failing to get my first *boche*'. Yet another, at the very moment of pointing his revolver at the back of a German at the Métro Bastille, found that he was no longer aiming at an enemy soldier, just at another human being. The *résistants* of Fabien's cell might have been determined, and with all the justifications Communist ideology afforded at their disposal, urging that internationalism required them to kill as many Nazis as possible to help their comrades on the Eastern Front. Yet the cause they served was still fragile and, like themselves, virtually untested in street violence.

Because of this, the killing of Moser caught the Germans momentarily by surprise. Their immediate thought seems to have been that it was prompted by lunacy or private vengeance and, when they did decide it had been politically motivated, their first suspects were Republican veterans of the Spanish Civil War rather than French

Communists as such. Even when Communists were blamed, the report sent by Rudolf Schleier, a diplomat working for Abetz in the Paris embassy, to Ribbentrop in Berlin still linked the killing specifically to the demonstration at the Porte Saint-Denis and the execution of Gautherot and Tyszelman. In fact, the death of these men had served only as an additional spur to a campaign already embarked on for larger political reasons.

Yet it was understandable that the Germans should have put the emphasis where they chose to. Some personal motive, some element of comrade directly avenging dead comrade, seemed necessary to explain the killing of Moser for one obvious reason. The anger the French felt at the Occupation always vented itself most forcefully against their fellow-countrymen who aided it rather than the Germans who had brought it about. Crowds gripped by patriotic fervour preferred to shout 'Death to Laval' rather than 'Death to Hitler', let alone 'Death to Otto von Stülpnagel'. It was Marcel Déat rather than a German whom the bloodthirsty member of Sartre and de Beauvoir's little group of would-be *résistants* proposed as a target. And when Paul Colette was arrested after his lone-wolf attempt to assassinate Laval and Déat, at the ceremony honouring the first recruits to the Légion des Volontaires Français held just six days after the killing of Moser, he was at pains to make it clear that he had aimed only at the French officials present, because 'the Germans were doing their duty'. The view that the Germans were doing their duty – or, more cynically, that they were just behaving like Germans – would survive the end of German correctness. Even during the time of SS atrocities in 1944 the deepest hatred would still be reserved for Frenchmen who dishonoured the name of France.

Nevertheless Fabien's example opened the floodgates to violence against Germans in the autumn of 1941. By the end of the year there had been about sixty-eight attacks. Some, like the derailment of military trains, were primarily acts of sabotage, but most were directed at personnel. In Paris the first to follow the Métro Barbès killing came on 3 September when Acher Semhaya – a Communist and Jew born in north Africa – shot and wounded an NCO at the entrance to the Hôtel Terminus near the Gare de l'Est. On 16 September a captain was wounded in the Boulevard de Strasbourg. During the next month the violence spread well beyond Paris. On 20 October a group of young Communists from Paris led by Gilbert Brustlein, one of Fabien's companions at the Métro Barbès, killed the local

Feldkommandant outside the cathedral in Nantes. (He screamed like a pig with its throat cut, Brustlein reported.) On the following day another young Communist *résistant* dispatched from Paris, working in liaison with a group of Spanish Republicans, succeeded in shooting an adviser to the military administration in Bordeaux. Back in Paris, a grenade attack killed two soldiers in the Rue Championnet at the end of November. And on 26 December, the first anniversary of the day when Vercors had stood among the crowds reading the news of Bonsergent's execution, another grenade wounded a member of the Feldgendarmerie in the Boulevard Montparnasse.·

The German authorities reacted harshly, despite their reluctance to admit the scale of the campaign against them or its success. Whenever possible, their public announcements sought to minimize their losses by speaking of attacks on Germans rather than the killing of Germans. In the case of the Feldkommandant in Nantes, they may even have helped to broadcast the widespread rumour that the killing resulted from a quarrel between homosexuals.* But in general the burden of their message was clear. Communists were blamed, even if the language of propaganda demanded that they be referred to as 'cowardly criminals in the pay of Moscow and Britain' or supporters of the 'Jewish-Marxist plutocratic alliance'. And the German response was spelled out by Otto von Stülpnagel as early as 22 August. Hostages would be shot in reprisal.

This was in line with the Reich's policy in its other occupied territories. Whenever a German was attacked, let alone killed, prisoners already detained would be treated as hostages, or if necessary hostages would be taken from the civilian population, and they would be executed. 'Reprisal constitutes a right of distress,' Stülpnagel wrote, 'and on this reef, on this fact, all moral and humanitarian arguments shatter.' Moreover, hostages would be executed in private: their disappearance *bei Nacht und Nebel*, the very obscurity of their fate, was designed to add to the deterrent effect of their death. In the immediate aftermath of the Métro Barbès killing three hostages died in this fashion and more died, in groups of ten or twelve, as further attacks on Germans in Paris mounted during September.

---

* When Vercors, for example, came to write his memoirs, *La Bataille du silence* (1967), he was still under the impression that what had happened in Nantes was 'a sordid business of underworld queers'.

At the end of the month Stülpnagel drafted a code for reprisal which specified the categories of people from which hostages could be drawn. They included Communists and anarchists, those detained for Gaullist sympathies, those detained for distributing hostile tracts, those detained for their suspected connection with acts of sabotage and terrorism, and even, curiously, 'French citizens of German ethnic origin', by which he meant former inhabitants of Alsace and Lorraine. Youths between the ages of 18 and 21 should not be executed unless there was reason to suppose that the authors of the attack provoking the reprisal came from the same age group. And, finally, their bodies should not be buried in a common grave lest the site become a focus for anti-German propaganda.

'The nightmare is beginning,' commented *La Gerbe* that autumn. The worst nightmare came after the death of the Feldkommandant in Nantes, the highest-ranking German yet to have been assassinated. Hitler himself originally demanded, via Keitel, the execution of 100 to 150 hostages but soon refined his order: fifty should die immediately, fifty more twenty-four hours later, and a final fifty after another twenty-four hours if there had been no new developments in the search for the assassins. In the event twenty-seven people from the camp at Châteaubriant and twenty from Nantes jail were shot on 22 October; the next day fifty hostages from the camp at Mérignac were shot in reprisal for the shooting of the Bordeaux military adviser. The majority of them were Communists, though the dead from Nantes included notables singled out by the Abwehr, among them a Socialist deputy mayor and Léon Jost, a veteran who had lost a leg in the First World War and was serving a three-year sentence for helping people to escape across the border into Spain.

Stülpnagel announced a halt to the killings on 27 October, stressing that he intended to give the French authorities a further chance to catch the assassins and the French people a further chance to lay information against them. The executions could easily be resumed. In fact, the autumn of 1941 had established the bloody cycle of attack and reprisal, counter-attack and counter-reprisal, which would stain the remaining years of the Occupation. As the pattern developed, so the *résistants* grew more determined and the Germans more indiscriminate, extending even the loose rules which Stülpnagel had established.

On 5 August 1942 (to take just one example) three Romanian *résistants* belonging to the FTP and the Main d'Oeuvre Immigrée, a subsidiary of the Communist Party, threw a stick of grenades into a group of airmen at the Jean-Bouin stadium in Paris. The Germans claimed that three of their men died and forty-two were wounded, though a trustworthy modern historian has calculated that in fact eight died and thirteen were wounded. So, while still seeking to minimize the deaths they suffered, the Germans had an interest in bumping up their total casualty list as an excuse for large-scale reprisals. Himmler himself urged a harsh response and Hugo Sperrle, commander of the Luftwaffe in France, demanded that three hostages should be executed for each dead German and two for each wounded German, making a total of ninety-three. The Germans did not have that many hostages at their disposal and were forced to claim extra ones from among the prisoners held by the French authorities; even then their total still fell short. Eighty-eight people were executed on 11 August in groups of five at fifteen-minute intervals. Their bodies were cremated at Père-Lachaise cemetery.

Most of these eighty-eight victims were Communists. Three were national leaders of the Communist youth movement and fourteen had been arrested for printing *L'Humanité*. The others included a rank-and-file member who had the bad luck to be the brother of the party's leader, Maurice Thorez, together with two men who had hidden him after he had escaped from internment. Also on the list were Fabien's father and father-in-law, and the father of a *résistant* executed the previous March: a policy directive by Himmler in July had made relatives of *résistants* legitimate hostages for no other reason than that they were relatives. A sizeable minority of those executed were foreigners, chiefly Hungarian, Belgian and Dutch. Only one of the dead had been formally condemned to death by a German military tribunal.

It was reported that many of these men went to their deaths, like the hostages at Châteaubriant before them, singing *La Marseillaise* and shouting '*Vive la France!*' The cause of resistance already had its songs and its slogans. By their deaths it gained another priceless asset: martyrs. Although they could not be remembered at physical shrines – the German custom of cremating the bodies or burying them separately was meant to prevent exactly that – they could be remembered by their words. In the last letter before he died in December 1941 the Communist deputy Gabriel Péri looked to the future, the future beyond the Occupation which young Communists in particular would help to bring about. He used a striking phrase, '*les lendemains qui chantent'* ('the tomorrows that sing'), whose currency was assured when the Communist poet Louis Aragon adapted it in one of his wartime poems. Elsewhere, other hostages and *résistants* wrote their last letters in the knowledge that they were bequeathing to the cause of resistance not just the fact of their martyrdom but noble words as well. 'I am going to die today, despite my innocence and my determination to follow the path of right. . . . My last wishes are that you should not weep too much for me. . . . I am looking death in the face and I am not afraid': thus René Laforge from his cell in Dijon in March 1942. His fellow-prisoner Jean Schellnenberger, known by the codename of Tue-Mouches (Flykiller), was hastier but more pungent: 'It's over. Goodbye. Be brave. We will not suffer.'

The picture that seems to emerge from the autumn of 1941 onwards is of two sides confronting each other across a line drawn with increasing sharpness, while the non-combatants kept to their houses during the extended hours of curfew imposed as the emergency grew. Yet this impression is misleading; however deep the hatred engendered by the Occupation, the battle lines which emerged were never drawn with satisfying clarity. In fact, the Métro Barbès killing prompted doubt and provoked disagreement among virtually all the interested parties: not just among the passive witnesses, who interpreted their need for security and a quiet life diversely as the violence intensified, but also among *résistants* and even among the Germans.

The German doubts were the simplest and the most simply resolved. For all his draconian attitudes Otto von Stülpnagel had never been entirely convinced of the wisdom of collective reprisals, fearing they might alienate public opinion. When it did not come from Berlin, the pressure to put people before the firing squad *en masse* had come from Helmut Knochen and his staff at the Sicherheitsdienst in Paris. This disagreement, typical of the division between the career soldiers of the Wehrmacht and the National Socialist Party loyalists, was settled in the customary fashion: by a victory for the loyalists. Stülpnagel was eased into retirement in February 1942 and replaced as Militärbefehlshaber by a cousin, Karl Heinrich von Stülpnagel, former chairman of the delegation to the Franco-German armistice commission. Karl Heinrich did not share his relative's doubts, though he was sufficiently aware of the need for euphemism to ban the use of the word *otage* in official communiqués.

He was by and large content to leave Karl Oberg, appointed head of the German security and police forces in France in May 1942, to push ahead as far as his shortage of manpower and his desire not to strain working relations with the French police allowed.

Since the chief of the French police was then René Bousquet, these working relations were grotesquely harmonious. The effect of the policy on reprisals, like German policy on deportations, was to draw Vichy ever more deeply and publicly into complicity with the occupiers. Pétain himself, who had detected an 'ill wind' blowing through the country only days before the Métro Barbès killing, made radio speeches condemning such attacks in September and October 1941: 'We laid down our arms at the armistice. We do not have the right to pick them up again to strike the Germans in the back.' As for the reprisals: 'Once again, a trickle of blood is running across our country. The price we are paying is frightful.' Though he spoke about the fate of the hostages in 'a broken voice' – his own phrase – his distress contained no condemnation of the Reich.

In fact, neither he nor any of those who served him uttered any word criticizing the Reich in public or, apparently, in private consultations about the hostage question. Vichy's ambassador in Paris, Ferdinand de Brinon, was in touch with Otto von Stülpnagel immediately after the Métro Barbès killing over a suggestion that six Communists be brought before a special French tribunal, whose judges would be instructed in advance to find them guilty, and then publicly executed in the Place de la Concorde. It is not absolutely clear who originated the idea, but the insistence on a French court (however remote from French traditions of justice) and a public execution would seem to bear de Brinon's fingerprints. As it transpired, the only three men submitted to this process were executed in the courtyard of the Santé prison, in obedience to the Reich's preference for privacy. Negotiations about the other three contributed to the delay in late August and early September before Stülpnagel embarked on his own campaign of reprisal.

Pierre Pucheu, the Vichy Minister of the Interior who later attempted to change sides, played a part in selecting the hostages who died at Châteaubriant. Exactly in what capacity or what spirit he acted is hard to establish. But, whether he was a moderator trying to reduce the numbers or a collaborator just making sure the victims were Communists, his mere involvement helped to assure his own trial and execution by the Free French when he threw himself on their mercy in north Africa in 1943. Similar uncertainty shrouds the bizarre proposal, made after the executions at Bordeaux, that Pétain should offer himself at the demarcation line as a hostage in lieu of all the others. One witness has him making the suggestion himself, while another records that the idea came from an aide. Both agree that the cabinet vetoed it. In any event, it was never made public, much less acted on: Christ-like rhetoric might have become the Marshal but actual martyrdom did not.

Other French people had no reason to keep their anguish to themselves. And it did not just concern the reprisals, though their savagery naturally provoked both horror and growing personal fear: who, after all, could count themselves safe from such increasingly random punishment by the occupiers? The anguish had begun with the killing of Moser itself, which 'was received everywhere with disapprobation', to quote from the diary kept by Georges Benoit-Guyod, a senior police officer. The Germans, who would complain how little understanding the French showed when it came to a matter like the yellow star, agreed with him on this point. 'The great majority of the population', wrote the first Stülpnagel in the official jargon of the day, 'reject these Communists as common criminals, and the Jews who are the moral instigators of these crimes.' Even after the end of German correctness the pent-up frustration people felt at the presence of the occupiers did not necessarily make them rejoice at the spectacle of a naval cadet sprawled dead on the floor of a Métro carriage. Blood, when it took that form, did not answer the anger and exhilaration which had overcome Vercors when he read the news of Bonsergent's execution. 'What we are presented with now', Benoit-Guyod wrote,

> is not a hand-to-hand fight but the cowardly assassination from behind of a defenceless man. So odious is the deed that it arouses spontaneous indignation, made more complex from a feeling that the killer, with the advantage of picking his time and place, has every hope of escaping, leaving behind innocent witnesses who are in great danger of being suspected instead of him.

Assassination, then, could seem doubly unfair: in its choice of victim and in its consequences for bystanders. The notion of fair play still influenced people to a surprising degree even in circumstances which seemed to have made such rules irrelevant. It had already made more than one member of Fabien's cell hold his fire before the

Métro Barbès killing, and objections persisted afterwards even in militant Communist circles. Some Communists felt that, far from being corporate acts dedicated to the cause of internationalism, the attacks were just displays of individual bravado. And, of course, it was on Communists that the burden of reprisal fell most heavily. One party official in Nantes even went so far as to call on the *résistant* who had killed the local Feldkommandant to give himself up – vainly, of course, since Gilbert Brustlein neither surrendered nor was captured, and the hostages still went to their deaths.

Any lingering myth of a resistance movement, let alone a nation, united in its assault on the Germans is destroyed by the reaction of some non-Communist *résistants*. Their doubts and objections took a different slant from those of the Communists but were even more emphatic. They were put succinctly on 23 October, the day the Bordeaux hostages died. 'It is completely normal and completely justified that Germans should be killed by the French,' the argument began, sharply distinguishing the disapproval it would go on to express from Pétain's horror at merely criminal acts: 'If the Germans did not want to meet death at our hands, all they had to do was to stay in their own country.' But, it continued,

> war requires tactics. It must be conducted by those entrusted with the task. . . . For the present, the watchword I give the occupied territory is not to kill Germans. I say this for one reason alone, which is that, at the moment, it is too easy for the enemy to respond by massacring our fighters, who are for the time being unarmed. As soon as we are in a position to go on the attack, the necessary orders will be given.

The voice that spoke these words – so confident of its right to attention, so sure of its authority – came via the BBC from London. It belonged, of course, to de Gaulle.*

B UT WHO, IN EFFECT, was de Gaulle in 1941? What influence did he really command? And what view of resistance did he hold? In June 1940 he had been, by his own description, 'nothing'. Before the war he had carved something of a reputation for himself with his views on military strategy, while losing the support of Pétain, his first

---

* Later versions of the text (in de Gaulle's *Mémoires de guerre*, for example) read 'to kill Germans openly', implying a distinction between public assassination and covert elimination.

hero and patron. The brief conflict of 1940 had brought him a few local successes on the battlefield, which went almost unnoticed amid the prevailing chaos, and the rank of general, which he scorned using for most of his years in exile. His experience of political office had come only in the last days of defeat, serving a dying government in a junior post. None of these things made him a nonentity – nobody who encountered de Gaulle ever called him a nonentity – but, by the same token, none of them made the French look to him as a future leader. And on 17 June 1940 he had apparently consigned himself to disgrace, if not oblivion, by flying to Britain.

There, to start with, he had few resources and few supporters. A month after his arrival he had still mustered only about 7,000 Free French to his cause; many exiled members of the armed forces preferred to serve under British command rather than pledge loyalty to him. Nor was Britain in any position to help de Gaulle make good these deficiencies: faced with massive problems equipping its own troops, the government actually encouraged many French soldiers who had been ferried across the Channel from Dunkirk to return home. But Britain gave de Gaulle two things. It recognized him as 'leader of all the Free French, wherever they may be', and it gave him access to a microphone at the BBC. The first gift, to be sure, both looked and was virtually meaningless. It certainly said nothing about how Britain as a whole, or even its War Cabinet, regarded de Gaulle. Instead, it expressed Churchill's personal fondness for the impulsive gesture and his instinct that he had found in de Gaulle a fellow-spirit, another man of destiny – 'the Constable of France', as he put it in quasi-Shakespearean language.

As for de Gaulle's right to speak to his fellow-countrymen on the radio, it was granted almost casually and it seemed equally insignificant. Certainly his first broadcast, made on 18 June, has acquired a status in popular memory it did not have at the time: hardly anybody in Britain knew or cared about it and the BBC did not think it worth recording. Few people in France heard it. Later, of course, many would convince themselves that they had and that they had been moved by it, but their memory was as misleading as the belief that de Gaulle had uttered a clarion call to civilian resistance. In fact, his insistence that France had lost a battle but not the war was directed specifically at fellow-officers in the hope they would ignore the coming armistice, as he had done. Vichy received it in this spirit and denounced him as a renegade general sowing sedition; in

August it would arrange for a military tribunal to try him and sentence him to death *in absentia*.

If de Gaulle eventually succeeded in turning Britain's modest and unpromising gifts into priceless assets, he did not do so just by proving himself a man of honour, a supreme patriot and a charismatic leader. He did so because of a shrewd political sense, a gift for manoeuvre. This led him to grasp from the start that what Britain had done for him could in fact have worsened his position, if that were possible. He had exiled himself from France when Vichy dominated the climate of opinion, and Vichy asserted everywhere that to remain in France was itself proof of honour and patriotism, while to leave was desertion. To go to Britain and accept British favours made the desertion far worse. By Vichy's standards it was treachery, but even to those of less extreme views de Gaulle had still thrown in his lot with an ally so strongly suspect as to seem virtually an enemy.

It was vital, then, that de Gaulle establish and maintain a certain haughty distance between himself and his host. It was vital that he make it plain he was still fighting for France, and hence accepting Britain as a provisional ally in a desperate hour, and not fighting for Britain. He must never look Britain's friend, much less Britain's servant, which of course was exactly how Vichy and the Reich sought to portray him as soon as they found him worth more than passing attention. De Gaulle's task seemed virtually impossible at the bleak time of Mers-el-Kébir in July 1940, when consistency with his own views obliged him to associate himself, in speeches beamed at France, with a country which had just killed French sailors and sunk the better part of the French fleet. It looked no easier in September, surveying the wreckage of the botched Anglo-Gaullist raid on Dakar. Then, de Gaulle's grandiose title of Governor General of French Equatorial Africa simply sounded like the claim of a puppet of Britain's imperial interests. It is small wonder that he should have admitted to thinking of blowing his brains out at this juncture.

Yet de Gaulle did manage the perilous balancing act which circumstances demanded if he was to survive with any credibility. Making it clear that he regarded Britain as an ally and partner – not as a bosom friend, much less an employer – came naturally to a man of his imperious and combative temperament. De Gaulle, moreover, was never an anglophile in the way Churchill was a francophile. If policy required him to be rude to the British, then (as Churchill grimly testified) 'he certainly carried out this policy with perseverance'. It answered, moreover, something deep in the world-view of a man born in 1890 and thus an impressionable 8-year-old when France and Britain had come to the brink of war in confronting each other over an obscure village on the Upper Nile called Fashoda.

To de Gaulle, France was not just a European country and Britain was not just her cross-Channel neighbour. France was a global empire and Britain was her global rival. Both these propositions were fundamental to his policy in the years 1940–4 and hence to the nature of his achievement. His imperial perspective made the insistence that France in 1940 had lost a battle but not the war something more than unrealistic defiance. It had shrewd practical sense for, whatever disaster might have overtaken metropolitan France, there was still some consolation to be found in her overseas territories. Vichy held them but with a weaker grip than it held the mainland, if only because it was not supported by the Reich, which had used the armistice agreement to confirm its lack of interest in the French empire. So prying these territories loose from their loyalty to Vichy – in some cases merely a technical loyalty – became a major goal. It was worth risking and suffering the humiliation at Dakar. It was even worth dispatching Admiral Muselier across the Atlantic in late 1940 to the two tiny French islands of Saint-Pierre and Miquelon off the Canadian coast. There the Admiral presided over a referendum of the 5,000 inhabitants which endorsed de Gaulle and the Free French rather than Vichy.

For all its air of comic opera, the Saint-Pierre and Miquelon episode showed de Gaulle's strategy in miniature. He had liberated French territory from Vichy by the popular assent of its French inhabitants; in however small a fashion, he had become the real, acknowledged leader of some of the French. He had done so, moreover, without consulting Britain and at the price of provoking American anger. This proof of his independence was not merely an extra advantage but an essential part of his purpose. Wresting power over French territory from Vichy: that was one part. Preventing rival nations from gaining power over French territory at a time of weakness: that was the second part. It explained de Gaulle's fury when the British landed on Madagascar (a French possession) without consulting or warning him in May 1942 and it explained his renewed fury over British intentions in Syria and the Lebanon in the autumn of the same year.

Above all, it explained his abiding preoccupation with north

Africa and his decision to make Algiers, not London, his headquarters from 1943. There his rival was not Britain but America. President Roosevelt never shared Winston Churchill's admiration for de Gaulle. Indeed, he disliked and distrusted him as 'just another French general'. His suspicion agreed neatly with the State Department's lingering hope that Pétain might yet be persuaded to 'stand up in his boots'. Reluctance to acknowledge de Gaulle led America to seek rival candidates of its own. The search was so intense that it even briefly included figures like General de la Laurencie, de Brinon's predecessor as Vichy ambassador to Paris but soon an opponent of the regime. His vision of a future France found no place for de Gaulle except as the recipient of a pardon for the way he had behaved. In north Africa after the Allied landings of November 1942 the preferred American candidate was Admiral Darlan, by then hopelessly tainted in the eyes of all but Vichy. And after Darlan was assassinated, America urged the claims of General Henri Giraud: a safer, more conservative figure than de Gaulle, with Vichy connections which might raise eyebrows but also with a daring escape from imprisonment in Germany to his credit. De Gaulle gritted his teeth, assented to a power-sharing agreement with Giraud as co-president of the Comité Français de Libération Nationale in May 1943, and then proceeded to undermine him ruthlessly. By November he was the Comité's sole president.

In such ways did de Gaulle achieve a measure of power on the international scene, and power, moreover, which announced his independence of political patrons. Some said it proclaimed his sheer bloody-mindedness. The familiar slur of enemy propaganda that he was merely the tool of Britain or the Allies certainly found no answering echo in the hearts of Churchill or Roosevelt. Prying loose those parts of the empire which Vichy could not defend, he also made sure that no other nation and no other nation's candidate got their hands on them. This achievement occupied a great deal of his energy: it was no light task, as Churchill sardonically rebuked him, to add Britain and America to Germany, Italy and Japan on the list of his enemies. Yet it had to go hand in hand with paying equally determined attention to mainland France herself. To gain power at the periphery of the empire while still being powerless at the very centre would have been futile. De Gaulle set about building his power inside France the same way the *résistants* were building theirs: by words.

The BBC microphone was his equivalent of their clandestine press. In all, he delivered sixty-eight radio speeches between 1940 and 1944, a campaign interrupted only when disagreements over Madagascar, the Middle East and Darlan's role in north Africa provoked Britain to suspend his access to the air waves. His speeches were supplemented by two regular series: *Honneur et patrie*, which consisted of five-minute talks usually given by de Gaulle's spokesman Maurice Schumann, and a magazine programme, *Les Français parlent aux Français*. If anything, the spoken word proved a more powerful medium than the printed word, since it allowed him to challenge Pétain – also a great believer in broadcasting – directly on his own ground. De Gaulle won. While the Marshal's words have faded into oblivion, de Gaulle's words have lodged in the public memory, like Churchill's. And like Churchill's words, even at the time they sounded as if they were destined to be remembered.

So the rise of de Gaulle's reputation in France belongs essentially to the history of broadcasting. Individual witnesses differ in their memories of when they first heard his voice or were struck by what he said, but the general pattern is clear: he had few listeners in June 1940, found an audience in 1941, and in the course of 1942 established a real following. For what they are worth, Vichy's statistics estimated that 300,000 people were regularly listening to him at the beginning of 1941 and that ten times as many were doing so a year later. And it was in the spring of 1942 that *résistants* began to take pleasure in the most barbed of all their jokes:

'Did you hear what happened near the Luxembourg gardens the other evening? It was just after nine o'clock. A Jew killed a German soldier, disembowelled him and ate his heart.'

'That's impossible. It's impossible for three reasons: Germans don't have hearts; Jews don't eat pork; and after nine o'clock in the evening everyone's listening to the BBC.'*

If de Gaulle's relationship with Britain over the affairs of empire was often one of suspicion and rivalry rather than partnership, the relationship with Britain created by his radio broadcasts proved altogether more harmonious, despite those periods when he was

---

* One of many versions of the joke (which has the Jew eating the German's brains) appeared in April 1942 in *Le Père Duchesne*, a clandestine journal for which Yves Farge wrote in Lyon.

deprived of the microphone. Indeed, the relationship was symbiotic. Between 1940 and 1942 the growth in de Gaulle's reputation and a change in attitude to Britain among the French went hand in hand, reinforcing each other. His appearances on the radio, with the official approval it implied, gave credibility to an obscure colonel – he still preferred that style to general – which he would otherwise have lacked. Yet by allowing a man so obviously independent-minded as de Gaulle to broadcast also helped to give Britain credibility, lulling suspicions and antagonisms which the events of 1940 had rekindled. It was entirely appropriate that by 1942 the slogan '*Vive de Gaulle!*' should have joined the V-sign, once Hitlerian but now firmly Churchillian, as the most common ways of demonstrating a spirit of resistance.

De Gaulle, then, had transformed his name from 'nothing' into the name of a cause, or at least a group of linked and strongly felt attitudes: hating the Occupation, despising Pétain, wanting to see the Germans out of France, above all refusing to give up and accept defeat. He had made himself into a symbol, a living symbol which subsumed the memory of those symbols from history that the *résistants* were also invoking: Clemenceau, Foch, Napoleon, Joan of Arc. And in his own estimation at least, he had done precisely what Pétain had hoped but miserably failed to do as leader of Vichy: he had become France.

Actually, the claim to be France in some indefinable but potent way had been implicit in de Gaulle's wartime utterances right from the moment of his arrival in Britain. Of course, it sits rather more easily in the French language and the French rhetorical tradition than it does in English, though it could also call forth derision and resentment from some of the French. That was as nothing compared to the fury with which Churchill denied it during one of his stormiest meetings with de Gaulle, over British intentions in Syria and the Lebanon in September 1942: 'You claim you are France! You are not France! I do not recognize you as France! Where is France?' This outburst drew from de Gaulle a reply which retrenched his position only by a whisker and did little to clarify it:

I am acting in France's name. I am fighting on the same side as England but not for England. I speak in the name of France and I am responsible for France. The French nation is convinced that I speak for France and will uphold me as long as that belief continues.

The problem was that a symbol is not necessarily also a leader. There is a gap between intangible power and actual status, a gap wide enough to exasperate even the man who had so generously acknowledged de Gaulle as 'leader of all the Free French' in 1940. When he spoke over the BBC to the French, de Gaulle's voice had grown to command great influence: nobody disputed that. Yet in real political terms, in conducting negotiations and in making decisions, what weight should it carry? That, precisely, was the question which caused him to fall out with Churchill in September 1942; it would cause even angrier exchanges between the two when the time came for the D-Day landings in 1944.

It was, besides, an equally sensitive issue in de Gaulle's relations with the resistance which had grown up in France. The rise of resistance mirrored his own rise; he had been regularly in touch with it, through agents, emissaries and sympathizers making the hazardous journey in and out of occupied territory; many of its members had found his name, what he symbolized, an invigorating and useful rallying cry. Yet de Gaulle and resistance inside France had begun their wartime careers separately, and for a long time they remained essentially apart. De Gaulle knew that. When he addressed the French in the aftermath of the assassinations and reprisals of the autumn of 1941, however, he spoke of the matter in very different terms. He spoke of resistance, a scattered and diverse phenomenon which had sprung from the grass roots, as if it were an army. And he gave it a *consigne*, which can indeed mean a 'watchword' but also means an 'instruction' or 'order'. If he was not already claiming to be a leader, he was certainly stating his ambition of creating a unified resistance and being acknowledged as its leader.

This could easily have made de Gaulle look presumptuous; certainly there was no shortage of cynics or opponents to cast doubt on the validity of his ambition or his motives for pursuing it. They pointed to his previous lack of interest: on their missions to France so far his Free French agents had confined themselves to gathering and reporting intelligence, without trying to promote internal resistance as such. They argued that, since resistance had grown from the grass roots, unification would weaken rather than strengthen it. As for de Gaulle's authority, they suggested that guerrilla warfare does not come naturally to tank officers and that de Gaulle himself showed little evidence of acquiring the necessary grasp of tactics. Even a man like Frenay, willing to work with and for him, suspected that de Gaulle sometimes viewed the resistance in France not so much as an ally as a rival: another potential threat to his own power which he needed to co-opt and neutralize. Communist *résistants*, in particular, were influenced by the Soviet Union's suspicion of de Gaulle and the rhetoric which denounced him as the tool of London bankers. Understandably, they were reluctant to yield the command they enjoyed over their own organizations.

All these factors militated against de Gaulle; some would prove intractable. In his favour he had not just the popular reputation he had built for himself but also the special skills of his chosen delegate-general, Jean Moulin. On his missions to France Moulin's task was essentially diplomacy practised in the most extraordinary and dangerous conditions: establishing agreement between different and even apparently irreconcilable personalities, finding common ground between opposed political viewpoints, chairing committees, building an organization piece by difficult piece. His first main achievement, in January 1943, was to get the three main movements in the Southern Zone – Frenay's Combat, d'Astier's Libération and the Communist FTP, led by Jean-Pierre Lévy – to work together and pledge allegiance to de Gaulle as the Mouvements Unis de la Résistance (MUR). The Armée Secrète was the MUR's military wing. The process was extended to the Occupied Zone with the creation of the Conseil National de la Résistance or CNR. The inaugural meeting at which Moulin presided in Paris in May 1943, a bare month before his arrest, was effectively a miniature parliament of resistance. No less than sixteen organizations were represented. They included political parties, the Communists and Socialists among them, and trades unions such as the Confédération Générale du Travail as well as leading resistance movements: Ceux de la Libération, Ceux de la Résistance, Combat, the FTP, Libération-Nord, Libération-Sud and the Organisation Civile et Militaire.

The work of unification continued after Moulin's death, culminating in February 1944 in the Forces Françaises de l'Intérieur, or FFI, embracing both the Free French fighting with the Allies abroad and *résistants* eagerly awaiting the Allies' arrival in France. The mere existence of these organizations indicates the extent to which Moulin and de Gaulle had succeeded. De Gaulle may never have got an army as inclusive, disciplined or effective as he had hoped, but he got at least the appearance of an army and that was enough for his purpose. It was, after all, in the interests of everybody to co-operate up to a certain point. The prize for de Gaulle and the Free French abroad was that Free France ceased to be merely an idea and got closer to being a workable reality. Free France came to life at the point of liaison between international politics, where she was an acknowledged ally of Britain, the Commonwealth and the USA, and mainland France, where she had men and women ready to fight.

The prize for *résistants* at the grass-roots level was equipment. Left to themselves, they could muster a few weapons from those in civilian hands before the war, those still in the hands of sympathetic army officers, those left lying around in the chaos of 1940, and sometimes those which Italian army deserters in the Italian Zone were willing to exchange for false identity papers. But neither they nor the ammunition they came with was anything like enough. Explosives and radio transmitters were virtually unobtainable. It was partly the sheer lack of *matériel* which made early resistance organizations concentrate on publishing journals and educating the public in hostility to the occupiers. Increased co-operation and increased contact with London opened up the possibility of parachute drops organized through the F, or British, section of SOE or through its RF section, directly answerable to the Free French military intelligence service run by André Dewavrin.*

The availability of supplies encouraged the growth of *réseaux*, or networks, with purely military goals beyond committing minor sabotage or establishing escape routes for those who wanted to get abroad. Heavy and fragile though they might have been, radio transmitters dropped from London gave *résistants* a significant role in providing intelligence: first about the Reich's plans for invading Britain, later about the defence of the Atlantic Wall and the development of the V1 and V2 rockets, always about the strength and disposition of German forces. Sabotage, which had started humbly with acts like cutting a telephone cable or throwing sand in the machinery of a factory turned over to production for the Reich, could begin to grow towards the large-scale plans well in place before D-Day: Plan Vert for the railways, Plan Bleu for the electricity supplies, Plan Violet for the telephone and telegram systems, and so on. Even by 1943 the FTP could claim that their 1,500 actions between the beginning of January and the end of March included 158 train derailments and

---

* Codenamed Passy, after the Paris Métro station.

110 attacks on engines in their yards as well as the destruction of bridges, barges and canal locks. That these figures may well have been exaggerated is beside the point: a year earlier they would have been too implausible for a resistance organization to advance them.

Much of this escalation in activity can be traced to the increase in parachute drops from the first trickle in 1941 and 1942 to the deluge from the beginning of 1943 until August 1944, when more than 8,000 drops brought more than 8,000 tons of supplies and 800 agents into France. Yet, impressive though they may sound when quoted out of context, such statistics do not record the almost universal frustration and disappointment which *résistants* themselves felt right up to D-Day and beyond. They complained of drops which did not arrive, of drops which went astray, of drops which fell into the hands of conservative ex-army officers who stockpiled rather than distributed them, and of drops bringing agents whom they did not necessarily trust rather than equipment which they desperately needed.

The scarcity of explosives showed how little London – the Free French or the British – appreciated the advantages of ground-level sabotage over aerial bombardment. As for the scarcity of weapons and ammunition, it left many *résistants* feeling as if they were serving in an unarmed army. At best only half of those who regarded themselves as troops had weapons by D-Day, and this generous estimate is extrapolated from contemporary reports which spoke, locally, of 150 weapons among 4,000 *résistants* in Lyon and 600 weapons among 15,000 or 16,000 in Paris. Almost all these weapons were light: revolvers, rifles and sub-machine guns rather than bazookas or anything heavy enough to answer German artillery. And very few of them came with enough ammunition to sustain more than a day's fighting.

So the reality of resistance always fell short of what de Gaulle proposed to himself when he gave his *consigne* to the French in October 1941. *Matériel* remained a problem. Beneath the façade of unification, so did all the differences and divisions stemming from the origins of resistance in separate and small-scale initiative. Memoirs by both *résistants* and the Free French often dwell bitterly on the gap between the perspectives of the internal and external resistance, those inside France and those abroad. Some of their complaints can be dismissed: it is, after all, in the nature of all soldiers to feel that only somebody in their particular position on their particular part of the battlefield can really understand the war. But some complaints point to fundamental issues. Many *résistants*, sceptical of the attempt to unify resistance under a central command, attacked de Gaulle and Moulin for their autocratic approach. For their part, de Gaulle and the Free French were troubled by the degree of autonomy still enjoyed by the various organizations in first the MUR and then the CNR – an autonomy expressed, for example, in their continuing to publish their separate journals.

If anything, the divergence of views that these journals expressed grew more, not less, marked as D-Day approached. Specific political agendas grew more important as the question of when and if the Germans could be expelled gave way to the question of who would inherit France once the Germans had gone. The old political parties from the Third Republic of whom so many people had already grown tired? The pioneers of some new vision of national community first glimpsed amid the comradeship of the early *résistants*? De Gaulle? Or the Communists? Certainly the friction between de Gaulle and the Communists – each still jealous of power, each still determined to assert priority – was the most clear-cut reminder of how much that was vital to the future of France lay undetermined.

Though the divisions in resistance often emerged through sparring between desk-bound bureaucrats and front-line troops, or between Gaullists and Communists, the issue on which they crystallized was very question of strategy which had prompted de Gaulle to give his *consigne* in October 1941. The attacks on Germans in the autumn of that year had brought reprisals on hostages and *résistants* too weak to defend themselves, let alone go on the offensive. What de Gaulle wanted instead was *résistants* with, above all, the soldierly virtues of extreme patience and willingness to wait on orders. In the meantime, they should train, prepare and equip themselves, and gather intelligence for future use by themselves and the Allies. The orders would come when the Allied landings came. Rather than just being liberated by foreigners – a fate which de Gaulle's experience of his allies quite naturally made him fear beyond measure – France herself would rise up to take an honourable part in her own liberation. That, really, was what resistance was all about.

It was a sensible strategy, particularly attractive to a man like de Gaulle, trained as a soldier, used to dealing with soldiers and steeped in military thinking. The contemporary term for it was *action à terme* (long-term action). Yet some contemporaries sneered at it as *attentisme* (wait-and-see-ism), another version of the passive opportunism which Vichy had threatened to make a national disease. The alternative was *action immédiate*, going out and starting to kill your enemies now, as Fabien had done at the Métro Barbès. The cry of '*A chacun son boche*' commended itself particularly to Communists, who took special satisfaction in helping the Eastern Front by giving the Reich as hard a time inside France as possible, but it did not just appeal to Communists. Being occupied is humiliating and humiliation leaves people with the desire to hit out. Sometimes the desire can grow so strong as to be overwhelming, and the Occupation was one of those times.

The dangers of both *action immédiate* and *action à terme* were obvious. *Action immédiate* brought wasteful and tragic consequences; nobody could doubt that after the autumn of 1941. Yet *action à terme* might prove too little and too late; if it did, it would be every bit as wasteful and tragic as its alternative. Some were already aware of this appalling dilemma, but in the event resistance was neither sufficiently disciplined nor sufficiently unified to make the choice. It took *action immédiate* and it took *action à terme*: it brought down on itself, and those about it, the worst consequences of both courses. France was doomed to suffer by fire and again by fire.

6

Settling Scores

It is a question of life or death! You will be hanged with
me, we will all be hanged if we do not know how to fight!
Be resolute, together we will win!

> Joseph Darnand, addressing *miliciens*,
> 28 November 1943

You backed England and we backed Germany; you won
and we lost.

> Louis Bastide, *milicien*, to Georges Chaillaud, *maquisard*,
> just before Chaillaud hanged him,
> 27 July 1944

RESISTANCE GOT ITS first impetus from two things: the Reich's
brutality in France and its failure on the Eastern Front, made
manifest by Field Marshal Paulus' surrender at Stalingrad in January
1943. They gave it the dual character it would continue to bear until
Liberation. For those already committed, resistance became a cycle
of revenge piled on revenge; for the rest, it depended on nervous
calculation of the fortunes in the war outside France. Yet neither
killings at home nor battles abroad were in themselves enough to
make resistance the mass activity it had become by Liberation. When
de Gaulle delivered his watchword of restraint over the BBC in the
autumn of 1941, he knew full well that the *résistants* he addressed fell
far short of being the army he might have hoped for, not just in their
lack of discipline and organization but in their numbers too.

The Reich's mistakes on the steppes of Russia and on the execution grounds of France continued to make more *résistants*, of course,
but the real boost to recruitment came from another aspect of its
policy. Or, rather, it stemmed from a lack of policy which had been

apparent from the start. Hitler had known exactly how to conquer France, but he had no real idea what he wanted to do with his conquest in the long run and events never gave him the leisure to address the issue. So expediency rushed in to fill the vacuum, the sort of expediency which would dictate virtually all the Reich's policies – except, perhaps, the Holocaust – in all its occupied territories after 1941. Its actions had much less to do with establishing a New European Order than with plundering to satisfy short-term needs.

Those needs were not just for money, materials and goods, though of course France was stripped of all these at a frightening rate from the moment of her conquest. By the end most of her wealth and resources was going to her conquerors (60 per cent of her national income just to pay the Occupation costs stipulated in the armistice), leaving the French to make what shift they could with shortages, inflation and the *système D*. But what the Reich needed above all was extra workers to produce weapons and military equipment. Simultaneously engaged on several fronts, its war machine could not be kept supplied just by German workers, and besides, able-bodied adult Germans were usually considered more valuable in Wehrmacht uniforms than in dungarees on the assembly line. Foreign labour was essential and France, the most highly developed industrial country which the Reich occupied, promised to be a particularly rich source. Whole sections of her manufacturing industry were quickly turned over to collaborative endeavour. Yet the French labour which made tanks and other military vehicles pour out of the Berliet and Renault factories was never enough. The discrepancy grew all the greater as the Reich's losses piled up and its reserves dwindled.

The history of the Reich's eventual failure is nowhere written more eloquently than in its increasingly desperate pursuit of the increasingly remote targets it set itself: the number of Jews to be crammed into the eastbound trains and the number of soldiers to be pressed into Wehrmacht uniforms as well as the number of foreign workers on the production lines in the factories of the Ruhr valley. Nothing charts the last stage of the Reich's failure in France more exactly than the history of its attempt to satisfy its demands for labour. It was not just that it failed in meeting the statistical goals which had become the overriding preoccupation of German bureaucrats and administrators. The very endeavour itself did more than any other single project the Germans undertook to drive a population, originally passive and demoralized, into the arms of resistance.

THE CAMPAIGN TO recruit French workers for German factories began in the atmosphere of correctness which surrounded the 1940 armistice. On one poster a Frenchman in dungarees pointed to Germany on the map of Europe: 'Hey, mate, come with us. We're having a good time and earning a good living in Germany.' On another, a smiling mother and child stood in the foreground while a man waved cheerfully to them from the background: 'The bad times are over. Dad is earning good money in Germany!' A third showed another happy woman: 'Jeannette loves working in Germany. She's found a fiancé who is also a skilled volunteer.' Make money in Germany: if you're a married man, you can support your family; if you're a single woman, you might even meet a nice French boy as well. The messages were as crudely genial as the poster which showed a Wehrmacht soldier taking French children under his friendly wing, and every bit as determined to present the Occupation as a wonderful chance for international friendship and co-operation.

However eager they may have been to believe German propaganda in the autumn of 1940, the French were not seduced. For all the difficulties people were suffering, the daily grind of shortages and poverty had not really set in sufficiently to provide the spur of financial desperation. By the time it had, people were less inclined to believe German promises; many had already become aware that the Germans were the problem and not the solution. So by the beginning of October 1941, more than a year after the recruiting drive had started, only about 48,500 people – 34,000 men and 14,500 women – had volunteered. The result was miserably small by comparison with the number of workers Germany had garnered from Poland (more than a million), Czechoslovakia (nearly 150,000) and Yugoslavia (more than 100,000). Given the very different circumstances of eastern and western Europe, this disparity was inevitable. So was the disparity between France's contribution and the contribution of her immediate neighbours, Belgium and Holland, smaller but subject to more draconian regimes: more than 120,000 workers from Belgium and 90,000 from Holland. But even tiny, neutral Switzerland had sent about 17,000 volunteers to the Reich, or a third of what France had managed.

Hitler's appointment, in March 1942, of Fritz Sauckel to head the drive to exploit foreign labour marked a change throughout Europe. In France, which Sauckel was quick to visit, it signalled the beginning of the end of any pretensions to correctness. New posters went up and new recruiting offices opened, in the major cities of the Southern Zone as well as in the Occupied Zone. By the end of May the total number of recruits had risen to about 150,000, of whom more than 60,000 had come forward in the previous couple of months. This gave the French authorities grounds for pointing to the good effects of their compliance, but it was not in Sauckel's nature to be satisfied with results that were merely promising. Relentless, unimaginative and brutal, he was the perfect servant of a war machine already well on the way to becoming unquenchable in its thirst for labour. He would be remembered as 'the slave-trader of Europe'.

The Vichy regime, of course, owed its very existence to the premise that deals could be struck with such men. And when Laval returned to power in the spring of 1942, he thought he spotted the chance for exactly the sort of bargaining on which he most prided himself. The Germans wanted more workers and they needed the help of the French authorities. Vichy for its part was desperately anxious to get back the prisoners-of-war the Reich still held. Almost two million had been taken in the battle of 1940. Some had escaped and others had been released – veterans of the First World War, for example, and the seriously wounded – but about one and a half million remained captive. They were of no practical use to the Reich, since the Geneva Convention forbade their being forced to do war-related work, but they had immense political value. For France their continued absence was a major blow to an economy already under siege; the fact that half a million of the POWs were farmworkers was particularly damaging to the rural economy by which Vichy set such store. Above all, their fate remained a stumbling block to Vichy's credibility in the eyes of the French, a clear warning that the government which claimed to have rescued national sovereignty was in fact proving impotent.

So Laval hammered out with Sauckel the scheme which he called the *Relève*, or relief shift: an exchange of POWs for workers.* He

---

* A later refinement also allowed POWs to waive their rights under the Geneva Convention and become 'free workers' in Germany.

announced it over the radio on 22 June in the same speech which voiced his hope for a German victory in Europe. The fact that he should have let slip those words, so dangerous to his cause, eventually so damning to himself, suggests the mood of careless triumph in which he spoke. Laval, whose career had certainly seen its ups and downs under Vichy as well as under the Third Republic, may well have imagined that the unveiling of the *Relève* was his finest hour. As a personal achievement, it was the ultimate proof of his skill in negotiation. It showed that both the Germans and the French needed him, something which both had in the past been inclined to doubt. As an achievement for Vichy, it vindicated his government's belief that collaboration was in the best interests of both France and Germany: it gave both sides what they most wanted.

In propaganda terms, going to work in a German factory could now be presented in a new light, not as self-interested or desperate but as doubly patriotic: a way at once of rescuing a fellow-countryman who had fought in the battle of 1940 and of helping the Reich's international crusade against Bolshevism. This, of course, was how Laval put the case in his radio speech and again at Compiègne in August when he welcomed the first trainload of POWs repatriated under the *Relève*. But the details of the scheme did not fully match the rhetoric. In his negotiations Laval had originally proposed that one French POW be returned for every two people who volunteered to work in Germany; Sauckel had countered by proposing one POW for every five workers. They had finally agreed on a ratio of one to three. So, for all the POWs to be returned under the *Relève*, something like four and a half million workers would have to volunteer.

It did not take much arithmetical skill to make this damaging calculation. The underground journals which were still the most effective sign of resistance delighted in reminding people of it. Indeed, they found the *Relève* an ideal target, and the continual burden of their attack was that what workers actually found in Germany bore little relation to what they had been promised. A typical item, from *L'Insurgé* in October, summed up conditions:

Journey	Long, little food, under German supervision
On arrival	Camps where workers are treated like cattle
Later	Sleeping in barracks, herded together
Work	Twelve hours a day, piece-work but no increase in wages

Wages	Enormous taxes and fines
Cost of living	Higher than in France
Food	Not even enough for Italians who are used to low subsistence
Freedom	Nil
Conclusion	Exploitation; prisoner's status. Thousands of workers killed by bombing.

This account did not exaggerate the bleak reality which French conscripts encountered at, for example, the Krupp arms factories or the Dora factory near Buchenwald. Here about 10,000 workers, mainly French and Russian, made V2 rockets in vast underground caverns where the atmosphere was thick with noise and powdered stone. They slept only four and a half hours a night, herded together in dormitories holding 2,500. The least failure to comply with the regimen was met with brutality; the only solace was peeing into the electrical systems of the rockets to sabotage them. Rumours of conditions in such places filtered back to France, supporting what the resistance journals alleged. Yet neither the rumours nor the counter-propaganda were absolutely necessary, so widespread was cynicism about all the claims which the Reich made and Vichy endorsed. The Occupation was, after all, a time when the only thing people could be sure of was that the official story would turn out to be a lie.

Such attitudes guaranteed the unpopularity of the *Relève* from the start. Rather than touching the patriotic workers depicted on the posters, Laval's appeal was answered largely by the same groups who had responded to previous recruiting drives: the desperate and the marginal. Typical volunteers in the latter part of 1942 were recent immigrants – north Africans, Spaniards and Italians from the Southern Zone, Poles from the Occupied Zone – and people from areas of high unemployment like the Alpes-Maritimes, the Var and the Aude. Their numbers were just about enough to help the scheme reach its first major target, particularly when those unlucky enough to be press-ganged by the Germans were added to the tally. Sauckel had wanted his grand total to reach 250,000 by the end of the year; in fact, it fell only about 10,000 short.

So the *Relève* had not failed immediately or disastrously, even though it had survived its first test only with difficulty and, indeed, with every sign that France's voluntary resources would quickly run dry. But even in ordinary circumstances, the short-term logic of the

Reich demanded that as soon as the books came close to balancing, the goal had immediately to be made more difficult. And, of course, the opening of 1943 was anything but ordinary for the Reich: it saw Paulus' Sixth Army collapse and surrender at Stalingrad. In February Hitler decreed the full mobilization of Nazi-occupied Europe. This new urgency meant that in France Sauckel was now looking for half a million more workers and looking for them in a hurry. Half were supposed to be found by March, and of this first contingent 150,000 were meant to be skilled workers.

Not even Vichy, with its gift for believing its own rhetoric, imagined such targets could be reached by jolly posters and talk of patriotic duty. Just going through the motions of compliance demanded that voluntary recruitment be replaced by compulsion. So, in the matter of supplying labour to the Reich as on virtually every other point in its dealings, the regime succumbed to the trap it had made for itself. Having begun by making small concessions which it claimed as triumphs of its bargaining skill, it had no alternative but to make large concessions which few could doubt were proof of its powerlessness. And no concession Vichy ever made to the Reich was more publicly damaging than when, on 16 February 1943, Laval was forced to bring in the Service du Travail Obligatoire (STO), or Compulsory Labour Scheme.

Originally the STO specified a two-year stint in Germany, for which men between the age of 20 and 22 were required to register. Miners and farmworkers, as well as the unfit, were exempt and students were granted deferrals until September; there was even a vague reassurance that not all those who were technically eligible would in fact be needed. Yet by 1944 successive changes to the regulations had enlarged the scope of the STO at every point. Farmworkers, for example, had lost their exemption and the age range of those eligible spanned men from 18 to 60 and childless women from 18 to 45. Not all of them had to work in Germany. Men over 45 and all the women could remain in France under the authority of Albert Speer's Organisation Todt, whose main achievement was to build the Atlantic Wall in anticipation of Allied landings.* Laval, who never doubted the damage the STO would do to his government and his

---

* It was named after Dr Fritz Todt, the civil engineer responsible for the autobahn system and the Siegfried Line before the war, who preceded Speer at the Ministry of War Production and Armaments. He died in 1942.

own reputation, succeeded at least in wringing these concessions from the Germans.

This small success earned him small thanks: people who had previously nicknamed Laval 'the horse-trader' now took to lumping him with Sauckel as 'the slave-trader'. Working for the Germans had lost all the overtones of patriotic duty that Vichy had sought to give it. Really, it was just like the deportation which the Jews were suffering – and this fate, surely, was what a patriotic government was there to protect patriotic Frenchmen from. Obviously, compulsory labour at home was preferable to compulsory labour abroad; obviously working for Speer was preferable to working for Sauckel. Some people trying to avoid going to Germany took grateful refuge in the Organisation Todt; a few even wore its khaki uniform and swastika armband with pride, for it was still a time when any uniform, however servile, conferred status and the appearance of authority. Yet the Todt organization was still only a lesser evil, and the majority of those eligible for compulsory labour had fallen directly under the shadow of what they did not doubt was a very great evil indeed.

It was certainly an evil great enough to resist. The enlargement of the STO's scope did not announce success but growing desperation at the impossibility of meeting the quotas which the Reich set. The failure of the STO is written unmistakably in the final tally. In the course of the Occupation the Reich had tried to press more than two million workers into its service in Germany, the majority of them after February 1943 as STO conscripts. Yet when Liberation came there were well under 800,000 French workers in Germany and this figure, of course, included not just STO conscripts but volunteers and POWs who had become 'free labourers'.

To put the failure another way, one out of every two people who should have served under the STO had not done so. Faced with their government's failure to protect them from the occupiers, one out of every two people had evaded the law. Practically, it was not hard. Draft-dodging is not difficult in most countries and most wars: officials can always be bribed to fill in a form wrongly or doctors persuaded to falsify a medical record. And draft-dodging in France during the Occupation was particularly easy. After all, respect for the law had steadily been eroded in those supposed to uphold and enforce it as well as in those who found themselves among its victims. So the faked or bought or stolen certificate of exemption from the STO took its place naturally among the other phoney documents – the certificates of discharge from the army, the ration books – which even respectable people found necessary for survival.

And those who could not slip smoothly through the bureaucratic net had other means of evading the STO. Leaving home was not so big a step in a society whose very concept of home had already taken such shocks, a society massively uprooted in 1940 and since then made sadly accustomed to the idea that people could disappear without questions being asked or official explanations given. In 1943 or 1944 leaving home could simply mean moving from one to another fragment of a family already divided and dispersed. For those who wished simply to lose themselves among strangers, France was conveniently rich in out-of-the-way rural areas where officialdom was stretched too thinly to make a proper check and farmers were too desperately short-handed to make inconvenient inquiries of any extra worker who turned up at their door.

In one of its main aspects, the history of the Occupation was the history of people being forced on to the road or forced into hiding. Those trying to avoid the STO were simply the latest to join all the other victims, all the other *débrouillards*: the people who had fled in the 1940 exodus, the people who had got stuck on the wrong side of the demarcation line at the armistice, the deserters and escaped POWs without convincing papers, the foreign exiles and refugees in fear of the internment camp, the Jews in fear of deportation. Officialdom acknowledged the existence and the growing number of this new group of missing people, this new group outside the law, in a succession of bureaucratic terms. At first, they were *insoumis* or *défaillants*: people who had failed to register for the STO by the specified date. Then they were *réfractaires*: definitely recalcitrants, definitely dodgers, a new type of law-breaker created by new laws but still nonetheless a law-breaker.

Many of the men first called *réfractaires* in 1943, of course, were just *réfractaires*: they changed places, found an obliging employer and did their best to keep their heads down for as long as possible. They usually seem to have succeeded. But for some, only a minority but still a significant number, evading the STO took them beyond the spirit as well as the technicality of what now passed for law. And in the course of 1943 they quickly adopted a name for themselves, different from *réfractaire* in its connotations and destined to become the most resonant new word of an era already fertile in its creation of new words. They called themselves *maquis*.

THE WORD *MAQUIS*, from the Italian *macchia*, entered the language by way of the Corsican dialect, which used it to describe the island's characteristic landscape of dense scrub and woodland. Nobody has ever managed to trace exactly how or why it came to be applied to the new type of resistance and the new type of *résistant*. Henri Frenay, the leader of Combat, first heard it used in this sense on New Year's Eve in 1942 – an appropriately symbolic date, though he did not trouble to record the details of the occasion. By the following June more or less everybody in France had grown familiar with it. *Maquis*, then, was slang of the purest sort, a spontaneous and popular coinage. And this in itself says a great deal about the phenomenon it described.

But what, exactly, did resisting the occupiers have to do with the Corsican landscape? What, really, did the word *maquis* connote and what purpose did its connotations serve for those who adopted it? On the most basic level, it filled the need for a term which rejected the sullen, negative overtones of *réfractaire*. *Réfractaires*, obviously, were just shirkers of duty, evaders of the law who should be dealt with by the proper authorities. Those *réfractaires* for whom evasion of the STO had become positive and militant naturally welcomed a word which proclaimed their stance. So why did they not just call themselves *résistants*, an established word which made the point clearly enough?

Until then resistance had been predominantly, though of course by no means exclusively, urban. Its main breeding ground had been the Occupied Zone, where people were exposed to the full force of the German presence without the intermediary buffer (notional rather than actual though it often was) which Vichy offered in the Southern Zone. Its characteristic habitat had been the urbanized and industrial north, where shortages cut deepest and German reprisals took their most public and savage form. And, of course, the northern cities also held the greatest concentration of all the diverse sorts of people – journalists or trades unionists, teachers or disillusioned soldiers, students or factory workers – most disposed by temperament and background to become *résistants de la première heure*.

By comparison, the countryside and particularly the countryside of the Southern Zone had seemed a more comfortable place, and so a place more given to indifference or apathy about the fate of the nation. People there found it easier to contrive ways around the food shortage – even to make a profit from the suffering in the cities – and easier to close their ears to the noise of distant conflict. The Southern Zone had, of course, lost whatever protection its status had given it when the Germans moved across the demarcation line in November 1942, establishing themselves as a dominating presence thoughout the whole country except for the little cluster of departments reserved to the Italians between the Mediterranean and Lac Léman in the south-east. This move, yet another decisive blow to Vichy's credibility, brought the reality of being occupied home to many rural areas which city-dwellers had previously despised for their complacency. Shortly afterwards the same rural areas looked attractive hiding places for *réfractaires* whose recalcitrance had turned into defiance.

The countryside often had more to offer than just literal shelter. By no means all the rhythms of rural life celebrated indifference to matters more wide-reaching than the next harvest. Political or religious history had given many areas their own proud traditions of rebellion and resistance. Foresters and farmers in the Morvan, for example, had been at odds with governments and tax-collectors long before the Marquis de Vauban had incautiously espoused their grievances in the seventeenth century. The Cévennes still held memories of the Camisards, the Protestants who had defied Louis XIV and fought their own local religious war in 1702. The Camisards offered not just an uplifting historical precedent but an exact and relevant model of how to use guerrilla tactics in the local terrain. Even the Cévenol Catholics on the borders with the Gard, the Hérault and the Ardèche had militant ancestors who had fought against Jacobinism during and after the Revolution. The Aude had an even earlier tradition in the Cathars and their struggles against the Albigensian crusades in the thirteenth century. During the Occupation it was invoked and kept alive in the local habit of using *les purs*, the old name for the Cathars, as an alternative way of referring to the Maquis.

With the growth of the Maquis, then, resistance was not just spreading to the countryside but taking on a different character, a rural character. That was what the common phrase, *prendre le maquis*, announced: it meant, simultaneously, joining the resistance and taking to the woods and the hills. It meant becoming an outlaw. Of course, *résistants* in the early years of the Occupation had been outside the law, to their own personal danger and their own personal cost. Their commitment implied a fundamental willingness – derived from political belief, religious faith or some more private sense of ethics – to set the law of the day, and much of the time their own safety with it, at nothing. Yet, for all that, they had not quite been outlaws in the traditional sense of the term.

The early leaders had usually been full-time workers for their cause, albeit sometimes virtually self-taught in the work required of them. They operated underground, adopted false identities, travelled long distances, moved to and fro across the demarcation line and periodically went in and out of the country, all with the aim of welding local pockets of resistance into a coherent system. Much of their task was diplomatic or bureaucratic. For all the hazards of his life in France and the brutality of the fate he met, Jean Moulin was an organizer and an ambassador. For his part, Henri Frenay was at pains to point out that he spent most of his time at the desk or the conference table with fellow-*résistants*: he never killed a German, never threw a bomb, never took part in a para-military raid.

Nor did many of his followers. If they were the makings of an army, they were not yet in any literal sense soldiers. Circumstances did not yet require them to be; indeed, circumstances usually made it vital that they should not be. Full-time, and hence paid, *résistants* were always in a small minority. Most were what came to be called *sédentaires* or *statiques*: they kept their ordinary identities and their ordinary jobs, drew their ordinary salaries, apparently maintained the ordinary round of their lives. This was not just useful cover, since in many cases it was essential to the nature of the work they were doing as *résistants*. It allowed journalists to gather information and gave them access to the means to print it. It allowed factory workers, railway workers, gendarmes and civil servants to gather intelligence which eventually made its way to the Free French and the Allies.

Being *maquis* was different. It originated, as the earliest resistance had done, in a spontaneous and popular movement of feeling. It grew, as the earliest resistance had done, by bringing diverse and unlikely people together. Their sheer variety was always the greatest strength, as also the greatest weakness, of those ranged against the Occupation. But being *maquis* had at its core the experience of young men – the 20- to 22-year-olds Laval first targeted when the STO was put into place – who fled the law, went on the roads, took to the woods and the hills, and found places of refuge. On the way they met up with each other and formed small bands. These attracted others whom the Occupation had already pushed into disenchantment or hiding. They were often older people with greater experience of hardship, politics and warfare: Spanish exiles who had fought in their country's civil war, soldiers who had refused to accept the armistice, exiles and refugees from the Reich and eastern Europe, Jews who had escaped the round-ups, even dispersed members of the north African regiments of 1940 and downed Allied airmen. The list of such people who could swell Maquis groups was by then formidably long. And to survive, these groups made contact with each other, with sympathetic local people, with resistance cells and networks already established.

Coalescence and enlargement meant that, in one sense, what was distinguishably *maquis* merged into the larger movement. Its bands became units in a growing network, elements in an emerging structure, almost lost in the alphabet soup of organizations dedicated to fighting against the Occupation. Even the word *maquis* became in many mouths just a synonym for any form of resistance. Yet being *maquis* also meant, as it always had to mean, belonging to a small band of outlaws. In the very name it adopted for itself, the Maquis looked back to the lawless country and the lawless traditions of Corsica. These quasi-legendary overtones – sometimes enforced by echoes of the Camisards or the Cathars – gave the Maquis glamour and dramatic force. Yet for its members to survive, let alone be effective, it also had from the start to adopt its own style of militancy, develop its own disciplines. To be *maquis* meant being both a bandit and a soldier.

A contemporary recruiting pamphlet was at pains to stress the arduous, even the forbidding aspects of an existence hiding in remote villages, sheltering in abandoned buildings, or simply camping out under canvas. 'Men who come to the Maquis to fight live badly, in precarious fashion, with food hard to find,' it announced:

> They will be absolutely cut off from their families for the duration; the enemy does not apply the rules of war to them; they cannot be assured any pay; every effort will be made to help their families but it is impossible to give any guarantee in this matter; all correspondence is forbidden.
>
> Bring two shirts, two pairs of underpants, two pairs of woollen socks, a light sweater, a scarf, a heavy sweater, a woollen blanket, an extra pair of

shoes, shoelaces, needles, thread, buttons, safety pins, soap, a canteen, a knife and fork, a torch, a compass, a weapon if possible, and also a sleeping bag if possible. Wear a warm suit, a beret, a raincoat, a good pair of hobnailed boots.

Even this sensible list does not entirely blot out the perilous charm which life in the Maquis could hold. 'Darkness falls in the forest,' wrote one young recruit about his first night with the Maquis in the Morvan:

> On one path, some distance from our camp, two boys stand guard over the safety of their comrades. One has a pistol, the other a service rifle, with a few spare cartridges in a box. Their watch lasts for two hours. How amazing those hours on duty in the forest at night are! Noises come from everywhere and the pale light of the moon gives everything a queer aspect. The boy looks at a small tree and thinks he sees it move. A lorry passes on a distant road: could it be the Germans? . . . Are they going to stop?

There is no reason to be condescending about this breathless, boyish excitement. It faithfully captures what being initiated into the Maquis felt like for the generation who were young in 1943 and 1944. They were embarking on a romantic adventure which quickly forged loyalties with new comrades; they were nervously confronting new dangers they barely understood; they were proudly learning new techniques of survival and battle. These essential features stand out in accounts by *maquisards* even after innocence had quickly given way to experience which made them regard danger and discipline as commonplace.

Group loyalty and group identification were always their most striking feature, though hardly the most surprising. The Occupation dispersed society, divided it, set it so profoundly at odds with itself as to endanger the very notion of society. It created both the circumstances and the need for people to fall back on, or to build, their loyalties at the microcosmic level. So France became a country of factions split into smaller factions and splintered again into tiny fragments, each passionate in its solidarity with itself, passionate in its warfare with the rest. This description applies as much to the *ultra-collabos* who set the tone in Parisian journalism, the thugs who joined the rival parties headed by Doriot and Déat, and the *zazous* who listened to swing as it does to the cells formed by the *résistants de la première heure* or the underground remnants of the Communist Party. But nowhere does it apply more strongly than in the Maquis. Loyalty, mutual trust and the close bonds of friendship were not just essential to survival on a daily basis; they gave a sense of identity back to people who otherwise had come close to losing all they had.

Maquis groups were quick to take on their own distinctive structure and, indeed, their own distinctive sub-culture, expressed in how they behaved, how they talked, how they dressed. The band which the young recruit in the Morvan had joined was only twelve strong, a sensible size well within the accepted recommendation that bands should never be larger than sixty and preferably much smaller. Smallness increased security, not least in helping to keep groups highly mobile, able to move from one base camp to another at short notice and without being detected. Enforced by experience, these precautions became part of the regimen which writers giving advice to the Maquis were soon urging as a matter of necessity:

> A *maquisard* should stay only where he can see without being seen. He should never live, eat, sleep except surrounded by look-outs. It should never be possible to take him by surprise.
>
> A *maquisard* should be mobile. When a census or enlistment [for the STO] brings new elements he has no means of knowing into his group, he should get out. When one of the members deserts, he should get out immediately. The man could be a traitor.
>
> *Réfractaires*, it is not your duty to die uselessly.

The extent to which a particular band kept to this discipline depended on the leader; so, in practice, did its entire fate. In other occupied countries militant bands of outlaws might operate on scrupulously democratic lines, hammering out communal decisions in the same way that their members had done in political parties, trades unions or local councils before the war. This was how the *andartes* in ELAS, the Greek People's Liberation Army, usually went about their business. In France, too, resistance had its committee aspect from the start, and as time went on committees would shape its higher levels, with all the delays and difficulties, the personal rivalries and political divisions, that such structures always entail. But the basic unit, the Maquis band, typically owed its existence to a single leader and organized itself under his example and authority. Leaders were usually older than most *réfractaires* and often not *réfractaires* at all, but people whom earlier experience of politics, war and persecution had driven into resistance, or people who held positions of influence in their local communities. From the beginning they were called *chefs*, or chiefs; soon they took on the military style of *capitaine* or *colonel*, ranks which many had held until the armistice and which now represented their positions in the new army they were training.

Their importance is reflected in the names that bands adopted. Significantly few were drawn to the abstractions – Combat, Liberté, Libération – favoured by the earlier, and largely urban, organizations. Some, relishing the romantic and legendary side of outlawry, took deliberately colourful titles: beasts of the jungle were an obvious favourite and groups like the Maquis Ours, Tigre, Loup, Lion, Eléphant, Puma and Rhinocéros proliferated. Some dedicated themselves to the memory of a dead martyr, some chose the name of their region, others were just cryptic. Many, however, took the name – or rather the codename – of their chief. The recruit who recorded his first night in the forest of the Morvan had joined a band which usually called itself the Maquis le Doc, brought together by a local doctor with all the right qualifications for leadership: military service before the war, standing in the community, and a strong and charismatic personality. Neighbouring bands included the Maquis Bernard, the Maquis Socrate, the Maquis Henri Bourgogne and so on.

The *noms de guerre* used by the other members of the group served a double purpose, practical in concealing their real names (necessary to protect their families, if for no other reason) and symbolic in proclaiming that the Maquis had given them a new identity. Their choices were sometimes boyish, sometimes learned, sometimes whimsical and sometimes purely functional, indicating the salient skill a member contributed to the band, as cook or mechanic or weapons expert. The young recruit to the Maquis le Doc was still old enough to have grown a goatee beard, so he became Le Bouc. Together with Riez, Le Prof, Fakir, Jumeau, Bouboule and Tarzan, his companions in arms included Clairon (Bugle), Sapeur (Sapper), Bûcheron (Lumberjack), Le Moto (Motorbike), and Canon (Gun) – the last, ironically, the first of them to die in battle. In other groups the men sometimes adopted women's names. Nicknames like Frisé (Curly), Double-mètre (Lofty) and Fil-de-fer (Skinny), already traditional in the classroom and the military barracks, turned up all over the place.

United in acceptance of their leader, bound to each other by a common purpose and a common discipline, answering to the names their new way of life bestowed on them, *maquisards* went further in devising a language for themselves, a slang of their own. They spoke of a sub-machine gun, normally a *mitraillette*, as a *miquette* or *sulfateuse*. In the Dordogne they took to calling plastic explosive *foie d'oie*, or goose liver. But the word most often in their mouths, the word they came closest to making their own, was *piquer*. It had always been one of the most broadly applied verbs in the language, and today the one-volume Larousse dictionary needs seven major categories to list all its various meanings, technical and colloquial. However distantly, they all derive from the original meaning of 'to prick' or 'to make a small hole'. Even *pique* and *piquant*, which the English language has borrowed, still carry the underlying idea of sharpness. In French by far the most common meaning of *piquer* in colloquial speech is 'to steal'. The difference between this usage and the formal *voler* is that *piquer* implies an indulgent or approving attitude; it concedes that theft can be committed for a good motive and in a good cause. Some French-English dictionaries seek to capture the nuance by rendering *piquer* as 'to nab' or 'to pinch'. What it really meant in the mouths of the Maquis was 'to liberate'.

Liberation as theft, theft as liberation: the practicalities of life in the Maquis intertwined the two. To pursue their goal of Liberation in the long term *maquisards* had first to survive, and to do this they had, like any outlaws, to steal – to liberate supplies or the money to buy supplies for themselves in the short term. Lack of equipment was an obstacle all *résistants* faced when they started out, but Maquis bands often had a basic, urgent need for food and clothing; cooking utensils, fuel, medical supplies were luxuries. Proper uniforms, beyond the ubiquitous beret, lay outside the means of most groups. The lack of proper weapons, felt by all *résistants*, was especially frustrating: the 300 *maquisards* in the Ain, otherwise organized and daring fighters, still had only twelve sub-machine guns, plus a few pistols and hunting rifles, between them, while the Maquis of Spezet in Brittany could muster only four pistols, two of which no longer worked.

The problem of weapons was not solved for the Maquis, any more than for other resistance organizations, by parachute drops which were inadequate in number, difficult to organize and prone to go astray. The obvious remedy of stealing or seizing weapons from the Germans was usually impossible until the chaos of the months following D-Day. Until then the Germans might be the real enemy in the guerrilla war, but that meant they were people to avoid, not to confront. *Maquisards* confined themselves to attacking other targets and satisfying day-to-day needs.

For money, they robbed railway stations, post offices, factories on pay day and banks. The Banque de France suffered major losses at branches in Saint-Claude (in the Jura) and Clermont-Ferrand; a whole shipment of money being moved by train from Périgueux to Bordeaux was stolen. A softer and more tempting target was offered by the Chantiers de Jeunesse, the pathetic substitute for military service which Vichy had established. Its emphasis on rural skills, such as forestry, meant that the *Jeunes* had exactly the sort of equipment the Maquis needed (except, of course, weapons). In January 1944, for example, a raid on the Paulhan factories supplying the *Jeunes* in the Cévennes yielded 1,980 pairs of khaki shorts, 1,455 khaki jackets and 1,640 canvases for tents, together with overalls and forestry jackets. This was a particularly rich haul, but one advantage even of smaller raids was that the *Jeunes* – conscripts, and for the most part faint-hearted and reluctant conscripts – would rarely put up opposition and sometimes even took the opportunity to defect. Maquis raids frequently had a secondary purpose, ideological or propagandist: if it was not recruitment, it could be punishment. This goal provided an obvious justification for choosing to descend on the suspected *collabos* or the known *pétainistes* when foraging through the towns and villages for food.

Outlaws, even just thieving outlaws without an ideological agenda or political aims, exist in a specific relationship to society. They steal in defiance of the established authorities, who are usually distant, but with the consent – even the connivance and applause – of the ordinary people who witness their deeds or hear tales of them told in the neighbourhood. Maquis theft both announced and consolidated its relations with local communities. When groups attacked *mairies* to get ration tickets (as they often needed to) some sympathetic mayors would allow themselves to be bound and gagged to make the raid look plausible. Afterwards, by way of extra help, they would sometimes give the authorities exaggerated accounts of the number and weaponry of the *maquisards* involved.

One historian of the Maquis has pointed to such incidents as demonstrating the emergence of 'a basic form of contract between the armed resistance and the population'. This is undoubtedly true but, in the circumstances of occupied France, it was essential to any such contract that the Maquis be more than a deserving cause or a romantic presence. It had to be a tangible power. At however local a level, it had to rival and overshadow official power, not just to prick or *piquer* it. As the Occupation entered its final phase, this claim was being made and this appearance sustained regularly by some of the larger networks of Maquis groups. The Maquis Bernard had set up its own system of taxation in the Auxois, demanding money and food on a scale which reflected people's friendliness or hostility to their cause. The leader in the Limousin, Georges Guingouin, had styled himself *préfet* and was running a system of price control which allowed farmers to charge higher rates than those imposed by Vichy. When the English philosopher A.J. Ayer arrived, as an SOE agent, in the south-west of France near Liberation, he found it 'in the hands of a series of feudal lords whose power and influence were strangely similar to that of their fifteenth-century Gascon counterparts'.

Henri Frenay had first heard the word *maquis* on the last day of 1942. Nothing showed more clearly just what it had come to mean nearly a year later than what happened on Armistice Day. Like May Day, Bastille Day and the anniversary of the battle of the Marne, Armistice Day was a critical date in the national calendar. On such occasions in 1942 crowds had gathered in several cities to shout '*Mort à Laval*', sing *La Marseillaise* or hear a message from de Gaulle reminding them they had need of their hope, their pride and their rage. These outbursts of popular feeling had marked the rise of resistance, so it was inevitable that the Maquis should have chosen 11 November 1943 to show how much further resistance had progressed in its command of numbers, organization, discipline, popular support and public gesture.

Henri Romans-Petit, regional leader in the Ain and the Haute-Savoie, chose for his demonstration the little town of Oyonnax, in the hills of the Jura overlooking the plain that stretches across to the Burgundian Côte. Nearly 300 *maquisards*, gathered from all over the region under conditions of strict security, descended on Oyonnax, bearing themselves like soldiers. Romans-Petit wore his dress uniform as a reserve captain in the airforce. Many of the other uniforms were motley and home-made, patched together from the military dress of 1939–40 and pickings from the *Jeunes*, but they were identifiably and emphatically uniforms. One group guarded the access roads; others secured the post office, the fire station, the *gendarmerie* and the German commissariat. In fact, the Germans were absent that day and the local gendarmes sympathetic or cowed.

Preceded by buglers and flanked by a white-gloved guard of honour, Romans-Petit led a parade through the streets to the memorial to the dead of the First World War, where a wreath in the shape of the cross of Lorraine was laid and the customary minute's silence observed.

Afterwards the *maquisards* led the inhabitants in singing *La Marseillaise* and went away again in as precisely drilled a fashion as they had arrived. There had been no disorder and no challenge to their power, but instead an admiring welcome from the people lining the streets. News of what Romans-Petit and his men had achieved spread rapidly in France; from London the BBC reported it and de Gaulle applauded it. The *maquisards* had 'occupied' Oyonnax – or, rather, 'liberated' Oyonnax – if only symbolically and for a day. And behind them they had left a promise and a threat in the inscription on their wreath at the war memorial. '*Les vainqueurs de demain à ceux de 14–18*', it said: 'From tomorrow's victors to those of 14–18'.

NEW LAWLESSNESS AND new authority, the revival of banditry and the making of a popular army: these ambivalences were at the heart of what the very word *maquis* brought to resistance. They would continue to invigorate and trouble it until Liberation, and beyond. And they had been apparent virtually from the introduction of the STO. Few people had imagined that the STO would succeed even in delivering the labour Germany demanded, much less in delivering it without further antagonizing the popular mood. Few had doubted that its failure would further destabilize the shaky structures which made up the political reality of France – the relationships between the Reich, Vichy and the ultra-collaborationist Right, and between each of these three forces and the rest of the French.

On one occasion when Sauckel presented his latest set of demands for labour, Laval is supposed to have retorted: 'Have you been sent by de Gaulle?' Otto Abetz, the German ambassador to Paris, told Sauckel that the Maquis should put up a statue of him inscribed 'To our number one recruitment agent'. Sauckel, however, was too committed to the short-term logic of his masters to be swayed by such protest. His problem was a shortfall in conscripts. If it could not be solved altogether, it could at least be reduced by ignoring the bureaucracy of the STO and turning to direct expedients, such as *shanghaillage*: swooping unannounced on villages or rounding up audiences as they left the cinema.

As for the wider implications of the problem, the Reich was used to ignoring Abetz, whose sensitivity to the mood of the French made his voice suspect in Berlin, and used to regarding Laval not as a policy adviser but as a tool, however unreliable. People who evaded the STO were law-breakers and people who turned *maquis* were criminals. They were not political opponents (a term which anyway had no place in the rhetoric of the Reich) but simply opponents of the civil order. And maintaining civil order, of course, was a task the Reich had from the start resolved to leave as much as possible and for as long as possible to the French.

The perspective from Vichy was different and altogether unhappier, even before the full scale of the problem which the STO landed in its lap had emerged. Naturally, it joined the Reich in denouncing *maquisards* as common criminals, labelling them *bandits* and *terroristes*, and calling for them to be stamped out. But it also acknowledged the need to distinguish between militants and the rest of the *réfractaires*. Many people had evaded the STO from motives of self-interest which fell far short of political defiance. They were to be condemned, as unpatriotic in an hour when France needed all the patriots she could muster, but not put beyond the pale. Rather than antagonizing them further, Vichy tried to woo them back into the fold, as Laval did when he announced an amnesty for *réfractaires* in October 1943, promising that those who registered themselves with the authorities would not be sent to Germany.

The amnesty failed, just as other attempts to solve the problem through the normal exercise of civil power did. The five departments of the Aveyron, the Lozère, the Hérault, the Aude and the Pyrénées-Orientales, for instance, had a list of 853 *réfractaires* to track down in the last months of 1943. They succeeded in finding only one. This miserable result might have been extreme, yet it suggested the scope of the crisis facing Vichy. The middle ground it sought to inhabit between the occupiers and all the various shades of French opinion had grown so narrow as to be virtually untenable. If there had ever been a time for resolving matters by diplomacy, negotiation and rhetoric, it had long since passed. Brutality was the order of the day, and Vichy had no choice but to engage battle with the Maquis.

However, it lacked soldiers. The whole point of the armistice, as the Reich had drafted it, had been to grant Vichy power on paper without actual power, a grand title and grand responsibilities but not the means to carry them out. Even the rump of its armed forces, the *armée de l'armistice*, had been disbanded after the Germans occupied the Southern Zone in November 1942. Hunting the Maquis was a task beyond the resources of ordinary gendarmes, whose loyalty was in any case increasingly suspect – like the loyalty of so many other servants of the state whose original inclination had been to go along with the new order of the day. The Groupes Mobiles de Réserve, the para-military police which Vichy had established in April 1941, could be called into the hunt but it was not by itself strong enough; besides, its morale and sometimes even its loyalty could not always be relied upon. To take on the Maquis, Vichy needed a new force, a new organization dedicated to the task, and there was nowhere left to recruit it except from the ultra-collaborationist Right.

Factions like Jacques Doriot's Parti Populaire Français, Marcel Déat's Rassemblement National Populaire and all the other quasi-Nazi *groupuscules* had always posed a tricky problem for Vichy. However negligible they might have seemed individually – and, of course, they had tended to operate individually and in rivalry with each other – their dissident voices had struck an answering chord in popular opinion which could not be ignored. Whether it was left to flourish outside Vichy or invited to take its place at the cabinet table, the ultra-collaborationist Right represented a threat. The best hope had always been to neutralize its energy and not to stimulate it.

The Reich, of course, had every reason for stimulating its energy, though like Vichy it had no desire to see it coalesce. The Reich had always been willing to bypass Vichy in its policy of sub-contracting the dirty work of the Occupation to the French whenever it could. It had already authorized and funded the ultra-collaborationist factions, while still taking care to keep the rivalries between them simmering. It had smiled on Jew-hunting gangs of thugs like Henri Laffont's so-called Gestapo of the Rue Lauriston. To operate the STO and combat the Maquis, it would come to depend more and more on such desperate bands, particularly in the dark months of 1944. The Comité Pour la Paix Sociale and the Ligue Pour l'Ordre Social et La Justice, both creations of Doriot and his PPF, were press gangs who worked for a salary and received a bounty for each victim of *shanghaillage*. The Selbstschutz (its name means 'self-defence') was a hit squad recruited in the autumn of 1943 from the PPF with German help. Typical of its work was the assassination in July 1944 of the politician Paul Laffont (who some thought might resume office at Liberation), along with a local doctor summoned by

Madame Laffont to treat the dying man. The killers looted Laffont's house and divided their spoil with the Germans.

Vichy could not ignore the threat to its own waning power from such private contracts between *ultra-collabos* and the Germans. Yet it also knew, now more than ever before, that by relying on *ultra-collabos* itself it might easily be unleashing forces it could not control. This is why Laval chose to ignore Doriot and Déat, their two most charismatic and powerful leaders, and fixed his attention instead on Joseph Darnand. Darnand had all the extremist qualifications. Before the war he had joined first Charles Maurras' Catholic and monarchist Action Française and then Colonel de la Roque's Croix du Feu, the most vocal of the *ligues* which had brought France to the brink of civil war in February 1934. Eventually he had found a permanent home with Eugène Deloncle's *cagoulards*, where his activities escaped prosecution only with the help of Xavier Vallat, the future head of Vichy's Commissariat Général aux Questions Juives.

Yet Darnand also boasted an impeccable military record and a cluster of medals, not just from the First World War but from the recent conflict as well; he had not succumbed to the lethargy of the phoney war or the defeatism of 1940. He was known, moreover, for his hostility to Germany as well as his admiration of Pétain. Rather than associating with the *collabos* of the Occupied Zone, he had spent the Occupation in Nice working for the *pétainiste* veterans' organization, the Légion Français des Combattants, and the Légion des Volontiers Français. From the largely respectable and complacent ranks of the Légion Français des Combattants he had created the Service d'Ordre Légionnaire, a cadre of toughs and ideologues bent on carrying the fight against Jews, Communists, Freemasons and Gaullists off the podium and on to the streets. In this idiosyncratic record Laval found the qualities that recommended Darnand to his service. The man was, he said, a fine soldier with 'about as much political intelligence as a kerbstone'.

The result was the Milice Française, or French Militia. Laval served as president and Darnand as secretary-general, but Laval's role was nominal: Darnand was the real driving force. The Milice was his creature and the direct successor to his Service d'Ordre Légionnaire. It inherited the SOL's composition and, indeed, many of its members: the same toughs and ideologues, the same sprinkling of the respectable bourgeoisie and even the disaffected aristocracy, made increasingly uncomfortable by the influx of common criminals. The Milice even declared its ancestry from the SOL in its marching song ('For those who brought about our defeat/ No punishment is harsh enough. . .') and the dress it adopted. The SOL had worn khaki shirts, black ties and berets – the last technically borrowed from the Chasseurs Alpins regiment but in practice a symbol of Frenchness favoured by the Maquis as well. To this uniform the Milice simply added dark blue jackets and trousers and, for its emblem, a white gamma: the zodiacal sign of the Ram, chosen for its connotations of strength and renewal.

Officially the Milice came into being in January 1943, before the introduction of the STO, the growth of *réfractaires* and the real emergence of the Maquis. Its oath of allegiance mentioned resistance only as one element in a litany of witch-hunting directed at all the familiar targets: 'I swear to fight against democracy, against Gaullist insurrection and against Jewish leprosy. . .'. At its creation there was a greal deal of talk about the good work the Milice could do in stamping out black marketeers, those other enemies of all right-thinking people. Yet these goals were quickly swallowed up in the realization that it was, as Pétain put it, 'the vanguard in maintaining order': in other words, effectively Vichy's only instrument for fighting the Maquis. Entering the popular vocabulary at more or less the same time, the words *maquis* and *milice* together defined the new realities: the one a little-known word for the back country of Corsica, which became a synonym for militant resistance; the other a familiar word meaning simply 'militia', which became a synonym for militant repression.

The Maquis and the Milice were enemies thrown up by the final chaos of the Occupation, in a sense twins symbiotically linked in a final hunt. But who was the hunter and who the hunted? Though they began by being hunted and remained outlaws and fugitives until Liberation, *maquisards* were quick to organize, quick to grow in self-confidence. They found in the Milice a target which was particularly easy to hate: *miliciens* were not, like Wehrmacht soldiers, German conscripts doing their job but French volunteers betraying their country. And they looked vulnerable: the Milice rarely enjoyed the local support that nourished the Maquis and, increasingly, it suffered from the knowledge that it was on the losing side in a battle which would not give quarter to the losers.

To start with, moreover, the Milice had problems equipping itself as great as any the Maquis faced. Its uniform might have included a leather belt and holster but *miliciens* were instructed to stuff the empty holster with paper. Weapons were scarce even among the Francs-Gardes, the inner cadre of full-time and salaried *miliciens*. The Germans were naturally reluctant to put guns in the hands of any of the French, whatever their political complexion or purpose, and Vichy was too fearful of the *ultra collabos'* power to urge the Milice's case with the Germans. As a result, *miliciens* began to fall victim even before they themselves had drawn blood in the hunt. The first died in April 1943 and his name was invoked at Milice rallies as crying out for vengeance; it soon headed a list of martyrs, for by October ten *miliciens* had been killed.

Numerically, these were low casualties in an organization which by then had attracted about 29,000 members (of both sexes), 10,000 of them Francs-Gardes. But the impotence that the casualties announced drove an unreflective man of action like Darnand wild with frustration. It made him threaten resignation. It even encouraged him to try flirting with the Free French abroad – though, of course, people incapable of stomaching Vichyite renegades like Admiral Darlan and Pierre Pucheu would have no truck with him. To make his position tenable, he finally had to swallow the hatred of Germans which had helped put medals on his chest in two world wars. In October he took the oath of loyalty to Hitler admitting him to the Waffen-SS; eleven of his leading henchmen quickly followed suit. Their new allegiance overcame technical objections to the Milice being given German weapons. The immediate fruit might only have been some fifty sub-machine guns – many of them British ones seized from parachute drops that had gone astray – but the larger result was to guarantee the bloodiness and bitterness of the fight in which Darnand was engaged.

Politically, it also signalled a new alignment in power, confirmed when Darnand entered the Vichy cabinet as Secretary-General for the Maintenance of Order in January 1944, with a portfolio as large as his title implied. Vichy had always kept as much distance as it could from the right-wing militants, and it had treated those whom the Germans recommended for cabinet appointments with particular caution. That was why it drew the line at Doriot, whose absence fighting on the Eastern Front could be given as grounds for rejecting him, and Déat, whose violent personal criticism of Pétain still made him unacceptable. Vichy would end up admitting Déat anyway in the following March, as Minister of Labour and National Solidarity. But before that it had already felt forced to take Darnand, the third name on the German list.

In doing so, it was admitting that what Laval had feared would happen had in fact come about: the servant had grown more powerful than the original master and, in so far as it called anybody master, reserved that name for the Germans. Sturmbannführer Darnand and his followers could even dream of the day when the Milice would be the *parti unique* in the new France. Vichy was being pushed yet further aside, not just in the larger war between the Germans and the Allies or even in the local battle between the Germans and the French. It was being pushed aside in the battle between the French and the French.

The most visible aspect of this battle was a cycle of assassinations cutting down public figures whose sympathies had been proclaimed by their previous careers. It amounted to a purge, growing in scope and savagery, of names familiar from the Third Republic as well as the Occupation. January, the month when Darnand took his seat at Vichy, saw the death of Victor Basch and his wife near Lyon. Basch, then 80, was a Jew whose record as a supporter of Dreyfus and a president of the League for the Rights of Man spoke faintly of the controversies and innocent hopes of a previous era. The *miliciens* who killed him belonged completely to their time. They included Paul Touvier – whose trial for his activities in the Milice would have to wait another fifty years – and Joseph Lécussan, Touvier's superior in Lyon and a friend of Darnand from their days together in the *cagoule*. Lécussan was known for his habit of carrying in his wallet a star of David cut from the skin of a Jewish corpse by sympathetic medical students in Toulouse, where he had also worked.

Jean Zay has already been mentioned, as a former member of Blum's Front Populaire government, additionally unfortunate in being both partly Jewish and a Freemason. Some of his enemies still remembered the youthful pacifism which had once led him to write disrespectfully of the French flag. This record had guaranteed his presence in the dock with Blum and other figures from the Third Republic at the show trial Vichy had attempted at Riom in 1942. After the collapse of the trial Zay continued to be held in prison at Riom. In 1944 the Deuxième Bureau, or intelligence section, of the Milice arranged to have him transferred to Melun. The *miliciens* who turned up to collect him on 10 June apparently told him they were really *maquisards* trying to free him. The story helped to explain the detour they took up a mountain road to a spot known as the Puits du Diable, or Devil's Well. There they shot him and hid his body so thoroughly that it was not discovered for more than two years.

By then the Maquis, too, had its hit squads and its hate-figures. An obvious target – probably the most obvious target – was Philippe Henriot, the broadcaster who (thought Gertrude Stein) had done more than any other single person during the Occupation 'to turn Frenchman against Frenchman'. He was still broadcasting in 1944, invoking all his considerable powers of rhetoric to condemn the Maquis as terrorists and Communists and to applaud the Milice as the last centurions in the defence of order. His influence had been further acknowledged in January, when Vichy appointed him Minister of Information and Propaganda as a way of placating the Reich for its failure to admit Doriot to the cabinet. In both capacities he showed a stubborn disregard for the threats against him which had become almost a commonplace in the pages of resistance journals. Those threats were realized in the early hours of 28 June. A group of *résistants* posing as *miliciens*, led by a hired killer named Desmoulin, bluffed their way into his flat at the Ministry building in Paris and murdered him in front of his wife.

Both sides in the battle made a special point of attending to ceremony, in creating public spectacles laden with emotion and propaganda. When the circumstances allowed, both the Maquis and the Milice buried their dead with the most punctilious formality; when the circumstances did not, they remembered and invoked their names in a formal litany. The ultra-collaborationist Right made Henriot's death into its greatest, as well as its last, ceremony of the Occupation. Streets were renamed in his memory. His coffin lay in state at the Hôtel de Ville where (it was claimed) 400,000 people filed past to pay their respects. His funeral, virtually a state funeral, was conducted in Notre-Dame by Monsignor Suhard, Cardinal-Archbishop of Paris, and memorial services were held in other big cities throughout France.

More practically, the orders for further killing went out. It was surely no coincidence that in the immediate aftermath of Henriot's death both the German authorities and their French sympathizers should have chosen to remember Georges Mandel. A former member of Blum's government and Reynaud's last cabinet, one of those who had stood firm with the Prime Minister in opposing an armistice, Mandel had been brought back and imprisoned after his incautious flight to Morocco on the *Massilia*. In 1942 he had been handed over to the Germans, who put him in Buchenwald along with Blum and Reynaud. But at the beginning of July 1944, within days of Henriot's death, they decided to return Mandel to France. He was lodged in the Santé prison to await, it was said, transfer to another prison near Vichy. The *miliciens* who collected him on 7 July stopped their convoy on its way through the forest of Fontainebleau on the pretext that the leading car had stalled. When Mandel got out to see what was the matter they shot him.

His murder followed so conveniently on the heels of Henriot's that it could only have been a direct reprisal. Yet the other deaths in the cycle lack this precise logic, however loudly they proclaimed that blood will have blood. Darnand liked to speak of a *règlement des comptes* but the accounting he called for – echoed, of course, with equal savagery from the camp of resistance – was never destined, or indeed meant, to be an exact affair: 1944 had simply become the time for settling scores, any scores, for revenging grudges, any grudges. Agreed on this common imperative, the sides in the conflict blur and become almost indistinguishable from each other. The Milice hit squads pretended to be the Maquis; the Maquis hit squads pretended to be the Milice. Sometimes it was impossible to tell which was really which, and sometimes it hardly mattered.

Historians have now established that the men who gunned down Maurice Sarraut, newspaper editor and man of influence in pre-war politics, outside his home in Toulouse in December 1943 belonged to the Milice. Contemporaries had no way to be sure. *Collabos* hated Sarraut for the mild liberalism of his Third Republic past, and *résistants* distrusted his willingness to listen to overtures from Vichy. Both sides had denounced him, and either could have killed him. When Mansuy, one of the *miliciens* who had killed Mandel, disappeared shortly afterwards during the liberation of Paris, one report claimed that he had died trying to assassinate de Gaulle at the Hôtel de Ville and another that he had died fighting the Germans on the barricades. Neither story can be confirmed or discounted, since 1944 saw so many obscure deaths and so many extraordinary changes of camp. In such a climate of hatred sometimes only the hatred remained certain, not the cause it served.

The leaders of Vichy, of course, were hardly better informed than anybody else, not even about the activities of their own creation, since the Milice had no reason to confide in them either before or after it carried out its operations. When Laval inquired about Jean Zay's fate he was told that Zay's car had been ambushed by *maquis-ards* who had spirited him away. He naturally suspected that 'those bastards in the Milice are hiding something from me', just as he again suspected the truth behind the claim that Mandel had died when the convoy transporting him had been ambushed. The thought shocked him for, despite their differences, he had felt a personal liking for Mandel. He certainly made it known that he would not accept the return of Mandel's fellow-prisoners, Blum and Reynaud, from German hands. But that was as far as his power went. As for Pétain, despite his condemnation of the Maquis and the soldierly respect he felt for Darnand, he too was left deploring the 'hideous reputation' the Milice had earned, vainly protesting in August that his authority was being used as a cover for introducing 'a system of terror'.

Echoes from the assassinations made themselves heard throughout the country. Henriot's murder did not call forth just Mandel's but also a spate of killings by *miliciens* in Lyon, Toulouse, Clermont-Ferrand and Grenoble; in Mâcon alone seven people died. The terrible war left its mark on every region – almost, it seemed, on every town and village. Growing desperation made the Milice more vicious: it tortured prisoners, killed prisoners, sometimes just dug the graves for those the Germans had killed. For its part the Maquis, still probably better armed and certainly in better heart, grew more daring and more indiscriminate in its attacks. When it targeted the chief of the Milice at Voiron, near Grenoble, in April 1944 it also killed his wife, his 10-year-old son, his infant daughter and his 82-year-old mother. The following month a communal grave was uncovered in the hills above Saint-Laurent in the Haute-Savoie, containing the bodies of eight police officials the Maquis had kidnapped from Bonneville. Henriot lived long enough to speak in his propaganda broadcasts of 'Soviet-style executioners' and, remembering the massacre of Polish officers in the forest outside Smolensk in 1940, of 'a French Katyn'.

Perhaps nowhere was the savage muddle more tellingly played out than in the town of Saint-Amand-Montrond, one of a handful of neighbouring places in the Berry which put forward rival claims to stand at the exact geographical centre of France. The news of the distant D-Day landings on 6 June encouraged the Maquis to liberate the town. The Germans were then virtually absent, and what was intended might have been only a symbolic gesture like the liberation of Oyonnax on the previous Armistice Day. Yet even Romans-Petit's demonstration had provoked a response, for the Germans attached as much importance to symbolism as did all the other parties to the Occupation. In nearby Nantua an SS battalion had rounded up 130 people for deportation a month later. A Maquis doctor had been found shot; two of his co-workers, one of them a captain of gendarmes who had helped to plan the Armistice Day demonstration, were tortured before being deported.

At Saint-Amand-Montrond the *maquisards* encountered a contingent of Francs-Gardes, whom they succeeded in taking prisoner before withdrawing. As well as thirteen *miliciens*, their hostages included several women; one was Simone, the wife of Francis Bout de l'An, a renegade intellectual and national figure in the Milice. His influence assured a quick response. Within a couple of days German troops and *miliciens* swooped on the town, looting houses and seizing people suspected of being connected to the Maquis: eleven were killed virtually on the spot and the rest were imprisoned and tortured. Even so, the Milice chief sent from Orléans to handle the affair still sought a negotiated solution. He was joined by the mayor and other dignitaries, including the archbishop of nearby Bourges. Their efforts bore fruit on 23 June, when the *maquisards* freed Madame Bout de l'An and the rest of their women hostages, except one who chose to remain behind. For its part the Milice released the hostages it had taken, though the Germans held on to theirs and eventually deported most of them.

Madame Bout de l'An had been spared and so, in large part, had Saint-Amand-Montrond: hysterical threats of razing the town and slaughtering its population had not been carried out. But thirteen *miliciens* remained in the hands of the Maquis, and Francis Bout de l'An, a nervous man determined to look tough, was not appeased. He was responsible for urging one aspect of the tragedy to its conclusion, while the Maquis independently completed the other. Their hostages posed a dilemma for the *maquisards*, made the more poignant by the fact that some of the men on either side had grown up together in the same town and knew each other well. If the hostages were freed, they would betray their captors' location; if they were kept, they would hinder their captors' efforts to keep on the move. On 29 July the *maquisards* decided to kill them, hanging them rather than risk giving their position away by the sound of gunfire.

Bout de l'An's chosen instrument was Joseph Lécussan, the *milicien* who had killed Basch and his wife the previous January. Armed with an emergency appointment as departmental *sous-préfet*, he conducted a *rafle* of Jews in Bourges. They were chosen not because they had anything to do with what had happened in Saint-Amand-Montrond but because the Jews were always to hand, always guilty. Thirty-six of them were taken from the Gestapo headquarters by lorry in successive groups on 24 July, 26 July and 8 August to an abandoned farm called Guerry, on the edge of the forest a few kilometres outside Bourges. There Lécussan and his helpers, French and German, threw them down the old well-shafts and piled stones and bags of cement on top.

T HOSE WHO LIVED, let alone fought, through the spring and summer of 1944 remember above all its *mentalité terrible*. When they use the phrase they are usually thinking in particular of the war between the French and the French. Yet *la guerre franco-française* was only one part of the larger war then grinding its way towards a decisive encounter. Even by the end of 1943 the Reich had suffered heavy reverses in its campaign in the east, and the east was just one of three fronts on a desperately overstretched battle line of more than 11,000 kilometres, or nearly 7,000 miles. Fortune was clearly deserting Hitler's cause. For all their caution and their delay, the western Allies were bound to strike a powerful blow and bring the issue to its climax. The landings would come and the landings would liberate France.

Or would they? Military historians now have little difficulty in explaining why the odds on D-Day and afterwards lay heavily in the Allies' favour. The inability of German intelligence to penetrate Allied planning and the inability of the Luftwaffe to hinder from the air any plan the Allies chose to launch across the Channel made it, in John Keegan's words, 'the smoothest of broad highways to the weak places in the Atlantic Wall'. The army defending the Wall was not the army which had overrun France in 1940: four years of fighting had taken a heavy toll on the Wehrmacht. Its ranks were padded with older men and younger boys, with *Freiwilligen* (volunteers) and *Hilfswilligen* (auxiliaries) from all the territories occupied by the

Reich, and with captured troops from the Red Army. There was even a handful of Koreans looking nervously across the Channel.*

The German high command had never been happy on the defensive, and by 1944 it was no longer in a state to mastermind a fluent, co-ordinated strategy such as *Sichelschnitt* had been. The division of authority between Rommel and Rundstedt in the task of repulsing the Allies was itself an awkward arrangement. Their lack of agreement made it worse: Rommel put his trust in stopping an invasion dead at the Atlantic Wall itself while Rundstedt (supported by Guderian, the architect of Panzer tactics) favoured a more flexible defence in depth. Hitler did not help matters. He was no longer given to bold ideas, as he had been in 1940, but instead to querulous, distrustful intervention: he pored over detailed battlefield maps, he reserved the deployment of vital Panzer divisions to his own direct command, he issued sudden, impossible orders. The July bomb plot did not improve his mood. Nor did the replacement of Rundstedt and then Rommel by Field Marshal Hans Günther von Kluge, and of Kluge in turn by Field Marshal Walther Model, clarify the Reich's strategy. In practice it did not amount to much more than a sullen resolve to fight where it stood and not to yield, come what may. And that, of course, was exactly the stance which the generals of the First World War had so bloodily discredited.

None of these factors, so clear in retrospect, was anything like as clear at the time. The Channel still seemed the near-impassable barrier it had traditionally been, the barrier that had defeated Hitler, and Napoleon too. Though obviously weakened, the Wehrmacht could still be suspected of untapped reserves of strength and endurance. As for Allied invasions, the landings in north Africa had given hope to sympathizers in France, but the memory of the disastrous raid on Dieppe in 1942 still lingered and news of the deadlock at Monte Cassino and Anzio was still fresh. In preparing the French for what might happen when the Allies landed on French soil, German propaganda made great play with the picture of an Allied snail creeping up the boot of Italy. Even the wait for the D-Day landings was slow, doubtful and agonizing; in the event, Liberation would prove equally so.

---

* They had been conscripted into the Japanese army when Korea was a Japanese colony, captured and conscripted by the Red Army during border fighting between Japan and the Soviet Union in 1939, then captured and conscripted again outside Moscow in 1941.

If hindsight clarifies the military situation favouring the Allies, it also compresses the events following D-Day into a rapid succession of images: Allied troops storming the Normandy beaches, de Gaulle marching down a Champs Elysées lined with cheering crowds, France free again. It did not happen like that. Hitler might have conquered France in a bare six weeks in 1940, but in 1944 the pace of military events was plodding. Liddell Hart later summed up Operation Overlord, as the battle in the north was codenamed, in remarking that it might eventually have gone according to plan but it had not gone according to schedule.

Even on D-Day itself, 6 June, the airborne troops found themselves dispersed and, in some cases, lost. At Omaha Beach, one of the five Allied landing places between Caen and Cherbourg, the Americans ran into an unexpectedly strong defence which they overcame only with sheer bloody-mindedness and the knowledge that there was nowhere to retreat to, only the sea behind them. It was the end of July before the Allies broke out from Normandy to the west, with the advance of General Patton's Third Army through Avranches, and mid-August before they closed the Falaise gap in the east. By then the battle had claimed 210,000 Allied casualties, about 40,000 of them killed; 240,000 Germans had been killed or wounded, and another 200,000 captured. Upwards of 50,000 French civilians had died and many towns – Lisieux, Coutances, Saint-Lô, Falaise, Argentan and Caen – had been left in smoking ruins. Paris, of course, did not suffer that fate but Paris, which had fallen little more than a month after the start of the 1940 invasion, had in 1944 to wait for its liberation until the last days of August, two and a half months after D-Day. Even then, the Allies' entry into the capital signalled a last-minute change of tactics which actually advanced their schedule.

After Paris had been liberated Hitler's loss of France was still desperately slow. Allied landings in the south, to split the German defences, had originally been planned to coincide with D-Day. But Operation Anvil was delayed by a shortage of landing craft and British reluctance to divert resources from the Italian campaign. Churchill even insisted its codename be changed to Operation Dragoon, because he felt dragooned into it by the Americans. It did not start until 15 August, when troops landed on the islands and beaches south of Cannes. They never met the terrible reverses which had plagued the Allies in the north from the moment the Americans found themselves bogged down at Omaha Beach. Yet it still took another month for the armies now advancing from north and south to make contact with each other, on the bleak plateau of the Châtillonais north of Dijon.

The Reich's defence was fiercest in the east. It was there, from the Belfort Gap and the Vosges up to the Ardennes, that its retreating armies were pushed in their escape from the Allied pincer. By mid-September the Allies had advanced to a line corresponding roughly to the pre-war border of France, though Strasbourg, in the disputed territory of Alsace and Lorraine, was not liberated until near the end of November. The battle of the Bulge, Hitler's counter-assault in the Ardennes at the end of the year, brought his armies almost to the Meuse near Dinant, where Rommel's crossing in 1940 had been one of the first warnings of the Reich's coming victory. This time the Reich was repulsed and lost 120,000 troops in the process. But it was teaching the western Allies the same lesson that the Red Army was learning on the Eastern Front: as it was forced back towards its heartland its armies grew ever more stubborn, ever more capable of springing surprises which almost threatened to reverse the tide of the war. Not until near the end of March 1945, nearly ten months after D-Day, did the troops who had started their advance on the beaches of the Channel and the Mediterranean actually cross the Rhine.

So, step by painful step, the occupiers were forced out of France in the last six months of 1944. There was no national date for Liberation. Each town and village still celebrates a different day, the gaps between them marking advances that often looked bogged down, pockets of German defence that often turned out to be unexpectedly tough. It proved the bitterest of ends to a bitter war. But what role, really, had France and the French played in this end? The very circumstances of 1944 made it impossible for France to be what cynics insisted she had been in 1914–18 and again in 1940, the helpless soil over which foreign armies raged. The hope and the pride and the anger – above all, the anger – to which de Gaulle had appealed as long ago as 1942 guaranteed that the French would not simply play the role of smiling, waving extras assigned them in the Allies' publicity photographs.

Officially, the landings marked the final unification of resistance. They were the moment when the Free French regiments hammered together abroad and bloodied in north Africa returned to the soil of the mainland. There they joined, not isolated cells of *résistants* or outlaw bands, but a popular army. It was significant that before the end of May 1944 the BBC had dropped the word *maquis* from its broadcasts. The preferred term was FFI, or Forces Françaises de l'Intérieur, the final umbrella organization to emerge from all the patient work by all the committees which de Gaulle had cajoled and bullied and inspired.

On neither side of the Channel did the reality match the official version. The real leaders of the battle knew that. The troops assembled for Operation Overlord were American, British, Canadian, Polish and French. The first, of course, were represented in greater numbers than those of any other nation. General Pierre Koenig – hero of the battle against Rommel's divisions at Bir Hakeim in June 1942 and now commander of the FFI – had been granted equal status with the generals of other nations under Eisenhower's supreme command. Yet, however necessary the presence of Koenig and the Free French might have been as a gesture of goodwill, and as further proof in the face of German propaganda that the Allies were not invading but liberating France, their military role was not thought significant. Out of the thirty-nine divisions assigned to Normandy, just one was Free French: the Deuxième Division Blindée (Second Armoured Division) under General Leclerc.* It did not land on D-Day itself, though it did join in the fighting at the Falaise gap. In Operation Dragoon, it is true, seven out of the American General Patch's eleven divisions were Free French – commanded by General Jean de Lattre de Tassigny – but the landings in the south were altogether a smaller and less favoured affair.

As for de Gaulle, his position was an anomaly. From the Allied point of view it was summed up by his place at the head of the list of worries Eisenhower drew up before D-Day, topping even the notorious uncertainties of the weather in the Channel. In the four years since Churchill's first generous welcome de Gaulle had made himself a perpetual stimulant but also a perpetual irritant, a symbol the Allies had to acknowledge but not a head of state they could bring themselves to recognize. His Comité Français de Libération Nationale was acknowledged as the provisional government of France by Czechs, Poles, Norwegians, Yugoslavs and Belgians – France's

---

* The *nom de guerre* of the Vicomte Jacques-Philippe de Hautecloque.

fellow-victims in distress – but not by the Americans and the British. France, so the Americans at first assumed, would simply join Italy under AMGOT, the Allied Military Government for Occupied Territories. American officials were trained at Yale and Charlottesville, Virginia, to assume the administration of the country once Vichy's representatives had been unseated. To counter the German Occupation marks which had flooded into France, special Liberation currency was printed, bearing the *tricolore* and the motto, *Liberté, Egalité, Fraternité*, but otherwise looking very much like dollar bills.

De Gaulle did not set foot on the mainland of France until 14 June, more than a week after D-Day itself and two days after Churchill had toured the Allied bridgeheads. Even then, he made only a one-day visit, landing at Courseulles-sur-Mer in the centre of Juno Beach and venturing a few kilometres inland to Bayeux, the first town of any size which the Allies had liberated. He went in the face of Allied reluctance expressed, in a private letter from Eden to Churchill, in the hope that he could be confined to shaking a few hands and not allowed to hold public reunions or attract crowds. The commonly repeated story that the first two Frenchmen de Gaulle did meet, both gendarmes, failed to recognize him might have been mere gossip among his many detractors, but it was not implausible nor to his discredit. To the French, de Gaulle was not then a public face, but a public voice.

He retreated again to Algiers, already a better power base than London and for the moment still a better power base than anywhere in France. When he did return to the mainland, landing at Cherbourg on 20 August, he did so merely on the pretext of inspecting the liberated areas and he again had to seek the Allies' permission first. But, after touring the ravaged landscape of Brittany and Normandy, he arrived on 22 August at Rambouillet, the country seat of Third Republic presidents, in the forest west of Paris. Installing himself there was a typically bold gesture, which he qualified by refusing to trespass on the presidential facilities beyond taking a volume of Molière to read from the library. He was watching events, certain of his role in them, certain of France's need of him.

What did France have to offer him, and what did he have to offer France? From his point of view the state of resistance was less than satisfactory, less than reassuring. The creation of a deeply divided people, it remained not just locked in a bitter war of the French against the French but also divided among itself. In some areas the Communists of the FTP were wary of joining the umbrella of the FFI; in others they joined in such numbers that they overwhelmed its Gaullist character. The very problems that weakened resistance in the fight against the Germans also warned that resistance had nurtured powerful rivals in a fight to inherit France once the Germans had gone.

But, of course, there were other ways of judging resistance than by looking at it from the perspective of de Gaulle and the Free French who had spent the war abroad planning for France's future. Local and various, its real strength lay in the grassroots where it had started and flourished. It was a guerrilla force, ferocious but patchy in the extent of its power. Like most guerrilla forces, it was reliably best at sabotage, at hindering rather than confronting its enemy. Before the landings, hindering the enemy was more a matter of morale than anything else. Blowing up a railway line or a radio transmitter or a factory merely inconvenienced the Germans, and always carried risks of reprisal, but it greatly cheered the people who set the charge – which is why they often used more explosive to make a bigger bang than was strictly necessary. After D-Day sabotage served a tactical function.

It could hinder the movement of German troops, whether reserves brought in from Germany or defeated remnants of the Wehrmacht retreating back home. Most critically, it could delay the arrival of reinforcements to stem the haemorrhage in the Atlantic Wall during the days immediately following D-Day itself. Most reinforcements were dependent on the railway, and railway lines and carriages were now particularly vulnerable to attack. One German infantry division, ordered on 6 June to make the 200-kilometre journey by rail from Redon in southern Brittany, was forced to complete its advance on foot. It did not start to arrive at the front until 11 June. Another infantry division took twenty-two days to get from Bayonne. Even Panzer divisions were vulnerable, since their tanks depended on special railway transporter cars for making long journeys. Das Reich, the Second Waffen-SS Panzer Division, was ordered to prepare to move north from Montauban, north of Toulouse, to Normandy on 8 June. The Loire, where Allied planes had bombed the bridges, need not have been an obstacle to a division which had tackled far bigger ones during its service on the Eastern Front. But a journey which should have taken seven days in the end took sixteen.

In some places, of course, *résistants* went beyond sabotage in aid of the Allies and took matters directly into their own hands. The very delays in the Allied advance themselves encouraged such local initiative. When General Patton's Third Army did finally break out of Normandy via Avranches at the end of July, it found its way through Brittany effectively cleared. The region's rural character had long made it a centre of resistance. Even before D-Day the *maquisards* had been confident enough to stage full-dress rehearsals of their plans to sabotage the railways; soon after D-Day they had brought rail traffic to a halt and fought pitched battles with the Germans. Now, with the news of Patton's advance, they liberated places like Saint-Brieuc, Quimper and Nantes by themselves. The Allies met virtually no opposition until they reached the U-boat bases at Brest, Lorient and Saint-Nazaire. In the south, it had been estimated that Operation Dragoon would take ninety days to reach Grenoble. But while the bulk of General Patch's force made its way slowly up the Rhône valley, an armoured-car regiment acted instead on a tip from de Gaulle and the FFI. It followed the Durance valley and the old Route Napoléon from Nice through Grasse, Digne and Gap, met by already victorious local *résistants* as it went. It reached the outskirts of Grenoble in six days.

General Eisenhower paid tribute to the work *résistants* had done in Brittany; after the war André Malraux cited their work in the Durance valley as one of the main achievements of which resistance could be proud. Both were models of co-ordination between local *résistants* and the Free French – the internal and external forces of the FFI – and between the FFI and the American troops. Yet such models were rare. The perspectives of these various parties to the liberation of France were too divergent and their communication lines too fragile to make concerted action the norm. In its absence, *résistants* were caught in a dilemma which could easily turn into disaster.

Their cause had grown formidably strong, particularly in the rural areas of the south. In some places it was so buttressed by local support that it amounted to a government waiting for the right moment to take over; in others it had driven the Vichy and German authorities so thoroughly on to the defensive that it seemed almost to have become the new government. But, when it came to it, resistance was still not an army which could rise up and hope to win, either by itself or as a third front to complement Operation Overlord and Operation Dragoon. France would be liberated, but not by an *insurrection nationale*. The dream of France liberating herself died hard, however. The idea of creating 'a real piece of free France inside the occupied territory' had attracted Jean Moulin as early as February 1943. The emphasis, endorsed by de Gaulle, on *action à terme* (or long-term action) had deferred it but pent-up energies in the long wait for D-Day lent it new urgency.

The Haute-Savoie was already a Maquis stronghold, so the temptation to make it a stronghold in a strictly military sense proved irresistible. From January 1944 onwards *maquisards* led by Théodose Morel, codenamed Tom, gathered on the Glières plateau, north-east of Annecy. By the end of February there were 460 of them, sworn to '*Vivre libre ou mourir*'. Conditions and equipment were rudimentary: the *maquisards* lived in summer chalets, liberated skis from the handful of winter holidaymakers and built igloos to use as gun emplacements. They had only light weapons and virtually no radios for staying in contact with each other. Yet they held propaganda value for the Free French in London, determined to insist that 'In Europe there are three countries resisting: Greece, Yugoslavia and the Haute-Savoie.' The propaganda helped to ensure parachute drops of weapons and supplies from the Allies.

And, together, the propaganda and the parachute drops ensured that the enemy took the *maquisards* on the Glières plateau seriously. When Vichy's Groupes Mobiles de Réserve failed to dislodge them, the Germans moved in. They launched an aerial bombardment in the middle of March and a full-scale attack near the end of the month: an Alpine Division of 7,000 men, with SS units, artillery cover, air support and a contingent of 1,000 *miliciens*. About 150 *maquisards* died as their stronghold fell; in the mopping-up operation about 200 more people were arrested, tortured, haggled over by the Milice and the Germans, and shot or deported. The propaganda war which had already misled both attackers and defenders about the strength of the fortress quickly obscured the precise numbers and fate of the victims.

Hope and frustration guaranteed that the failure in the Haute-Savoie would be played out again in the Auvergne. De Gaulle's Comité Français de Libération Nationale had assigned the region a critical role in taking mass action; the local head of the FFI believed that continuing to play a waiting game would only demoralize his forces. On 20 May he began gathering them at Mont Mouchet in the

Margeride and in the Gorges de la Truyère under the banner, 'Free France starts here'. Estimates of their number vary wildly, from 3,500 to 11,000, though the lower figure is the more likely. German attacks during the course of June dislodged them from Mont Mouchet and harried them from refuge to refuge, killing at least 125 of them and wounding an equal number. In the widening pattern of reprisal which the Occupation had made familiar, several villages were destroyed and about 70 local civilians died.

The *maquisards* on the Glières plateau were beaten during the build-up to D-Day; those on Mont Mouchet were beaten while the battle for Normandy was already under way. The *maquisards* on the Glières plateau got propaganda support from the Free French abroad and parachute drops from Allied planes; those at Mont Mouchet got no parachute drops and stood in an ambiguous relationship to the Free French abroad. Their action accorded with the dream of a third internal force rising up against the occupiers, yet Free French broadcasts were already careful to avoid the phrase *insurrection nationale*, which expressed the dream announced by the banner on Mont Mouchet. And on 10 June, as the Germans were attacking Mont Mouchet, General Koenig phrased the Gaullist suspicion of sudden uprisings and Maquis fortresses as an emphatic command to the FFI: 'Keep guerrilla activity below its maximum level. . . . Do not mass together. . . . Form small separate groups.'

This division in perspective and strategy played a larger role in the fate of the last attempt at a Maquis fortress. Ironically, its site was the Vercors, the plateau south-west of Grenoble which had given Jean Bruller his pseudonym for resistance writings like *Le Silence de la mer* and which had struck Jean Moulin as the ideal spot to create 'a real piece of free France'. Eugène Chavant, regional head of the FFI in the Isère, summoned his followers to gather there on hearing the news of the D-Day landings. Some 3,000 had gathered by 9 June, and their number continued to grow as the weeks wore on. The restoration of the French Republic was declared on 3 July. Bastille Day, fittingly, brought a massive drop of supplies – part of the largest such operation the US Air Force had launched in daylight, 360 Flying Fortresses and a guard of fighters spreading over the Lot, the Corrèze and the Dordogne as well as the Vercors plateau. But, for all their abundance, the supplies did not include badly needed heavy weapons. More disquieting, there was no sign of the French troops the *maquisards* had hoped would be dropped in to join them. And most disquieting of all, there was no news of Allied landings in the south – the fighters on the plateau had no way of knowing they had been put off until 15 August – and no sign of Allied reinforcements.

In the middle of June the Germans had driven the Maquis back from the village of Saint-Nizier-du-Moucherotte near the northern tip of the plateau, severing its connecting link with Grenoble. When it came in the last days of July, the main attack was the operation on the Glières plateau writ larger and more bloodily. It even depended on the same Alpine division, given air cover by the Luftwaffe and supported by SS glider troops, Alpine commandos and a Panzer unit from Lyon. By the time the action had ended, it had claimed the lives of 630 *maquisards*, including some who had been shot where they lay wounded in a field hospital, and 200 others, including local villagers and a medical team treating the wounded.

A particular note of bitterness was added to this grim tally in the telegram Chavant sent to Algiers on the night of 21–22 July, as the attack began. It pleaded one last time for the help – men, food and equipment – he had been counting on from the start and had still been hoping for over the last few weeks. If help did not come, the defenders of the Vercors would be forced to agree with what was already being bruited about: that the high-ups in London and Algiers understood nothing of the situation on the ground, that the high-ups in London and Algiers were criminals and cowards. 'That's what we are saying,' the telegram ended: 'criminals and cowards.'

The Free French in London and Algiers, of course, could reasonably point out how many groups in the Maquis were pleading for help, how little help there was available and how much of it was dependent on American and British allies now engaged in their own battle. They could point to the success of the Vercors defenders in holding up a significant number of German troops and to the combined strength which the defenders had mustered, even in their defeat. They could pay tribute to the heroism of the Maquis at Vercors, while pointing to the tactical folly of mass assembly by forces whose strength lay in remaining small and mobile.

All these points were made in the recriminations which followed the Vercors disaster. At root, though, it joined the disasters on the Glières plateau and at Mont Mouchet in underlining the dilemma in which resistance, with its particular combination of angry strength and military weakness, was now caught. The French had already expressed it, like most of the sadder truths the Occupation had taught them, in a joke circulated and repeated in one form or another throughout the country (by the diarist Galtier-Boissière in Paris and by Gertrude Stein in the Haute-Savoie, for example). On the crowded platform of a bus a German soldier accidentally treads on a Frenchman's foot. Surprised into reacting instinctively, the Frenchman lashes out and hits him. As soon as he does so, another Frenchman forces his way from the other end of the bus and hits the German too. All three are taken to a police station, where the German and the first Frenchman soon clear up their misunderstanding and apologize to each other. The second Frenchman is then required to explain himself, and says: 'When I saw the German get hit, I thought it meant I had the right to hit him too.' At least, that is what he says in one version. In another, he says: 'I thought it meant the war was over.'

The joke and its variant endings encapsulate all the potential for muddle in the tactical debate between *action immédiate* and *action à terme* which the killing at the Métro Barbès in August 1941 had made public. Those sceptical of *action immédiate*, as de Gaulle had long since declared himself to be, could now regard the dead of Glières, Mont Mouchet and the Vercors as the victims of rashness on a grand scale. Those sceptical of *action à terme* could now ask with added urgency when the 'right moment' for action would come. It had not come with the imminence of Allied landings, it had not come with Allied landings in the north, it had not come with the daily expectation of Allied landings in the south. So would it ever come? Or would the 'right moment' slip by, leaving France to be liberated by foreign allies, leaving four years of French anger unappeased?

It would have taken more than tactical advice, however wisely measured, to stem such feelings. In the event, they surfaced in local hope and local pride as well as in local anger. Take, for instance, the case of Annonay, a town in the Ardèche which already had a claim to fame as the scene of the Montgolfier brothers' ballooning experiments in the eighteenth century and which was eager to stake another as the first place in France to be liberated, the first place to liberate itself. The conditions were apparently ideal, since the Germans were absent and the gendarmes, as well as the postal and telegraph workers, were sympathetic. *Maquisards* from both the FFI and the FTP proclaimed an end to the Occupation in Annonay at about ten o'clock on the morning of 6 June, just hours after the first landings on the Normandy beaches. They went on to mark the occasion by sending a vengeful telegram to Pétain and Laval demanding that they present themselves before a local tribunal to answer for their deeds.

The telegram went unanswered, of course, but Annonay's liberation also proved nearly as brief and symbolic as the liberation of Oyonnax the previous Armistice Day. A combined force of Groupes Mobiles de Réserve and Milice entered the town on 19 June, with a column of Germans not far behind them. The *maquisards*, who had already had to face criticism from some inhabitants for being rash and premature, made a tactical withdrawal. A skirmish took place on the outskirts of the town and two *maquisards* arrested while trying to help a wounded comrade were executed, but no mass reprisals were visited on Annonay. The Germans withdrew the same day, leaving the Groupes Mobiles de Réserve in charge. They in turn withdrew on 15 July, leaving Annonay in an official no man's land until August.

By the standards of the time, these exchanges of power had a cautious, almost courtly air. Elsewhere local struggles brought savagery in their wake. The consequences of the attempt to liberate Saint-Amand-Montrond in the immediate aftermath of D-Day have already been described. At Tulle, in the Corrèze, *maquisards* of the FTP fought a fierce battle with defenders of the German garrison on 7 and 8 June, killing more than fifty of them, executing at least ten of the prisoners they took and briefly managing to fly the *tricolore* over the town before the arrival of German reinforcements forced them to withdraw. The next day the Germans hanged ninety-nine men from trees, telegraph poles and the balconies of houses.

The soldiers who carried out the reprisal belonged to Das Reich, the Waffen-SS Panzer Division making its way in the face of Maquis harassment from Montauban to the Normandy front. Their journey left a terrible mark on the country between. Some of the tanks that arrived in Tulle had prisoners from an earlier engagement strapped to their front as protection from Maquis fire. And on 10 June another company of 120 men from Das Reich swooped on the village of Oradour-sur-Glane, north of Limoges, to carry out the most notorious of all the atrocities committed during the Occupation. They arrived in the early afternoon and by midnight they had killed 642 people, virtually the entire population. The men were herded together in barns and shot. The women and children were crowded into the church which was then burned to the ground along with all the other buildings of Oradour.

In the half-century since it took place the Oradour massacre has been kept alive in the memory of the French in several different ways. It was decided after the war to preserve the ruins of the village as a shrine. The trial in 1953 of twenty-one of the men responsible brought the troubling reminder that not all were German; fourteen of the accused were Alsatian conscripts (or *malgré-nous*), most of them aged between 17 and 19 in 1944.* Historians still puzzle over the reason for the massacre and find it a mystery. Why should Oradour have been chosen? It had no record of Maquis activity. Did it suffer for one of the ambushes in the area which Das Reich could not revenge more directly? Or did it suffer by mistake, confused with its militant near-namesake Oradour-sur-Vayres, 40 kilometres away? But of all these ways of remembering Oradour the most potent is embedded in colloquial speech, which has made the word *oradour* a generic term for all the other *villages martyrisés* of 1944 as well: places like Ascq, near Lille, where 86 people died in April, and Maillé, south of Tours, where 126 people died in August. *Oradour* is the name for the helplessness of France and the French, even at the hour of Liberation.

P ARIS, OF COURSE, was at once the greatest prize and, potentially, the greatest victim. Hitler appreciated its importance, as much symbolic as tactical. 'In history the loss of Paris always meant the loss of France,' he reminded General Dietrich von Choltitz, the newly appointed Kommandant, on 22 August 1944.† As soon as he had deftly trapped it in the curving blade of *Sichelschnitt* in 1940, he had rushed to visit the capital in person. 'It would have pained me greatly if I had had to destroy Paris,' he added later. But by 1944 his attitude

---

*Sturmbannführer (Major) Otto Dickmann, who commanded the men at Oradour, had died fighting in Normandy; his second-in-command, Hauptsturmführer (Captain) Kahn, disappeared without trace.

† General Hans von Boineburg-Lengsfeld, the previous Kommandant, and Karl Heinrich von Stülpnagel, the Militärbefehlshaber, were replaced because of their involvement in the July bomb plot against Hitler. On his way back to Berlin, Stülpnagel stopped at Verdun, where he had served in the First World War, and tried to kill himself. He was hanged on 30 August 1944.

had hardened into a vengeful determination to leave only scorched earth behind him in any retreat from the Allies. 'Paris must be destroyed from top to bottom before the Wehrmacht leave,' he is supposed to have told Choltitz: 'do not leave a single church or cultural monument standing.'

De Gaulle needed no reminding of what Paris meant. Its fate was uppermost in his mind, too, on 22 August, when he installed himself at the presidential seat at Rambouillet. He had been urging the importance of liberating Paris as soon as possible after the Allied landings since at least the previous November, long before he had any idea of the actual form which Operation Overlord would take. He had even wrung from Eisenhower – virtually unique among Allied generals in his sympathetic attitude to de Gaulle – the promise that the honour of liberating the capital should go to French, and not British or American, troops.

Eisenhower was conceding less than de Gaulle might have hoped. Alone among the parties to the battle, the Allies refused to give Paris high priority. By 22 August they had encircled it from the west – Patton's army touched the Seine both upstream and downstream, only about 60 kilometres away in either direction – but they still hoped to avoid making a direct move. Paris was a far trickier proposition than anything the battle of Normandy had presented, and the battle of Normandy had itself been difficult enough. Its concentration of both people and cultural monuments ruled out aerial bombardment and heavy artillery barrages, so taking the city would soak up time and lives in a campaign already behind schedule and high in casualties. Once it was taken, feeding its population would drain supplies urgently needed for the armies advancing on Germany. Besides, the Allied commanders comforted themselves, the capture of Paris was not tactically essential: in his memoirs General Bradley was still calling it a pen-and-ink job on the map. The best thing to do was to bypass Paris, let the German defence start to wither away and not attempt any direct assault until the middle of September.

This soldierly logic overlooked the reality of what was happening in Paris. People there heard the first news of the D-Day landings with less excitement than people in the rural south. Some reports even suggested a metropolitan indifference to what happened in the provinces, a belief that events were not truly national until, and unless, they reached the capital. But all the signs soon warned that events were going to reach Paris. In the course of four years Parisians had grown used to seeing Wehrmacht soldiers – originally so smart, so disciplined, so correct – looking shabbier and shabbier. Now the soldiers flooding back from the Normandy front had the look of a defeated army. One young teenager stumbled accidentally on a convoy of ambulances drawn up outside a military hospital:

> The drivers were utterly exhausted. On stretchers in the ambulances, their hastily applied bandages soaked in blood, lay wounded men, most of whom could only have been three or four years older than I was. Some were crying, their faces racked with pain. The heat was so intense that the windows were down. A lament rose from the convoy, the mingling of a hundred moanings, sobbings and hoarsely murmured cries, which was an even more overwhelmingly strange thing than the sight of these very young men rolling their heads in agony on their stretchers.

Remembering the incident years later, he added that 'the temptation to feel sorry for them did not cross my mind'.

Most of the soldiers flooding in did not stay long, and when they left much of the city's permanent garrison went with them: first the *souris grises* (as the French called the women auxiliaries), then the security forces and the SS with Darnand's orphaned *miliciens* in their wake, and then even the new Militärbefehlshaber, General Kitzinger, and his staff, leaving Choltitz in sole command. By 17 August Galtier-Boissière could write with malicious pleasure in his diary of '*la grande fuite des Fritz*': 'the mass flight of the Fritzes'. But, for all the military traffic which jammed the streets, it was not a disorderly rout, not even strictly a flight. Hitler was still hoping to construct, First-World-War style, a second line of defence along the Somme. Now a bridgehead, Paris was being battened down for a siege. Siege conditions replaced the hardships of ordinary life: food grew even scarcer and the power supply even less reliable, the newspapers stopped publishing, the radio ceased to broadcast, restaurants closed. Public transport failed as its workers went on strike, followed by the postal workers, the nurses and the police.

In this growing discontent what role could organized resistance assume? It was divided in its loyalties, between Gaullist and Communist, and in its impulses. Alexandre Parodi, de Gaulle's political delegate to the territories which the Allies had not yet liberated, and Jacques Chaban-Delmas, the military delegate, urged restraint. Henri Tanguy, codenamed Colonel Rol, head of the FFI in Paris and a Communist veteran of the Spanish Civil War, was eager to take up arms. His feeling was shared not just by other Communists but by people like his own second-in-command, Colonel de Margueritte, codenamed Lizé, whose patience with clandestine planning had reached an end. They were deterred only by the weakness of the forces at their disposal. Whatever their true number – Chaban-Delmas put it at 15,000 to 16,000 – it was Rol's own gloomy estimate that between them they boasted only 600 weapons, mainly rifles and sub-machine guns.

The police broke the stalemate. In time of revolution their loyalties always carry decisive weight and in Paris in 1944 the police were disaffected, on strike and still armed. On 19 August they took over the Préfecture de Police on the Ile de la Cité and hoisted the *tricolore*, the first time the French flag had been flown in the capital for over four years. Countless Parisians had been watching for such a gesture, checking the swastikas on the public buildings (as Simone de Beauvoir was doing at the Palais du Luxembourg each morning) to see when they would disappear. Other *tricolores* started to sprout as the news spread, on local police stations, *mairies* and schools, challenging and replacing the emblem which the Germans had made the most visible and potent symbol of their domination. Nor, beneath the symbolism, did the underlying significance of what was happening escape Parisians: the great French bureaucracy, whose established structures and habits of smooth administration had been an essential prop to the Reich, as to Vichy, had openly broken ranks at last.

After their initial surprise Colonel Rol and his FFI moved quickly to take advantage of the moment. Fighting soon broke out in the Boulevard Saint-Germain and the Boulevard Saint-Michel. In the Place Saint-Michel, Galtier-Boissière found himself caught in the crowd forced to flee into side streets when the officer leading a column of German lorries fired several bursts from his sub-machine gun. Shots were exchanged with the Germans holding the Palais du Luxembourg, the former seat of the Senate, and the Luxembourg Gardens. People started building barricades, sometimes under the very eye of the few patrols still about. By the end of the day about 150 *résistants* and about 50 Germans had died. By then Parodi, as determined as Colonel Rol to seize the opportunity for the Gaullists, was already starting to move de Gaulle's appointees into the ministry buildings which had been cleared.

The actual moment when uprisings begin often takes leaders of all the various sides by surprise. And as they continue, uprisings take on a momentum of their own outside the control of leaders. What had started in Paris had at first caught Choltitz, Parodi and Rol unawares; in the next few days it underlined their growing powerlessness. For his part, Choltitz had come to Paris unwilling to put it to the torch as Hitler wanted but nevertheless determined to defend it. The enemy he envisaged, however, were the Allied armies and not the people of Paris; he had disposed his scanty forces in anticipation of a siege from without. Knowledge of his tactical weakness made him welcome the offer from Nordling, the Swedish Consul-General, to arrange a truce. Parodi, for his part, was equally agreeable: a negotiated truce with the Germans, leading to a negotiated handover of the city to the Gaullists, looked to him exactly the sort of triumph his cause sought. Colonel Rol, when first consulted, vetoed the truce because he thought events on the street were running his way and then, on 22 August, agreed to it because he thought events had run sufficiently his way.

By this point these manoeuvrings counted for less than the underlying momentum of the events themselves and the impression they made on those watching from outside Paris. The best informed was undoubtedly de Gaulle at Rambouillet. So what, exactly, did he see? He saw Paris threatened by three dangers. It might be the scene of a popular uprising bloodily put down: another Warsaw. It might be the scene of a popular uprising, largely Communist in character, which succeeded: another July Commune. It might be the scene of chaos which would force the Americans to intervene: another dominion of the Allied Military Government for Occupied Territories. The last possibility was hardly less disagreeable than the others.

In fact, de Gaulle's information made the prospect of Paris becoming another Warsaw look the least likely danger. Choltitz had shown his willingness to negotiate; indeed, he had even made clear to Nordling his willingness, if not to surrender outright, at least to bow to the arrival of a superior army. This reassurance, combined with his political shrewdness, made de Gaulle actually oppose the truce which Parodi, his own delegate, was trying to make stick. Apart from affirming de Gaulle's faith in the French, the ferment in Paris also rattled the Americans, particularly since their intelligence reports and grasp of the issues were inadequate. The situation, in short, made the Americans change their mind about the need to liberate Paris and made them remember that the honour had been promised to French troops.

On the evening of 22 August the order was given to Leclerc's Second Armoured Division, quartered south of Argentan, to advance immediately on Paris. As it passed Rambouillet the next day, de Gaulle impressed on Leclerc the urgency of gaining his objective before a second Commune was established and before the Americans arrived. By the evening of 24 August two of Leclerc's three columns, approaching Paris from the south, had reached Fresnes. Rather than wait till the next day, he sent forward a token contingent of less than 150 infantrymen and a mere handful of Sherman tanks. Just before nine-thirty, after slipping into the city by the Porte de Gentilly, they stopped outside the Hôtel de Ville on the Rue de Rivoli. It took some moments for passers-by to notice their arrival and realize they were not German.

By the time Leclerc's main forces entered the city early the next morning they were already passing into history and into myth, fondly remembered as *la Deuzième DB* just as the people who wore their FFI armbands were known to everyone as *les fifis*. They were far from being unopposed, since satisfying honour and placating Berlin demanded that Choltitz muster at least a show of defence. He managed it by the time-honoured expedient of not letting his men know of his willingness to yield up the city. Heavy fighting took place round the Ecole Militaire and Les Invalides. The Foreign Office building on the Quai d'Orsay was set ablaze. German snipers in the Tuileries Gardens did particular damage. Trouble-spots held out and mopping-up operations continued for several days.* Yet the outcome of the battle had been decided by the afternoon of 25 August, when Choltitz agreed to go to the Préfecture de Police and sign the document of surrender which Leclerc presented to him.

Paris had fought a battle, but a small battle by the standards Europe was then setting, and Paris had escaped the disaster which had seemed to threaten it only days before. The nature of the victory, moreover, was already clear in the surrender document itself. As a

---

* The sporadic nature of the fighting helped to make estimates of losses no more trustworthy than any of the other statistics offered for Liberation. Leclerc calculated that he lost 76 men, with another 200 wounded; the FFI put losses among Parisians at about 1,600, about 600 of them non-combatants. Claims that about 3,000 Germans died may well be too high; the figure of nearly 17,000 German prisoners is plausible.

mere general of one division out of many in the Allied armies fighting in France, Leclerc might not technically have had the right to treat with the enemy at all; at most, he should have acted only on behalf of the Allied Supreme Command. In fact he identified himself as representing the provisional government of France. There was no mention of the Americans or the British, and there would have been no mention of the Paris FFI either had not Colonel Rol, who turned up late and uninvited to Leclerc's meeting with Choltitz, insisted on his right to put his name on the document as well.

Leclerc's concession to Colonel Rol angered de Gaulle when he arrived in Paris later on 25 August, but in fact there was no need for anger. For the time being at least, the Communists had been side-lined as effectively as the Americans. AMGOT, of course, was already dying on the vine in liberated areas: people scorned its spe-cially printed currency as *fausse monnaie* and derided its hastily trained American administrators as Sixty-Day Wonders. Starting with Bayeux, the first town to be liberated and the first to see de Gaulle himself, they turned instead to the commissioners de Gaulle had been prudently readying for the task at his base in Algiers. In Paris itself Parodi had already made sure that de Gaulle's appointees were at their desks in their appropriate ministries. The way was securely paved for de Gaulle's triumphal progress at the head of the parade which passed next day from the Arc de Triomphe and down the Champs Elysées to a thanksgiving service in Notre-Dame. And as he passed, the crowds lining the route not only cheered him: they confirmed him as their leader by acclamation.

Men do not become leaders by popular acclamation just through shrewd political manoeuvring, though de Gaulle had certainly proved his mastery of this skill. Nor do they become leaders by popular acclamation just through the example of their courage, though de Gaulle had certainly set this example since June 1940. They become leaders by popular acclamation if they have a vision which answers a need, deeply and widely felt, and if they have at their command the language which makes people realize how deeply and widely they feel their need of the vision. De Gaulle had both the vision and the language. To a people who had spent four years humiliated and divided he had a healing myth to offer, a myth which promised to heal humiliation and heal division, which promised even to heal history. His rhetoric conjured the myth into life as present reality when he told the colleagues who had gathered to greet him at the Hôtel de Ville, just hours after his arrival in Paris, what the messy events barely finished in the capital signified:

> Paris, Paris abused, Paris broken, Paris martyred but Paris liberated by her own people, with the help of the armies of France, with the help and support of the whole of France, that is to say of fighting France, that is to say of the true France, the eternal France.

EPILOGUE

Division and Its Aftermath

I'm very small and weak compared to you who have the
Germans to defend you. I have the French, it's true, which
is why I'm not going to ask you to account for what you
did, since they will.

Letter from Georges Mandel's daughter
to Laval, 24 July 1944

Pétain was a great man who died in 1925.

De Gaulle

FRANCE 'LIBERATED BY her own people, with the help of the
armies of France, with the help and support of the whole of
France, that is to say of fighting France, that is to say of the true
France, the eternal France': the vision that de Gaulle extrapolated
from events in Paris and offered his audience at the Hôtel de Ville in
August 1944 was not a flight of rhetoric meant to catch the enthusiasm of the passing moment. De Gaulle's perorations were never
fugitive or hasty; they all had the monumentality of granite. This
one spoke to both the immediate past and the immediate future.
Its reading of history implied the programme for France which
de Gaulle had already started to enact.

Obviously it is not hard to challenge the Gaullist myth on its own,
strictly historical, terms. France had not been liberated by France,
much less by the whole of France. She had been liberated by the
Allied armies, in which the French army formed only a minority, and
by *résistants* who – though their numbers had grown as the Allied
armies approached – were still, as they had always been, only a
minority of the French. (And *résistants*, of course, were not just

French: they included refugees from Spain, Germany and eastern Europe and agents from Britain, Canada and the USA.) Even this minority was as divided in its eventual goals as it had been in its tactics. And it in turn was divided from all the other minorities – Vichyites and *pétainistes, collabos* and *ultra-collabos* of whatever motive or complexion – who had shaped France's experience of the Occupation and Liberation.

To offer even such a literal correction to the Gaullist myth is already to indicate the problems confronting de Gaulle. He himself combined his idealistic vision with extreme practicality, tempered his belief in *la France éternelle*, one and indivisible, with a realistic estimate of her present state. Even as he led the parade down the Champs Elysées toward Notre-Dame the day after his speech at the Hôtel de Ville he knew, so his memoirs would record, that rival ambitions as well as devotion kept pace with him. '*C'est la mer!*' he exclaimed of the crowds who cheered, finding in the sea of people the living embodiment of France's unity but still laconically noting that the 'reefs of politics' remained visible.

Even the thanksgiving service at Notre-Dame itself confirmed his wary instincts. Machine-gun fire was heard as he entered the cathedral and more shooting broke out when he was inside, making much of the congregation dive for cover, though he himself characteristically remained, in the words of one admiring witness, 'standing, alone, in full view at the throne of kings'. At the time nobody could identify who fired the shots, and historians can still only report the various rumours which clustered round the incident. Germans or *ultra-collabos* making a last defiant gesture? Quite possibly, for despite the agreement between commanders street-fighting was still going on. Communist *résistants* staging a coup? Unruly *résistants* making their dissatisfactions known? In such fragile and dangerous times those possibilities could not be discounted either.

When the service did go ahead it was not conducted by the appropriate cleric, despite de Gaulle's deep respect for protocol. Monsignor Suhard, Cardinal-Archbishop of Paris, had made his sympathies too publicly known during the Occupation: blessing and absolving men of the Légion des Volontaires Français on their way to fight with the Wehrmacht on the Eastern Front, welcoming Pétain on his single visit to Paris in April 1944 and, most recently, officiating at Henriot's funeral in the very cathedral where de Gaulle now stood. He later wrote Suhard a letter blandly disclaiming any personal antagonism but, on the day of the thanksgiving service itself, armed police firmly kept the Monsignor out of the way in his archepiscopal palace.

Disaffected *résistants* on the one side and tainted *collabos* on the other, both required a firm hand. 'Nothing can be done except through order,' de Gaulle insisted: 'Nothing and, above all, nothing great can be done except through order.' Special times demand special measures, special times justify special powers. Pétain had told the French people much the same thing in 1940, but he had had the Germans to back him up and even then he had never quite succeeded in gaining the unquestioning obedience he sought. And what authority, really, did de Gaulle now possess? For all his popularity and his triumph in Paris, surely he was just (as one of the unconverted bluntly put it) 'the provisional head of a provisional government of a provisional republic'? Céline had called Pétain *Philippe le Dernier*: people were soon calling de Gaulle *Charles le Temporaire*.

It was typical of de Gaulle that he had equipped himself not just with a vision of *la France éternelle* but with a constitutional argument as well. He had been advancing it since the early days of his flight to Britain in 1940, always feeling the need for more than the proof of rhetorical grandeur or lonely courage to justify his stand. In his eyes the Third Republic had never ceased to exist, and he was now the caretaker best qualified to put it back into working order. This was why, surprising and even disappointing some of his audience, he had not proclaimed the restoration of the Third Republic at the Hôtel de Ville as the *maquisards* on the Vercors plateau, for example, had thought it necessary to do in July. Its restoration did not need to be proclaimed. The Third Republic had always been there because Pétain had acted illegally and unconstitutionally in everything he had done: in forming a cabinet with the sole purpose of seeking an armistice and in founding the Vichy state with powers that the National Assembly had no right to grant him. He had staged a *coup d'état* and led a government without rightful claim to power or obedience.

Their attitudes to the Republic had always marked a critical difference between de Gaulle and Pétain. Indeed, they underlined the critical difference between the two, ultimately no mere question of constitutional law but a fundamental matter of loyalty and temperament. Otherwise, cynics might say, they bore a disconcerting resemblance to one another. Both were soldiers who rose to power in a time of crisis and achieved power by popular acclamation. Both, in soldierly fashion, lectured on the need for order and professed disdain for sectarian politics. Both claimed to represent France without being elected by the French; both, indeed, virtually claimed to be France. Yet where Pétain was the last and most powerful enemy of the Republic, de Gaulle was its last and most powerful ally. In his speeches he could, and did, endow the words *la République* with as much resonance as *la France*. After four years filled with the voices of autocracy and revolution, at a time when those voices had not yet been stilled, his insistence on *la République* reassured fears (which his manner did not always put at rest) that he was just another autocrat, another revolutionary, another opportunist soldier taking advantage of the moment. He was there to defend the essential continuity of French government – and that was, at least, the most tangible part of *la France éternelle*.

F RANCE 'LIBERATED BY her own people, with the help of the armies of France, with the help and support of the whole of France, that is to say of fighting France, that is to say of the true France, the eternal France': the healing myth de Gaulle offered the nation's hurt pride had at its heart a tribute to resistance. Yet however flattering it might have been to the nation at large, the very generosity of his tribute was also contentious. By depicting resistance as a national activity, in effect retrospectively welcoming the whole nation into resistance, de Gaulle was belittling the real *résistants*.

In a sense, that is exactly what he intended. What de Gaulle wanted, his critics said (and, some added, what he had wanted all along) was a resistance without *résistants*. Resistance was proof of *la France éternelle*; *résistants* were trouble. Communist *résistants* probably had neither the intention nor the power to stage a coup, though in the atmosphere of 1944 it was easy to be suspicious of them on this score. Yet they had certainly achieved a far stronger position than de Gaulle had wanted and, indeed, they would go on to fight bitterly and tenaciously for their position in the history of resistance and in present politics as *le parti des fusillés*: the party with more martyrs to its credit than any other group could claim. Other *résistants*, not Communist but touched by the radicalizing experience of resisting, had nourished themselves with the hope that their struggle would end with a new order and a new society, not just with the old Republic revived. Others, particularly the Maquis bands of the rural south, had got used to making their own law and were reluctant to submit themselves to the normal bureaucracies of French administration.

Many *résistants*, always more comfortable with de Gaulle as a symbol, a point of reference, than as an actual leader, had got their first real taste of the disillusionments to come at the very moment of their success. The ranks of resistance, of course, had swollen first as the tide of the war changed, then again as Allied landings grew imminent and finally beyond all original proportion as the Allied armies advanced. In Paris, for example, de Gaulle's delegate Chaban-Delmas had put the strength of the FFI at between 15,000 and 16,000 in mid-August, and he may well have been overestimating it. Yet by 25 August, when Leclerc's division arrived, there were between 50,000 and 60,000 people wearing FFI armbands on the streets. It was only natural for experienced *résistants* to be contemptuous of the last-minute converts and to nickname them *résistants du mois d'août* or *RMAs* and, in other areas, *septembristes*. Dominique Ponchardier, veteran of the military intelligence network Sosies, was not alone in feeling he was in a 'world of false noses' or in beginning to suspect that people with real noses, like himself, 'were the real *cons*'.

When *résistants* found not just the latecomers but the whole of France given equal status with themselves in de Gaulle's rhetoric, their suspicion was confirmed. And in some cases it hardened into active resentment when they discovered that after being thanked they were to be curtly disempowered. In Paris Colonel Rol had already found himself pushed to the sidelines by a combination of de Gaulle's soldiers and de Gaulle's commissioners. The scenario repeated itself in other cities and led to angry confrontation when de Gaulle toured the south-west in September. In both Toulouse and Bordeaux the *résistants* who turned out to greet him were disconcerted by the hollow brevity of his tribute to them. They were annoyed to see how much more he preferred the company of his appointed commissioners and of what they contemptuously referred to as *naphtalinés* or *naphtalinards*: mothball men, officers released from the army in 1940 who had put their uniforms on again after several years of inactivity. A final sour note was struck when in both places de Gaulle made a special point of ordering

SOE agents held locally in high regard to leave the country immediately.*

So what role remained for *résistants*? What outlet could the energies which had been building up over four years now find? Officially the preferred solution was for them to enlist in the regular army and join in the Allied advance on the German border. As many as 135,000 of them finally did. Some 75,000 had already done so by November, enough to relieve the African troops in de Lattre's regiments before winter came and to play a substantial part in liberating Alsace and Lorraine. Those who died fighting there included, for example, Colonel Fabien, famous for the assassination at the Métro Barbès. He had been a Communist. Yet many fellow-Communists regarded enlistment with suspicion and refused to volunteer. Nor did life in the army prove a happy solution for other *résistants*, particularly those who found themselves assigned ranks inferior to the *naphtalinés*; for some, who had commitments at home, it was no solution at all.

For others, fighting the Germans in the east was not the fulfilment of their task but a diversion from what resistance had come to mean. Resistance, of course, had begun with the urge to get rid of the occupiers, the dream of a day, however vaguely or distantly perceived, when the Germans would be pushed out of their local Kommandantur, pushed out of Alsace and Lorraine, finally pushed back across the Rhine. Yet because that day had for so long looked distant, resistance had increasingly become engaged with another task closer to hand: fighting the French who were betraying France. Even before *la guerre franco-française* had broken out resistance had committed itself to a language of national recrimination – the French denouncing the French – quite as vehemently as Vichy had done. Let us take revenge on those in France who brought about our defeat, Vichy had said. Let us take revenge on those in France who made the shameful peace, *résistants* had answered. With the escalation of violence, giving revenge its specific, local and personal aspect, resistance had announced a doctrine of accountability. These scores will be settled, these deeds will be avenged, these people will be punished, its journals and spokesmen had continually warned.

---

* The Toulouse agent was Roger Landes (Aristide), who held dual Franco-British citizenship, and the Bordeaux agent was George Starr (Hilaire). Both worked for the RF (Gaullist) section of SOE, subject to General Koenig's orders.

They never failed to add: and it is we who will do it. So Liberation had become, in one of its most deeply desired aspects, a day of national judgement.

THE FRENCH TERM for this national judgement is *épuration*, which can be translated as either 'purification' or 'purge'. The very different connotations of these words create an ambiguity entirely befitting a process violently argued at the time and afterwards disputed by historians with hardly less bitterness. Nothing about the *épuration* has ever been safely beyond controversy: not even how long it lasted or how many victims it claimed, much less what it showed about the nation just starting to emerge from the ordeal of the Occupation.

The most basic difficulty, of course, stems from the question of what period the term *épuration* is taken to cover. *Résistants* had already started the business of judgement and punishment by 1942, long before D-Day. And in a sense the *épuration* continues today, or rather it has been resumed in the wake of Klaus Barbie's trial in the late 1980s. The last tainted survivors of the Occupation are still sporadically appearing before the courts accused of crimes against humanity: René Bousquet, the police chief who helped to organize the Paris *grand rafle*, in 1993; Paul Touvier, the *milicien* who worked with Lécussan and Barbie in Lyon, in 1994; and Maurice Papon, who carried out *rafles* and deportations of Jews in the Gironde, in 1996.

Two critical phases lie within this broad span, though they overlap and merge indistinctly into each other. The first, straddling D-Day by a margin of months on either side, was the time of rough justice: summary executions by *résistants*, and their lately arrived hangers-on, sometimes in gangs acting in the heat of the moment but also, increasingly, as people's courts or military tribunals. The second phase saw the official creation of special courts, handing out death sentences and lesser punishments with an attempt at due process. They were established in mid-September 1944, while a special High Court for leading collaborators was formed a couple of months later.

The problem of distinguishing these phases, however, does not account for the conflicting statistics attached to the *épuration*. The number of summary executions has been particularly contentious. Estimates have varied from the huge total of 100,000 or even 150,000 deaths between 1942 and 1945, widely bandied about soon afterwards, to the figure of about 10,000 deaths, half before and half after D-Day, later calculated by historians such as Peter Novick and the Comité d'Histoire de la Deuxième Guerre Mondiale. Plainly, the discrepancy is not simply mathematical but ideological. The first, wildly inflated, figure is a last flourish of Vichy apologetics, designed to present the regime as an upholder of order at first defied and then swept away by a Reign of Terror as bad as anything the revolutionary fervour of the 1790s had achieved.*

Yet the lower and much more trustworthy figure of 10,000 deaths cannot be passed over in silence either. Many of the victims were from the Milice, whose losing battle with the Maquis had already descended into mutual savagery by the eve of Liberation. The diary of a *maquisard* in the Haute-Savoie, for example, recorded the fate but not the name of this captured *milicien* at the end of July:

> Aged twenty-nine, married three months ago. Made to saw wood in the hot sun wearing pullover and jacket. Made to drink warm salted water. Ears cut off. Covered with blows from fists and bayonets. Stoned. Made to dig his grave. Made to lie in it. Finished off with a blow in the stomach from a spade. Two days to die.

A month later, after Liberation had come to Nîmes, nine *miliciens* were put up against the wall of the Roman arena and shot. The FFI captain in charge of the proceedings later called them 'normal, expeditious and legal' and identified the judges simply as 'the people of France and the victims of fascism'.

Miliciens were by no means the only targets. Indeed, many had left with the departing Germans and many had taken pains to make themselves scarce. So the attention of the kangaroo courts run by *résistants* easily turned, in a lengthening list of grievances, to informers, people who had denounced their neighbours, black marketeers, people who had denounced black marketeers, and officials whose management of food supplies had caused resentment. The court martial which first met in Périgueux on 7 September had found 172 people guilty by the third week of October. Thirty-three of them had been condemned to death, though the sentence on one had been reduced at the representation of his neighbours. Some who died had

---

* Extreme advocates of this view included Sisley Huddleston, an English journalist granted French citizenship by Vichy during the Occupation, in books such as *Terreur, 1944* (1947) and *France: The Tragic Years, 1939–1947* (1955).

undoubtedly been active members of the Milice, but the scanty dossiers also show that one man had left the Milice the previous January; another, who denied working for the Germans, was known to have had a lot of money to spend and had been seen leaving a haunt of the Gestapo; a third had been accused of making defeatist remarks and 'threatening patriots'. Not all the eighty victims executed by the Maquis Bernard at the Château de Pressac, north of Limoges, were *collabos* by any stretch of the imagination; some were victims of the internecine war between Communists and Socialists. And in the Dordogne at Issigeac the mayor, the priest, the doctor and the dentist died because they had protested against the local Maquis leader's plan to open a brothel.

In Paris the Vel d'Hiv, where the Jews had been held in 1942, housed a new generation of victims, and Drancy, the waiting room for Auschwitz, was taken over by *les fifis* for their prisoners. In the panic among the *collabos* and suspected *collabos* some, like the writer Drieu la Rochelle, killed themselves and others fled. People who had taken to referring to the magazine *Je suis partout* ('I am everywhere') as *Je chie partout* ('I shit everywhere') now renamed it *Je suis parti* ('I've cleared out'). Some of the smart set who had clustered round Otto Abetz stayed behind and tried to make what peace they could with the new order. Coco Chanel, known for her anti-semitism and her admiration for the occupiers, hurried to give out bottles of Chanel No. 5 to American GIs. She was arrested – at the Ritz, fittingly enough – but released soon afterwards. Sacha Guitry, the actor, playwright and impresario who had been so prompt to produce documents quelling the rumour that he was Jewish, now equipped himself with a letter from Abetz claiming his contact with the Germans had been limited because many of them considered him 'non-Aryan'. It did not prevent him being held in Fresnes prison and suffering a permanent shadow over his reputation.

The actress Arletty, who had had a German lover, was one of Guitry's fellow-prisoners, though she was granted parole so that the shooting of Marcel Carné's *Les Enfants du paradis* could be finished. Paris was alive with rumours of what had become of her. Some said her breasts had been cut off, which was not true. Others said her head had been shaved, which might have been true and would account for the turban she wore in the film. But the fate of the *collabos horizontales*, the women accused of having slept with the occupiers, was usually more public.

History has acquired its most abiding image of the *épuration* by mob hatred and mob justice in the spectacle of women forcibly paraded through the streets naked or half-naked, often carrying their babies, and sometimes with swastikas branded on their bare scalps or between their breasts. Many were prostitutes, and virtually all were called prostitutes by their tormentors. These ceremonies took place throughout the country in August and September, usually in the atmosphere of a savage carnival and sometimes as the organized prelude to the victims' imprisonment, or worse. In most parts of the country people simply used the verb *tondre* (to shave) in describing them, but in the Midi they used *plumer*: to pluck, as one plucks a chicken. In Paris they spoke of *la coiffure de '44*: the hairstyle of '44. The practice seems to have spread spontaneously: it may well have been encouraged by the early incidents at Chartres, reported to the rest of France by the BBC from London, and by local resistance journals, but it took its energy from local anger and not official approval. Certainly, the legal formulae which soon defined collaboration specifically exempted mere personal contact with German troops.

Yet in the autumn of 1944 vengeance and witch-hunting, public rumour and private malice still held the sinister power that had fuelled the previous four years. For some the national judgement could not be too comprehensive or too harsh; for others it had already gone far enough to disgust. This conflict was being voiced among *résistants* in the Gard in September. A captain of the local FFI put the case for vengeance in its most compellingly simple terms: 'I'll simply say that the majority of the FFI have been outlaws. They are lads from the mining areas . . . they have been hunted; they have been imprisoned; they have been tortured by *miliciens* whom they now recognize. It is understandable that they should now want to beat them up.' A local doctor in the Maquis put the objection with equal force: 'When I read the communiqué on the executions, I felt the signature at the bottom should read, Feldkommandantur.'

His words had already been anticipated the previous month by a Maquis leader in Périgueux, when he cautioned that, however great the need for judgement, 'we must respect ourselves'. And even before Liberation de Gaulle's spokesman Maurice Schumann, broadcasting from London in November 1943, had warned of a danger as old as history, as old as war: 'If the defeated enemy succeeds in making us forget the very principles in whose name we have stood up to them . . . they will have taken away from us the moral victory, which when all is said and done is the only thing that counts.'

It was inevitable that the danger he feared should now threaten France. The Occupation had left too much anger, too much frustration and too much shame for the violence suddenly to cease. Nor could a leader in de Gaulle's position hope to touch its underlying impulse. In practical terms, however, he could do a great deal and there was no doubt in which direction his efforts lay: 'Nothing can be done except through order. Nothing and, above all, nothing great can be done except through order. What is order? It is the order of the state, of the Republic, which the government of the Republic represents and must enforce.' It was in the name of order, the government and the Republic that he moved to take the *épuration* from *résistants* and put it in the hands of the special courts created in mid-September and in action in Paris by mid-October.

The first person they sentenced to death was Georges Suarez, who had taken over *Aujourd'hui* when its first editor, Henri Jeanson, had realized how strictly it would be forced to toe the German line. Suarez was quickly followed, first into the dock and then to the execution ground, by Laffont, Bonny and the other *gestapistes* of the Rue Lauriston and by the three surviving *miliciens* who had killed Georges Mandel. Yet the fact that the first collaborator to die by due process should have been a journalist was prophetic. Mob justice had already found a favourite target in *collabos horizontales*. In the streets collaboration was most expressively, most satisfyingly identified with sexual collaborators. The courts bore down more harshly on writers, journalists and broadcasters than they ever would on businessmen or bureaucrats. In the dock collaboration was most expressively, most satisfyingly identified with intellectual collaborators.

Some, like Henriot and Drieu la Rochelle, might have been beyond reach of the law but others could still be called to account: the radio traitors Jean Hérold-Paquis, with his slogan of '*Car, comme Carthage, l'Angleterre sera détruite*' ('Since, like Carthage, England shall be destroyed'), and Paul Ferdonnet, who had spoken of the British as *les sales anglais* and the Jews as 'a cursed race'; Jean Luchaire, doubly damned for his influence in the press and by association with his daughter Corinne, a notorious sexual *collabo*; even Charles Maurras of Action Française, old, deaf and irrelevant, so wrapped in the bitterness of a past age that he received his sentence (of prison, not death) with 'This is the revenge of Dreyfus.'

The trial of Henri Béraud of *Gringoire*, a violent anglophobe but no lover of Germany, first stirred unease. De Gaulle commuted his death sentence. Unease grew louder with the case of Robert Brasillach. His work for *Je suis partout* had included some of the most rancorously effective writing of the entire Occupation. Nobody doubted Brasillach's talent and nobody doubted his sincerity either. Perhaps the purest, or at any rate the most purely intellectual, of the *ultra-collabo* set, he had boasted '*Nous ne sommes pas des convertis*' ('We are not converts') in the triumphalist phase of the Occupation and boasted again '*Nous ne sommes pas des dégonflés*' ('We are not cowards') as the Allied armies approached. He had given himself up in September and, standing in the dock the following January, he looked, as Simone de Beauvoir remarked, 'ready to die well'. He acknowledged his death sentence by saying 'It's an honour.'

It drew protest from François Mauriac (whom *Le Canard enchaîné* nicknamed 'Saint Francis of the Assizes'), joined by Valéry, Claudel, Cocteau, Colette and, with some misgivings, Camus. Their plea for mercy toward Brasillach could be dismissed as the reaction of a literary milieu which, while ready to exact its own punishment through the blacklist, was always protective of its own in the face of the wider world. De Gaulle, at any rate, did dismiss the protest and let Brasillach die: perhaps justice did not demand his death, he conceded, but preservation of the state did. The underlying issues, however, would not go away. De Gaulle had urgent reason to put the *épuration* into the care of the courts: to leave it in the hands of *résistants* would have been unthinkable. Yet doing so raised deeply troubling questions about the order, the government and the Republic he most wanted to defend.

For one thing, the trials themselves often showed how little due process could differ from rough justice in the immediate aftermath of the Occupation. Their outcomes were sometimes foregone conclusions. The jurors were picked from people of impeccable resistance credentials: *résistants* might need to be disciplined and made subject to proper authority but they could not be excluded from this process of all processes. And besides, the slightest suggestion that undetected *collabos* might be sitting in judgement on accused *collabos* could not be countenanced. Yet most of the qualified judges available had also served Vichy, and not just served the Vichy state but sworn the required oath of personal loyalty to Pétain. Defending counsel rarely failed to make this point in the acrimonious quarrels which filled the courtrooms. Somewhere in the course of these quarrels, too, the debate between the need for vengeance and the need for restraint continued, but no longer as a debate about *résistants* or a debate between *résistants*. It was a debate about the policy of de Gaulle's state.

It found de Gaulle and his fragile state particularly vulnerable. Since June 1940 he had based his stand on the unconstitutionality of the Vichy regime and the illegality of the armistice. Less than a month after arriving in Britain he had spelled out the future implication: 'liberated France will punish the people responsible for her disasters and the architects of her servitude'. His Free French had used the BBC and the other channels open to them to repeat the threat against 'the architects of her servitude' with a specificity – and sometimes a violence of language – which could rival the rhetoric of *résistants* inside France. And in March 1944, before he returned to mainland France, de Gaulle had launched the official *épuration* in Algiers when he gave his assent to the execution of Pierre Pucheu, the former Vichy minister who had tried to change sides.

Yet de Gaulle also made it clear he felt a reluctance to see Pucheu die, a desire – albeit one the practical politician in him could quell – to avoid such extremities. It stemmed from his awareness, as Liberation approached, of the need for national healing: the need he announced at the Hôtel de Ville in the vision of France liberated by 'the whole of France, that is to say of fighting France, that is to say of the true France, the eternal France'. How then to reconcile the need for national healing and the clamour for national judgement? In fact, the majestic cadences of his Hôtel de Ville speech themselves imply a path to compromise in the way that the clauses following 'the whole of France' at first appear to amplify the phrase but on closer inspection really narrow it. The whole of France, it seems, was not quite the whole of France after all; there were some French people who were not really part of the true France, the eternal France.

The architects of France's servitude had to be punished, and those who had assisted in that servitude had to be excluded from the otherwise embracing vision which de Gaulle proposed. The latter part of this proposition was soon given definite and precise status in the legal formula introduced to deal with lesser forms of collaboration: the crime of *indignité nationale*, or national unworthiness, and the punishment of *dégradation nationale*, or national degradation, which involved the loss of the right to vote, the right to stand for election, the right to hold public office, the right to practise certain profes-sions and so on. Such measures might have carried uncomfortable echoes of Vichy itself, which had appealed to unity and then launched witch-hunts, and some in France in 1944 heard the echoes with disquiet. But de Gaulle lacked Vichy's vindictive clarity and its love of lengthening its list of victims; he sought to bury as much of the past as could decently be buried beneath compromise. The same logic which had acknowledged resistance as a majority activity demanded that collaboration be identified with a distinct and tiny minority.

So the legal *épuration* went ahead, but with caution. On this point, at least, the statistics are relatively clear. Military and civilian courts tried or examined 160,287 cases in all: 45 per cent of them resulted in acquittals or the decision not to prosecute, 25 per cent in convictions leading to prison sentences and another 25 per cent in convictions leading to sentences of *dégradation nationale* as the primary punish-ment. Some 7,037 people were condemned to death but only about 1,500 were actually executed. The rest of the death sentences were commuted to prison sentences, a presidential prerogative which, while he held office, de Gaulle approached with extreme seriousness. The work of the courts tailed off dramatically between 1948 and 1953, when an amnesty law effectively halted the *épuration*. By then there were 1,500 people in prison for acts committed during the Occupation. By 1964, when Jean Moulin's ashes were installed in the Panthéon, there were none.

THE POLITICAL FUDGE de Gaulle proposed might have been more sensible than any of the other options open to France, but in practice it satisfied nobody. It was attacked by those who thought the national judgement too wide and too harsh, and by those who found it too narrow and too mild. The illusion of a nation reunified and the hope of a nation radically cleansed soon disappeared. France was left to live with an immediate legacy of political volatility in the post-war years, announced in October 1945 when the electorate voted against continuing the Third Republic and confirmed the following January when de Gaulle resigned from office. But France was also left with a longer, more subtle legacy: the sense that history held shameful and unresolved truths, truths it might be better to ignore or to examine but which never lost their power to trouble.

At the heart of this 'poisoned memory' (as Robert Frank calls it) lay Vichy and what Vichy had done. In the chaos of 1944, however, it had looked briefly as if Vichy had been swept away unnoticed. Just days before the liberation of Paris the Germans took Laval and Pétain to Belfort and then into Germany; a more willing retinue of lesser politicians and *ultra-collabos* went with them. At the Hohenzollern castle of Sigmaringen, overlooking the Danube, their pretence at government finally collapsed into the squabbles of the nursery. Pétain and Laval sulked while the rest played tug-of-war for whatever remnants of power they imagined were still left for the Reich to bestow. Doriot was Hitler's favoured candidate as the new leader of France but Fernand de Brinon, the ambassador to Paris whom Galtier-Boissière called a 'greedy tapir', had hopes which he sought to advance by styling himself Graf von Brinon.

And there the story of Vichy should by rights have ended, finding its last and most fitting chronicler in Céline. His account of his stay among the refugees at Sigmaringen, *D'un château l'autre*,* remains an unrivalled epitaph on the final disarray of *'la fin des fins'*. For some, of course, Sigmaringen did mark the effective end. Doriot died in February 1945 when his car was strafed by Allied planes – or possibly German planes, said agitated rumour in the echoing corridors of the castle. Soon after his funeral the rest began to slip away. Céline, canny as ever, was the first; the others soon followed, to continue the fight elsewhere or just to elude the Allies. Some, like Darnand and de Brinon, were soon caught; others, like Abel Bonnard, the Minister of Education, managed to evade notice a little longer. A few, like Déat and Darquier de Pellepoix, former head of the Commissariat Général aux Questions Juives, managed to die in hiding.†

Yet Pétain insisted on returning to France. Simply staying on French soil in 1940 had, after all, been his first and most vehement policy, the guarantee of purity which had distinguished him from those, like Reynaud, who had advocated a government in exile, and those, like de Gaulle, who had actually left. Ever since he had been wrenched so unceremoniously from Vichy he had maintained that he was a prisoner and withheld support from the rivals who struggled

---

* Published in 1957.

† Darnand and de Brinon were executed, de Brinon's execution on 15 April 1947 being the last of the *épuration*. Bonnard, Déat and Darquier were condemned to death *in absentia*. On Bonnard's eventual return to France he received a short suspended prison sentence.

to succeed him. He had finally taken to his bed in passive protest. Now, still trusting vaguely in himself and his reputation as the Victor of Verdun, he demanded the right 'to defend his honour' and managed to slip across the Swiss border on 24 April 1945, his eighty-ninth birthday. Two days later he was back on French soil holding out his hand to General Koenig, who had been deputed to meet him. Koenig refused to shake it.

Laval returned rather less willingly, not expecting anyone to shake his hand. His case was rushed before the specially appointed High Court early in October, to quieten criticism that the *épuration* was faltering and to get the matter out of the way before France's first post-war elections later in the month. Laval's lawyers objected to the lack of time to prepare his defence and withdrew from the case. Laval took the job on himself with desperate bravado, haranguing the judges and trading insults with the jury. Halfway through the proceedings he retired to his cell and refused to appear in the dock, so he was not in court to hear the inevitable death sentence pronounced. Even his execution was botched. He tried to kill himself the night before, but the cyanide he had kept hidden in his jacket had lost some of its potency. In the morning his stomach was pumped out so that he could be dragged before the firing squad, vomiting and barely conscious.

Laval's trial struck even an opponent like the Protestant leader Pastor Marc Boegner as 'a scandal beyond description'. But Laval's career had for a long time looked bound to end as it did, in a raucous judgement which clarified nothing, a bitter vengeance which could shame even his enemies. Pétain's trial, in the previous July, had been a muted affair by comparison, yet it was the more telling in its power to embarrass. Privately, de Gaulle shared the widely felt regret that the Marshal had not just stayed quietly abroad. National healing could not embrace him but national judgement could not despatch him as it could Laval. Too many people remembered his record at Verdun. Too many people remembered their relief on hearing that France had been consigned into his hands in 1940 and their stubbornly maintained hope that he was, after all, playing a double game with the Germans. Many conservative Catholics still hankered after the social values he had promulgated from Vichy; even many *résistants* were charitable enough still to regard him as just the deluded or senile tool of schemers like Laval.

Pétain began his defence by reading a statement which repeated

the justification he had offered in his last broadcast to France before
he had gone to Sigmaringen: 'If I could no longer be your sword, I
wanted to be your shield.' The sword-and-shield analogy would be
trotted out many times more by Pétain's apologists in the post-war
years, though its weaknesses were as glaring as ever. They began with
the simple and obvious objection that if Pétain had been the shield
then presumably the sword – if it was anything or anyone – had been
de Gaulle. Yet each had, privately as well as publicly, regarded the
other as a traitor. It was ridiculous to imply even in the most general
terms that some sort of common endeavour had joined the work of
Vichy and the work of resistance. Vichy had rooted itself so firmly in
the assumption that the Reich would win the war that it had never
been able to find any other rationale for its existence.

The trial did not illuminate these arguments; indeed, it did not try
to illuminate anything. After his opening statement Pétain left his
defence in the hands of counsel and retreated into silence, sometimes dignified but usually drowsy, breaking it occasionally to insist
he could not hear the question he was being asked or could not
remember the answer to it. The long parade of witnesses consisted
largely of politicians and soldiers concerned above all to defend their
own reputations: Blum, Daladier, Reynaud, even President Albert
Lebrun whom nobody had been listening to even in 1940. Some, like
General Weygand and of course Laval, were literally rehearsing their
defence for their own trials. Had Reynaud seriously raised the
possibility of an armistice? Had Weygand said that Britain's neck
would be 'wrung like a chicken'? Had Pétain approved Laval's public
expression of his hope for a German victory? The dreary performance brought with it the reminder that it had, after all, been
French history which prompted Marx to observe that events always
happen twice, the first time as tragedy and the second time as farce.

In passing the death sentence on Pétain his judges expressed the
hope that it would be commuted on the grounds of his age.
De Gaulle quickly obliged. Pétain was finally moved to the Ile d'Yeu,
a bleak slab of rock off the Brittany coast with only a tiny fishing
community for population, where a former military garrison was
turned into a prison for a single prisoner. Sinking into senility which
nobody could write off as a convenient stratagem, he still clung to
life as if simply continuing to live was the only means left of out-
facing his detractors. His death a few months after his ninety-fifth
birthday in 1951 renewed the embarrassment that his name and

memory still had the power to provoke. The authorities granted relatives and friends permission to bury him in his marshal's uniform, though *dégradation nationale* had stripped him of the rank, but insisted he be buried on the island itself, almost off the edge of the map of France. The plot Pétain had reserved for himself in the Douaumont cemetery on the field of Verdun was left empty. Despite periodic applications from a dwindling band of admirers and apologists it has remained so: a gap in the neat rows of official commemoration, the public memory.

Sources and Further Reading

These notes do not attempt anything like a bibliography of the available literature on the Occupation, or even of the part of it I myself have consulted. They merely list the works most likely to interest general readers and those which I found most useful in my research, with a few comments on how they influenced what I wrote. Though I have usually relied in my text on my own translations from French sources, I include details of published translations for the sake of readers without French.

GENERAL

Historical Studies

Henri Amouroux, *La Grande Histoire des Français sous l'Occupation*, 10 vols. (Paris: Robert Laffont, 1976–93) and *La Vie des Français sous l'Occupation* (Paris: Fayard, 1961): blandly journalistic in approach but rich in detail
Jean-Pierre Azéma and François Bédarida (eds.), *La France des années noires*, 2 vols. (Paris: Editions du Seuil, 1993): a useful introduction to the present state of scholarship, with contributions from, among others, Stanley Hoffmann, Jean-Louis Crémieux-Brilhac, Robert Frank, Robert O. Paxton, Henry Rousso, Jean-Pierre Rioux, Claude Lévy and H. R. Kedward
H.R. Kedward, *In Search of the Maquis: Rural Resistance in Southern France, 1942–1944* (Oxford: Clarendon Press, 1993) and *Resistance in Vichy France: A Study of Ideas and Motivations in the Southern Zone, 1940–1942* (Oxford: Oxford University Press, 1978): the best of recent studies
Henri Michel, *Paris allemand* (Paris: Albin Michel, 1981) and *Paris résistant* (Paris: Albin Michel, 1982)
Henri Noguères, with Marcel Degliame-Fouché and Jean-Louis Vigier, *Histoire de la Résistance en France de 1940 à 1945*, 5 vols. (Paris: Robert Laffont, 1967–81): comprehensive but uneven

Robert O. Paxton, *Vichy France: Old Guard and New Order, 1940–44* (London: Barrie and Jenkins, 1972): a groundbreaking re-evaluation, more influential than any other recent study of Vichy, if not the entire Occupation

David Pryce-Jones, *Paris in the Third Reich* (London: Collins, 1981): notably rich in social detail

Lucien Steinberg, with Jean-Marie Fitère, *Les Allemands en France 1940–1944* (Paris: Albin Michel, 1980): particularly useful for its detailed account of the Reich's administration

General readers may wish to start with Ted Morgan, *An Uncertain Hour: The French, The Germans, The Jews, The Barbie Trial and the City of Lyon, 1940–1945* (London: Bodley Head, 1990), whose preoccupations are as ramifying as its title. Two recent studies which have helped stimulate international comparisons with the fate of France are Madeleine Bunting, *The Model Occupation: The Channel Islands under German Rule, 1940–1945* (London: Harper Collins, 1995) and Mark Mazower, *Inside Hitler's Greece: The Experience of Occupation, 1941–44* (New Haven and London: Yale University Press, 1993).

Biographical Studies and Collections of Speeches, etc: Pétain, Laval, de Gaulle and Churchill

Marc Ferro, *Pétain* (Paris: Fayard, 1987), the standard biography for 1940 onwards, supplemented by Jean-Claude Barbas' edition of Pétain's speeches, *Discours aux Français. 17 juin 1940–20 août 1944* (Paris: Albin Michel, 1989)

Jean-Paul Cointet, *Pierre Laval* (Paris: Fayard, 1993), also Fred Kupferman, *Laval* (Paris: Masson, 1976), neither completely superseding Geoffrey Warner, *Pierre Laval and the Eclipse of France* (London: Eyre and Spottiswoode, 1968)

Jean Lacouture, *De Gaulle: Le Rebelle 1890–1944; Le Politique 1944–1959; Le Souverain 1959–1970* (Paris: Editions du Seuil, 1984, 1985 and 1986), translated by Patrick O'Brian as *The Rebel, 1890–1944* (London: Collins Harvill, 1990) and by Alan Sheridan as *The Ruler, 1945–1970* (London: Harvill, 1991). Of de Gaulle's writings: *Mémoires de guerre*, 3 vols., *L'Appel 1940–1942, L'Unité 1942–1944* and *Le Salut 1944–1946* (Paris: Librairie Plon, 1954, 1956 and 1959), translated by Jonathan Griffin as *The Call to Honour 1940–1942* (London: Collins, 1955) and by Richard Howard as *Unity, 1942–1944* and *Salvation, 1944–1946* (London: Weidenfeld and Nicolson, 1959 and 1960); Vol. 1, *Pendant la guerre: juin 1940–janvier 1946*, of *Discours et messages*, 5 vols. (Paris: Plon, 1970); and Vol. 3, *juin 1940–juillet 1941* (1981), Vol. 4, *juillet 1941–mai 1943* (1982) and Vol. 5, *juin 1943–mai 1945* (1983) of *Lettres, notes et carnets*, 12 vols. (Paris: Plon, 1980–8). See also François Kersaudy, *Churchill and de Gaulle* (London: Collins, 1981)

Martin Gilbert's 12-volume biography of Churchill (London: Heinemann, 1966–88): Vol. 5, *Prophet of Truth: Winston S. Churchill, 1922–1939* (1976); Vol. 6, *Finest Hour: Winston S. Churchill, 1939–1941* (1983); and Vol. 7, *Road to Victory: Winston S. Churchill, 1941–1945* (1986). Also *Winston S. Churchill: His Complete Speeches, 1897–1963*, ed. Robert Rhodes James, 8 vols. (New York and London: Chelsea House Publishers in association with R.R. Bowker and Co., 1974), especially Vols. 6 (1935–42) and 7 (1943–9)

Memoirs, Reminiscences and Contemporary Diaries

Simone de Beauvoir, *La Force de l'âge* (Paris: Gallimard, 1960), trans. Peter Green as *The Prime of Life* (London: André Deutsch and Weidenfeld and Nicolson, 1962)

Henri Frenay, *La Nuit finira* (Paris: Robert Laffont, 1973), trans. Dan Hofstadter as *The Night Will End* (London: Abelard, 1976)

Jean Galtier-Boissière, *Journal 1940–1950*, with a preface by Henri Amouroux (Paris: Quai Voltaire, 1992), comprising the diaries published earlier by Editions La Jeune Parque as *Mon Journal pendant l'Occupation* (1944), *Mon Journal depuis la Libération* (1945), *Mon Journal dans la Drôle de paix* (1947) and *Mon Journal dans la Grande Pagaïe* (1950)

André Gide, Vols. 5 (1939–42) and 6 (1942–9) of *Journal* (Paris: Gallimard, 1946 and 1950), trans. Justin O'Brien as Vol. 4 (1939–49) of *The Journals of André Gide* (London: Secker and Warburg, 1951)

Jean Guéhenno, *Journal des années noires (1940–1944)* (Paris: Gallimard, 1947)

Ninetta Jucker, *Curfew in Paris: A Record of the German Occupation* (London: Hogarth Press, 1960)

Arthur Koestler, *Scum of the Earth*, The Danube Edition (London: Hutchinson, 1968)

Paul Léautaud, Vols. 13, 14 and 15 of *Journal Littéraire* (Paris: Mercure de France, 1963)

Jean-Paul Sartre, 'Paris sous l'Occupation', *La France libre*, Vol. 9, No. 49 (15 November 1944), translated as 'Paris under the Occupation' in *French Writing on English Soil: A Choice of French Writing Published in London Between November 1940 and June 1944*, selected and trans. J.G. Weightman (London: Sylvan Press, 1945); republished in French, with 'Qu'est-ce qu'un collaborateur?' and 'La République du silence', in *Situations, III* (Paris: Gallimard, 1949)

Gertrude Stein, *Wars I Have Seen* (London: Batsford, 1945)

Janet Teissier du Cros, *Divided Loyalties*, with a preface by D.W. Brogan (London: Hamish Hamilton, 1962)

Vercors (pseudonym of Jean Bruller), *La Bataille du silence* (Paris: Presses de la Cité,1967), trans. Rita Barisse as *The Battle of Silence* (London: Collins, 1968)

Sources and Further Reading

PROLOGUE: VERDUN AND ITS LEGACY

Alistair Horne, *The Price of Glory: Verdun 1916* (London: Macmillan, 1962), remains the standard account of the battle itself. For its aftermath I am particularly indebted to: Pierre Servent, *Le Mythe Pétain: Verdun ou les tranchées de la mémoire* (Paris: Editions Payot, 1992) and Eugen Weber, *The Hollow Years: France in the 1930s* (London: Sinclair-Stevenson, 1995). Among memoirs of the inter-war years Elliot Paul, *A Narrow Street* (London: The Cresset Press, 1942; published as *The Last Time I Saw Paris* in the USA), paints a picture of unrivalled vividness.

CHAPTER 1: INVASION AND EXODUS

I am particularly indebted to: Alistair Horne, *To Lose a Battle: France 1940* (London: Macmillan, 1969); Jacques Benoist-Méchin, *Soixante Jours qui ébranlèrent l'Occident: 10 mai–10 juillet 1940* (Paris: Robert Laffont, 1981; originally published 1956), translated as *Sixty Days That Shook the West* (London: Jonathan Cape, 1963); Jean-Louis Crémieux-Brilhac, *Les Français de l'an 40*, 2 vols. (Paris: Gallimard, 1990); Herbert R. Lottman, *The Fall of Paris, June 1940* (London: Sinclair-Stevenson, 1992); Nicole Ollier, *L'Exode* (Paris: Culture, Art, Loisirs, 1969); and Pierre Ordioni, *Les Cinq Jours de Toul (du 18 au 22 juin 1940)* (Paris: Robert Laffont, 1967).

For eye-witness accounts: Clare Boothe (Clare Boothe Luce), *European Spring* (London: Hamish Hamilton, 1941); James Lansdale Hodson, *Through the Dark Night: Being Some Account of a War Correspondent's Journeys, Meetings and What Was Said to Him, in France, Britain and Flanders during 1939–1940* (London: Victor Gollancz, 1941); General Sir Edmund Ironside, *The Ironside Diaries 1937–1940*, ed. Colonel Roderick Macleod, DSO, MC, and Denis Kelly (London: Constable, 1962); Neville Lytton, *Life in Unoccupied France* (London: Macmillan, 1942); and Antoine de Saint-Exupéry, *Pilote de guerre* (New York: Editions de la Maison Française, 1942), trans. Lewis Galantière as *Flight to Arras* (London: William Heinemann, 1942).

CHAPTER 2: VICHY AND THE NEW EUROPEAN ORDER

In addition to Robert O. Paxton, *Vichy France*, I am indebted to: Michèle Cointet, *Vichy Capitale 1940–1944* (Paris: Perrin, 1993); Hervé Couteau-Bégarie and Claude Huan, *Darlan* (Paris: Fayard, 1989); Eleanor M. Gates, *End of the Affair: The Collapse of the Anglo-French Alliance, 1939–40* (London: George Allen and Unwin, 1981); W. D. Halls, *The Youth of Vichy France* (Oxford: Clarendon Press, 1981); John Hellmann, *The Knight-Monks of Vichy France: Uriage, 1940–1945* (Montreal and Kingston: McGill-Queen's University Press, 1993); Henri Michel, *Le Procès de Riom* (Paris: Albin

Michel, 1979) and *Vichy, année quarante* (Paris: Robert Laffont, 1966); Alan S. Milward, *The New Order and the French Economy* (Oxford: Clarendon Press, 1970); Viktor Reimann, *The Man Who Created Hitler: Joseph Goebbels* (London: William Kimber, 1977); Norman Rich, Vol. 2, *The Establishment of the New Order,* of *Hitler's War Aims* (London: André Deutsch, 1974); Aviel Roshwald, *Estranged Bedfellows: Britain and France in the Middle East during the Second World War* (New York and Oxford: Oxford University Press, 1990); Dominique Rossignol, *Vichy et les Franc-Maçons: La Liquidation des sociétés secrètes 1940–44* (Paris: Editions Jean-Claude Lattès, 1981); and Andrew Shennan, *Rethinking France: Plans for Renewal 1940–1946* (Oxford: Clarendon Press, 1989).

For Hitler at Rethondes, see William L. Shirer, *The Collapse of the Third Republic: An Inquiry into the Fall of France in 1940* (London: Heinemann and Secker and Warburg, 1970). For the uses of Joan of Arc, see Marina Warner, *Joan of Arc: The Image of Female Heroism* (London: Weidenfeld and Nicolson, 1981), and Gabriel Jacobs, 'The Role of Joan of Arc on the Stage of Occupied France' and Nick Atkins, 'The Cult of Joan of Arc in French Schools, 1940–1944', in *Vichy France and the Resistance: Culture and Ideology,* ed. H.R. Kedward and R. Austin (London: Croom Helm, 1985).

CHAPTER 3: ARE YOU IN ORDER?

David Pryce-Jones, *Paris in the Third Reich,* is a treasure trove of detail. I am also indebted to: Bertram M. Gordon, *Collaborationism in France during the Second World War* (Ithaca and London: Cornell University Press, 1980); André Halimi, *La Délation sous l'Occupation* (Paris: Editions Alain Moreau, 1983); Antoine Lefébure, *Les Conversations secrètes des Français sous l'occupation* (Paris: Plon, 1993); and Pascal Ory, *Les Collaborateurs, 1940–1945* (Paris: Editions du Seuil, 1976).

For novels and memoirs, see: Jean Dutourd, *Au bon beurre* (1952); François Maspero, *Le Sourire du chat* (Paris: Editions du Seuil, 1984), trans. Nancy Amphoux as *Cat's Grin* (London: Penguin, 1988); Maurice Sachs, *La Chasse à courre* (Paris: Gallimard, 1949), trans. Richard Howard as *The Hunting* (London: Calder and Boyars in association with Sidgwick and Jackson, 1967), and *Le Sabbat* (Paris: Gallimard, 1945), trans. Robin King in an abridged form as *Day of Wrath: Confessions of a Turbulent Youth* (London: Arthur Barker, 1953) and trans. Richard Howard as *Witches' Sabbath* (London: Jonathan Cape, 1965); and Jean-Michelle Belle, *Les Folles Années de Maurice Sachs* (Paris: Bernard Grasset, 1979).

CHAPTER 4: PRESENCE AND ABSENCE

I am particularly indebted to H.R. Kedward, *Resistance in Vichy France,* for drawing my attention to the significance of Sartre's point about presence and absence in 'Paris sous l'Occupation'; and to Michael R. Marrus and Robert O. Paxton, *Vichy et les Juifs* (Paris: Calmann-Lévy, 1981), translated by the authors as *Vichy France and the Jews* (New York: Basic Books, 1981). Also: Jacques Adler, *Face à la persécution: les organizations juives à Paris de 1940 à 1944* (Paris: Calmann-Lévy, 1985), translated by the author as *The Jews of Paris and the Final Solution: Communal Response and Internal Conflicts, 1940–1944* (New York and Oxford: Oxford University Press, 1987); Asher Cohen, *Persécutions et sauvetages: Juifs et Français sous l'Occupation et sous Vichy*, preface by René Rémond (Paris: Cerf, 1993); Edward Crankshaw, *Gestapo: Instrument of Tyranny* (1956; reprinted London: Greenhill Books, 1990, and Novato, California: Presidio Press, 1991); Saul Friedländer, *Quand vient le souvenir . . .* (Paris: Editions du Seuil, 1978), trans. Helen R. Lane as *When Memory Comes* (New York: Farrar, Straus, Giroux, 1979); André Kaspi, *Les Juifs pendant l'occupation* (Paris: Editions du Seuil, 1991); André Labarthe, 'Paris interdit', anonymously in *La France libre*, Vol. 4, No. 20 (15 June 1942), translated as 'A Forbidden City' in *French Writing on English Soil: A Choice of French Writing Published in London Between November 1940 and June 1944*, selected and trans. J.G. Weightman (London: Sylvan Press, 1945); Maurice Rajsfus, *Des Juifs dans la collaboration: l'UGIF (1941–1944)*, preface by Pierre Vidal-Naquet (Paris: Etudes et Documentations Nationales, 1980); and Claudine Vegh, *Je ne lui ai pas dit au revoir. Des enfants déportés parlent. Entretiens avec Claudine Vegh* (Paris: NRF, Gallimard, 1979), trans. Ros Schwartz as *I Didn't Say Goodbye*, with an afterword by Bruno Bettelheim (New York: E.P. Dutton, 1984).

CHAPTER 5: LIVING IN FEAR, LIVING IN HOPE

I am again indebted to H.R. Kedward, *Resistance in Vichy France*, not least for his remarks about the evolution of a Resistance rhetoric. Also: Daniel Cordier, *Jean Moulin: l'inconnu du Panthéon*, 3 vols. of a projected 6 (Paris: Editions Jean-Claude Lattès, 1989–1993); M.R.D. Foot, *S.O.E. in France: An Account of the Work of the British Special Operations Executive in France 1940–1944* (London: HMSO, second edition 1968); and George Millar, *Maquis* (London: William Heinemann, 1945).

CHAPTER 6: SETTLING SCORES

I am particularly indebted to H.R. Kedward, *In Search of the Maquis* (the source of the quotation beginning 'a basic form of contract'). Also: Philip Beck, *Oradour: Village of the Dead* (London: Leo Cooper, 1979); Jacques Delperrié de Bayac, *Histoire de la Milice* (Paris: Fayard, 1969); Max Hastings, *Das Reich: Resistance and the March of the 2nd SS Panzer Division through France, June 1944* (London: Michael Joseph, 1981); Edward L. Homze, *Foreign Labor in Nazi Germany* (Princeton, New Jersey: Princeton University Press, 1967);

John Keegan, *Six Armies in Normandy: From D-Day to the Liberation of Paris June 6th–August 25th, 1944* (London: Jonathan Cape, 1979); (for Henri Romans-Petit and Oyonnax) Raymond Ruffin, *Ces Chefs de maquis qui gênaient* (Paris: Presses de la Cité, 1980); (for Saint-Amand-Montrond) Tzvetan Todorov, *Une Tragédie française: Eté 1944: Scènes de guerre civile* (Paris: Editions du Seuil, 1994), trans. Mary Byrd Kelly as *A French Tragedy: Scenes of Civil War, Summer 1944* (University Press of New England, 1996); and Alban Vistel, *La Nuit sans ombre: Histoire des mouvements unis de résistance, leur rôle dans la libération du Sud-Est* (Paris: Fayard, 1970).

EPILOGUE: DIVISION AND ITS AFTERMATH

Antony Beevor and Artemis Cooper, *Paris After the Liberation, 1945–1949* (London: Hamish Hamilton, 1994); Alain Brossat, *Les Tondues: un carnaval moche* (Paris: Editions Manya, 1992); Herbert R. Lottman, *The People's Anger: Justice and Revenge in Post-Liberation France* (London: Hutchinson, 1986); Peter Novick, *The Resistance Versus Vichy: The Purge of Collaborators in Liberated France* (New York: Columbia University Press, 1968); Frederic Pottecher, *Le Procès Pétain* (Paris: Editions Jean-Claude Lattès, 1981); Henry Rousso, *Un Château en Allemagne: La France de Pétain en exil, Sigmaringen 1944–45* (Paris: Editions Ramsay, 1980) and *Le Syndrome de Vichy: De 1944 à nos jours* (Paris: Editions du Seuil, second edition 1990), trans. Arthur Goldhammer as *The Vichy Syndrome: History and Memory in France since 1944* (Cambridge, Mass., and London: Harvard University Press, 1991); and Paul Webster and Nicholas Powell, *Saint-Germain-des-Prés* (London: Constable, 1984).

Chronology

Events outside mainland France are in italics.

1919
28 June   Treaty of Versailles signed.

1923
11 January   *French army occupies the Ruhr after Germany defaults*
                           on reparations.

1930
January   National Assembly votes in favour of building
                           the Maginot Line.
1 July   *Last Allied troops leave the Rhineland.*
12 December   *Last Allied troops leave the Saar.*

1933
30 January   *Hitler becomes Chancellor of Germany.*

1934
6–7 February   Right-wing demonstrations force Daladier's
                           government to resign.

1935
26 February   *Goering becomes Commander-in-Chief of the newly*
                           constituted Luftwaffe.
16 March   *Hitler introduces conscription.*
3 October   *Italy invades Abyssinia (Ethiopia).*

1936
7 March   *Germany moves its army into the Rhineland.*
5 May   Blum's Front Populaire Français elected.
28 June   Doriot founds the Parti Populaire Français.
8 July   *Spanish Civil War begins.*
8 August   Blum's government refuses help to Spanish
                           Republicans.

14 October	*Leopold III of Belgium revokes the Franco-Belgian treaty and declares his country neutral.*
27 October	*Hitler signs treaty with Mussolini.*

1937
30 January	*Hitler formally withdraws from the Treaty of Versailles.*
22 June	Blum's Front Populaire government falls.

1938
11–12 March	*The Reich annexes Austria in the Anschluss.*
13 March–8 April	Blum's second government.
30 September	*Munich agreement between France, Britain, Germany and Italy concedes Sudetenland, in north-west Czechoslovakia, to Germany.*

1939
15 March	*Germany invades all of Czechoslovakia.*
28 March	*Spanish Civil War ends.*
7 April	*Italy invades Albania.*
4 May	Déat publishes 'Mourir pour Dantzig?'
22 May	*Germany and Italy announce formal alliance.*
23 August	*Germany makes non-aggression pact with the USSR.*
24 August	*Britain and Poland sign pact of mutual assistance.*
25 August	French government bans Communist publications, *L'Humanité* and *Ce Soir.*
1 September	*Germany invades Poland.*
3 September	*Great Britain, New Zealand, Australia and France declare war on Germany.*
10 September	*Canada declares war on Germany.*
6–17 September	France launches Saar offensive.
17 September	*The USSR invades eastern Poland.*
26 September	French government outlaws the Communist Party and other Communist organizations.
27 September	*Warsaw surrenders.*
29 September	*Poland is divided between Germany and the USSR.*
30 November	*The USSR invades Finland.*

1940
20 February	Chamber of Deputies expels Communist deputies.
21 February	*Building of the concentration camp at Auschwitz begins.*
29 February	Ration cards introduced.
13 March	*Finland signs armistice with the USSR.*
21 March	Reynaud replaces Daladier as Prime Minister.
28 March	Agreement between France and Britain prohibits either country from making a separate peace.
7 April	*Germany invades Denmark and Norway.*

9 April	*Denmark surrenders.*
10 May	*Germany begins its western offensive against Belgium, Holland and Luxembourg. Winston Churchill forms coalition government in Britain.*
13 May	German army enters France by crossing the Meuse at Dinant and Sedan.
15 May	*Dutch army surrenders.*
18 May	Reynaud appoints Pétain Deputy Prime Minister.
19 May	Weygand replaces Gamelin as Commander-in-Chief of the French army.
20 May	German army establishes Panzer corridor to the Channel near Abbeville.
22 May	Panzers take Boulogne and Calais.
24 May	British Expeditionary Force begins to fall back on Dunkirk.
26 May–3 June	British Expeditionary Force and some French troops evacuated from Dunkirk.
28 May	*King Leopold orders Belgian army to surrender.*
5 June	De Gaulle becomes Under-Secretary of State in the Ministry of War.
9 June	*Norway surrenders.*
10 June	French government leaves Paris for the Loire valley. *Italy declares war on France and Britain.*
11 June	Weygand declares Paris an 'open city'.
14 June	German army enters Paris. French government moves from the Loire valley to Bordeaux.
15 June	Strasbourg and Verdun fall.
16 June	French cabinet rejects plan for Anglo-French union. Reynaud resigns and is replaced by Pétain.
17 June	Pétain's broadcast calls for an armistice. Lyon and other cities of more than 20,000 declared 'open'. De Gaulle flies from Bordeaux to Britain. Moulin attempts suicide.
18 June	De Gaulle broadcasts from London, calling for continuation of the struggle.
22 June	Franco-German armistice signed at Rethondes.
23 June	Hitler visits Paris. Laval enters Pétain's government as Deputy Prime Minister.
24 June	France signs armistice with Italy.
25 June	Armistice comes into force.
28 June	*British government recognizes de Gaulle as leader of the Free French.*
29 June	Pétain's government leaves Bordeaux for Clermont-Ferrand.

30 June	Pétain's government forms the Chantiers de Jeunesse. *Germany occupies the Channel Islands.*
1 July	Pétain's government moves from Clermont-Ferrand to Vichy.
3 July	*British navy sinks the French fleet at Mers-el-Kébir.*
5 July	Pétain's government breaks off diplomatic relations with Britain.
10 July	National Assembly votes the Third Republic out of existence, handing power to Pétain. *Battle of Britain begins.*
11 July	Pétain establishes the Vichy regime with himself as Head of State.
22 July	Vichy begins to review citizenship of those naturalized since 1927.
2 August	Stringent rationing introduced. Military tribunal at Clermont-Ferrand condemns de Gaulle to death.
3 August	Abetz installed as German ambassador in Paris.
4 August	*Italy invades British Somalia.*
7 August	Third Reich annexes Alsace and Lorraine.
17 August	Germans ban Jews who fled to the Southern Zone from returning to the Occupied Zone.
29 August	Légion Français des Combattants formed in the Southern Zone.
14 September	*Italy attacks Egypt.*
23–24 September	*Forces loyal to Vichy repel Anglo-Gaullist attempt to take Dakar.*
25 September	*French planes bomb Gibraltar.*
27 September	German decree requires a census of Jews in the Occupied Zone. Vichy dissolves the Communist Party. *Germany, Italy and Japan sign Tripartite Pact.*
3 October	Vichy introduces first Statut des Juifs, defining Jewishness and banning Jews from higher public service and positions influencing public opinion.
4–5 October	Mass arrest of Communists in Paris.
7 October	*German army attacks Romania.*
12 October	*Hitler postpones invasion of Britain until spring 1941.*
22 October	Laval meets Hitler at Montoire, near Tours.
24 October	Pétain meets Hitler at Montoire.
28 October	Laval appointed Vichy's Foreign Minister. *Italy attacks Greece.*
30 October	Pétain advocates collaboration in a radio broadcast.

11 November	First public demonstration against the occupiers, in Paris.
13 December	Pétain dismisses Laval.
15 December	The ashes of Napoleon's son, the Duc de Reichstadt, are interred in Les Invalides.
18 December	De Brinon becomes Vichy ambassador to the Germans in Paris.
23 December	Jacques Bonsergent executed for 'attacking' a German officer in Paris.
25 December	Darlan meets Hitler at La Ferrière-sur-Epte.

1941

1 February	Déat forms the Rassemblement National Populaire.
7 February	*Je suis partout*, right-wing journal edited by Brasillach, reappears.
9 February	Darlan becomes Foreign Minister and vice-president of the Council of Ministers.
13 February	Pétain meets Franco at Montpellier.
February	*Le Juif Süss* (by Veit Harlan, 1940) shown in Paris cinemas.
March	Vichy establishes Commissariat Général aux Questions Juives (CGQJ), headed by Xavier Vallat.
2 March	*Germany attacks Bulgaria.*
6 April	*Germany attacks Yugoslavia and Greece.*
17 April	*Yugoslavia surrenders.*
27 April	*Greece surrenders.*
11 May	Vichy celebrates Joan of Arc's feast day.
14 May	First *rafle* of Jews in Paris.
20 May–1 June	*German forces overwhelm Crete.*
26 May – 13 June	Miners strike in the Pas-de-Calais and the Nord.
27 May	Protocols of Paris allow Germans to use military airfields and ports in the French Empire.
2 June	Vichy's second Statut des Juifs, requiring a census of Jews in the Southern Zone and excluding Jews from commerce and industry.
7 June	*Anglo-Gaullist forces invade Syria.*
22 June	*Germany, Italy and Romania declare war on the USSR.*
7 July	Légion des Volontaires Français contre le Bolchevisme (LVF) founded.
12 July	*Britain and the USSR reach Mutual Assistance Agreement.*
14 July	*Vichyite forces surrender to Anglo-Gaullist forces at Acre (Syria).*

22 July	Vichy law authorizes confiscation of Jewish property and enterprises.
20 August	*Rafle* of Jews in Paris. *Siege of Leningrad (St Petersburg) begins.*
21 August	Colonel Fabien kills a German at the Métro Barbès-Rochechouart in Paris.
27 August	Paul Collette tries to assassinate Laval and Déat after an LVF ceremony at Versailles.
3 September	German soldier shot at Gare de l'Est, Paris. *Gas chambers first used at Auschwitz.*
5 September	Exhibition on 'Le Juif et la France' opens in Paris.
27 September	*Italy surrenders in Ethiopia.*
2–3 October	Eugène Deloncle organizes the blowing-up of seven Paris synagogues.
4 October	Vichy announces anti-trades union *charte du travail* (labour charter).
20 October	Feldkommandant of Nantes shot. *Moulin arrives in London.*
22 October	German shot in Bordeaux. Germans execute twenty-seven hostages at Châteaubriant and twenty at Nantes.
23 October	Germans execute fifty hostages at Bordeaux.
29 October	Germans license Doriot's Parti Populaire Français.
29 November	Vallat establishes the Union Générale des Israélites de France, supposedly to let the Jews manage their own affairs.
1 December	Pétain meets Goering at Saint-Florentin.
7 December	*Japan attacks Pearl Harbor.*
8 December	*The USA and Britain declare war on Japan.*
10 December	*Japan invades the Philippines.*
11 December	*Germany declares war on the USA.*
25 December	*Hong Kong surrenders to the Japanese.*

1942

1/2 January	Moulin returns to France on his first mission as de Gaulle's representative.
16 January	*Japan invades Burma.*
20 January	*Wannsee meeting commits the Reich to Final Solution.*
4 February	Service d'Ordre Légionnaire, predecessor of the Milice, is formed.
15 February	*Singapore falls to the Japanese.*
20 February–15 April	Blum, Daladier, Gamelin and other Third Republic leaders tried at Riom.

3 March	Allied bombing of France begins with RAF raid on the Renault works at Billancourt.
19 March	Vallat sacked from CGQJ, replaced by Darquier de Pellepoix.
21 March	*Hitler appoints Sauckel to head the drive to exploit foreign labour.*
27 March	First trainload of Jews leaves Drancy for Auschwitz.
27–28 March	RAF raid on the submarine base at Saint-Nazaire.
March	Franc-Tireurs et Partisans (FTP) formed.
18 April	Laval returns to office, replacing Darlan. Bonnard becomes Minister of Education.
29 April	*Japan takes control of central Burma.*
29 May	Jews over the age of 6 in the Occupied Zone are required to wear the yellow star.
1 June	Germans transfer responsibility for security in France from the army to the SS, headed by General Oberg.
22 June	Laval announces the *Relève* in a speech which also hopes for a German victory.
16–17 July	*Grand rafle* of Jews for deportation to Auschwitz.
5 August	First Jews from camps in the Southern Zone sent to Drancy *en route* for Auschwitz.
11 August	At Compiègne, Laval greets the first French prisoners-of-war returned under the *Relève*.
13 August	*Switzerland closes its borders to Jewish refugees.*
19 August	Anglo-Canadian raid on Dieppe fails.
23 August	Pastoral letter by Archbishop Saliège of Toulouse condemns deportation of the Jews.
13 September	*Siege of Stalingrad begins.*
23 October	*Battle of El Alamein begins.*
8 November	*Allies begin landings in North Africa.*
11 November	Germans occupy Southern Zone.
27 November	French fleet at Toulon scuttled.
28 November	Armistice Army disbanded.
11 December	Vichy regime orders Jews in the Southern Zone to have *Juif* or *Juive* stamped on personal documents.
24 December	*Darlan assassinated in Algiers.*
1943	
18 January	*Siege of Leningrad (St Petersburg) lifted.*
24 January	Germans destroy the Vieux Port in Marseille.
27 January	*Siege of Stalingrad ends.*

31 January	The Milice Française is founded, with Laval as president and Darnand as secretary-general.
January	At Moulin's initiative, Combat, Libération-Sud and the FTP join forces as the Mouvements Unis de la Résistance (MUR).
14 February–20 March	*Moulin back in London.*
16 February	Service du Travail Obligatoire (STO) introduced.
February	Henriot begins regular broadcasts on Radio-Paris.
1 March	Demarcation line abolished for 'full French nationals'.
11 April	Laval and Sauckel announce scheme for transforming French POWs into 'free workers'.
24 April	First *milicien* killed by *résistants*.
28 April	Déat forms the Front Révolutionnaire National.
12 May	*German and Italian forces in Tunisia surrender.*
27 May	Moulin presides at the inaugural meeting of the Conseil National de la Résistance (CNR) in Paris.
30 May	*De Gaulle arrives in Algeria. Comité Français de la Libération Nationale (CFLN) established, with Giraud and de Gaulle as co-presidents.*
9 June	Germans arrest General Delestraint, head of the Armée Secrète.
21 June	Klaus Barbie captures Moulin and other leading *résistants* at Caluire (Lyon).
9 July–17 August	*Allies conquer Sicily.*
20 July	*German forces retreat after battle of Kursk.*
25–26 July	*Mussolini replaced by Badoglio in Italy.*
3 September	CFLN condemns Pétain and Vichy ministers as traitors.
8 September	Germans take over Italian-occupied territory in southern France. *Italy agrees an armistice with the Allies.*
9 September	*Allies land in Italy at Salerno and Taranto.*
11 September	*Germans occupy Rome.*
23 September	*Mussolini re-establishes Fascist government in German-occupied northern Italy.*
1 October	*Allies enter Naples.*
3 October	Résistants *and Free French troops liberate Corsica.*
13 October	*Italy declares war on Germany.*
9 November	*De Gaulle becomes sole president of reorganized CFLN.*
11 November	*Maquisards* 'occupy' Oyonnax and other towns to commemorate Armistice Day.
2 December	*Miliciens* assassinate Maurice Sarraut, newspaper editor, in Toulouse.

1944

1 January	Darnand becomes Vichy Secretary-General for the Maintenance of Order.
6 January	Henriot becomes Vichy Minister of Information and Propaganda.
10 January	Victor Basch, former president of the League for the Rights of Man, and his wife murdered.
22 January	*Allies land at Anzio.*
27 January	Authority of the Milice extended to the north of France. *Leningrad relieved.*
1 February	Forces Françaises de l'Intérieur (FFI) officially created.
26 February	Darquier sacked from CGQJ, replaced by Charles Mercier du Paty de Clam.
16 March	Déat becomes Vichy Minister of Labour and National Solidarity.
20 March	*Pierre Pucheu, ex-Vichy Minister of the Interior, executed in Algiers.*
26 March	*Maquisards* defeated in battle on the plateau of Glières.
1 April	SS troops massacre eighty-six people at Ascq, near Lille.
6 April	Barbie raids the children's refuge at Izieu.
26 April	Pétain makes his first and only visit to Paris during the Occupation.
2 June	*CFLN declares itself the provisional government of the French Republic.*
2–20 June	Germans attack mobilized forces of the Auvergnat Maquis at Mont Mouchet and the other bases to which they flee.
5 June	*Allies enter Rome.*
6 June	D-Day landings.
7–9 June	*Maquisards* occupy Tulle but withdraw on arrival of an SS division, which hangs ninety-nine local men.
10 June	SS troops massacre 642 people at Oradour-sur-Glane, near Limoges.
14 June	De Gaulle returns to French soil, entering Bayeux.
17 June	Hitler pays his last visit to France, meeting Rommel and Rundstedt at Margival, near Soissons.
20 June	*Miliciens* assassinate Jean Zay.
28 June	*Résistants* assassinate Henriot.
5 July	Hitler sacks Rundstedt as Supreme Commander

	in the West, replacing him with Field Marshal Gunther von Kluge.
7 July	*Miliciens* assassinate Mandel.
12 July	Vichy ministers hold their last council meeting.
14 July	USAF makes its largest daytime drop of supplies to the Maquis in the Lot, the Corrèze and the Dordogne as well as the Vercors plateau.
20 July	*Attempt to assassinate Hitler fails at Rastenburg.*
21–23 July	The Maquis defeated on the plateau of the Vercors, losing 630 men.
24 July–8 August	*Miliciens* and Germans kill thirty-six Jews at Guerry, near Bourges.
31 July	General Patton's Third Army breaks out from Normandy at Avranches.
5 August	Pétain condemns the actions of the Milice.
7 August	Hitler appoints General Dietrich von Choltitz Kommandant von Gross-Paris.
15 August	French and Allied troops land in Provence.
17 August	Last trainload of Jews leaves France for Auschwitz.
18 August	Germans take Laval from Paris to Belfort.
19 August	Street fighting begins in Paris.
20 August	Germans take Pétain from Vichy to Belfort; his last speech as Head of State is broadcast. De Gaulle lands at Cherbourg. Germans kill 100 prisoners at Saint-Genis-Laval, near Lyon.
21 August	SS troops massacre 126 people at Maillé, near Tours.
22 August	General Leclerc's Second Armoured Division ordered to advance on Paris.
24 August	Reconnaissance column of Leclerc's Division enters Paris in the late evening.
25 August	Leclerc's main force arrives in Paris; Choltitz surrenders; de Gaulle arrives and makes speech at Hôtel de Ville.
26 August	De Gaulle heads parade from the Arc de Triomphe to Notre-Dame.
7 September	Germans take Pétain, Laval and members of the Vichy cabinet from Belfort to Sigmaringen.
12 September	General Leclerc's Free French troops, advancing south, and Lattre de Tassigny's forces from Provence meet at Nod-sur-Seine in Burgundy.
15 September	Special courts created to try collaborators.
14 October	*Athens liberated.*

23 October	*Britain, the USA, the USSR and Canada officially recognize de Gaulle's government.*
28 October	Armed organizations apart from the police and army dissolved.
18 November	Special High Court created to try leading collaborators.
24 November	General Leclerc's Second Armoured Division enters Strasbourg.
16–26 December	*The battle of the Bulge: German counter-offensive in the Ardennes almost reaches the Meuse near Dinant before being repelled.*

1945

19 January–6 February	Brasillach tried, sentenced and executed.
26 January	*Soviet troops enter Auschwitz.*
22 February	*Doriot killed by strafing planes near Sigmaringen.*
7 March	*Allies cross the Rhine.*
12 April	*Allies liberate Buchenwald and Belsen.*
14 April	Reception committee, including de Gaulle, Frenay and François Mitterrand, welcomes the first *déportés* to return to France.
24–27 April	Pétain returns to France via Switzerland and is arrested.
26–28 April	*Partisans capture and execute Mussolini.*
29 April	*Allies liberate Dachau.*
8 May	*VE Day: official date of German surrender.*
23 July–15 August	Pétain tried, convicted and sentenced to death.
1 August	Laval arrives back in France, from Austria.
15 August	*VJ Day: Japan surrenders after atomic bomb attacks on Hiroshima (6 August) and Nagasaki (9 August).*
17 August	Pétain's sentence commuted to life imprisonment.
3–10 October	Darnand tried, sentenced and executed.
4–9 October	Laval tried, convicted and condemned to death.
15 October	Laval executed.
21 October	Elections confirm de Gaulle as President.
20 November	*Nuremberg trials of twenty-one leading Nazis begin.*

1946

20 January	De Gaulle resigns.
10 September	Court in Lyon sentences Paul Touvier, former *milicien*, to death in his absence.
1 October	*Verdicts delivered at Nuremberg trials.*
13 October	Referendum on the constitution of the Fourth Republic.
16 October	*Leading Nazis found guilty at Nuremberg hanged.*

1947

4 March — Court in Chambéry sentences Touvier to death *in absentia.*

15 April — De Brinon becomes the last person to be executed under the *épuration.*

1949

23 June — René Bousquet, former Vichy Chief of Police, given suspended sentence of five years' *dégradation nationale.*

23 July — Otto Abetz sentenced to twenty years' hard labour (but does not serve full sentence).

1951

5 January — First amnesty law revokes punishment of those sentenced to *dégradation nationale* or prison terms of less than fifteen years.

23 July — Pétain dies at the age of 95 on the Ile d'Yeu, where he had served his prison sentence.

6 November — Association pour Défendre la Mémoire du Maréchal Pétain formed.

1953

12 January–13 February — Twenty-one SS soldiers, fourteen of them from Alsace, tried in Bordeaux for the Oradour massacre.

3 August — Second amnesty law effectively ends the *épuration.*

1954

14 April — Last Sunday in April declared a national day commemorating the victims and heroes of the deportation.

1958

1 June — De Gaulle becomes President.

28 September — Constitution of the Fifth Republic adopted.

1964

18–19 December — Moulin's ashes transferred to the Panthéon.

26 December — National Assembly suspends the statute of limitations for crimes against humanity as defined by the Nuremberg Trials and the UN Charter.

1965

19 December — De Gaulle re-elected President.

1969

15 June — Pompidou becomes President.

1970
9 November   De Gaulle dies.

1971
April   Marcel Ophuls' film *The Sorrow and the Pity* released in cinemas (but not shown on French TV until October 1981).
23 November   Pompidou commutes sentence passed against Touvier in his absence.

1983
5 February   Barbie extradited from Bolivia to France and indicted for crimes against humanity.

1985
April   Release of Claude Lanzmann's film *Shoah*.

1987
11 May–4 July   Barbie tried in Lyon and sentenced to life imprisonment.

1989
24 May   Touvier arrested in Nice for crimes against humanity.

1991
25 September   Barbie dies in prison.

1993
8 June   Bousquet assassinated while awaiting trial for crimes against humanity.
16 July   Anniversary of the *grand rafle* marked as a national day of remembrance.

1994
19 April   Touvier sentenced to life imprisonment.

1996
17 July   Touvier dies in prison.
18 September   Judges in Bordeaux rule that Maurice Papon, former Vichy official in the Gironde, should stand trial for crimes against humanity.

Acknowledgements

My researches have been made more fruitful as well as more pleasant by the staff of the Musée de la Résistance en Morvan at Saint-Brisson, the Musée de la Résistance at Mussy-sur-Seine, the Library of the Institut Français in London, the Imperial War Museum and Cambridge University Library. I owe a particular debt to Raymond and Christine Chalumeau, Xavier Debard, Maurice Raquin and Jean Renard for their patience in answering my questions. In Britain I have been helped by Annette Kelley, Anna Saunders, Mary Turner and Victoria Turner, as well as by my agent Andrew Lownie and, at John Murray, Grant McIntyre and Gail Pirkis.

Index